THEORY OF THE NOVEL

Theory *of the* Novel

GUIDO MAZZONI

Translated by
ZAKIYA HANAFI

Harvard University Press

Cambridge, Massachusetts
London, England
2017

Originally published as *Teoria del Romanzo,* © 2011 by Società
editrice Il Mulino, Bologna.

Second printing

The diagram on page 12 is reprinted from *The Political Unconscious: Narrative as a
Socially Symbolic Act* by Fredric Jameson, page 21 (Routledge Classics Edition) and
page 36 (Cornell University Press Edition). Copyright © 1981 by Cornell University. Used
by permission of the publishers, Routledge in the United Kingdom and Commonwealth, and
Cornell University Press throughout North America and the rest of the world.

Library of Congress Cataloging-in-Publication Data
Names: Mazzoni, Guido, 1967– author.
Title: Theory of the novel / Guido Mazzoni; translated by Zakiya Hanafi.
Other titles: Teoria del romanzo English
Description: Cambridge, Massachusetts : Harvard University Press, 2017. | Includes index.
Identifiers: LCCN 2016008613 | ISBN 9780674333727 (alk. paper)
Subjects: LCSH: Fiction—History and criticism—Theory, etc. | Literature—Philosophy.
Classification: LCC PN3331 .M2813 2016 | DDC 809.3—dc23
LC record available at http://lccn.loc.gov/2016008613

Contents

Translator's Note

Unless otherwise stated, all citations from foreign literary works are taken from the standard English editions. Where no English version exists, or when the English version is either partial or too old to be reliable, citations have been translated directly from the originals. In these cases, the punctuation and the use of capital letters have been modernized. The titles are shown in English if the translated version has entered into common use (for example, the *Republic, War and Peace, The Man without Qualities*) and in the original language if the translated version has not entered into common use. The original title in both cases is shown in the note along with the original publication date if it is known and if the information serves to provide a historical context for the text. When passages from secondary literature are quoted, the English-language version is used whenever possible. When this is not available, they have been translated directly from the originals. In certain cases, some changes have been made to ensure that the critical passages accurately reflect the literary work under discussion. Some foreign-language titles and expressions have been translated into English to aid understanding.

I REALIZE THAT, despite my precautions, nothing is easier than to criticize this book should anyone ever think of doing so. Those who wish to take a closer look will, I think, discover a dominant thought which binds together, so to speak, the various sections of the whole book. But the range of the topics which I have had to deal with is very wide and anyone attempting to single out one fact to challenge the body of facts, to quote one idea wrenched from the main body of ideas, will manage to do so with ease. I should, therefore, like people to do me the favor of reading my work in the same spirit that has guided my efforts and to judge this book by the overall impression it leaves, just as I myself have come to my opinions not for a particular reason, but through the mass of evidence.

—Alexis de Tocqueville, *Democracy in America*

AND SUDDENLY a long-forgotten, meek old teacher, who had taught him geography in Switzerland, emerged in Pierre's mind as if alive. "Wait!" said the old man. And he showed Pierre a globe. This globe was a living, wavering ball of no dimensions. The entire surface of the ball consisted of drops tightly packed together. And these drops all moved and shifted, and now merged from several into one, now divided from one into many. Each drop strove to spread and take up the most space, but the others, striving to do the same, pressed it, sometimes destroying, sometimes merging with it.

"This is life," said the old teacher.

"How simple and clear it is," thought Pierre. "How could I not have known before?"

—Leo Tolstoy, *War and Peace*

Introduction

Truth and Literature

Why the Novel Matters

> Nothing is important but life. . . . For this reason I am a novelist. And being a novelist, I consider myself superior to the saint, the scientist, the philosopher, and the poet, who are all great masters of different bits of man alive, but never get the whole hog.
>
> The novel is the one bright book of life. . . . In this sense, the Bible is a great confused novel. You may say, it is about God. But it is really about man alive. Adam, Eve, Sara, Abraham, Isaac, Jacob, Samuel, David, Bath-Sheba, Ruth, Esther, Solomon, Job, Isaiah, Jesus, Mark, Judas, Paul, Peter: what is it but man alive, from start to finish? Man alive, not mere bits. Even the Lord is another man alive, in a burning bush, throwing the tablets of stone at Moses's head.

This is the most important passage in "Why the Novel Matters," an essay written by D. H. Lawrence in 1925 and published posthumously in 1936.[1] Here we find a theory of the novel expressed in bold, elementary formulas—one that circulated widely among the writers of the nineteenth and twentieth centuries. More sophisticated versions of the same ideas can be found in the works of Honoré de Balzac, Émile Zola, Henry James, Virginia Woolf, and E. M. Forster.[2] A few years before "Why the Novel

---

1. David Herbert Lawrence, "Why the Novel Matters," in *Phoenix: The Posthumous Papers* (New York: Viking Press, 1936); reprinted in *Study of Thomas Hardy and Other Essays*, ed. Bruce Steel (Cambridge: Cambridge University Press, 1985), 191–198. Regarding the dating of the essay, see Steel's introduction," p. L.

2. Honoré de Balzac, "Avant-propos" (1842) to *La Comédie humaine*; English translation "Author's Introduction" to *The Human Comedy*, trans. Ellen Marriage in *The Works of*

Matters," in speaking about literature in general but thinking about the novel he was working on at the time, the greatest of Lawrence's contemporaries had written that "real life, life finally uncovered and clarified, the only life in consequence lived to the full, is literature."[3] Most likely, over the coming decades, novelists of the twenty-first century will continue to repeat the same ideas.

What makes Lawrence's essay interesting is precisely its crudeness: by simplifying the thought process and removing any nuances, it unabashedly presents an opinion that many writers and readers have shared over the past two centuries, thereby making it easily recognizable. The superficial intentions of "Why the Novel Matters" are easy to decipher: Lawrence wants to make himself important, to endow his works with an absolute value and challenge anyone with the same ambitions who might threaten his supremacy. And yet, if we reflect on the assumptions that make a piece like this possible, we understand that what lies hidden behind the mediocrity of his claims is an entire epochal landscape. Today we take his words for granted: we might agree or disagree with him, but what we read strikes us as plausible. When we compare Lawrence's ideas to other ways of viewing how the various human sciences relate to each other, though, some of his judgments no longer seem obvious. Asserting that the novel is the only book of life, placing it ahead of religion, philosophy, and science, is hardly a gesture to be taken for granted. In order for a statement like this to be even conceivable, the European cultural horizon had to have already gone through two of the most profound metamorphoses in its history. The first, more limited one transformed literature; the second, which was more extensive, transformed the relations between literature and other forms of knowledge, and, ultimately, those between literature and truth.

Honoré de Balzac, ed. by George Saintsbury (Boston: Dana Estes, 1901) vol. 1, pp. liii–lxix; Émile Zola, "Le Naturalisme au théâtre" (1879–1880); English translation "Naturalism on the Stage" in *The Experimental Novel, and Other Essays,* trans. Belle M. Sherman (New York: Cassell, 1893), 123–125; Virginia Woolf, "Life and the Novelist" (1926), in *The Essays of Virginia Woolf,* vol. 4, *1925–1928,* ed. Andrew McNeillie (London: Hogarth Press, 1994), 400–412; Edward Morgan Forster, *Aspects of the Novel* (1927) (London: Penguin Books, 2005).

3. Marcel Proust, *Le Temps retrouvé*; English translation *Finding Time Again*, trans. Ian Patterson, in *In Search of Lost Time*, 6 vols, general editor Christopher Prendergast, vol. 6 (London: Penguin Press, 2002), 204.

Between the mid-sixteenth century and the beginning of the nineteenth, a genre long considered an unpretentious form of entertainment—the novel—became the primary art practiced in the West, the art that portrays the extensive totality of life,[4] or, as a contemporary novelist put it, the flagship that literature ranges against systematic thought, against science and philosophy.[5] No other aesthetic language has inspired so many critical texts and so much thought over the past two hundred years. Writers who were once accused of ruining the canons of taste and morality have been introduced into school curricula; works intended for quick consumption have received the kind of attention philology reserves for safeguarding cultural monuments for posterity. Three centuries ago, an interest of this sort would have been unimaginable: in 1740, at the beginning of a decisive decade for the history of the novel in Lawrence's homeland, no one in England or elsewhere would have ranked the novelist ahead of the saint, the philosopher, or the scientist.[6] The metaphor of the novel as the book of life appeared in the mid-1700s but began to be used the way Lawrence did only toward the end of that century; and only over the course of the nineteenth century did the prestige of the novel become consolidated. The most striking premise of "Why the Novel Matters" thus represents a geological change in the system of literary genres starting from the second half of the eighteenth century. The first question this book explores lies within the confines of literature: Chapters 2 to 8 describe the birth of the novel, its rocky rise, and its modern evolution.

Books of Life

But this discontinuity in the sphere of literature was part of a broader transformation. To illustrate it, I offer a genealogy of the metaphor with which we began. The book of life is an image charged with history: over the course of time many works, many genres, and many disciplines have claimed to be the book of life.[7] The most distant example, that of the Bible,

---

4. György Lukács, *Die Theorie des Romans* (1920); English translation *The Theory of the Novel,* trans. Anna Bostick (Cambridge, MA: MIT Press, 1971).

5. Walter Siti, "L'orgoglio del romanzo," in *L'asino d'oro* 10 (1994): 67.

6. See Jerry C. Beasley, *Novels of the 1740s* (Athens: University of Georgia Press, 1982), 1.

7. See Hans Blumenberg, *Die Lesbarkeit der Welt* (Frankfurt am Main: Suhrkamp, 1981).

is also the one Lawrence refers to. But it is not hard to come up with other precedents: for Galileo the book of nature was written in the language of mathematics;[8] more than a century later, Voltaire used the same image to talk about philosophy,[9] giving metaphorical shape to an idea that has existed ever since Parmenides, Plato, and Aristotle made abstract thought the highest form of human discourse.[10]

Lawrence is replicating a venerable intellectual move. He is reusing an age-old critical genre: the *paragone*. In its Renaissance form, the *paragone* compared the merits of two arts (poetry and painting, for example), but its archetype has a wider scope and a more extensive genealogy.[11] The first comparison between families of discourses developed in Greece between the sixth and fourth centuries BCE, when a set of practices and texts that slowly acquired the name of philosophy broke off from the practices and texts of the epic poets. The first major example of a *paragone* is found in the *Republic,* where Plato endorses the superiority of concepts over mimesis, and the primacy of philosophy over the imitative arts. This line of thought gave rise to an opposition between the irrational languages of the poets and the rational languages of the philosophers and scientists, namely, the cornerstone of European metaphysics—the assumption that in the self-representation of our culture is said to distinguish "the path of Western thought . . . from all Oriental wisdom."[12]

But while the genre of the *paragone* was formed in a Platonic mold, Lawrence spoke from a completely different historical perspective. Between the end of the eighteenth century and the beginning of the nineteenth century, a

8. Galileo Galilei, *Il Saggiatore* (1623); English translation *The Assayer,* in *The Controversy on the Comets of 1618,* trans. Stillman Drake and C. D. O'Malley (Philadelphia: University of Pennsylvania Press, 1960).

9. Voltaire, *Zadig ou la Destinée* (1747); English translation *Candide, Zadig and Selected Stories,* trans. Donald M. Frame (Bloomington: Indiana University Press, 1961), chap. 3, p. 109.

10. See Ernst Robert Curtius, *Europäische Literatur und lateinisches Mittelalter* (1948); English translation *European Literature and the Latin Middle Ages,* trans. Willard R. Trask (Princeton, NJ: Princeton University Press, 2013), chap. 11.

11. Curtius, *European Literature and the Latin Middle Ages,* chap. 11; Paul Oskar Kristeller, "The Modern System of the Arts: A Study in the History of Aesthetics," part 1, *Journal of the History of Ideas* 12, no. 4 (1951): 496–527, and part 2, 13, no. 1 (1952): 17–46.

12. Hans-Georg Gadamer, "Philosophie und Poesie," in Gadamer, *Kleine Schriften IV* (1977); English translation "Philosophy and Poetry," in *The Relevance of the Beautiful,* trans. Nicholas Walker (Cambridge: Cambridge University Press, 1986), 131.

cultural transformation redefined the relations between the books of life. During the eighteenth century there arose the discursive formation of modern aesthetics, which investigated and prior to that recognized the content of truth crystallized in the discourses of the arts. Between the end of the eighteenth century and the beginning of the nineteenth century, many writers and philosophers celebrated the force of art with new insistence. This current of thought toppled ancient hierarchies. If it is true that the texts grouped today under the category of mimesis have always been important, it is equally true that only in the past two centuries have they been so for the reason cited in "Why the Novel Matters." The idea that a narrative form could be superior to science, religion, and philosophy— because only fiction grasps "life"—is recent. It is an idea that can exist only once the aesthetic sphere is no longer conceived of as entertainment, decoration, or the allegorical rewriting of already known moral, historical, cosmological, and theological truths, but rather as an alternative model of knowledge to the world-picture propagated by philosophy, science, and religion. It can exist only once we begin to think that life, or its innermost core, eludes conceptual language.

In the past two centuries, mimesis and fiction have acquired a new status. Whether or not we agree with Lawrence, there is no denying that the art of storytelling holds truths that are vital to us: the claims stated in "Why the Novel Matters" could be made only after the order of discourses had undergone a metamorphosis. The significance of the novel and the reason a species of entertainment gained so much importance over a period of two and a half centuries is incomprehensible unless one understands that its rise is the sign of a ground-shifting transformation in the relations between literature and truth, between literature and philosophy, and between mimesis and truth that took place on the thresholds of the modern age.

Games of Truth

There does exist a third way of expressing the relationship between books of life, however, that differs from and comes later than the ones we find in Plato's *Republic* and "Why the Novel Matters." I will explain it starting from the end—from when the theoretical folds that this threshold contains had been entirely unfurled.

At the beginning of the 1980s, having agreed to write the "Michel Foucault" entry in a dictionary of philosophers slated for publication in 1984, Michel Foucault, under a pseudonym, attempted to explain the meaning of his work in a few short pages. He states that what he pursued, book after book, was an extended inquiry into "games of truth": the discursive practices that define what is true and what is false, what form the discourse of truth must take, and who and what the subject and object of knowledge are.[13] Through these mobile structures, situated in and exposed to becoming, he explains, being is constituted as experience and reality enters into language as something that can be thought or represented.[14] The expression "games of truth" is a new term for what a decade and a half earlier, at the height of *The Archaeology of Knowledge,* he had called "discursive formations."[15] Most likely, during the years separating *The Archaeology of Knowledge* (1969) from the dictionary entry, Foucault had been influenced by Ludwig Wittgenstein and his concept of "language games."[16] The two formulas describe objects that differ in part, because Wittgenstein's idea applies to common, fluid practices (giving orders, describing objects, reporting events),[17] while Foucault's notions designate knowledges codified by centuries-old history (medicine, grammar, psychiatry, political economy).[18] Still, the affinities are more interesting than the differences. For Wittgenstein as for Foucault, language and culture do not form coherent wholes that can be talked about in the singular; instead, they compose heteroclite, fractured territories that are born, die, transform themselves, overlap, clash, and interweave following the unpredictable, impossible-to-deduce

13. Michel Foucault, "Foucault, Michel 1926–" (1984); English translation by Catherine Porter, in *The Cambridge Companion to Foucault,* ed. Gary Gutting (Cambridge: Cambridge University Press, 1994), 314–319.

14. Michel Foucault, *Histoire de la sexualité, II. L'Usage des plaisirs* (1984); English translation *The History of Sexuality,* vol. 2, *The Use of Pleasure,* trans. Robert Hurley (New York: Vintage Books, 1990), 6ff.

15. Michel Foucault, *L'Archéologie du savoir* (1969); English translation *The Archaeology of Knowledge,* trans. A. M. Sheridan Smith (New York: Pantheon Books, 1982), 31.

16. On the similarities between Wittgenstein and Foucault, see Arnold I. Davidson, *The Emergence of Sexuality: Historical Epistemology and the Formation of Concepts* (Cambridge, MA: Harvard University Press, 2001), chap. 7.

17. Ludwig Wittgenstein, *Philosophische Untersuchungen* (1953); English translation *Philosophical Investigations,* trans. Gertrude Elizabeth Margaret Anscombe (Oxford: Basil Blackwell, 1986), §§23ff.

18. Foucault, *Archaeology of Knowledge,* 31; Foucault, "Foucault, Michel 1926–," 314.

transformations of a prelinguistic entity that Wittgenstein calls "forms of life" and Foucault "historical *a prioris*." The discourses that form a part of these complex volumes are not bound by unchanging norms, but by constantly moving regularities subject to transformations.[19] Both linguistic games and games of truth are transcendental structures marked by a historical and geographic origin. Culture as a whole is the sum of all the discursive regions. Between the various provinces there is no rational hierarchy, like what joined the forms of Absolute Spirit together in Hegel's philosophy, since no language can claim to have a privileged access to truth.

Now: to compare games of truth and books of life without presupposing that one of these codes has a theoretical privilege over the other means to conceive of knowledge as a constantly changing sum of incommensurable language games that follow a very different paradigm than what prevailed after the clashes between philosophy and rhetoric, and between philosophy and poetry, out of which Western metaphysics arose. The latter is founded on the idea that only a certain use of language, that of thought, is able to grasp the thing-in-itself. The act of thinking shared by everyone is developed rigorously by philosophy or science, which is to say, by the discourses that encircle, reformulate, and put into order all other types of discourses. Whoever compares games of truth without granting any theoretical privileges effectively destroys the Platonic hierarchies. An overturning of this sort was made possible over the past few centuries by two decisive transformations. Subsequent to these, other ways of understanding the genre of the *paragone* arose that were very different from the one on which the edifice of Platonism had been founded. The first coincided with the Romantic consecration of the arts and the development of modern aesthetics, which is to say, with the recognition that truth can reside in a medium other than the concept. But the truly crucial threshold, the one that undermined Platonism, emerged in the second half of the nineteenth century.

For the history of culture, the names of philosophers are primarily metonymies: they indicate the collective flows of thought that certain authors intercept, refine, and transmit to following generations. Nietzsche is the name we use to demarcate the beginning of this new epoch. According to the cultural perspective signified by this metonymy, every one of our affir-

---

19. Foucault, *Archaeology of Knowledge,* 37–38.

mations comes out marked by a prioris that cannot be established, and all the disciplines that strive to express the truth are a preunderstanding among preunderstandings, a genre among genres, starting with philosophy—the form of knowledge that has accredited itself with the power to dismantle all presuppositions and to craft discourses free of blind spots. A century later, the intellectual attitude that Nietzsche inaugurated was dubbed the linguistic turn, and it spread throughout contemporary culture, reviving, in a completely different historical landscape, some of the assumptions implicit in the theories of language and knowledge that Plato had fought against, namely, rhetoric and sophistry.[20] This third way of understanding the genre of the *paragone,* corresponding to a later historical phase than modern aesthetics or the stances defended by Lawrence, constitutes the most deeply rooted premise of this book. Every discourse we have about the world (philosophy, science, religion, poetry, fiction) comes into being marked by a blind a priori and bears an image of the content sedimented in its form. This image is latent and prior to the manifest content that the individual work strives to communicate. To think abstractly, to tell with words, to tell with images, to paint, to calculate, to experiment in laboratories—none of these are neutral activities. Rather, they constitute the core of a discipline, they give a face to an idea of reality that each discipline constructs. The form of the discourse imposes an order on the world: it creates an ontology. In this sense, the prime content of every philosophical work is sedimented in the medium of thought; the prime content of film lies in the use of motion-images and time-images; the prime content of every narrative is crystallized in the form of the story, and so on.

During ordinary communication, the assumptions on which games of truth are based remain implicit: indeed, if ordinary communication exists at all, if we can speak to each other with a reasonable expectation of being understood, this is precisely due to the fact that the rules of speech are removed from analytical processes and assumed to be valid. Etymologically, that which is "implicit" is what remains folded away. In order to unfold it we rely on thought, on the linguistic game to which we assign the task of bringing to the surface the levels of meaning that, like the geological layers hidden under the visible crust of the earth, remain crushed in the assumptions of our utterances. The act of thinking is made up of many movements

---

20. See Barbara Cassin, *L'Effet sophistique* (Paris: Gallimard, 1995).

that become possible or impossible, conceivable or inconceivable, depending on the planes of the discourse that are opened up by a form of life and a cultural model. To unearth these assumptions, the philosophical paradigm that we associate with Nietzsche's name makes use of the methods of *deconstruction* and *genealogy.* To know ourselves, to state the foundations of our own identity, means taking our discourses apart and locating them in the historical and geographic ground from which they emerged and to which they will one day return. Ever since cracks appeared in the edifice of Platonism; ever since the disciplines that for centuries or millennia claimed direct access to the nature of things discovered themselves to be marked by partial preunderstandings and by a contingent origin; ever since the historicist, perspectivist, and multicultural idea that thought is born situated and that transcendentals change over time and space refused to be subordinated to abstract thought; ever since truth was conceived as an unconscious, collective *illusio,* and the will to truth itself became problematic, genealogy and deconstruction have become the starting point of every philosophy—or, better yet, they have become the starting point of every philosophy seeking to repeat the Kantian critical act in our epoch, staying true to the founding idea of European speculation, namely, that one must commence from the foundations, begin from the beginning. In this kind of cultural landscape, a discipline like literary theory, which is historically accustomed to comparing discourse genres and explicating what is implicit in their structures, possesses a weight comparable to what formal logic might have had when metaphysics was still untouched by the linguistic turn. Naturally, neither morphological analysis nor historical-geographic anamneses are removed from the vicious circle: their internal forms and histories are thoroughly contingent and remain subject to other analyses and anamneses. Still, they do have the logical and chronological advantage of disclosing what normally remains closed from view: they possess the privilege of belonging to a later phase.

Literature and Reality

There are two ways of understanding the practice of genealogy. In the Homeric poems and in the Bible, genealogies set out family and intraspecific lineages that link each individual to his or her ancestry; in the work of Nietzsche, genealogies restore ideas to layers of reality existing before ideas and—to take up the expression used earlier and transform it into a metaphor—they adopt an extraspecific look. *On the Genealogy of Morals,* for example, does not limit itself to tracing the entire history of prejudices on good and evil: it also unmasks the relations of power from which ethical rules are said to derive. This book adopts a primarily intraspecific approach: I reconstruct the family history of the novel, beginning from its rootedness in the language games of fiction and mimesis, and only at the end do I tie the internal history of the texts to history *tout court.* Taking this approach means putting forward a model of the relationship between literature and reality. Let me clarify this by turning to the book on literary theory that most clearly explains it.

In *The Political Unconscious* (1981), Fredric Jameson reflects on the paradigms that the critic employs to think about the connections between culture and the world. He refers to a passage by Louis Althusser that sets out three ways of imagining the relationship between the totality of social life and its parts.[21] The first views reality as a network of small local events, of precise relations that a certain minimal cause entertains with its effect. Althusser defines this paradigm as *transitive,* Jameson as *mechanical.* Homologous to the schemas of modern natural sciences, the mechanical schema abounds in positivist-style histories of culture, which focus on the molecular relations that constitute the kernel of every historical narrative: the influence of one writer on another, of a historical event on a cultural circle, of a milieu on an artistic form, of a publishing choice on a literary genre.

The second paradigm, called *expressive,* conceives of the parts in connection to a whole endowed with an inner essence. It separates the areas of the real that express the core of the totality from the sectors that are peripheral and derivative. Appearing in the metaphysics of Leibniz, perfected by the metaphysics of Hegel, a model of this sort gives form to the histories of culture and arts that descend from the tradition of *Geistesgeschichte* but also from the Marxist sociology of culture in its popularized version. Reality is divided into levels, and the levels are arranged according to a

---

21. Louis Althusser and Étienne Balibar, *Lire "Le Capital"* (1965); English translation *Reading "Capital,"* trans. Ben Brewster (London: Verso, 2009), chap. 9; Frederic Jameson, *The Political Unconscious: Narrative as a Socially Symbolic Act* (Ithaca, NY: Cornell University Press, 1981), chap. 1.

hierarchy that leads from the inner essence, or structure ("the ultimately determining instance of economic organization"), to superstructural phenomena (the history of culture), passing via the intermediate planes (politics, ideology, the history of intellectuals). Because the movements of the structure and the movements of the superstructure are believed to be homologous, the latter are interpreted as reflections or consequences of the former.[22] The theory of layers is not an exclusively Marxist schema of thought: every "school of suspicion" identifies a plane that is "the ultimately determining instance" (the mode of production, the will to power, the unconscious) on which the others are dependent, just as phenomena are on their essence.[23]

The third, *structural* paradigm comes from the metaphysics of Spinoza, and, according to Althusser, it represents the great theoretical novelty of Marx's *Capital*. In the expressive model, the essence of the whole is present in a single, deep dimension that imprints its mark on the layers situated on the surface. In the new model, the whole is inherent in each of its modes of being: "the whole existence of the structure consists of its effects."[24] According to Jameson, this paradigm reworks the Marxist theory of levels while reinstating Marx's original insight:

> Where the latter either conceived or, in the absence of a rigorous conceptualization, perpetuated the impression of "the ultimately determining instance" or mode of production as the narrowly economic—that is, as one level within the social system which, however, "determines" the others—Althusser's conception of mode of production identifies this concept with the structure as a whole. For Althusser, then, the more narrowly economic . . . is however privileged, not identical with the mode of production as a whole, which assigns this narrowly "economic" level its particular function and efficiency as it does all the others. . . . This is the sense in which this "structure" is an absent cause, since it is nowhere empirically present as an element, it is not part of the whole or one of the levels, but rather the entire system of *relationships* among those levels.[25]

---

22. Jameson, *The Political Unconscious*, 92ff.

23. See Paul Ricœur, *De l'interprétation: essai sur Freud* (1965); English translation *Freud and Philosophy: An Essay on Interpretation*, trans. Denis Savage (New Haven, Conn.: Yale University Press, 1977), 32ff.

24. Althusser and Balibar, *Reading "Capital,"* 189.

25. Jameson, *The Political Unconscious*, 35–36.

Jameson illustrates this paradigm with the accompanying diagram:

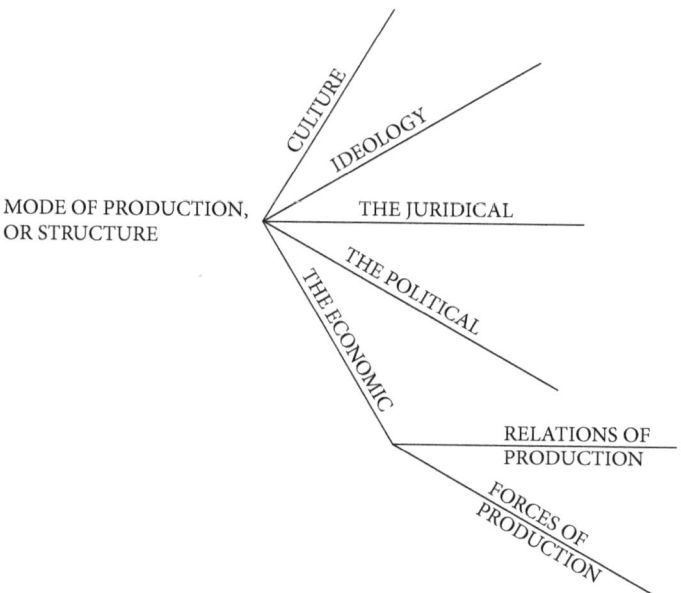

It is important to understand that these mechanical, expressive, and structural causalities do not exclude each other; rather, they describe different planes of being, each having a validity of its own in a multiplanar world in which complex systems of causes are at work. The studies that stem from the mechanical model, for example, plausibly explain why there exists a relationship between the development of the novel and the growth in the number of readers that took place during the eighteenth century, or between the evolution of literary genres and the publishers' decisions. It is undeniable that Samuel Richardson's success was partly due to the rise of a new readership, and that the architecture of Dostoevsky's works—his way of dividing the text into chapters or building dramatically styled scenes—also stems from the fact that his works were published as serials. In the same way, the expressive paradigm captures real processes: often mocked, the thesis of Marxist literary sociology that the birth of the modern novel was a reflection of the capitalist economy and middle-class individualism continues to return because it has a solid foundation in reality. However, while it is true that each of the paradigms dwells on a legitimate layer of causes, the perspective that this book adopts is inspired above all by the third schema of thought and by its ontological decision. In keeping with

Capital, Jameson defines "mode of production" as the totality of things and relations. Still, this philosophical vocabulary does not necessarily have to be applied to the structural model: the paradigm that Althusser and Jameson describe maintains its essential traits even when a different metaphysics and a different language are used to give a name to the whole. The metaphysics and language that I will adopt descend from historicism and from the *Lebensphilosophie* of the late nineteenth century: I will talk about "forms of life" and "epochs." Obviously, a choice of this sort can hardly be justified in the space of a few pages. In the sectorial perspective of this study, what will make it legitimate or illegitimate is the effectiveness or ineffectiveness of the book you are now reading.

A form of life in an epoch of its history is composed of regional systems: practices, social relations, institutions, linguistic games, and disciplines. Although the parts of the whole are linked by mechanical and expressive relations of causality, there is no "ultimately determining instance" that combines all the others together, like an essence that sums up all the phenomena. Instead, there are causal relations moving between the systems into which reality is divided, each of which expresses an aspect of the whole that partly or wholly escapes the other systems. While vulgar Marxist sociology interprets the aesthetic sphere as a secondary outgrowth of an underlying primary structure, this book starts from the conviction that an essential aspect of the Western form of life takes shape and becomes an object of knowledge only through mimesis and fiction. The reason for this, as we will see, is because only in mimesis and fiction do human beings become aware of themselves as individual, particular beings, thrown into time, located in a world, and placed among others. To retrace the intraspecific history of the ways in which people's lives have been narrated means to reassess the history of the ways in which this dimension of the real was anchored in language and transformed into experience. I will therefore reconstruct a sectorial genealogy, and at the end I will attempt to understand if and how our form of life comes out of this regional perspective illuminated.

What Is the Novel?

In its common sense meaning, as conveyed by contemporary dictionaries, the novel is a narrative of a certain length, mainly fictional and mainly in prose. The limitations of this formula are obvious: most novels are written in prose, but prose is not a necessary characteristic; most novels tell fictional stories, but some describe real events; the length allows us to distinguish the novel from what we define as a short story or novella, but it turns out to be impossible to establish precise criteria.

Let us give up on dictionaries, then, and turn to the genre theories that have appeared during the past few centuries. One of the most influential came out of the writings of Friedrich Schlegel. His critical fragments and *Dialogue on Poetry* contain ideas that became widespread throughout the 1800s and were further developed in the 1920s and 1930s by Mikhail Bakhtin. The novel, writes Schlegel, is the first important literary form to be born outside the age-old norms, both written and nonwritten, that governed ancient and classicist poetics: it is devoid of rules, changes constantly, and absorbs the other genres. Over the course of the nineteenth century, these theories would lead to celebrated, eloquent reformulations:

> Thus the critic who, after reading *Manon Lescaut, Paul et Virginie, Don Quixote, Les Liaisons dangereuses, Werther, Elective Affinities, Clarissa Harlowe, Émile, Candide, Cinq-Mars, René, Les Trois Mousquetaires, Mauprat, Le Père Goriot, La Cousine Bette, Colomba, La Rouge et le Noir, Mademoiselle de Maupin, Notre-Dame de Paris, Salammbô, Madame Bovary, Adolphe, M. de Camors, L'Assommoir, Sapho*, etc., still dares to write "This is a novel, that is not" seems to me to be endowed with a perspicacity remarkably like incompetence. . . . Is there a set of rules for writing a novel, any deviation from which would require a story to bear a different name?
>
> If *Don Quixote* is a novel, is *Le Rouge et le Noir* one as well? If *Monte Cristo* is a novel, what about *L'Assommoir*? Is it possible to make a comparison between Goethe's *Elective Affinities*, Dumas's *Les Trois Mousquetaires*, Flaubert's *Madame Bovary*, Monsieur O. Feuillet's *M. de Camors* and Zola's *Germinal*? Which of these works is a novel? What are these famous rules? Where do they originate from? Who made them? By virtue of what principle, whose authority, and what reasoning?[26]

For Bakhtin, the changeability of the novel descends from its supposedly comic and popular origins; for Schlegel, it represents instead the literary correlative of the right to creative freedom and personal idiosyncrasy, the

---

26. Guy de Maupassant, *Pierre et Jean* (1887–1888); English translation *Pierre et Jean*, trans. Julie Mead (Oxford: Oxford University Press, 2001), 3–4.

cult of the particular on which was founded the epoch that Schlegel called Romantic and we call modern.[27] This anarchy presents itself in many ways. According to the normative poetics that Antonio, the character in the *Dialogue on Poetry,* expounds, the best novels are those that give themselves over to autobiographical confession or play with subjective humor: "What is best in the best novels is nothing but a more or less veiled confession of the author, the profit of his experience, the quintessence of his originality."[28]

What Schlegel has in mind is the autobiographical and humorous fiction of Sterne and Jean Paul and *Jacques the Fatalist* by Diderot.[29] But the novel takes another characteristic form as well, which we find in the works of Richardson, Fielding, Goldsmith, and Fanny Burney, and which clashes with Antonio's theory:

> Yet I appreciate all the so-called novels to which my idea of romantic form is altogether inapplicable, according to the amount of self-reflection and represented life they contain. And in this respect even the followers of Richardson, however much they are on the wrong track, are welcome. From a novel like *Cecilia Beverley,* we at least learn how they lived there in London in boredom, since it was the fashion, and also how a British lady for all her daintiness finally tumbles to the ground and knocks herself bloody. The cursing, the squires, and the like in Fielding are as if stolen from life, and *Wakefield* grants us a deep insight into the world view of a country preacher.[30]

There are thus two ways of telling stories about individuals: by focusing on the subjective angle of particularities, confessions, and idiosyncrasies; or by dwelling on the objective angle, on the multiplicity of the outer world, on the variety of everything that exists. About twenty years later, in reflecting on the evolution of painting and the novel, Hegel expressed a similar idea when talking about the freedom enjoyed by contemporary artists:

27. See Friedrich Schlegel, *Fragmente*; English translation *Lucinde and the Fragments*, ed. Peter Firchow (Minneapolis: University of Minnesota Press, 1971).

28. Friedrich Schlegel, *Gespräch über die Poesie* (1800); English translation, *Dialogue on Poetry and Literary Aphorisms*, ed. Ernst Behler (University Park: Pennsylvania State University Press, 1968), 103.

29. Schlegel, *Lucinde and the Fragments*, fragment 78, p. 152: "Many of the very best novels are compendia, encyclopedias of the whole spiritual life of a brilliant individual."

30. Schlegel, *Dialogue on Poetry*, 103.

Bondage to a particular subject-matter and a mode of portrayal suitable for this material alone are for artists today something past, and art has therefore become a free instrument which the artist can wield in proportion to his subjective skill in relation to any material of whatever kind. . . . In this way every form and every material is now at the service and command of the artist.[31]

The first volume of the *Aesthetics* ends with extraordinary predictive lucidity by tracing out the two long roads mimesis would take from that moment on: "the imitation of external objectivity in all its contingent shapes" and "the liberation of subjectivity, in accordance with its inner contingency."[32] What he means by this is the desire to portray contingent lives and forms of life in their objective particularity, as happens in the novels that the nineteenth century would call "realistic"; and the impulse of modern individuals to express themselves and their individual difference, as happens in the introspective genres and mimetic forms that overlay the things they represent with the patina of subjectivity.

What is the novel today? If we were looking for a concise formulation that belonged to neither Schlegel nor Hegel nor Bakhtin but that neatly encapsulated an idea central to their theories, we might say this: *Starting from a certain date, the novel became the genre in which one can tell absolutely any story in any way whatsoever.* The boundless multiplicity of forms of life, whether real or possible, can be narrated from inside or outside consciousness, and at the same time any style can be adopted, allowing the variety of the subjective imagination to be revealed. Whoever goes into a bookstore and browses the shelves where novels are stacked expects to find a bit of everything: long and relatively short texts, stories about ordinary lives and invented worlds, fictional stories and true stories, adventure and the everyday, plausible and implausible plots, realism and estrangement, self and world, seriousness and contingency, highs and lows, prose but also verse. The fluidity of the boundaries is reflected in the fluidity of the terms that designate the form. Rarely do contemporary bookstores have a specific shelf dedicated to something called "novels," while we often

---

31. Georg Wilhelm Friedrich Hegel, *Vorlesungen über die Ästhetik;* English translation *Aesthetics: Lectures on Fine Art,* vol. 1, trans. T. M. Knox (Oxford: Oxford University Press, 1975), 605–6.
32. Ibid., 801.

come across a section dedicated to the genre called *fiction* by French and English speakers, and *narrativa* by Italian speakers. Publishers reproduce the same division: novels, autobiographies written for artistic purposes, and short stories are grouped under the same series, almost as if they were a subspecies of a wider species. This means that our culture conceives of every narrative written with aesthetic intentions as part of a single family, inside of which the differences matter less than the similarities. The same anarchic fluidity is at work in the conscious and unconscious minds of writers: faced with the empty page, modern storytellers know that they have absolute freedom, at least in principle. In theory, the poets and playwrights of our times also move in a realm of abstractly unlimited possibilities, but then, in the practice of writing, only the writer who uses the narrative form is able to encompass all the other genres. In the past couple of centuries, there continue to appear novels written in verse (from Pushkin's *Eugene Onegin* to Vikram Seth's *The Golden Gate*), novels written in dialogical and theatrical forms (*Requiem for a Nun* by Faulkner), and novels that contain lyric poetry (from Pasternak's *Doctor Zhivago* to *Scuola di nudo* by Walter Siti). Few boundary lines are discernible in this apparently formless space. Rules that dictionaries incorporate into their definitions (prose and length) are the most uncertain and least relevant. Starting from a certain date, novels began to primarily use prose, but this has yet to completely triumph; novels are longer than novellas and short stories, but a rigid criterion is impossible to establish. Moreover, the boundary that separates a long narrative from a short one is hardly insurmountable: many of the things that can be said about the modern novel are equally true for the modern short story, because the two genres belong to the same species. The structural boundaries are other than these.

The first is *the narrative form*: in more or less straightforward or unusual ways the novel tells a story. Although some works shift the barycenter of the text toward nonnarrative elements, the language game of storytelling remains implicit in the family resemblance we think about when talking about the novel. The second is *the possibility to make free use of any content and any style*. This is why the novel clearly distinguishes itself from the narrative forms that premodern literary theory rigidly codified, namely, the ancient *epos* and historiography. While these narrate defined topics in a defined style, the novel remains changeable and multiform. To ask what the novel is, what image of the world lies deposited in its structure, why this way of representing people and things has become so important, means to answer two questions: What does it mean to tell a story? What does it mean to tell a story about absolutely anything in any way whatsoever?

In Chapter 1, I attempt to answer the first question through a theory of narrative and, more generally, through a theory of mimesis. Normally, literary criticism tackles a question of this sort from a timeless point of view, according to a method first put into practice by the Russian Formalists during the 1910s and 1920s, later picked up on by the discipline that Tzvetan Todorov, in 1969, called "narratology."[33] The discursive formations of the story and mimesis became truly definable when they came up against a real boundary. In the West, the borders that today still separate mimesis from concept and literature from philosophy have a birth date: they were fixed during the discursive battle that took place between the sixth and fourth centuries BCE in ancient Greek culture. At the conclusion of these conflicts there arose the theoretical boundaries that still shape our ways of conceiving reality. *Theory of the Novel* takes its point of departure from this original split.

The clash retraced in the first chapter is fundamental for other reasons as well. As we shall see, fiction did not have the capability of telling any story in any way whatsoever. This became a reality because the linguistic institutions emerging between the sixth and fourth centuries BCE generated forms of censorship and control over stories that maintained their hegemony for thousands of years, until modern literature swept them away. Chapters 2, 3, and 4 recount the birth of the novel, according to the modern meaning of the term, along with how this took place between the mid-sixteenth century and the beginning of the nineteenth century. At the conclusion of a dialectical, tortuous process, Western narrative was emancipated from the two structures of sense that had hindered the anarchic mimesis of particularities. The first was the Platonic-Christian subordination of the arts to a normative morality and to disciplines that come to know reality through the medium of the concept; the second was the classical and classicist poetics on the separation of styles, which broadly influenced European literature until the late eighteenth century. These a prioris bound the narrative of ordinary lives to an apparatus of ideas and principles that came prior to the disorder of ordinary lives. Instead, the novel allowed stories to

---

33. See Tzvetan Todorov, *Grammaire du "Décaméron"* (The Hague: Mouton, 1969), 10.

be told about beings and the contingent circumstances that surround them with a richness, plasticity, and new importance, introducing a definitive break in the ways we represent reality and construct invented worlds. When this transformation wielded its effects, the existence of private, common individuals secured an unprecedented linguistic space in European culture and the novel entered into the modern epoch of its history, as we shall see in Chapter 5. Chapters 6, 7, and 8 trace out a historical morphology of the modern novel, from the birth of the nineteenth-century paradigm to the emergence of modernist and postmodernist fiction. The Conclusion reflects on the global meaning of the novel as a game of truth and on the aspects of contemporary life that narrative forms allow us to understand. Every page in this book leads to this epilogue.

CHAPTER ONE

A Theory of Narrative

People and Leaves

In the ninth book of the *Iliad* Agamemnon sends Odysseus, Ajax, and Phoenix to appease Achilles's wrath. The three ambassadors arrive at the camp of the Myrmidons while the hero is beginning to sing an epic song accompanied by a lyre he has won in the war. Patroclus listens, seated in front of him. The song is interrupted by the arrival of the guests; taken by surprise, with lyre still in hand, Achilles gets up to welcome them.

> Now they came beside the shelters and ships of the Myrmidons
> and they found Achilleus delighting his heart in a lyre, clear-sounding,
> splendid and carefully wrought, with a bridge of silver upon it,
> which he won out of the spoils when he ruined Eetion's city.
> With this he was pleasuring his heart, and singing of men's fame,
> as Patroklos was sitting over against him, alone, in silence,
> watching Aiakides and the time he would leave off singing.
> Now these two came forward, as brilliant Odysseus led them,
> and stood in his presence. Achilleus rose to his feet in amazement
> holding the lyre as it was, leaving the place where he was sitting.
> In the same way Patroklos, when he saw the men come, stood up ...[1]

This is the most ancient Western representation of storytelling, the practice that Plato would later identify using the inclusive term of *mimesis.*

---

1. Homer, *Iliad*, trans. Richmond Lattimore (Chicago: University of Chicago Press, 1967; first ed. 1951), 9.185–95.

What he means by this in the *Republic* is the wider set of practices that includes the more limited subset of storytelling, according to a taxonomic schema that has come down to us through the ages. There are two other similar scenes in the *Odyssey,* in the first and eighth books. One takes place during a banquet, when the Proci force Phemius the bard to sing a poem on the return of the Achaeans to their homeland; the other is when Odysseus, as a guest at the table of Alcinous, asks Demodocus to recount the fall of Troy.[2] The function of the epic song is hedonistic, commemorative, celebratory, and pedagogic. For nonprofessional singers, it is a pleasurable pastime; for the bards, who perform during banquets, it is their job to sing stories that hold a symbolic weight in the life of the community, about the deeds of gods and heroes.

For the culture that the ancient Greek *epos* bequeathed to us, the origin of stories is memory. The daughters of Mnemosyne, the Muses, confer on the singer a power that seemed prodigious to archaic Greek culture: to show parts of reality that elude the present because they no longer exist or have yet to occur. Those who dedicate themselves to the storytelling inspired by the Muses acquire the power to describe beings and events belonging to a world that has disappeared or has yet to appear, "as if you were there yourself or heard from one who was," to use Odysseus's words in praise of Demodocus's art.[3] Hesiod explains the powers of Mnemosyne using the formula that Homer employs to describe the powers of Calchas, the diviner: to know all things of the present, the past, and the future.[4] In the Neo-Latin tongues and in English, a linguistic equivalent for the ability to recall a fragment of life that is removed from the present or has yet to arrive is found in the etymology of one of the terms used to translate *mimesis:* representation. In theory, all beings and events can escape from the cyclical continuity of occurrences to take on a symbolic existence through

2. Homer, *Odyssey* 1.150–154, 1.325–327, 8.487ff.

3. Homer, *Odyssey* 8.491.

4. Homer, *Iliad* 1.70; Hesiod, *Theogony,* lines 32, 38. For more on this comparison, see, among others, Jean-Pierre Vernant, "Aspects mythiques de la mémoire en Grèce" (1959); English translation "Mythic Aspects of Memory," in *Myth and Thought among the Greeks,* trans. Janet Lloyd with Jeff Fort (Brooklyn, NY: Zone Books, 2006), 115–138; and Marcel Detienne, *Les Maîtres de vérité dans la Grèce archaïque* (1967); English translation *The Masters of Truth in Archaic Greece,* trans. Janet Lloyd (Brooklyn, NY: Zone Books, 1996), 39ff.

stories. If so, it would be possible to know all that comes to pass on the earth, as the Sirens promised Odysseus in their bid to tempt him.[5] Nevertheless, only a superhuman memory, like what the Sirens claim to possess or like that of the gods, would have the capacity to remember the past in its entirety. Human memory, limited like all mortal things, discriminates and erases: lacking the capacity to remember everything, the bard chooses a restricted canon of events and condemns a virtually infinite number of beings and actions to oblivion. This is why the Greek *epos* defines itself by naming its own content, that is, the events worthy of being safeguarded in the story: "the glorious deeds of heroes,"[6] the "works of the gods and men."[7]

To the culture that produced the *Iliad* and the *Odyssey* it seemed obvious that the deeds of the gods should be brought back into the present: in the Homeric poems it is taken for granted that divine actions are worthy of being passed down. But when it comes to telling the stories of human beings, the difference between memorable events and unmemorable ones becomes problematic and charged with significance. Unlike the gods, human beings are legion, they are born in obscurity, and they are subject to the cyclic movement of nature, which replaces particular individuals with other equivalent ones. This is the brutal law governing the condition of all ephemeral beings. One of the most well-known similes in the *Iliad* offers a visual expression of it:

> As is the generation of leaves, so is that of humanity.
> The wind scatters the leaves on the ground, but the live timber
> burgeons with leaves again in the season of spring returning.
> So one generation of men will grow while another
> dies.[8]

There does exist an afterlife in the Homeric world, but it offers no consolation for death: the shades who crowd Hades wander around as a mass of spent individuals drained of vitality and painfully inclined to sigh for

---

5. Homer, *Odyssey* 12.191.
6. Homer, *Iliad* 9.189.
7. Homer, *Odyssey* 1.338.
8. Homer, *Iliad* 6.146–149.

life.[9] The only form of true survival known to this ancient world is the memory of human actions preserved in stories.

The *Iliad* and the *Odyssey* are studded with *nomoi* and *ethe*—general observations that transform the poems into a community encyclopedia designed to offer ethical, legal, political, and technical precepts. The simile of the leaves contains one of these universals. These four lines, crystallized into a comparison, state a law that governs the existence of finite beings; they present a condensed ontology. If we were to translate it into a language that would become possible only many centuries later, after the development of philosophy, the thought being expressed would sound like this: "Like all finite beings, living and dead, human beings are caught in a dialectic between difference and repetition. This is because each individual is threatened by the seriality implicit in the structure of being (one lineage of people succeeds another; after one leaf comes another) and in the structure of thought (language dissolves the differences between particular individuals in the identity of common names, seeing that beings are unlimited but words are few). The specific fates of Achilles or Odysseus are swallowed up in the indistinguishable fate of 'human beings' in general, just as the uniqueness of each leaf is swallowed up in the fate of 'leaves' in general." An assumption of this sort is what sustains the ethics of warrior glory and legitimizes the commemorative and celebratory activity of the bards: each with his own weapon does battle against the seriality of finite beings. Heroic acts and the stories sung about heroic feats arise from the other side of an opposite, complementary destiny: the fate of those who see their existence disappearing into a mass of equivalent lives, unable to impress a sign of their difference in the fabric of the world, and destined to be lost in the infinite cycle of endlessly similar beings.

In archaic Greek culture, the contradiction between biological life and symbolic survival was expressed by the conflict between the parts that

---

9. In book 11 of the *Odyssey*, Odysseus goes down into Hades and, seeing Achilles, calls out to him as a happy man—a seemingly appropriate epithet for someone who received the honors of a god when alive and who is treated like a king in the land of the dead. But Achilles replies that he would exchange his condition with that of a plowman or a slave, even, just to be able to return to life and be something more than the lord of the washed-out shades. See *Odyssey* 11.478–491.

compose human identity: the *body* and the *proper name*.[10] The body belongs to the order of nature, the proper name to the order of culture. While animals possess a body but have no name, there is no human being who lacks a name, as Alcinous remarks to Odysseus.[11] Proper bodies and proper names are subject to the same destiny: the former lose their specific features after death; the latter can vanish into the universality of common names, as in the simile of the leaves, which refers to people in general but not to a particular individual. However, there is one fundamental difference: while the biological existence of bodies puts individuals on an equal footing by condemning them to death, the cultural existence of names has the capacity to give a different weight to each being, bringing differences into relief in the memory. Common people leave few narrative traces and they are lost in a panoply of individuals who, like the dead, are *nonymnoi,* or "nameless." The less valiant warriors preserve a trace of their own identity, but only in the form of pure sound, a sign without an aura, dispersed in the midst of countless other, similar signs that make up the long lists of warriors fallen in battle. Only those who accomplish exceptional feats propagate the glory of their proper name and are able to survive symbolically in storytelling.[12] The attempt to resist death and the will to distinguish oneself in life ultimately respond to the same desire: to stand out from the obscure background of the mortal condition, to push back against the limits that imprison beings who are subject to *physis,* to escape the threat that hangs over the living.

The singers are primarily concerned with one side of this twofold ontology: their focus is on particular beings, not on general laws; their works offer a chain of stories, not a reflection on the constants that govern lives.

10. See Jean-Pierre Vernant, "Mortels et immortels: le corps divin" (1986), in *L'Individu, la mort, l'amour* (1989); English translation "Mortals and Immortals: The Body of the Divine," in *Mortals and Immortals: Collected Essays* (Princeton, NJ: Princeton University Press, 1991), 27ff.

11. Homer, *Odyssey* 8.550–554.

12. Hesiod calls the dead *nonymnoi,* "without name" (*The Works and Days,* line 154). On the antithesis between the dead and heroes, see Jean-Pierre Vernant, "Le Mythe hésiodique des races: essai d'analyse structurale" (1960), and "Le Mythe hésiodique des races: sur un essai de mise au point" (1966); English translation "Hesiod's Myth of the Races: An Essay in Structural Analysis" and "Hesiod's Myth of Races: A Reassessment," in *Myth and Thought among the Greeks,* 25–87. Also by Vernant, "La Belle Mort et le cadavre outragé" and "Mort grecque, mort à deux faces," in *L'Individu, la mort, l'amour,* 76.

Although the gods are immortal, they cause or undergo transformations similar to those that afflict humans. Although the universal maxims running through the poem are eternal, they are preserved in memory only with regard to particular events.[13] Although it is possible to formulate laws and concepts in the form of *nomoi* and *ethe,* the logic of the poems is suited for dwelling on the singular, the accidental, and the ephemeral. About twenty-eight centuries later, we perfectly understand this short-sightedness: we find exactly the same thing in the stories that crop up all around us—because the outlook on the world adopted by the Homeric poems is still implicit today in the language game of storytelling as it has been passed down to us. What image of reality is communicated when telling a story? What lies hidden in the act of narration?

Mimesis and Concept

The gesture of beginning with the ancient Greeks has often accompanied philosophies of history based on the idea that culture develops organically and the end is contained in the beginning. This is not my intention. I turn to genealogy only because I want to pinpoint when the structures of sense that still shape our discourses today first came to be established. Mimesis and narrative were defined only when they came up against *fines,* that is, real boundaries. For a long time, ancient Greek culture relied on the works of Homer and Hesiod as its primary discourse of truth: they transmitted mythical tales, historical memory, cosmologies, moral philosophies, *nomoi,* and *ethe.* Between the sixth and fourth centuries BCE, this apparatus of knowledge was shaken by violent criticisms, and the authority of storytellers began to come under fire in the name of another idea of knowledge that was confusedly in the process of forming. The attacks that Pythagoras, Xenophon, Hecate of Miletus, Heraclitus, and others directed against the mythical tales and works of Homer and Hesiod, the allegorical readings of the *Iliad* and the *Odyssey* that spread from the third decade of the sixth century BCE,[14] are the sign of a slow transformation that changed the idea

13. Eric A. Havelock, *Preface to Plato* (Cambridge, MA: Belknap Press of Harvard University Press, 1982).

14. On this period of change, see, among others, Jean Pépin, *Mythe et allégorie: les origines grecques et les contestations judéo-chrétiennes* (Paris: Aubier, 1958), 95ff.; Jesper Svenbro, *La Parole et le Marbre: aux origines de la poétique grecque* (Lund: N.p., 1976),

of knowledge and culminated at the beginning of the fourth century BCE in one of the texts that was crucial for the history of games of truth in the West: Plato's *Republic*.

Plato was the first to use the term *mimesis* as a unitary category for grouping together all the imitative arts.[15] The field was defined precisely

101ff.; Marcel Detienne, *L'Invention de la mythologie* (1981); English translation *The Creation of Mythology*, trans. Margaret Cook (Chicago: University of Chicago Press, 1986), 82ff.; Silvia Gastaldi, *Paideia/mythologia*, in Plato, *La Repubblica*, trans. and ed. with commentary by Mario Vegetti, vol. 2 (Naples: Bibliopolis, 1998), bks. 2 and 3, pp. 348ff. On the competition between forms of knowledge as a basic characteristic of archaic Greek culture, see Geoffrey Ernest Richard Lloyd, *Magic, Reason, and Experience: Studies in the Origin and the Development of Greek Science* (Cambridge: Cambridge University Press, 1979); also by Lloyd, *Adversaries and Authorities: Investigations into Ancient Greek and Chinese Science* (Cambridge: Cambridge University Press, 1996), and *The Ambitions of Curiosity: Understanding the World in Ancient Greece and China* (Cambridge: Cambridge University Press, 2002).

15. The words *mimos* (mime as genre and the mime as an actor), *mimeisthai* (to mimic), *mimema* (the result of the act of mimicking), and *mimetes* (he who mimics) can be found starting in the fifth century, especially in reference to the genre of mime and dance. Initially the act of *mimeisthai* signified the effects of a performance that was more than an aesthetic representation. It denoted primarily the deception practiced by the *mimetes* vis-à-vis those who watched, in other words, the relationship that is established between the imitator, the person imitated, and the removal of identity that imitation entails. In the first half of the fifth century BCE, this set of words could denote poetic-musical works as well as visual ones, but as early as the end of the sixth century BCE, Simonides had associated painting and poetry. See Hermann Koller, *Die Mimesis in der Antike: Nachahmung, Darstellung, Ausdruck* (Bern: Francke, 1954); Gerald F. Else, "Imitation in the Fifth Century," *Classical Philology* 53, no. 2 (April 1958): 73–90; Göran Sörbom, *Mimesis and Art: Studies in the Origin and Early Development of an Aesthetic Vocabulary* (Stockholm: Svenska Bokforlaget, 1966); Jean-Pierre Vernant, "Naissance d'images," in *Religions, histoires, raisons* (1978); English translation "The Birth of Images," in *Mortals and Immortals: Collected Essays*, ed. Froma I. Zeitlin (Princeton, NJ: Princeton University Press, 1991), 164–185; Gregory Nagy, "Early Greek Views of Poets and Poetry," in *The Cambridge History of Literary Criticism*, vol. 1, *Classical Criticism*, ed. George A. Kennedy (Cambridge: Cambridge University Press, 1989), 1–77; and especially Stephen Halliwell, *The Aesthetics of Mimesis: Ancient Texts and Modern Problems* (Princeton, NJ: Princeton University Press, 2002), 15ff. In works by Plato, the term *mimesis* has many meanings, and the imitative activity is judged in different, sometimes contradictory ways (a detailed analysis can be found in Halliwell, *The Aesthetics of Mimesis*, chaps. 1–4, in Stefan Büttner, *Die Literaturtheorie bei Platon und ihre anthropologische Begründung* [Tübingen: Francke, 2000], and in Daniele Guastini, *Prima dell'estetica: Poetica e filosofia nell'antichità* [Rome: Laterza, 2003], chap. 2). I will focus on the most important meaning for the history of effects, namely, the mimesis that Plato explains in several passages in the *Republic* and that make him "the greatest enemy of art Europe has yet produced" (Friedrich Nietzsche, *Zur Genealogie der Moral: Eine Streitschrift* [1887]; English translation *On the*

because it came up against an objective limit.[16] The author of the *Republic* was actually refining a knowledge that during the millennia to come would put into question the value of the imitative arts, one that, when juxtaposed with the activities of poets and painters, made these seem similar enough to be called by the same name. The frontier Plato traced out between the new paradigm and the old games of truth arose out of a retrospective, teleological narrative, because the cultural spaces the *Republic* distinguished between so peremptorily were only clearly separated from each other in the fourth century BCE.[17] Plato talks about a "quarrel from of old"[18] that divided poetry and philosophy, but in reality, this conflict only became conceivable in the years of his youth—only at the end of the fifth century were the terms *poiesis* and *philosophia* applied to genres that were distinguishable by form and content.[19] But while it may be true that some aspects of the story told by the *Republic* are skewed, it is equally true that it was legitimized a posteriori by subsequent history. Plato's work gives a name to the process that led European culture to exacerbate the tension between poetry and thought and to separate out two different cultural platforms: knowledge that mimics versus knowledge that reasons, imitation versus abstract thought, mimesis versus concept. Despite the criticisms that Western metaphysics and Platonism have endured over the past century and a half, still today, one hundred and forty years after Nietzsche and forty years after the linguistic turn, these discursive families continue to trace out the boundaries of the disciplines through which we come to know the world. Although challenged by theory, in practice the antithesis remains impregnable: the disciplines of arts and philosophy or arts and sciences remain separated by institutional and, therefore, objective borders. To receive

Genealogy of Morals, ed. Keith Ansell-Pearson, trans. Carol Diethe [Cambridge: Cambridge University Press, 2007], 114).

16. See Lloyd, *Magic, Reason, and Experience,* 100ff.; Andrea Wilson Nightingale, *Genres in Dialogue: Plato and the Construct of Philosophy* (Cambridge: Cambridge University Press, 1995).

17. Nightingale, *Genres in Dialogue,* 60ff.; Andrew Ford, *The Origins of Criticism: Literary Culture and Poetic Theory in Classical Greece* (Princeton, NJ: Princeton University Press, 2002), 46ff.

18. Plato, *Republic* 10.607b, in *Plato in Twelve Volumes,* vols. 5 and 6, trans. Paul Shorey (Cambridge, MA: Harvard University Press, 1969).

19. Maria Michela Sassi, *Gli inizi della filosofia: in Grecia* (Turin: Bollati Boringhieri, 2009), chap. 5.

a salary as a bearer of legitimate knowledge on any subject whatsoever, one's knowledge must have been expressed in a reasoned form: imitators are compensated only inasmuch as they are experts of an art, as specialists in "creative writing."

Instead, at the beginning of the fourth century, stories were still a direct source of knowledge and the architrave of Greek *paideia*. The *Republic* reexamines the role this tradition should have in the pedagogic system of an ideal state. In Plato's opinion, imitators should be either censored or expelled from the city. Some of his arguments are motivated by the way mimesis appeared in the first half of the fourth century BCE. The *Republic*'s condemnation was provoked in part by the bodily and musical nature of the contemporary epic and dramatic recitation: the forms of cultivated mimesis that we moderns are accustomed to are much less visceral than the ones Plato was alluding to. In this regard, some of the criticisms we find in the *Republic* belong to the past. Others, however, are fixed forever in the cognitive habits of the West.

Plato deploys multiple arguments in his attack against mimesis, but the most important and lasting objections are two. The first, which had been around for a long time,[20] was moralistic in nature: poets corrupt customs. They describe the gods in the process of performing unworthy actions; they show us that just people may end up unhappy and unjust people happy; they invent characters and plots that are different from how the world should appear if it were governed according to the idea of the good. Stories like this, says the character of Socrates, are likely to incite the "tender and impressionable" young to immoral actions and thoughts. Furthermore, poets have the capacity—a disturbing one for Plato—to imitate anything: they tell stories about good and evil with equal ease; they give themselves over to a protean changeability that is at odds with the stability that virtuous men should demonstrate.[21]

---

20. Svenbro, *La Parole et le Marbre*, chap. 3 and following; Detienne, *The Creation of Mythology*, 82ff.; Gastaldi, *Paideia/mythologia*, 349.

21. Plato, *Republic* 3.395c–396e. The assumption implicit in these stances, traces of which are found in Xenophon as well, is that the effect of a mimetic act does not depend on the effectiveness of the representation, but on the moral quality of the object represented. Imitating unworthy objects, or appreciating the imitations of unworthy objects, means taking on the reprehensible qualities of those things. As we shall see later, a trace of this idea remains in the aesthetics of European classicism.

The second criticism, concentrated primarily in the tenth book, is theoretical in nature and largely new. Imitators, says the character of Socrates, are incapable of teaching the truth, because the act of representing itself is what leads them so far astray from the truth. Because knowing means to penetrate beneath the surface of phenomena to capture their unchanging essences—the Ideas that lie under particular appearances—whoever imitates will never go beyond the ephemeral aspect of people and things.[22] Socrates explains this using an example that would become famous. The true bed is the Idea, the eternal form of the bed created by god; what we find in the real world are instead determinate, individual beds built by carpenters who are inspired by the general idea of "bed." Not only is a painting the imitation of an individual bed, it is seen from a limited perspective and painted by a painter who has no authentic knowledge of what he is depicting. The behavior of poets is no different. They remain obtusely attached to the singular, the phenomenal, the momentary, and the superficial; they do not represent people as they should be but rather show them burdened with particularities and emotions; they produce "inferior things" (*phaula*) with respect to the truth, ones best suited only to seduce the lower region of the soul, the changeable part stirred by the passions.[23]

These moralistic and theoretical criticisms cleared the way for the emergence of a position that exerted considerable influence on European culture. Although the moral and theoretical stances both derived from the same origin, they had different outcomes. To know that which is, a reasoning thought is required to discern principles: norms, regularities, and essences need to be established just as much to identify vices and virtues as to decipher natural laws. Here we have the first expression of a conflict between the two language games that would vie for hegemony over legitimate knowledge for the next two thousand years: imitation versus abstract thought, mimesis versus concept. Out of this original clash there arose local disputes between discursive formations built on these foundations: literature versus philosophy, the imitative arts versus science. After remaining latent for centuries, the conflict surfaced in the work of Plato and became rooted in European culture. With the completion of this process, "the history of Western

---

22. Plato, *Republic* 10.598b–601c.
23. Plato, *Republic* 10.603a–605c.

literary theory can be summed up as a continuous debate on the classical dictum that poets are liars."[24]

Plato expressed himself through the form of his works as well as through theory. It is true that certain devices (the use of myths and the dialogue genre) arose during a phase in history when the border between philosophy and poetry had not yet been demarcated, but it is equally true that Plato made every effort to mark this boundary, by separating mimesis from thought and creating a division between them. While poets speak of particular, visible beings, philosophers relate particularities to the universality of abstract, invisible ideas. While poets recount singular episodes that stand out from the serial foundation of life, philosophers ponder regularities. While the syntax of the poets is made to tell of deeds happening in time and space, philosophers bind the parts of reality together through analytical, atemporal turns of phrase. While mimesis speaks of beings and appearances, philosophy speaks of being and essences. While poets take their authority from the Muse and speak without intermediaries, philosophers discuss other people's *doxa,* the mechanism of abstract thought referring to the presence of a second person, whether overt or introjected.[25] This division between games of truth is what made a discourse on the a priori assumptions of discourses possible. It is no coincidence that the *Republic* reflects on the processes of rational thought as well as attempting to pin down the presuppositions of mimesis and narrative. A process of this sort had to take place before it became possible to challenge the linguistic foundations of knowledge and ask the question that concerns us now: What implicit content, what image of the world, lies sedimented in the act of telling a story? I will start with mimesis to make our way to narrative.

24. See Hans Blumenberg, "Wirklichkeitsbegriff und Möglichkeit des Romans," in *Nachahmung und Illusion,* ed. Hans Robert Jauss (Munich: Fink, 1969); English translation "The Concept of Reality and the Possibility of the Novel," in *New Perspectives in German Literary Criticism,* ed. Richard E. Amacher and Victor Lange (Princeton, NJ: Princeton University Press, 1979), 29–48, quote from 29.

25. "A silent inner conversation of the soul with itself has been given the special name of thought." Plato, *Sophist* 263e.

The Hidden Contents of Mimesis

The main content sedimented in mimesis is the *adoption of an ontology*. Mimesis moves in a specific territory of being: it inhabits the realm of particularities; it addresses the sublunar world. Gods, abstractions, super-human or subhuman beings, fantastic characters, universal laws, relation-ships, causes, categories, logical classes become objects of representation only if they take on a sensible and episodic appearance or serve as a back-ground to a work focused on the imitation of finite beings. When abstract entities are central to the text and take the form of ideas, the public living in an epoch whose culture is already familiar with other discursive formations and other models of truth perceives the occurrence of a code-switching, the advent of a different language game.

We can translate the preunderstanding immanent in mimesis into con-temporary philosophical vocabulary. The culture of the twentieth century offers two lexicons well suited for this purpose: the reflection of phe-nomenology on the concept of the lifeworld and that of Anglophone an-alytic philosophy on the vision of the world said to be implicit in the common sense of human beings. The ontology that mimesis presupposes resem-bles the general structures of the *Lebenswelt* as it is imagined by Husserl or the set of beliefs—"commonplaces of the least refined thinking"—that the descriptive metaphysics of P. F. Strawson tries to identify.[26] The *Leb-enswelt* presupposes that reality is composed of objects and beings included in a horizon;[27] naive realism imagines that the world is made of "partic-ular things, some of which are independent from ourselves," that history is made of "episodes in which we may or may not have a part," and that the constitutive elements of the real are bodies and persons.[28] Husserl is not always unequivocal on this point, but his philosophy seems to assume that

26. See Edmund Husserl, *Die Krisis der europäischen Wissenschaften und die transzen-dentale Phänomenologie: Eine Einleitung in die phänomenologische Philosophie* (1936); En-glish translation *Crisis of European Sciences and Transcendental Phenomenology*, trans. David Carr (Evanston, IL: Northwestern University Press, 1970), §37; and Peter Fredrick Strawson, *Individuals: An Essay in Descriptive Metaphysics* (London: Routledge, 1959), 10ff.

27. Husserl, *Crisis of European Sciences*, §§37 and 38.

28. Strawson, *Individuals*, 15.

the lifeworld is relatively atemporal;[29] Strawson, on the other hand, is explicit in saying that naive realism is a fixed core "which has no history—or none recorded in histories of thought."[30] A comparative look at the discursive formations of our culture shows the frameworks of the *Lebenswelt* or naive realism to be everywhere, but not as much in the language game of abstract thought as in the parallel and concurrent one of mimesis. We are capable of deciphering the rocky images on cave walls or the epic stories of extinct peoples. When faced with a painting coming from a distant time and space, with marks traced out using conventions that vary widely from our own, we still understand that certain figures mean a person or an animal, a woman or a man, a seated or standing character, a warrior or a farmer. When reading a story written thousands of years ago in a culture we know nothing about, we are still able to get a rough sense of what is happening. The continuity that the structures of imitation show throughout the ages suggests that the elementary forms of the *Lebenswelt*, the foundations of naive realism, really can transcend times and places. It would almost seem as if mimesis contained a supratemporal grammar of the finite experience. In the case of figurative arts, these primary forms are implicit in the bond with what E. H. Gombrich called "the message from the visible world;"[31] in the case of mimesis in general, the common element is a link with particularity. The arts that are entirely detached from these minimum common bonds, such as abstract painting or pure poetry, cease to appear mimetic.[32] When images do not portray objects or people, figurative art no longer appears figurative; when words ignore finite beings, there arise nonimitative genres and discourses. If the lower boundary of mimesis is the sign that becomes sound or pure form, as it does in music or abstract painting, the upper boundary is the sign which, by refraining from representing the finite, becomes pure concept or pure abstraction.

29. Husserl, *Crisis of European Sciences,* §36.

30. Strawson, *Individuals,* 10.

31. Ernst H. Gombrich, *Art and Illusion: A Study in the Psychology of Pictorial Representation* (1960) (Princeton, NJ: Princeton University Press, 1977), 181.

32. On the minimum common bonds that appear to remain despite the perpetual changeability of mimetic styles, see also Jean-Marie Schaeffer, *Pourquoi la fiction?* (1999); English translation *Why Fiction?* trans. Dorrit Cohn (Lincoln: University of Nebraska Press, 2010), 95.

The skeleton that lies beneath mimesis is thus an ontology whose primary structures are unchanging. On the surface of representation, mimetic works depict the world in its mutability; because if it is true that the imitators operate in a specific ontological realm, each being is particular only thanks to the distinctive traits that make it this entity and not another. Mimesis is the only language game capable of portraying the real or possible modes that particularities can assume. Between the second half of the seventeenth century and the first half of the eighteenth century, in order to make the novel more noble, critics resorted to an argument that was remarkably successful: they said that the new genre filled a vacuum in traditional historiography. Because novels recount the history of private lives and manners, they preserve the traces of things too fugitive and ephemeral to have a place in official discourses. This observation applies to more than just the novel: much of what we know about forms of life that have disappeared, or about forms of life that are contemporary but unknown, comes to us thanks to the language game of mimesis as it functions in the writing of history, chronicles, news reports, and in the arts. Imitation thus stands at the center of a double movement: on the one hand, it suggests the fixed persistence of a *Lebenswelt* that traverses all ages and cultures; on the other, it shows us the forms that particular life has assumed in different epochs and cultures. It does so by revealing the modes that cover the ontological skeleton of naive realism and by dwelling on transient aspects: appearances, features, gestures, characters, customs, morals, environments, ways of thinking. Of course, imitative works are an *interpretation* of the surface, not a copy: the image of the modes of being that reaches us is filtered by the techniques artists use, by the perceptual schemas of a given culture, and by the aesthetic fashions of a certain epoch. That said, the documentary and memorial value of the arts is crucial: without mimesis, we would lose the traces of an entire ontological realm, the most fragile and fugitive one. While other language games leave out the changing forms of life, mimesis acts as a storehouse or repository of the contingent.

The Confines of Mimesis

A metaphysics that conceives of reality as a jumble of beings and particular events; a system of signs that seeks to convey the multiplicity of life and life forms: these are the premises of what I shall call the *mimetic relationship with the world,* the precondition and rule of the genre we are talking about. But to understand its meaning we need to reflect on a crucial problem posed with immediacy by the Homeric poems and the *Republic:* it is not obvious that the mimetic relationship with the world should always exist or that it should always be considered valuable. Mimesis is bounded by a lower limit and an upper limit beyond which different language games come into play.

Other ways of interpreting reality are implicit in the simile of the leaves—ones that, if taken literally, would make the discourse of the bards impossible. If beings succeed each other, generation after generation, always different but always the same, then individuals and individual forms of life may or may not be: their existence is similar to other existences; their life is ephemeral and replaceable. They are pure contingency. Like inessential slivers of a totality that looms over them, they mean something only as fleeting moments of a cyclical motion or as interchangeable tokens of a law or concept. The tautological individual and the particular case of a universal law are two sides of one and the same way of regarding life. For those who adopt an outlook of this kind, the only seat of truth—of meaning and value—if it exists, is the history of the species, conceived as a sequence of perpetually equal beings who follow one another according to the logic of repetition. Anyone who took literally the ontology expressed by the simile of the leaves would be incapable of telling stories: in his or her eyes, there would never be any deeds worthy of telling; the differences between individuals would be insignificant. An image of this vacuum in the Homeric poems is the lot to which the minor heroes are consigned: those who are incapable of countering the seriality of life with their deeds are accordingly excluded from epic song or mentioned fleetingly in the lists of dead warriors.

The lower limit of mimesis is revealed in contemplating the idea that there is nothing to say, that nothing deserves to be represented, because every fragment of finitude is too banal to break free from interchangeability and come back into the present. Dostoevsky opens the fourth part of *The Idiot* (1868–1869) with a question vital to our inquiry. Since society is mostly composed of normal individuals who are devoid of dramatic traits, how can we tell the life stories of "ordinary, completely 'usual' people"? "How can [a novelist] present them to the reader so as to make them at least somewhat interesting?"[33] For the narrator of *The Idiot*, the nature of the subject matter would appear to be equally difficult: he takes it for granted that there are more adventurous lives or more representative existences worthier of appearing in a story. By lending the question an absolute—which is to say, theoretical—meaning, we soon realize that the issue is more complicated. What counts is not the intrinsic quality of the story, but the attitude of the imitator, the willingness to capture a difference where another type of gaze would see only dull, annihilating sameness. During the same period Dostoevsky was writing his novel, Tolstoy was finishing *War and Peace*—a work featuring the lives of many people whom the narrator of *The Idiot* would have judged too common to deserve attention. And yet the theoretical problem remains: potentially, the things that a narrator talks about are always tautological, closed up in their own individuality, irrelevant for the universal, because the material of stories is not the generality of an idea but rather the particularities of contingent lives and forms of life. Any attempt to excite interest in this level of the real comes up against an objection that can always be raised: "Why should I care about certain occurrences?" "What is it to me?" Ever since official truths took the form of abstract thought, the interest that stories arouse is always a precarious outcome and never an unquestionable premise. Only language games operating within the domain of the concept can say, with aggressive assurance, *de te fabula narratur*; people who tell stories can never be so sure. This lack of concern for the fate of particular beings, or for the sensible appearance of finite things, is the lower boundary of mimesis: it is the white light that cancels out all the other colors that make the representation of finitude possible.

The upper boundary of mimesis is implicit in the comparison with the leaves. What do these few lines tell us? Like what happens in passages that stop the narrative flow to describe laws, the simile breaks the rules of a discursive formation whose aim is to represent the singularity of finite beings. It interrupts the way of portraying reality that the listeners of the *epos* are used to and introduces a new language game. What we are witnessing is a reversal of the direct relation between the concrete and the abstract,

33. Fyodor Dostoevsky, *Idiot* (1868–1869); English translation *The Idiot*, trans. Richard Pevear and Larissa Volokhonsky (New York: Random House, 2002), 462.

the particular and the universal, the visible and the invisible. The comparison exploits the possibilities inherent in the morphology and syntax of natural languages, because they are sedimented in the existence of common names and in the ability to make judgments in the form of atemporal expressions governed by the verb "to be." Instead of focusing on singular events—on the fate of *this* person or *this* leaf—the simile states the timeless, spaceless law that governs a class of entities, depriving each individual of his or her difference and refraining from situating the event in space and time. Although the degree of abstraction remains very low, these four lines—as well as other passages in the *Iliad* and the *Odyssey* where *nomoi* and *ethe* are introduced—briefly interrupt the game of mimesis to arrive at a type of knowledge that grasps laws and ideas above or below singular beings. In 1873, a classical philologist who had recently abandoned the restricted field of his discipline revisited the image of the leaves to reflect on the nature of concepts:

> Every concept originates through our equating what is unequal. No leaf ever wholly equals another, and the concept "leaf" is formed through an arbitrary abstraction from these individual differences, through forgetting the distinctions; and now it gives rise to the idea that in nature there might be something besides the leaves which would be "leaf"—some kind of original form after which all leaves have been woven, marked, copied, colored, curled, and painted, but by unskilled hands, so that no copy turned out to be a correct, reliable, and faithful image of the original form.[34]

It was precisely in those years that Nietzsche began to deconstruct the idea of truth that Plato had transmitted to the West over two thousand years earlier, separating abstract thought from mimesis and postulating a necessary correspondence between the structures of being and the structures of thought. Thanks to the new *doxa* for which Nietzsche stands as the origin and metonymy, today we can reflect on games of truth, on the content hidden in linguistic acts and discursive formations. This is the case even for philosophy and the sciences, which have claimed and continue to claim a link between their languages and things in themselves. The preun-

---

34. Friedrich Nietzsche, "Über Wahrheit und Lüge im außermoralischen Sinn" (1873); English translation "On Truth and Lie in an Extra-Moral Sense," in *The Portable Nietzsche*, trans. Walter Kaufmann (London: Penguin Books, 1982), 46.

derstanding implicit in philosophy is opposed to the one implicit in mimesis: the former imagines the world as a territory that converges, the second as a territory that proliferates.

Between Nothingness and Ideas:
The Mimetic Discontinuity

The gaze of the imitator thus appears to stand midway between nothingness and ideas, between the attitude of those who view no phenomena as worthy of being separated out from the flow of occurrences and that of those who take a reflective, abstractive stance, seeking out the laws hidden in the flow of singularities. In both cases, mimesis opposes the serial nullification threatening all finite beings. The decision to represent something is an act charged with meaning: it signifies a belief that particular actions, people, or things, whether real or possible, deserve to be isolated from the limitless expanse of equivalent entities. They deserve to capture our attention and—to use the term that accompanied the rise of the modern novel in the seventeenth and eighteenth centuries—to be "interesting."

The *issue of selection* is thus central to the mimetic relationship with the world. By distinguishing between narratable events and unnarratable events, between what deserves to be brought back into the present and what does not, the Homeric bards made explicit a question that the epochs of mimetic abundance and democracy conceal or ignore. In the eyes of modern readers, interest in the events of particular beings is seemingly an unquestionable fact. At a time when our current horizon of expectations was still in the process of being formed, Sir Walter Scott used a famous line from Terence: "Homo sum, humani nihil a me alienum puto" (I am a human being, I consider nothing that is human as alien to me).[35] Living in an egalitarian and expressivist epoch, we contemporaries believe it to be obvious that stories about our fellow human beings, about all of them, are in theory worthy of attention. The Homeric bards believed instead that to represent the lives of some mortals, to bring them back into the present, was never an act to be taken for granted. While it may be true that imitation

---

35. Sir Walter Scott, *Alain-René Le Sage* (1822), in *Sir Walter Scott on Novelists and Fiction*, ed. Ioan Williams (London: Routledge and Kegan Paul, 1968), 125; Terence, *Heautontimorumenos* 1.1.77.

is inherent in human beings from infancy, as we read at the beginning of Aristotle's *Poetics,* not every event is necessarily worthy of narrative interest. When viewed from the higher perspective of the gods or in terms of the vast movement of nature, the exploits of human beings can even appear uninteresting, because irrelevancy threatens all particular beings (as the simile of the leaves clearly states and as Apollo repeats in answer to Poseidon[36]) and because particular beings are potentially infinite in number, and therefore all the same in their uncontrollable multiplicity. In the eyes of those who accept the mimetic relationship, the world presents itself as a dispersed totality of events, individuals, and particular forms of life that come into existence, mature, cross paths, die, and, in the end, are easily confused due to their very number. To restore the totality of what is happening or could happen, imitators must surrender themselves to what Hegel called the "bad infinity," which is to say, the unlimited sum of multiple small, singular stories. It is a condition that the most ambitious projects of nineteenth-century narrative approached when the novel form began to compete with philosophical systems in representing the extensive totality of life: in the comprehensive, multivolume collection of Balzac's *Human Comedy* and Zola's *Les Rougon-Macquarts*[37] or in the architecture of the great polyhistorical novels of the nineteenth and twentieth centuries, from Tolstoy's *War and Peace* to Hermann Broch's *Sleepwalkers,* from George Eliot's *Middlemarch* to Vasily Grossman's *Life and Fate.* In the twentieth century, literature discovered other lines of flight, shifting attention to the complexity of the inner life[38] or to the inexhaustibility of small, everyday experiences.[39]

> The bad mimetic infinity has been the object of a literary representation in a story by Danilo Kiš, "The Encyclopedia of the Dead" (1983). A woman who speaks in the first person imagines coming across a work entitled *The Encyclopedia of the Dead,* which tells the life story of every person who ever existed, with an extraordinary wealth of details. Written by a religious sect or by an organization that promotes an egalitarian vision of the world, the encyclopedia seeks to rectify the injustice of history by giving each

36. Homer, *Iliad* 21.463–466.
37. See Lukács, *The Theory of the Novel,* 109ff.
38. Virginia Woolf, "Modern Fiction (1919–25)," in *The Essays of Virginia Woolf,* vol. 4, *1925–1928,* ed. Andrew McNeillie (London: Hogarth Press, 1994), 160.
39. Georges Perec, *L'Infra-ordinaire* (Paris: Seuil, 1989).

human being a place in the collective memory. Not surprisingly, the only prerequisite for a person to be included is that his or her name cannot have appeared in any other encyclopedia. This monumental work, begun shortly after 1789, is fascinating. It is written in a style that pauses on every action and every detail, as if every single thing were worthy of interest:

> This is what I consider the compilers' central message—nothing in the history of mankind is ever repeated, things that at first glance seem the same are scarcely even similar; each individual is a star unto himself, everything happens always and never, all things repeat themselves ad infinitum yet are unique. (That is why the authors of the majestic monument to diversity that is *The Encyclopedia of the Dead* stress the particular; that is why every human being is sacred to them.)[40]

The spirit that animates the *Encyclopedia* is diametrically opposed to the ruthless mimetic selection that governs the Homeric poems: instead of the story of a few glorious deeds and a few extraordinary heroes, we have narrative commemoration democratically extended to include all beings deprived of fame. Kiš is well aware that a work of this sort is only possible in a culture that has made each and every person valuable, as in Europe starting in 1789, when the Christian idea of the sacredness of the individual became secularized in the Declaration of the Rights of Man and of the Citizen.[41] But what the story does not say—or says only indirectly, through its form—is that a work like *The Encyclopedia of the Dead* cannot exist, or can exist only in a tale inspired by Borges, because in the real world mimesis leads inevitably to a violent discrimination between discontinuities worthy of being told and the vast pool of uninteresting stories.

For these reasons, the choice of subject to be represented is crucial: it distinguishes the few living beings who deserve to leave a trace behind from the infinite mass of beings who remain unnoticed. The act of separating the narratable from the unnarratable is given all the importance it deserves by

40. Danilo Kiš, *Enciklopedija mrtvih* (1983); English translation *The Encyclopedia of the Dead*, trans. Michael Henry Heim (Evanston, IL: Northwestern University Press, 1997), 51.

41. The *Encyclopedia* project also recalls the project of the Tower Society in *Wilhelm Meisters Lehrjahre*: to collect the autobiographical confessions of its members in an archive. See Johann Wolfgang von Goethe, *Wilhelm Meisters Lehrjahre* (1795–1796); English translation *Wilhelm Meister's Apprenticeship*, trans. Eric A. Blackall in cooperation with Victor Lange (New York: Suhrkamp, 1989), bk. 8, chap. 5.

the Homeric bards. For them a work is defined first and foremost because it represents certain stories and not others, because it creates a discontinuity among continuities of irrelevant actions that are always the same, because it opens up a difference in the isonomy to which finite beings are subject. In our language game, the choice of topic occupies the same place that the object choice occupies in the psychic life described by Freud: it is the cornerstone of the edifice, the original decision that gives form to the region of possibilities. A simple list of the discontinuities imitators have extracted from the flow of real or imaginary phenomena says a great deal about a historical period: it shows which parts of the collective and personal life are deemed worthy of an emotional investment; it identifies the experiences, desires, and ways of life considered interesting. To understand epochal movements, it is enough to reflect on the mere content of their literature, figurative arts, or cinema.

Stories

These are the main features of mimesis, and verbal narrative is a subset of mimesis. How should this subset be defined?

Literary criticism of the twentieth century was thoroughly preoccupied with, and even obsessed by, understanding the a prioris of narrative. These efforts engendered a family of theories whose results, although incommensurable, do agree on a basic definition. I will present it in the words of what was for many years the most widely used introductory book on narrative studies in English-speaking countries: "by narrative we mean all those literary works which are distinguished by two characteristics: the presence of a story and a story-teller."[42] The term *story,* in this case, is intended to signify a series of episodes arranged in a form, what Aristotle in his *Poetics* called *mythos:* the assemblage of incidents (*synthesis ton pragmaton*), the structure that holds together the disparate elements that make up the narrated event.[43] What is a story?

---

42. Robert Scholes, James Phelan, and Robert Kellogg, *The Nature of Narrative: Revised and Expanded* (Oxford: Oxford University Press, 2006), 4. The first edition of *The Nature of Narrative,* published in 1966, was written by Scholes and Kellogg alone.

43. Aristotle, *Poetics* 6.1450a, trans. Anthony Kenny, Oxford World Classics (Oxford: Oxford University Press, 2013). For more on mythos as *synthesis ton pragmaton,* see Aris-

One of the main objectives of twentieth-century narratology was the attempt to answer this question by formulating "the minimal story" or "the minimal complete plot"—in other words, a statement that would express the degree zero of all stories:

> The minimal complete plot consists in the passage from one equilibrium to another. An "ideal" narrative begins with a stable situation which is disturbed by some power or force. There results a state of disequilibrium; by the action or a force directed in the opposite direction, the equilibrium is re-established; the second equilibrium is similar to the first, but the two are never identical.[44]

> It seems to us that the credit of an absolute generalizability can be granted at the point of departure (position of a proper name-subject, possibility of a process of *modification* or *preservation* that predicates the becoming of this subject).[45]

> A minimal story consists of three conjoined events. The first and third events are stative, the second is active. Furthermore, the third event is the inverse of the first. Finally, the three events are conjoined by three conjunctive features in such a way that (a) the first event precedes the second in time and the second precedes the third, and (b) the second event causes the third.[46]

But the first attempts to isolate the minimal story actually date back to ancient times. In book 10 of Plato's *Republic,* in one sentence, Socrates's character defines the content of mimetic poetry (*mimetike*). This is a relatively abstract term, but Socrates talks concretely about Homer, Hesiod, and the tragedians—all authors who tell stories. The definition of *mimetike* thus coincides in actuality with the definition of a minimal story:

> Mimetic poetry ... imitates human beings acting under compulsion or voluntarily, and as a result of their actions supposing themselves to have fared well or ill and in all this feeling either grief or joy.[47]

totle, *La Poétique,* Greek text with a French translation and notes, by Roselyne Dupont-Roc and Jean Lallot (Paris: Seuil, 1980), 198.

44. Tzvetan Todorov, *Poétique de la prose* (1971); English translation *The Poetics of Prose,* trans. Richard Howard (Ithaca, NY: Cornell University Press, 1978), 111.

45. Claude Bremond, *Logique du récit* (Paris: Seuil, 1973), 328.

46. Gerald Prince, *A Grammar of Stories: An Introduction* (The Hague: Mouton, 1973), 31.

47. Plato, *Republic* 10:603c.

The second attempt is to be found in Aristotle's *Poetics*, in a controversial passage in which *mythos* is said to be *synthesis ton pragmaton* and the minimal tragic plot is described:

> Tragedy is mimesis of action (*mimesis praxeos*) and is acted by living persons, who must of necessity have certain qualities of character and thought—for it is these which determine the quality of an action; indeed thought [*dianoia*] and character [*ethos*] are the natural causes of any action and it is in virtue of these that all men succeed or fail—it follows then that it is the plot [*mythos*] which is the mimesis of action. By "plot" I mean here the arrangement of the incidents.[48]

Beneath the superficial differences, the formulations by Plato, Aristotle, and the twentieth-century narratologists resemble each other. What they have in common is an original insight: every story imagines reality in a certain way simply because it is a story and not some other type of discourse (a work of science or philosophy, for example). Along with the plot form, crystallized in its structures, there comes a preunderstanding of life. I will isolate a few of the pivotal points.

1. *Particular beings. Mimetike,* we read in the *Republic,* talks about human beings. Narratology made short work of the rigidity of this idea;[49] and yet the protagonists of narrative do retain an ontological characteristic of people: they are particular beings. Since human beings will inevitably conceive the world starting from themselves, most stories use anthropomorphic heroes even when talking about gods, animals, cells, or allegories. This applies both to stories that use the medium of words and to those that use the medium of images.

2. *Plurality.* In his description of the heroes involved in plots, Plato uses the plural ("human beings acting"). Narratives tend to exhibit the constitutive plurality of particular beings: first and foremost, they assume that there are many people, that their life paths cross each other, that they experience continuously the presence of others, inside and outside themselves. The extreme examples of solipsism, from *Robinson Crusoe* to the novels by Beckett,

---

48. Aristotle, *Poetics* 6.1449b–1450a.

49. Bremond cites biology articles describing the first phase of cell division in a thoroughly narrative form: Bremond, *Logique du récit,* 111, 328.

always presuppose the physical or interior existence of second and third persons. A plot presupposes that there are many individuals whose paths interweave.

3. *Individuation*. As particular beings, the protagonists of plots must necessarily possess distinctive traits that identify them. There are three identifying marks: a body, a name (or any sign in place of a name: "K.," "the Unnamed"), and the set of qualities that makes each of them a specific individual. Aristotle condensed all this into the word *ethos*.[50] Modern culture tends to separate out two families of elements and to distinguish between character and manners—along the lines of an opposition between inside and outside, personal and collective, the domain of psychology and the domain of sociology that was invented on a precise date, acquiring rigor over the past few centuries, and a questionable philosophical legitimacy, considering its founding premises would be easy to deconstruct. However that may be, the particular beings that enter into plots are marked by distinguishing characteristics. And it does not matter whether the characterization refers to a single being or to a universal type: mimesis, as we have said, is the linguistic game that preserves the memory of contingent forms of life, whether real or imaginary, like a gigantic inventory of accidental existences.

4. *Imbalance*. For Plato as for Aristotle, the human beings described by *mimetike* and *mimesis* engage in action. The centrality of action is an essential feature of the ancient literary aesthetic, which insists on the public, visible, and sensible nature of the life imitated by the poets, to the detriment of the life that is lived in the semi-invisible regions of thought and the passions. In the text of the *Poetics* as it has come down to us, Aristotle returns several times to this point: poetry is the representation of what human beings do and what they say in the external world. True mimesis has as its object actions, and not characters; the primary goal of the poet is the creation of a *mythos,* of a plot, and not the static description of an *ethos*. But the insistence on action, as well as reflecting the underlying logic of the ancient poetics, is also what allows Plato and Aristotle to express in the philosophical vocabulary of their epochs an insight that would

50. See Frédérique Woerther, *L'Èthos aristotelicien* (Paris: Vrin, 2007).

run through the Western theory of narrative art: for there to be a plot, the particular beings described must undergo transformations; there is no story without metamorphosis.

From a theoretical point of view, the premise of plots does not necessarily require that there be public action—only that there be a change in state. Visible action was actually the way ancient culture identified the phenomenon of change. Classicist poetics that arose during the sixteenth century used phrases from Aristotle and Plato to refute the verbatim texts of the *Republic* and the *Poetics* in order to argue that, since even the inner life undergoes becoming, there may exist a mimesis and a *mythos* of the affects. But the essential element remains unchanged: the syntax of the story line is not made to represent static situations; the beings represented in plots are ontologically restless and out of balance: "and does not the fretful part of us present many and varied occasions for imitation, while the intelligent and temperate disposition, always remaining approximately the same, is neither easy to imitate nor to be understood when imitated."[51] This is the sense of one of the most famous incipits of the modern novel: "Happy families are all alike; every unhappy family is unhappy in its own way."[52]

5. *Time and space.* In plots, the first vehicle of imbalance is mere becoming: "between the activity of narrating a story and the temporal character of human experience there exists a correlation that is not merely accidental but that presents a transcultural form of necessity."[53]

> A celebrated passage from *The Man without Qualities* illustrates the consequences of this correlation. In chapter 122 of volume 1, Ulrich is walking around the streets of Vienna. He is restless and unhappy: his affair with

---

51. Plato, *Republic* 10.604e.

52. Leo Tolstoy, *Anna Karenina* (1875–1877); English translation *Anna Karenina*, trans. Richard Pevear and Larissa Volokhonsky (London: Penguin Books), 1. In "Berenice" (1835) by Edgar Allan Poe we read: "Misery is manifold. The wretchedness of earth is multiform." *The Collected Works of Edgar Allan Poe: Tales and Sketches*, ed. Thomas Mabbott (Cambridge, MA: Belknap Press of Harvard University Press, 1978), 209.

53. Paul Ricœur, *Temps et récit*, vol. 1 (1983); English translation *Time and Narrative*, vol. 1 (1983), trans. Katherine McLaughlin and David Pellauer (Chicago: University of Chicago Press, 1984), 52.

Gerda has ended badly; the Parallel Action proved to be a failure. All around him, in contrast to the restlessness that he feels running through him, the city transmits an impression of peacefulness. Suddenly, with a shift from the lived experience to reflection that is typical of Musil's style, Ulrich begins to ponder the essence of happiness. In his view, happiness originates from a "foreshortening of the mind's perspective" (*perspektivische Verkürzung des Verstandes*) that brings close things into sharp focus and allows distant things to fade, creating a world where one feels at home. This form of simplification, which Ulrich has lost forever, is also the law of stories:

> It struck him that when one is overburdened and dreams of simplifying one's life, the basic law of this life, the law one longs for, is nothing other than that of narrative order, the simple order than enables one to say: "First this happened and then that happened . . ." It is the simple sequence of events in which the overwhelmingly manifold nature of things is represented, in a unidimensional order, as a mathematician would say, stringing all that has occurred in space and time on a single thread, which calms us; that celebrated "thread of the story," which is, it seems, the thread of life itself. Lucky the man who can say "when," "before," and "after" [*"als," "ehe" und "nachdem"*]! Terrible things may have happened to him, he may have writhed in pain, but as soon as he can tell what happened in chronological order, he feels as contented as if the sun were warming his belly. This is the trick the novel artificially turns to account: Whether the wanderer is riding on the highway in pouring rain or crunching through snow and ice at ten below zero, the reader feels a cozy glow, and this would be hard to understand if this eternally dependable narrative device, which even nursemaids can rely on to keep their little charges quiet, this tried-and-true "foreshortening of the mind's perspective," were not already part and parcel of life itself. Most people relate to themselves as storytellers. They usually have no use for poems, and although the occasional "because" [*weil*] or "in order that" [*damit*] gets knotted into the thread of life, they generally detest any brooding that goes beyond that; they love the orderly sequence of facts because it has the look of necessity, and the impression that their life has a "course" [*Lauf*] is somehow their refuge from chaos. It now came to Ulrich that he had lost this elementary, narrative mode of thought to which private life still clings, even though everything in public life has already ceased to be narrative and no longer

follows a thread, but instead spreads out as an infinitely interwoven surface.[54]

Musil nicely captures a crucial element of plot as form: his observations on the thread of the story can apply to all types of *mythos*. Human beings connect what happens in space and time using syntactic links of a logical or historical type. While the causal or final linkages ("because," "in order that") expand the dimensions of reality, associate different planes with one another, and lengthen the intelligence, narrators are limited to saying "when," "before," and "after": they foreshorten the intelligence and delude themselves into thinking that life has a "course" and follows a single thread, the thread of the story. Theoretical knowledge, governed by the medium of thought and "concerned with the primary causes and principles,"[55] runs endlessly along the chains of reflection that transform life into an immense surface of cross-references. Instead, those who tell stories narrow their understanding of reality and introduce a simple order into chaos, surrendering themselves to the myopic and reassuring dimension of chronology. If the dominant links were not temporal, the language game of stories and the genre of narrative would transform into other games and other genres. Incidentally, this is why *The Man without Qualities* is considered an experimental novel: the anomalous role Musil's book assigns to the essayistic search for causes and principles makes it unusual for narrative fiction.

While the primary connections governing plots are chronological in nature, time presupposes a diametrically opposed dimension that this passage from *The Man without Qualities* does not take into consideration. In addition to being subject to becoming, the particular beings that narrative tells about are also located in space: Achilles, Odysseus, Agamemnon are found camped around Troy; Ulrich, Gerda, Arnheim, Section Chief Tuzzi exist in Vienna in 1913. Stories never talk about dislocated human beings, about humankind-in-itself or about a general human type, as do the abstract discursive formations (philosophy, theology, natural sciences, the

---

54. Robert Musil, *Der Mann ohne Eigenschaften*, vol. 1 (1930); English translation *The Man without Qualities*, vol. 1, trans. Sophie Wilkins and Burton Pike (New York: Knopf, 1995), chap. 122, pp. 708–709.

55. Aristotle, *Metaphysics* 1.981b.

human sciences); and even when the character is an *everyman,* the generic subject is always treated as a being located in a place. The concept of "chronotope" that Bakhtin develops in the most beautiful of his essays on the novel admirably expresses the unbreakable link between time and space that every story establishes.[56]

6. *Desire.* The first of the dynamic forces that stirs up plots is the mere presence of time as a manifestation of an imbalance to which finite beings are ontologically exposed simply by becoming. But this subjugation to the chronological chain is not the only vehicle of change at work in plots: next to the pure succession of instants we find another force that acts in time but does not coincide with chronology. When defining the degree zero of *mimetike,* Plato explicitly dwells on this point: "Mimetic poetry . . . imitates human beings acting under compulsion or voluntarily, and as a result of their actions supposing themselves to have fared well or ill and in all this feeling either grief or joy." In other words, anthropomorphic beings are subject to a perpetual instability of the passions, between the extremes of joy and grief. In seeking the ontological element that lies behind this phenomenal observation, we can say that we are happy or unhappy, we feel joy or grief, because a primordial lack runs through us, an essential imbalance that we call by the name of need, desire, or longing; when this force comes to a stop, we might declare ourselves to be happy, fortunate, or simply content. It is difficult to imagine a plot that does not include this potential restlessness and use it as a secondary driving force for stories along with the mere presence of time. A *mythos* begins because a character is looking for something or loses something and ends when the imbalance is righted: people enter into the plot as needy and desiring entities.

Narrative and Existential Analytics

Particular beings subject to time and located in a space, identified by a proper name, a body, a character, and manners; restless beings, because

---

56. Mikhail Bakhtin, "Formy vremeni i chronotopa v romane" (1937–1938); English translation "Forms of Time and of the Chronotope in the Novel," in *The Dialogic Imagination: Four Essays,* trans. Michael Holquist and Caryl Emerson (Austin: University of Texas Press, 1981), 84–258.

they are vulnerable to becoming and to desire; beings whose lives intersect with the lives of others, acting, speaking, and formulating thoughts, experiencing passions, living in a social system, until the imbalance is righted and the story reaches its end: this is the matter of stories. Now: when you try to put a complete, minimum plot down on paper, you arrive at a sentence that corresponds to a theory of human action.[57] This is a crucial point. Minimal stories produce what Martin Heidegger called an "existential analytic,"[58] or a concise description of the mode of being of human beings. *This is the case because only plots incorporate into their form the basic scaffolding of our lives qua existences that are finite, identified, situated, and off balance. All other language games have a relationship of pure exteriority with these a prioris, starting with abstract thought, which banishes from its processes the singular, temporal, spatial, intersubjective, anecdotal, and circumstantial nature of what individuals do and think. In the process, abstract thought transforms the particular life into the content of a discourse whose style produces statements divorced from particularity.* It is important to understand that the image of the world sedimented in plots is not the life of finite beings, but an interpretation of this life. Some of the most perceptive criticisms that the plot form received in the twentieth century allow certain aspects of the preunderstanding crystallized in plots to be captured, as if in a mirror image. The protagonist of Jean-Paul Sartre's *Nausea* (1938), Antoine Roquentin, reflects on the transfiguration of experience that takes place in stories:

> For the most banal event to become an adventure, you must (and this is enough) begin to recount it. This is what fools people: a man is always a teller of tales, he lives surrounded by his stories and the stories of others, he sees everything that happens through them; and he tries to live his own life as if he were telling a story.
>
> But you have to choose: live or tell. . . . Nothing happens while you live. The scenery changes, people come in and go out, that's all. There are no beginnings. Days are tacked on to days without rhyme or reason, an interminable, monotonous addition. From time to time you make a semi-total: you say: I've been travelling for three years, I've been in Bouville

---

57. See Todorov, *Grammaire du "Décaméron,"* 10.

58. Martin Heidegger, *Sein und Zeit* (1927); English translation *Being and Time*, trans. John MacQuarrie and Edward Robinson (New York: Harper and Row, 1962), §4 and following.

for three years. Neither is there any end: you never leave a woman, a friend, a city in one go. And then everything looks alike: Shanghai, Moscow, Algiers, everything is the same after two weeks. . . .

That's living. But everything changes when you tell about life; it's a change no one notices: the proof is that people talk about true stories. As if there could possibly be true stories; things happen one way and we tell about them in the opposite sense. You seem to start at the beginning: "It was a fine autumn evening in 1922. I was a notary's clerk in Marommes." And in reality you have started at the end. It was there, invisible and present, it is the one which gives to words the pomp and value of a beginning. "I was out walking, I had left the town without realizing it, I was thinking about my money troubles." This sentence, taken simply for what it is, means that the man was absorbed, morose, a hundred leagues from an adventure, exactly in the mood to let things happen without noticing them. But the end is there, transforming everything. For us, the man is already the hero of the story. His moroseness, his money troubles are more precious than ours, they are gilded by the light of future passions.[59]

Forty years later, in Georges Perec's writings on the notion of the "infra-ordinary," we find another frontal attack on the presuppositions of plots. According to Perec, "official discourses," starting with canonical narrative forms, never capture the gray, static background of our existence:

My "sociology" of everyday life isn't an analysis. It's just an attempt at description, or more precisely, a description of what no one ever looks at—because you're there, or you think you're there, they're too familiar and normally there's no language for them. Like enumerating the cars that go through the Mabillon intersection, or the gestures that a driver makes when he gets out of his car, or the different ways passers-by hold the newspapers they've just bought. It's a deconditioning: it's not about trying to capture what the official (institutional) discourses call an event or important, but what lies below that—the infra-ordinary, the background noise that fills every minute of our daily lives.[60]

59. Jean-Paul Sartre, *La Nausée* (1938); English translation *Nausea*, trans. Richard Howard (New York: New Directions, 1964), 39–40.

60. Georges Perec, *Entretien avec Jean-Marie Le Sidaner* (1979), in *Entretiens et conférences*, critical edition ed. Dominique Bertelli and Mirielle Ribière (Nantes: Joseph K., 2003), 93–94.

For the logic of plots, what is essential are the stories of particular beings, with their paths, their turning points, their denouements identified
from the perspective of the ending. What happens thus takes on a retrospective order and the elements that fail to fit into this preunderstanding
are cut out of the text. While the day-to-day perception of life ignores the
temporality and hierarchies by which plots organize reality, *mythos* separates the essential from the contingent. It introduces a *telos* into the disorder and creates the ordered, contrived areas of intensity that Sartre called
"adventures." Viewed from the perspective of the infra-ordinary, the syntax
of plots is unrealistic. It is no coincidence that authors such as Sartre and
Perec have attempted to sabotage the canonic narrative form: while the
author of *Nausea* used the genre of the diary, Perec employed the schema
of the list, which arranges events according to a different logic than that of
the story line.

Hence, plots are not a copy but an interpretation of the human world:
they attach importance to certain dimensions of being and leave out others.
Furthermore, they are *synthesis ton pragmaton*—a posteriori synthetic
constructions. The inventor of plots possesses a breadth of vision that is
lacking in the protagonists. Particular beings do not grasp the totality in
which they are immersed, because the whole that contains them eludes
them in two respects. In the first place, with respect to time: finite beings
are suspended between a beginning and an end; stories make complete
sense only when they end, while the living have no knowledge of what will
become of them.[61] In second place, with respect to the world: finite beings
do not grasp the synchronic totality in which they are immersed because
their perspective is limited. They do not see everything that others are
doing; they do not properly perceive the suprapersonal forces that influence life; they cannot understand in advance what will prove to be essential in the expanse of perceptions, passions, and microevents that make up
every instant. But while finite beings are ontologically short-sighted with
respect to the whole, the creator of plots can see the whole network of

61. Frank Kermode, *The Sense of an Ending: Studies in the Theory of Fiction* (London:
Oxford University Press, 1967), chap. 1; Paul Ricœur, *Temps et récit,* vol. 2 (1984); English
translation *Time and Narrative,* vol. 2, trans. Kathleen McLaughlin and David Pellauer (Chicago: University of Chicago Press, 1986), 19ff. See also Peter Brooks, *Reading for the Plot:
Design and Intention in Narrative* (Cambridge, MA: Harvard University Press, 1992), especially chap. 4.

causes and relations. Plots arise out of a vision of the whole: like Homer's Muses, the person who creates them knows all things of the present, the past, and the future.

When considered from the point of view of the infra-ordinary, plots are not realistic, but they are when considered from the perspective of their basic ontological grammar. Although the *mythos* to which we belong escapes our ordinary perception, we are objectively part of a plot. According to Frank Kermode, the degree zero of every plot is the *tick-tock* of a clock—the pair of sounds that give form to occurrences by marking in mere succession a beginning and an end.[62] However, there does exist an example of an elementary plot that is even closer to our experience and to the stuff of stories. It is the sequence we find in vital records and on tombstones: a proper name, a place and date of birth, a place and date of death. In the formless expanse of all that exists, this series of signs isolates a particular individual; it situates him or her in a space and a time; it imagines the individual as being in an original state of imbalance that, in the end, is destined to be objectively righted. The plot is the hyphen connecting the two dates and the two places. This line encapsulates what is essential for us, the living.

Narrators

By narrative, therefore, we mean literary works distinguished by the presence of a story and a narrator. So far we have discussed what is implicit in stories; now we need to reflect on the figure of the narrator, especially those who tell stories using words. This is the specific difference between verbal narrative and other genres with a plot.

Every story has four categories of interpreters: the author (or authors), the narrator (or narrators), the hero (or heroes), and the reader (or readers). The first and fourth remain outside the work; the second and third enter into the text connected by a relationship that is at the same time symmetrical and asymmetrical. Both express points of view and generate an interpretation of reality in which they are seen as protagonists or spectators. In every story, even in the most monologic, there is an element of relativism and prospectivism waiting to be activated: anyone's desires, values, and

62. Kermode, *The Sense of an Ending*, 44ff.

words can become our own, even those of an enemy; even Hector and Priam can elicit our compassion and fear. For the same reason, the narrator holds only one of many possible points of view; his or her word is partial. While concepts tend to establish immutable truths, narratives leave open the theoretical possibility that the story can be told from a different perspective. But to this symmetry of position there corresponds an asymmetry: the narrator and the protagonist both have a right to speak, but their accounts lie on different planes. Bakhtin refers to this imbalance as the concept of *extralocality* or *extralocation* (*vnenachodimost'*).[63] The storyteller is located in another sphere of reality that is external to the one inhabited by the characters: the narrator transcends the characters, views them from outside, knows more about them, and introduces them into a context.[64] The roles can be reversed, and the same individual may act at times as a narrator and at others as a character, but this does not change the nature of the two roles. As an intermediate figure between the author and the protagonist, the narrator gives tangible form to the presence of a mediation in the text.

> A comparison with the theater is helpful in understanding this point. In their classic form, texts of dramatic literature reproduce speeches and human gestures without the filter of an intermediate voice. The illusionistic idea behind this convention is the principle of the transparent fourth wall, as it is called in modern theater theory.[65] Narrative, instead, presup-

63. Mikhail Bakhtin, "Avtor i geroj v èstetičeskoj dejatel'nosti"; English translation "Author and Hero in Aestheric Activity," in *Art and Answerability: Early Philosophical Essays*, ed. Michael Holquist and Vadim Liapunov, trans. Vadim Liapunov (Austin: University of Texas Press, 1990), 12–14 and fn. 28. Bakhtin uses the concept of extralocality to describe the relationship between author and hero, but clearly this concept has a broader scope and can also shed light on the relationship between the author and the narrator and between the narrator and the hero.

64. In the same way, the author's sphere of reality is even further removed than the one occupied by the narrator. The author can take away the authority of whoever is telling the story, for example, when there are multiple narrators, or when the narrator's unreliability is suggested.

65. See Johann Wolfgang von Goethe and Friedrich Schiller, "Über epische und dramatische Dichtung" (1797); English translation "On Epic and Dramatic Poetry," in *Correspondence between Schiller and Goethe from 1794 to 1805*, trans. George H. Calvert, vol. 1 (New York: Wiley, 1845), 379–392; Bertolt Brecht's notes and essays on the topic of "non-Aristotelian drama," in *Schriften zum Theater. Über eine nicht-aristotelische Dramatik* (1957), partly

poses a filter: the appearance and actions of the protagonists, the physical and cultural space that surrounds them, the thoughts and passions that animate them, do not exist in sensible form in front of the viewer—they come to life only by means of an interpreter's words. Although there is no lack of exceptions, hybrid cases, and pioneering texts, this distinction is absolutely clear. Indeed, ever since the tripartite division of modern literary genres was declared, the expedients to which theatrical works resort in order to introduce forms of narration or commentary external to the events being acted out on stage are said to be epic or lyric, as if the theory recognized that they do not belong to the main core of dramatic art.[66] The works of classic modern drama written for the stage are *tranches de vie*, slices of life that unfold before the eyes of the viewers. In these types of texts, the mediation of the form has ideally taken place *before* the play that the audience sees being acted out on stage: when the work gets to the spectators, the story seems inseparable from how it is presented. Narrative, on the contrary, disconnects the story from its telling. It separates the plot events from the voice that gives form to them and displays the act of narrating along with what is being narrated. While the language game of theater involves three figures (the author who creates the plot, the characters who give substance to it, and the spectator who watches it staged), the language game of stories interjects a fourth figure between the author, the protagonists, and the readers.

Narrative mediation shows that the mimetic activity is a reading, not a copy, of the world. The hermeneutic nature of mimesis, which is implicit in all arts, is made explicit in stories because the narrator makes the subjective, interpreting aspect of mimesis into something substantial: he or she embodies the synthetic, a posteriori gaze that is inherent in the plot form. Because the narrator has a view of the ending and the plot in its entirety,

---

translated in *Brecht on Theatre*, ed. and trans. John Willett (New York: Hill and Wang, 1964), especially 46–47 and 57–60; Peter Szondi, *Die Theorie des modernen Dramas* (1956), English translation *Theory of the Modern Drama: A Critical Edition*, ed. and trans. Michael Hays (Minneapolis: University of Minnesota Press, 1987), especially "Introduction: Historical Aesthetics and Genre-Based Poetics."

66. See Goethe and Schiller, "On Epic and Dramatic Poetry"; Brecht, *Brecht on Theatre*; and Szondi, *Theory of the Modern Drama*.

he or she sees what remains hidden to the protagonists—the entire course of a fate or a story line, the sense of a life.[67]

Levels of Reality

While the figure of the narrator embodies the hermeneutic nature of mimesis, the narrator who uses words gains an understanding of the world modeled on the possibilities afforded by language. In one way, any sensible immediacy is evacuated. What the Greeks called *poiesis,* what for two and a half centuries we have called "literature," can aspire to an illusionistic copy of reality only when the text transmits words spoken in public, as happens in the theater;[68] in all other cases, literary mimesis translates sensory data into the medium of language. The image-based arts are spared the challenges of such abrupt code switches. But this loss of immediacy is accompanied by a parallel gain: precisely because literature exceeds the realm of the sensible, it appropriates the territories our culture comes to know through the medium of language, starting with levels of reality that transcend the senses. In most of the stories told in words, beings move between two ontological layers. There is the realm of visible action, audible speeches, events, and objects that are perceived through the senses and that the narrator translates into words. And then there is the silent space occupied by entities that do not take a public form, except through signs or symptoms: thoughts, passions, invisible regularities that we resort to in order to explain lives and behaviors, in the same way we saw at work in the simile of the leaves. To represent the invisible and the inaudible, the theater is forced to adopt epic expedients: for example, when the chorus of a tragedy explains the events that took place before the play begins or the moral of the story; or when a character speaks his or her thoughts out loud

---

67. In 1797, Goethe and Schiller reflected on this aspect of narrative in their correspondence on the differences between epic and drama. Drama is an art of pure presence, an art in which the action takes place in front of the viewer; instead, the epic form assumes that the story being told is in the past and that the narrator already knows the ending. While theater spectators are carried along by the action as it unfolds before their eyes, in the present and without any visible mediation, the narrator introduces a form of distance between his or her words and the story being told. See Goethe and Schiller, "On Epic and Dramatic Poetry," 379–392.

68. This is the sense of the distinction between *mimesis* (in the narrow sense) and *diegesis* found in the *Republic.* Plato, *Republic* 3.392d.

and lapses into a soliloquy that is unlikely to happen in real life. Film-makers are granted more freedom, but the devices they have at their disposal (the interior monologue, the voice-over) fall outside the normal medium of the art, which partly explains why they are rarely used. The verbal narrator can instead interpret the invisible parts of the real through words, because the supersensible abstractness of language allows her or him to reveal characters' thoughts, to show the superpersonal mechanisms that drive them, and to comment on the vicissitudes of their fates. Narrative mediation discloses two levels of reality.

1. In the early decades of the twentieth century, at the same time that Western narrative assigned a new value to the life of the psyche, a critical topos took hold. The conviction spread that verbal narratives alone are capable of entering into the intimate sphere of someone different from us (another character or another period of our *I*). Verbal narratives, it was said, can show what no other discursive formations have the capacity to reveal. A similar sentiment is expressed in Proust's *Swann's Way* (1913),[69] in Alain's *Systeme des beaux-arts* (System of Fine Arts) (1920),[70] and in E. M. Forster's *Aspects of the Novel* (1927).[71] Revisited on a number of occasions over the past few decades,[72] the idea achieved its final form in *The Logic of Literature* (1957) by Käte Hamburger: "Epic fiction is the sole epistemological instance where the I-originarity (or subjectivity) of a

---

69. Marcel Proust, *Du côté de chez Swann* (1913); English translation *Swann's Way*, trans. Lydia Davis, in *In Search of Lost Time*, vol. 1 (London: Penguin Books, 2002).

70. Alain, *Système des beaux-arts* (1920, 1926) (Paris: Gallimard, 1963), 319ff. ("Du roman.")

71. "It is the function of the novelist to reveal the hidden life at its source"; "[the characters in novels] are people whose secret lives are visible or might be visible: we are people whose secret lives are invisible." Forster, *Aspects of the Novel*, 56, 70.

72. Käte Hamburger, *Die Logik der Dichtung* (1957); English translation *The Logic of Literature*, trans. Marilynn J. Rose (Bloomington: Indiana University Press, 1993); Dorrit Cohn, *Transparent Minds: Narrative Modes for Presenting Consciousness in Fiction* (Princeton, NJ: Princeton University Press, 1978), 5ff.; also by Cohn, *The Distinction of Fiction* (Baltimore: Johns Hopkins University Press, 1999), 19ff.; Ann Banfield, *Unspeakable Sentences: Narration and Representation in the Language of Fiction* (Boston: Routledge and Kegan Paul, 1982), 260 and passim; Belinda Cannone, *Narrations de la vie intérieure* (Paris: PUF, 2001), 3ff.; Jean Louis Chrétien, *Conscience et roman I: la conscience au grand jour* (Paris: Minuit, 2009).

third-person qua third person can be portrayed."[73] While conceptual types of knowledge, from the premodern "sciences of the soul" to the psychoanalyses of the twentieth century, reveal the hidden dimensions only by reifying their content—by translating thoughts and passions into an object that the analytical gaze breaks down—narrative gains access to the inner world of third persons while continuing to treat individuals as subjects. What abstract thought tends to deprive of autonomy, narrative allows to come to the surface: the point of view of the other as a being who is different but equivalent to the I.

While it may be true that not all epochs and cultures interpret thoughts and passions as processes belonging solely to our interior world, there is no doubt that our thoughts and passions are the locus of an ontological asymmetry. When it comes to this aspect of our existence, each of us knows different things from other people, because when speaking about ourselves, each of us has access to levels of reality inaccessible to others, or at least not to the same extent. Written narrative can penetrate beyond the opacity of second and third persons without taking away their subjectivity. It is the only language game capable of doing so, because the sciences of the soul, the various schools of psychology and psychoanalysis, treat the psychic life of others as a thing, because the theater remains an "art of the silhouette"[74] as far as the mimesis of the interior life is concerned, and because the cinema relies on the interpretation of visible signs. Much of what our culture knows about the "treasure of the psyche" is "the fruit of the exploration of the soul by storytellers."[75] This possibility for introspection is what distinguishes narrative fiction from historical narrative based on sources and evidence. *Mythos* split into stories about historical events and stories that were invented during the same epoch when philosophers began to criticize the knowledge transmitted by poets. This division of duties and obligations led to different rules and possibilities: historians make it their task to report only things we can be certain about and they claim the right to occupy the domain of truth; storytellers agree to occupy the domain of fic-

---

73. Hamburger, *The Logic of Literature*, 83.

74. Thomas Mann, "Versuch über das Theater" (1908), in *Essays I 1893–1914*, ed. Hermann Kurzke and Stefan Stachorski (Frankfurt am Main: S. Fischer, 2002), 130.

75. Paul Ricœur, "L'Identité narrative," *Revue des sciences humaines 95*, no. 221 (January–March 1991): 43–44. See also Cohn, *Transparent Minds*, 5ff., 58ff.; Cohn, *The Distinction of Fiction*, 19ff.; Banfield, *Unspeakable Sentences*, 260.

tion, but in exchange retain the capacity (implicit in *diegesis*) to enter into people's hidden lives.

2. In addition to gazing into the invisible region of the inner life, storytellers have access to another realm that is barred to the senses: they can explain people's behavior through concepts, revealing the invisible regularities that abstract thought grasps in the realm of the visible. To a greater or lesser extent, every narrative made of words is enveloped in a conceptual ether composed of vocabularies that change over the course of the centuries. The simile of the leaves in Homer, the historical and sociological parts of Balzac's novels, and the essayistic parts of *The Man without Qualities* refer to completely different lexicons. What does not change, though, is the act of transcending the space of sensible appearance and interpreting actions in the light of laws. It does not matter whether the space of ideas is introduced by a first or a third person, whether it occupies long digressions or is concentrated into a word, or whether it is serious or ironic. Even the simplest act of describing a character by a concise adjective ("good," "bad," "tranquil," "upset"), even the use of a causal or final association, refers implicitly to the same concepts with which ethics, rhetoric, the human sciences, and common sense have attempted over the centuries to interpret behaviors. One of the most famous aphorisms nestled in Proust's *In Search of Lost Time* says that a work of art in which theories are expounded is like an object with its price tag still attached.[76] Apart from the fact that few works of art contain as many theories as Proust's novels, almost never do we come across narratives that entirely eschew concepts. Stories are emerged lands surrounded by the ideas with which we make sense of what happens.

Being in the World

What, in summary, is the basic preunderstanding crystallized in narrative? There is a page in Hegel's *Aesthetics* in which he talks about this very question:

> In drama, he [the character] creates his fate *himself,* whereas an epic character has his fate made for him, and this power of circumstances

---

76. Proust, *Finding Time Again*, 109.

[*diese Macht der Umstände*], which gives his deed the imprint of an individual form, allocates his lot to him, and determines the outcome of his actions, is the proper dominion of fate. . . . This destiny is the great justice and it becomes tragic not in the dramatic sense of the word in which the individual is judged as a *person*, but in the epic sense in which the individual is judged in his whole situation; and the tragic nemesis is that the greatness of the situation is too great for the individuals.[77]

Hegel is reflecting on the difference between drama and *epos*, but what he says holds true for all other types of stories. Like any art that incorporates a plot, narrative represents particular individuals in their dependence on time; but unlike the theater, it has the capacity to capture the dialectic between the hero or heroine and *die Macht der Umstände,* the power of circumstances. While theatrical tragedy judges individuals as *persons,* in the legal sense of the term—considering the actions for which individuals are subjectively or objectively responsible—stories do not make personal fortune or misfortune depend solely on the intrinsic value of subjective actions, but on the relationship between human action and the force fields in which individuals find themselves enmeshed. The verbal story encompasses in its structures both the subjection of individuals to time and their belonging in a world. In this way, it shows the objective tragedy of the human condition: it shows that happiness or unhappiness do not stem only from the merits or demerits of the individual, but also and above all from the power of circumstances.

As a genre of contingencies, narrative allows endless stories to exist by carving open an ontological region from the brutally changeable surface. Beneath the surface, however, one encounters an immovable structure, the same one that has been tapped for thousands of years in the attempt to establish the minimal story. "There are countless forms of narrative in the world," we read in the opening to a famous essay that was decisive in the development of narratology.[78] But whatever the subject matter, the telling of stories signifies a concern with the ontological realm populated by contingent lives and forms of life. It means that we are attending to the

---

77. Hegel, *Aesthetics*, vol. 2, pp. 1158–1181; pp. 1093–1100; quote from pp. 1070–1071.

78. Roland Barthes, "Introduction à l'analyse structurale des récits" (1966); English translation "An Introduction to the Structural Analysis of Narrative," *New Literary History* 6, no. 2 (Winter 1975): 237–272; quote from 237.

stories of finite beings, whether real or possible, showing the interweaving of their destinies, the happiness or unhappiness that awaits them as they exist in the midst of others and circumstances. It means that we accept a discourse that incorporates into its basic grammar the minimal scaffoldings of the human condition qua accidental existence, differentiated by dispositions, cast into a time and a space, bound to others, and located in a world. This is what narrative is.

CHAPTER TWO

The Origin of the Novel

Historical Semantics

The first defining characteristic of the novel as we understand the term today is its narrative form. The second is its capacity to tell all sorts of stories in all sorts of ways. This unprecedented mimetic anarchy, the genre's distinguishing trait, is inscribed in the history of the words that define it.

In the major European languages, the names used to refer to the novel belong to two completely different families of terms: one group includes *le roman, der Roman,* and *il romanzo;* the other, *the novel* and *la novela.* The first group is the most ancient.[1] It descends from the expression *romanice loqui,* which in medieval Latin meant "to speak like those who live in the lands of the former Roman empire," that is, in a language derived from Latin. Originally, the old French *romanz* indicated any one of the Neo-Latin language varieties. Starting from the twelfth century, through a metonymic drift, *romanz* began to signify speech or written text in a Romance language, especially when talking about a vernacularization and a narrative. In the second half of the twelfth century, *romanz* could refer to a narrative work of a certain length written in a vernacular and in verse that was intended to be read rather than sung and that was centered around

1. On the historical semantics of this family of terms, see Curtius, *European Literature and the Latin Middle Ages,* 30ff; Aurelio Roncaglia, *Tristano e Anti-Tristano. Dialettica di temi e d'ideologie nella narrativa medievale* (Rome: Bulzoni, 1981), 92–115, republished in *Il romanzo,* ed. Maria Luisa Meneghetti (Bologna: Il Mulino, 1988).

content taken from the cultures of antiquity (the "matter of Greece and Rome"), from Celtic legends (the "matter of Britain"), from Byzantine and Oriental subject matter, and from contemporary histories. Understood in this sense, the term was distinct from *estoire, conte, fable,* and *chanson de geste.* However, the boundaries were not always clear. For example, the *chanson de geste* could be called a *romanz* but never the other way around, because *chanson de geste* had a more specific meaning, primarily indicating an epic genre that was sung. Through a mechanism of symmetry and opposition, *romanz* (later *roman*) subsequently referred to narratives in verse that, unlike the *chanson de geste,* were intended to be read privately and not sung. In the thirteenth century, the term expanded to include narrative works in vernacular prose that told stories similar to those in the verse romances. In Italian, the word *romanzo* was used exclusively for the literary genre from the outset, seeing as the Neo-Latin language was always referred to as the "vulgar tongue" (*volgare*). In the fifteenth and sixteenth centuries, *romanzo* referred to chivalric or pastoral narratives written in prose or verse. The German "Roman" is a Gallicism that was acquired during the 1500s.[2]

What French, Italian, and German indicated using words derived from *romanice loqui* was referred to in English and Spanish using words that derived, primarily, from the Italian literary genre of the *novella* and, secondarily, from the Latin adjectives *novellus* and *novus.* The English word *novel,* appearing for the first time in the fifteenth century, originally meant "something new," "a novelty." The adjective *novel* preserved this meaning until the beginning of the eighteenth century. However, as early as the mid-sixteenth century, the noun *novel* referred to the Italian genre of the *novella,* following a usage that was solidified during the seventeenth century.[3] In the late 1600s, *novel* primarily indicated works inspired by the French *nouvelle,* a term that arose in its turn from the Spanish *novela* and the Italian *novella.*

---

2. Friedrich Kluge, *Etymologisches Wörterbuch der deutschen Sprache,* 22nd ed. (Berlin: De Gruyter, 1989), 604–605.

3. In *The Anatomy of Melancholy,* for example, Burton speaks about "*Bocace* Novells." See Richard Burton, *The Anatomy of Melancholy,* vol. 2, ed. Nicholas K. Kiessling, Thomas C. Faulkner, and Rhonda L. Blair (Oxford: Clarendon Press, 1990), part 2, sec. 2, memb. 4, subsection 1, p. 79.

During the same years when *novel* became the English translation of *nouvelle,* French literary criticism was galvanized by a battle between the defenders of the *nouvelle* and the defenders of the genre that the *nouvelle* had supplanted in the taste of cultured readers—the Baroque *roman.* The French opposition between *nouvelle* and *roman* gave rise to the English opposition between *novel* and *romance* that sparked discussion in British literary circles throughout the eighteenth century. For a long time the meaning of the two terms continued to fluctuate: *novel* and *romance* often overlapped and were confused until the oscillation gradually subsided between the last decades of the eighteenth century and the beginning of the nineteenth.[4] From that moment on, *novel* signified stories set in the world of everyday life, while *romance* indicated love or adventure stories set in a time and space other than those of the ordinary world. Over time, the opposition proved to be asymmetrical, because the word *novel* acquired a narrow sense and a wide sense: it came to define a work in a realistic, everyday setting as well as the great mixed genre that arose out of a combination between the *novel* in the narrow sense and the *romance.* In other words, it became equivalent to what in France and Italy was called the *roman* or *romanzo.*[5] From this point on, if strictly necessary, I will use the word *novel* in italics when referring to the narrow sense of the term, and, when necessary, I will use the word *romance* in italics when it is directly opposed to the *novel.*

4. See the essays collected in *Novel and Romance, 1700–1800: A Documentary Record,* ed. Ioan Williams (London: Routledge and Kegan Paul, 1970); Homer Obed Brown, *Institutions of the English Novel: From Defoe to Scott* (Philadelphia: University of Pennsylvania Press, 1997), passim; William B. Warner, *Licensing Entertainment: The Elevation of Novel Reading in Britain, 1684–1750* (Berkeley: University of California Press, 1998), 8ff.

5. Today this use is entirely common, as can be seen from the titles of English-language critical writings on subgenres that at one time were *romances* par excellence, namely, the Hellenistic novel and the heroic Baroque novel (for example, Thomas Hägg, *The Novel in Antiquity* [Berkeley: University of California Press, 1983]). It is significant that Showalter and DiPiero chose to use the word "novel" in their monographs on the early modern French prose narrative: English Showalter, *The Evolution of the French Novel, 1641–1782* (Princeton, NJ: Princeton University Press, 1972); Thomas DiPiero, *Dangerous Truths and Criminal Passions: The Evolution of the French Novel, 1569–1791* (Stanford, CA: Stanford University Press, 1992). In *The True Story of the Novel* (New Brunswick, NJ: Rutgers University Press, 1996) by Margaret Doody, "novel" refers to all types of the genre. On the widespread use of the word "novel" in recent decades, see Thomas Pavel, *La Pensée du roman* (Paris: Gallimard, 2003), 45. (Translator's note: An expanded English version, entitled *The Lives of the Novel: A History,* is now available from Princeton University Press [2015].)

In Spain, *romanz* and *romance* ultimately referred to a very precise genre, namely, a short composition on a chivalrous topic in a lyric-narrative style, usually written in verse. Until the beginning of the seventeenth century, the semantic spectrum of the term *novela* was similar to that of the Italian *novella* from which it derived. When Cervantes's *Exemplary Novels* (1613) altered the basic framework of the genre, extending the length of the texts and making them more complex, the word *novela* adapted to these changes.[6] But until the 1760s, *historia* remained the most common term for indicating long stories in prose, although *novela* also took on this meaning from time to time.[7] In the second half of the eighteenth century, Spanish literary critics used the terms *novela* and *romance* synonymously, just as *novel* and *romance* continued to be used interchangeably in English. In Spain at the height of the nineteenth century, the word *romance* could still be applied to the prose narratives of Sir Walter Scott.[8] *Novela* assumed the meaning it has today beginning mostly from the nineteenth century on, when it occupied the semantic spectrum that the term *romanzo* had in Italian.

The words used by European cultures to designate the genre of the novel thus have two different genealogies and a similar history: both refer, originally, to medieval forms (the courtly romance and the *novella*); both acquired their current meanings as a result of a semantic expansion. At the beginning, they signified narrative forms with fairly well-defined boundaries; in the end, they indicated a corpus of protean texts, an aggregate of works that can effectively tell stories about absolutely anything in any way whatsoever. It should be noted that the medieval categories already lent

6. See Guiomar Hautcoeur Pérez-Espejo, *Parentés franco-espagnoles au XVIIᵉ siècle: poétique de la nouvelle de Cervantès à Challe* (Paris: Champion, 2005), 28.

7. In 1637 Andrés Sanchéz de Espejo's *Rélacion* alluded to the "novela de don Quijote." In 1722 the translator of a Byzantine novel wrote in the preface that "Heliodoro . . . ideó una novela, que llamó Historia de l'Etiopía." (Heliodorus invented a novel that he called History of Ethopia). See Joaquín Álvarez Barrientos, *La novela del siglo XVIII* (Madrid: Júcar, 1991), 26–27.

8. Russell P. Sebold, *La novela romántica en España: Entre libro de caballerías y novela moderna* (Salamanca: Ediciones Universidad de Salamanca, 2002), chap. 1. This fluctuation was also affected by the uncertain history and origin of the words in English, which at the beginning of the nineteenth century were still unsettled: the subtitle of *Ivanhoe* (1820), like other novels by Scott, is *A Romance*.

themselves to a more narrow use and a wider one: *roman* could indicate a courtly romance or a general narrative in prose; *novella* could indicate a short story that was related to the new forms emerging thanks to the *Novellino* or *The Decameron*, or a short story on a general topic.[9] Although the initial terms may have been elastic *ab origine*, the crucial semantic expansion that transformed the categories of *romanzo, roman, novel,* or *novela* into what they are now occurred between the mid-sixteenth century and the beginning of the nineteenth. It was this transformation alone that made it possible to retrospectively include in the same literary family narrative in Latin prose from the first century CE, narrative in Greek prose from the third century CE, medieval narrative in verse and prose, and narrative prose written in the modern epoch. Only thanks to this transformation could such diverse works as *Satyricon, Aethiopica, Yvain, Orlando furioso, Gargantua and Pantagruel, The Princesse de Clèves, Robinson Crusoe,* and *The Sorrows of Young Werther* end up in a single genre and take on a name that, in many cases, is entirely antihistorical. Later, when the terms *romanzo, roman, Roman, novel,* or *novela* evolved to signify a long narrative with indefinite characteristics, the category broke away from its contingent geographical origin to become a general type: at that point, we began to talk about Chinese novels, Japanese novels, or Indian novels.

The Question of Origins

Research into the origin of the novel, an unavoidable topos of modern criticism, has produced conflicting results: the novel began with the *Odyssey;* the novel began with Socratic dialogue and the seriocomic genres of ancient literature; the novel developed in ancient Greek culture from Oriental precedents; the novel has a medieval origin; the novel emerged in the mid-

---

9. The polysemic nature that the term *novella* had in Boccaccio's time is captured well in the prologue to *The Decameron*: "I intend to present a hundred tales or fables or parables or histories (call them what you like) [intendo di raccontare cento novelle, o favole o parabole o istorie che dire le vogliamo]." However one interprets the "or" that comes after "tales" (as a synonym of "namely" or as a synonym of "or"), as a book of *novelle, The Decameron* is presented as a mixed work. This is a sign that the word *novella* had a variety of uses and that the genre could accommodate various types of materials taken from fables, parables, and histories, but also from romances. See Giovanni Boccaccio's *Decameron*, ed. Vittore Branca (Turin: Einaudi, 1987), "Proemio," 8–9; English translation *Decameron*, trans. John Gordon Nichols (New York, Alfred A. Knopf), "Prologue," 4.

sixteenth century with Spanish picaresque narrative; the novel emerged in
the mid-sixteenth century with the rediscovery of ancient prose narrative;
the novel arose in the 1700s in England. These strikingly divergent theories often stem from a shared attitude. Hans Robert Jauss likens discussions
on the nature of literary genres to the disputes of medieval philosophy on
the nature of universals. He distinguishes among three stances: for some,
genres are essences *ante rem*, pure forms that precede the texts, like Ideas:
for others, they represent taxonomic categories *post rem* that readers
apply to a magmatic, dispersed reality; for others still, they record an objective, historical continuity between works belonging to one and the
same family, like universals *in re*.[10] Almost all theories on the origin of
the novel depart, intentionally or unintentionally, from the idea that the
genre has its own essence. Even when the changeability of the genre is emphasized, these theories never give up on the conviction that the novel is
bound by an identity *ante rem* and that any texts unrelated to the definition are in some way spurious. Bakhtin can serve as a typical example of this
ambiguity. On the one hand, he resumes and develops Schlegel's idea of the
novel as a genre under continuous change; on the other, he identifies a
privileged lineage that supposedly embodies the entelechy of the novel. By
this he means the pluridiscursive and polyphonic tradition that arose out
of Socratic dialogue, the seriocomic genres of ancient literature, and the
anthropological substrate of popular humor.[11] This same attitude can be
found in many critics, even though the theories they put forward differ
from Bakhtin's. Ian Watt locates the origin of the novel in eighteenth-
century England, because the true novel, in his view, is based on "formal
realism."[12] Margaret Doody opens the chronological table prefacing her
True Story of the Novel with Xenophon's *Cyropaedia,* because the true
novel, in her opinion, must "includ[e] the idea of length (preferably forty or
more pages), and . . . it should be in prose."[13]

---

10. Hans Robert Jauss, "Theorie der Gattungen und Literatur des Mittelalters" (1972);
English translation "Theory of Genres and Medieval Literature," in *Toward an Aesthetic of
Reception,* trans. Timothy Bahti (Minneapolis: University of Minnesota Press, 1982), chap. 3.

11. See Mikhail Bakhtin, "Slovo v romane" (1934–1935); English translation "Discourse
in the Novel," in *The Dialogic Imagination,* 259–422.

12. Ian Watt, *The Rise of the Novel* (1957) (Berkeley: University of California Press,
2001), chap. 1.

13. Doody, *The True Story of the Novel,* 10.

Whether consciously or unconsciously, all these theories end up modeling an unstable aggregate of works in the same way common sense models things: as a fixed given, as a simple presence. But the entities studied by the history of culture ("the novel" or "secularization," "the middle ages" or "modernism") are not things: rather, they are universals *in re,* or to use another philosophical vocabulary, they are language games. They exist qua clusters of heterogeneous texts held together by a shared family resemblance, by a public web of terms, expectations, habits, and examples that create a field of works and then trace out its boundary lines. When this web has yet to form or has ceased to exist, the literary territory takes on another form or disappears. This means that the history of presuppositions and the history of objects are tied together by an inextricable, ontological knot: things make an appearance in the human world only when practices and words provide them with an identity. This is why it makes no sense to recount the history of a literary institution as if we were talking about a *res.* What we need to do instead is reconstruct the dialectic between the object and the words that enabled the object to be defined in the first place. The *Aethiopica* were not always considered a novel: they became such when we started to locate them in the same class of medieval texts that already bore the name of *roman.* This sort of retrospective identification, which is neither obvious nor necessary, should be the point of departure for all critical inquiries.

When did the novel come into being? *As we recognize it today, the genre emerged at the end of a transformation that took place between the mid-sixteenth century and the end of the eighteenth. Around 1550, the word "novel" referred for the most part to a narrowly defined, specific literary form. Around 1800, it referred to what it does today—a polymorphic space providing a home for stories of a certain length that do not fall within the confines of more rigidly codified narrative genres (epic poems, works of history, and the* chanson de geste). The same expansion took place in all the European lexicons for all terms related to the genre: *le roman, der Roman, la novela, il romanzo.*[14] In 1550 the family resemblance linking

14. The history and origin of the English names are more intricate because during the eighteenth century, instead of just one word for the territory we are describing, there were two. The meaning of *novel* and *romance,* as we were saying, became gradually more specific. They never referred to separate genres, but rather to variants of a single whole—different modes of a single narrative space. This space was referred to using the dittology *novel and*

the texts we now call by the name of novel was only vaguely perceived; in 1800 the terms *novel, roman, Roman, novela, romanzo* already meant what they mean today.

The First Corpus

As the word transformed, so did the object: between the middle of the sixteenth century and the end of the eighteenth century many strains of written narrative proliferated that, despite their dissimilarities, ultimately ended up forming a family—their differences were less important than their similarities. I will briefly list the subgenres that merged into the territory of the novel. This list is likely incomplete: readers who are familiar with the literature from these centuries will be able to fill in the gaps. My interest lies less in tracing out the exact confines of a literary space with shifting boundaries than in identifying the main families of works that compose it.

> The first group of texts to take the name of *romance* was *medieval and Renaissance courtly narrative* in verse and prose on the matters of Britain, France, and Rome. The first attempts to codify the cultural object named *romanzo*—by Fórnari, Giraldi, and Pigna[15]—refer to this tradition, which

romance, as it appears in Defoe's preface to *Moll Flanders* ("The World is so taken up of late with novels and romances"). Or one of the two terms was used, as in one of the most important eighteenth-century treatises on the novel, *The Progress of Romance* (1785) by Clara Reeve. In this case, the word *romance* sometimes had a restricted meaning, indicating a subgenre that was juxtaposed to the *novel*, and at other times it had a wider meaning, indicating the genre that came out of combining the *novel* and the *romance*—the equivalent of the French *roman*. By the beginning of the nineteenth century, it was abundantly clear that *novel* and *romance* were species of a single genus: "the word *novel* is a generical term; of which romances, histories, memoirs, letters, tales, lives, and adventures are the species" (Edward Mangin, *An Essay on Light Reading, as It May Be Supposed to Influence Moral Conduct on Literary Taste* [London: James Carpenter, 1808], 5). See Brown, *Institutions of the English Novel*; Warner, *Licensing Entertainment*, 8ff.; James Raven, "Britain, 1750–1830," in *The Novel*, vol. 1, *History, Geography and Culture*, ed. Franco Moretti (Princeton, NJ: Princeton University Press, 2006), 429–444.

15. Simone Fórnari, *La Sposizione di M. Simon Fórnari di Rheggio sopra l' "Orlando furioso" di M. Ludovico Ariosto*, 2 vols. (Florence: Lorenzo Torrentino, 1549–1550); Giovan Battista Pigna, *I romanzi* (1554), critical edition by Salvatore Ritrovato (Bologna: Commissione per i testi in lingua, 1997); Giovan Battista Giraldi Cinzio, *Discorso dei romanzi* (1554), ed. Laura Benedetti, Giuseppe Monorchio, and Enrico Musacchio (Bologna: Millennium, 1999).

had been revitalized during the early decades of the sixteenth century by two books destined for enormous success in Europe: *Amadis of Gaul* (the work predates the sixteenth century, but the first printed edition is from 1508) and *Orlando furioso* (1516–1532).

In the mid-sixteenth century, modern European literatures rediscovered the ancient *Greek novels*. Longus was translated into English in 1537–1539, into French in 1559, into English in 1587, and into German in 1615. Achilles Tatius was translated into French in 1545, into Italian in 1546, into English in 1597, into Spanish in 1617, and into German in 1626. Heliodorus was translated into French in 1547, into German and Spanish in 1554, into Italian in 1556, and into English in 1567.[16] The Greek works, usually called *histories,* were compared to chivalric narrative, in verse and in prose, which took the name of *roman, romanzo,* or *romance.* This is because readers recognized the similarities in structure, and because the plots originating in antiquity had already appeared in the genre called the *roman* during the Middle Ages (the so-called matter of Rome). Ancient Greek narrative would have a decisive influence on the European Baroque novel: from Cervantes's *Los trabajos de Persiles y Sigismunda* (1617), to the French heroic novels by Gomberville, la Calprenède, and the Scudéry brother and sister, to the most famous of the Italian novels of the seventeenth century, *Calloandro fedele* (1640–1641) by Giovanni Ambrogio Marini.

The *pastoral narrative* in verse and prose was directly or indirectly descended from ancient times. Sannazaro's *Arcadia* had revived pastoral themes between the end of the fifteenth century and the beginning of the sixteenth (the first printed edition was in 1504), but the genre experienced its greatest popularity after the first modern translations of Longus's *Daphnis and Chloe* (Annibal Caro, 1537–1539; Amyot, 1559) and after Jorge de Montemayor's *Diana* (1559).[17] The tradition continued with a profusion of important works like Cervantes's *Galatea* (1585), Sidney's *Arcadia* (the first printed editions are from 1590–1593), Lope de Vega's

---

16. See Carol Gesner, *Shakespeare and the Greek Romance: A Study of Origins* (Lexington: University Press of Kentucky, 1970), appendix: "A Bibliographic Survey," 145–162; Laurence Plazenet, *L'Ébahissement et la Délectation: réception comparée et poétique du roman grec en France et en Angleterre au XVIe et au XVIIe siècle* (Paris: Champion, 1997), 13.

17. See Françoise Lavocat, *Arcadies malheureuses: aux origines du roman moderne* (Paris: Champion, 1998).

Arcadia (1598), and Urfé's *Astrée* (1607–1627). The chivalric narrative, the pastoral narrative, and the Greek novel formed the area that English-language literary criticism called the *romance* in opposition to the *novel*.

At the beginning of the nineteenth century, when the distinction between *novel* and *romance* was still in the process of stabilizing, Sir Walter Scott presented the work of Alain-René Lesage in Ballantyne's Novelists' Library. To illustrate the genealogy from which the author of *Gil Blas* (1715–1735) descended, Scott invented an intelligent category that was destined for success: the *comic romance*.[18] In the mid-twentieth century, in a work that changed the interpretation of the English novel, Ian Watt arrived at this category independently when he spoke of the *inverted romance*.[19] Scott argued that the comic romance had developed mainly in Spain, citing *Lazarillo de Tormes*. In reality, the origin of this family of texts is more remote. Works like Petronius's *Satyricon* (first century CE), *The Golden Ass* (second century CE), Lucian's *A True Story* (second century CE), Luigi Pulci's *Morgante* (1478–1483), Rabelais's *Gargantua and Pantagruel* (1532–1564), the picaresque narrative in its comic variant, *Le Berger extravagant* (1627–1628) by Charles Sorel, and *Le Roman bourgeois* (1666) by Antoine Furetière all share a resemblance: they are pluristylistic narratives, but dominated by a lower register; they include adventurous elements; and they can be read as the comic reverse of the serious *romance*. Indeed, the parody is often quite explicit. It was in this context that the expression *anti-roman* arose: Charles Sorel used it in *Le Berger extravagant*.[20] The tradition of the mock-heroic comic narrative, which especially influenced the work of Fielding, also contributed to the birth of the comic romance.[21]

18. Scott, "Alain-René Le Sage," 125. The expression has a precedent in Scarron's *Roman comique*.

19. Watt, *The Rise of the Novel*, 11.

20. Sartre used the term *anti-novel (anti-roman)* again in his preface to Nathalie Sarraute's *Portrait of a Man Unknown* to refer to twentieth-century experimental narrative that deconstructs the rules of plot and character: Jean-Paul Sartre, *Portrait d'un inconnu* (1957); English translation *Portrait of a Man Unknown*, trans. Maria Jolas (New York: George Braziller, 1965), vii–xiv.

21. See Clotilde Bertoni, *Percorsi europei dell'eroicomico* (Pisa: Nistri-Lischi, 1997), 208ff.; and by the same author, "Guizzi parodici e storie senza eroi. Il romanzo sette-ottocentesco e la tradizione eroicomica," in various authors, *Gli "irregolari" della letteratura: Eterodossi, parodisti, funamboli della parola* (Rome: Salerno, 2007).

Even an unclassifiable text like *Don Quixote* (1605–1615) falls into the category of the comic romance. According to a well-known interpretation, Cervantes's masterpiece is said to stage the death of the *romance,* which is swallowed up by the prose of the world. Leaving aside opinions on the genre of this indefinable work, there is no doubt that up until the Romantic period the predominant reading of the text was as a parody: even *Don Quixote* was interpreted as a comic romance.[22]

The Life of Lazarillo de Tormes and of His Fortunes and Adversities (the first surviving printed edition dates from 1554) ushered in the *picaresque narrative.* The genre was revived fifty years later with *Guzmán de Alfarache* (1599–1604) by Mateo Alemán and was enormously popular in Spain and Europe. But while *Lazarillo* and *Guzmán* were fueled by a serious moral intention, at the beginning of the seventeenth century the picaresque genre was pulled back into the comic romance tradition.[23] Widely translated, the Spanish stories influenced French writers, especially Charles Sorel (*Histoire comique de Francion,* 1623–1633), Paul Scarron (*Le Roman comique,* 1651–1657), and Lesage (*Gil Blas,* 1715–1735). One of the most important narrative works in seventeenth-century Germany, *Simplicissimus* (1668–1669), by Grimmelshausen, descends from the picaresque tradition. Many eighteenth-century novels that were retrospectively classed in the *novel* genre are connected to this family, starting with Tobias Smollett's *The Adventures of Roderick Random* (1748) and Fielding's *Tom Jones* (1749).

Another corpus of texts in the comic romance tradition, related to the picaresque novel but with its own specific identity, is the *humorous novel of the eighteenth century:* from Sterne's *Tristram Shandy* (1760–1767), to Diderot's *Jacques the Fatalist* (written between 1765 and 1784, but not published until 1796), to the works of Jean Paul. This literary lineage would

22. Angel Flores and M. J. Bernadete, eds., *Cervantes across the Centuries* (New York: Gordian Press, 1969); Peter E. Russell, "'Don Quixote' as a Funny Book," *Modern Language Review* 64 (1969): 312–326; Anthony J. Close, *The Romantic Approach to "Don Quixote": A Critical History of the Romantic Tradition in "Quixote" Criticism* (Cambridge: Cambridge University Press, 1978); Horst Weich, "'Don Quichotte' et le roman comique français du XVIIᵉ et du XVIIIᵉ siècle," *Cahiers de l'association internationale des études françaises* 48 (May 1996): 241–261.

23. See Francisco Rico, *La novela picaresca y el punto de vista* (1970); English translation *The Spanish Picaresque Novel and the Point of View,* trans. Charles Davis (Cambridge: Cambridge University Press, 1984).

become an essential landmark for the first theorists of the truly modern novel, especially for Friedrich Schlegel. The freedom with which the humorous tradition mixed its contents and forms also contributed to the novel becoming perceived at a certain point as the genre that can be used to tell about anything in any way whatsoever.

One part of the texts later integrated into the literary space of the novel is related in various ways to the medieval genre of the *novella* and its sixteenth- and seventeenth-century transformations. In the mid-sixteenth century, short narrative enjoyed renewed popularity thanks to Matteo Bandello's *Novelle* (1554–1573) and Margaret of Navarre's *Heptaméron* (1558). Passing from Italy into Spain, the genre underwent a crucial transformation with Cervantes. In the preface to his *Exemplary Novels* (1613), the author of *Don Quixote* credits himself with being the first person to write *novelas* in the Castilian language.[24] But his interpretation of the genre transcended the boundaries set by the Italians. Cervantes lengthened the plot, introduced narrative techniques from the Greek romances, imbued the events with hidden moral senses, and to all intents and purposes inaugurated a new form that was remarkably successful in Spain and later exported to France.[25] In addition to these changes, he also introduced the publishing practice of circulating the novellas autonomously, detached from a unifying frame and presented as "comic stories" or "tragic stories."

During the seventeenth century, *novelas* and tragic stories became codified, meeting with considerable success throughout Europe and changing people's perception of the genre. Out of this metamorphosis came the French *nouvelle* of the second half of the seventeenth century: a type of book that, in the print types of our time, filled about a hundred or a hundred and fifty pages and told a love story between people of high rank, in a nonromance setting. The success of Madame de La Fayette's *The Princesse de Clèves* and the theoretical debate it set off during the last two decades of the seventeenth century solidified the features of the genre.[26]

---

24. Miguel de Cervantes, *Novelas ejemplares* (1613); English translation *Exemplary Stories*, trans., with introduction and notes, by Lesley Lipson (Oxford: Oxford University Press, 2008), 5.

25. See Frédéric Deloffre, *La Nouvelle en France à l'âge classique* (Paris: Didier, 1967), chap. 2; Hautcoeur Pérez-Espejo, *Parentés franco-espagnoles au XVIIᵉ siècle*, 27ff.

26. See Joan DeJean, *Tender Geographies: Women and the Origins of the Novel in France* (New York: Columbia University Press, 1991), 94ff.; Camille Esmein, "Le *tournant histo-*

Many of the most important narrative works from the eighteenth century are *epistolary novels with a love theme*. The genre began with Ovid's *Heroides* and continued to be practiced during the Hellenistic period. It made its way through the Middle Ages (the letters of Abelard and Heloise and Boccaccio's *The Elegy of Madame Fiammetta*) and then flourished again during the age of Renaissance humanism, thanks mainly to the success of *The Tale of Two Lovers* (1444) by Aeneas Silvius Piccolomini and the development of a women's epistolary literature during the sixteenth century.[27] Practiced continuously in the sixteenth and seventeenth centuries, epistolary fiction produced works that would prove to be remarkably influential, such as Gabriel de Guilleragues's *Letters of a Portuguese Nun* (1669). During the eighteenth century, the genre met with enormous success and contributed significantly to the development of the novel: this was the form charged with the mimesis of passions.[28] Some of the texts that were decisive for the history of the eighteenth-century novel had an epistolary structure: Richardson's *Pamela* (1740) and *Clarissa* (1748), Rousseau's *Julie, or The New Heloise* (1761), Burney's *Evelina* (1778), and Laclos's *Dangerous Liaisons* (1782). *The Sorrows of Young Werther* (1774) also belongs in some respects to the tradition of the romantic epistolary novel, although Goethe interpreted the genre in a completely new way.

The territory of the novel also covers works that resist any exact classification. We might call them *stories of individuals*[29] or *writings about personal experience*. From 1550 on, these stories gained in prestige and number, aided by the cultural atmosphere of the Reformation and the Counter-Reformation as well as the rebirth of Pauline and Augustinian thought, all of which played different roles in fostering autobiographical

rique comme construction théorique: l'exemple du 'tournant' de 1660 dans l'histoire du roman," *Théorie et histoire littéraire, Fabula LHT (littérature, histoire, théorie)*, June 16, 2005, http://www.fabula.org/lht/0/esmein.html; also by the same author, *L'Essor du roman: discours théorique et constitution d'un genre littéraire au XVIIᵉ siècle* (Paris: Champion, 2008), 11ff.

27. Thomas O. Beebee, *Epistolary Fiction in Europe, 1500–1850* (Cambridge: Cambridge University Press, 1999), 108ff.

28. See Jean Rousset, "Une forme littéraire: le roman par lettres," in *Forme et signification: essai sur les structures littéraires de Corneille à Claudel* (Paris: Corti, 1962).

29. The expression appears in Michael McKeon, *The Origins of the English Novel, 1600–1740* (1987) (Baltimore: Johns Hopkins University Press, 1991), 95ff.

writing. In Protestant countries, the sacrament of confession was replaced by the practice of keeping a private journal. In Catholic countries, the spiritual exercises and example of Ignatius of Loyola transmitted models for writing about oneself. Protestant and Catholic Augustinianism transformed Augustine's *Confessions* into the archetype of sixteenth- and seventeenth-century introspective literature.[30] In addition to promoting the spread of spiritual autobiographies, religious culture reinforced the tradition of biographies, generating lives of the saints, lives of converted sinners, and exemplary lives of good Christians.

But writings about experience and stories of individuals also developed outside the religious sphere, through the secular genre of the *letter,* for example, which Petrarch had transformed into a vital component of literary humanism. At the beginning of the sixteenth century, the authority of Erasmus contributed to propagating a new model of epistolary writing that was open to the multiplicity of life and to the subjectivity of the author, based on a flexible, interiorized application of the rules of rhetoric.[31] The letter proved to be important for the development of fiction in general. It provided a rhetorical framework for the romantic epistolary novel. It also lent itself to telling about experiences, voyages with realistic pretensions, or imaginary journeys based on the device of estrangement, as in the genre introduced by Giovanni Paolo Marana's *Letters Writ by a Turkish Spy* (1684) and consolidated by Montesquieu's *Persian Letters* (1721). The second half of the seventeenth century and the eighteenth century also witnessed an extraordinary outpouring of secular biography (the Plutarchian tradition, biographies of artists, writers, and scholars) and secular autobiography (from an anomalous work like Michel de Montaigne's *Essays* to the rebirth of the classic genre of *commentarii,* which in French culture was called *mémoires*).[32]

---

30. See Andrea Battistini, *Lo specchio di Dedalo. Autobiografia e biografia* (Bologna: Il Mulino, 1990), 33ff.

31. Marc Fumaroli, "Genèse de l'épistolographie classique: rhétorique humaniste de la lettre, de Pétrarque à Juste Lipse," *Revue d'histoire littéraire de la France* 88 (1978): 886–905.

32. See Beasley, *Novels of the 1740s,* chaps. 3–5; Franco D'Intino, *L'autobiografia moderna. Storia forme problemi* (Rome: Bulzoni, 1998), 29–37; J. Paul Hunter, *Before Novels: The Cultural Contexts of Eighteenth-Century English Fiction* (New York: Norton, 1990), chaps. 12–14; Marc Fumaroli, "Les Mémoires du XVIIᵉ siècle au carrefour des genres en prose," *XVIIᵉ siècle* 94–95 (1971): 7–37; René Démoris, *Le Roman à la première personne: du classicisme aux Lumières* (1975) (Geneva: Droz, 2002), 59ff.

Courtly, pastoral, and Greek romances, *novelle, novelas,* and *nouvelles,* romantic epistolary novels, and writings about personal experience all took their place on the genealogical tree of the novel. There were also literary or paraliterary forms that, although not belonging to the genre, had a profound influence on it.

Between the sixteenth and seventeenth centuries two forms appeared that were related to secular biography, but with a more static and analytical bent: the *character* and the *prose portrait.* Both descended from classical rhetoric. The character sketch experienced a second vogue after Casaubon's publication of *The Characters of Theophrastus* (1592 and 1599), first in England and then throughout Europe.[33] The prose portrait had a poetic prehistory,[34] developing mainly in French literature of the *âge classique.*[35] Both had an influence on how characters were represented in novels.[36]

Midway between writings about experience and pure invention, *travel literature* remained popular throughout the Middle Ages and the early modern period. While some of the stories presented themselves as reports of real-world experiences, others were described as works of the imagination or utopias. Regardless of their realistic status, this form influenced some of the works that entered the canon of the European novel, from

33. Benjamin Boyce, *The Theophrastan Character in England to 1642* (Cambridge, MA: Harvard University Press, 1947); John William Smeed, *The Theophrastan "Character": The History of a Literary Genre* (Oxford: Clarendon, 1985).

34. Lina Bolzoni, *Poesia e ritratto nel Rinascimento,* ed. Federica Pich (Rome: Laterza, 2008).

35. Gisela Ruth Köhler, *Das literarische Porträt: Eine Untersuchung zur geschlossenen Personendarstellung in der französischen Erzählliteratur vom Mittelalter bis zum Ende des 19. Jahrhunderts* (Bonn: Romanistischer Verlag, 1991), 141ff.; Jacqueline Plantié, *La Mode du portrait littéraire en France 1641–1681* (Paris: Champion, 1994).

36. See Peter Brooks, *The Novel of Worldliness: Crébillon, Marivaux, Laclos, Stendhal* (Princeton, NJ: Princeton University Press, 1969), 57ff. and passim; Smeed, *The Theophrastan "Character,"* chap. 10; Barbara Carnevali, "L'Observatoire des moeurs: les coutumes et les caractères, entre littérature et morale," in *Pensée morale et genres littéraires,* ed. Jean-Charles Darmon and Philippe Desan (Paris: PUF, 2009), 159–178; and by the same author, "Mimesis littéraire et connaissance morale: la tradition de l'éthopée,'" *Annales* 45, no. 2 (2010): 291–322.

Defoe's *Robinson Crusoe* (1719) to Jonathan Swift's *Gulliver's Travels* (1726–1735).[37]

The development of the novel has to be considered in relation to the mass of *popular writings* that occupied the same market segment later occupied by the *novel* and the *romance:* miraculous or edifying anecdotes, stories of wonders or monsters, secret histories, scandal sheets, letters, sermons, treatises of popular theology, devotional manuals, catechisms, moral debates on the events of the day, *exempla,* observations on contemporary customs, books of jests and manners, and guides to the duties of Christians, men, women, mothers, fathers, gentlemen, merchants, servants, shopkeepers, innkeepers, soldiers, and sailors.[38] With the spread of printing, this jumble of writings expanded throughout Europe. Some of the subgenres that formed one part were of medieval origin and therefore had a well-established history. The picaresque novel, for example, developed on the back of popular narrative forms like criminal biographies and jest books: the story of Ginés de Pasamonte in *Don Quixote* is a good illustration of how important and pervasive bandit tales were in the popular imagination, in Spain as in other countries. It is no coincidence that the first English translation of *Lazarillo de Tormes* was by David Rowland, who had previously been known for his stories about criminals.

Symbolic Thresholds: 1550

Here, then, is a concise list of the subgenres that shaped the space of the literary novel between the second half of the sixteenth century and the second half of the seventeenth. There are many reasons why the year 1550 can serve as the first historical threshold.

1. In the mid-sixteenth century, European literatures rediscovered the Greek novel. Between 1553 and 1554 the first picaresque narrative appeared. During the same timespan, the first treatises on the genre called the *romanzo*

---

37. Percy G. Adams, *Travel Literature and the Evolution of the Novel* (Lexington: University Press of Kentucky, 1983); Riccardo Capoferro, *Frontiere del racconto. Letteratura di viaggio e romanzo in Inghilterra, 1680–1750* (Rome: Meltemi, 2007).

38. See Hunter, *Before Novels,* chaps. 10 and 11.

appeared: Simone Fòrnari's *Sposizione sopra l'"Orlando furioso" di M. Ludovico Ariosto* (1549–1550), Giraldi Cinzio's *Discorso intorno al comporre dei romanzi* (first print edition 1554), and Giovan Battista Pigna's *I romanzi* (1554).[39]

2. Around 1550, the categories indicating the genre we are exploring began to be used in a more extended sense. This took place when some of the new narrative texts, or those that had been recently rediscovered, were introduced into the same literary territory occupied by courtly literature. Amyot's preface to his translation of Heliodorus (1547) is an emblematic text in this respect. Following antihistorical, typological lines of reasoning, he compares *Aethiopica* to medieval romances as if they were the same type of books:

> And, on the contrary, the majority of books of this sort (*livres de ceste sorte*) that were anciently written in our language—in addition to possessing no learning, no knowledge of antiquity, or anything (in a word) from which one might derive some utility—are also often so ill-conceived and so far removed from any probable appearance that they seem more akin to the fevered deliriums of a sick person than to the inventions of any man of wit and judgment.[40]

The crucial semantic expansion for the words derived from *novus-novella* began over half a century later, when the Spanish *novelas* lengthened and complicated the plots of the Italian *novelle*.

3. Around 1550, the new literary territory that was gradually taking shape around terms deriving from *romanice loqui* and from *novus-novella* began to bifurcate, following a schema that, through a few intermediate steps, punctuated the history of the novel during the following centuries. The dividing line rested on a cornerstone of classical literary theory, patterned on the opposition between poetry and history that Aristotle had laid out in the ninth chapter of his *Poetics*:

39. On the date of composition of Giraldi's and Pigna's works, and on the controversy that divided them, see the introduction, remarks, and appendixes to Giraldi Cinzio, *Discorso dei romanzi*, esp. 12–25.

40. Jacques Amyot, "Le Proësme du translateur," in *L'Histoire aethiopique de Heliodorus, contenant dix livres, traitant des loyales et pudiques amours de Théagènes thessalien et Chariclea aethiopienne, nouvellement traduite de grec en françoys* (Paris: Longis, 1547), not paginated.

A poet's object is not to tell what actually happened but what could and would happen either probably or inevitably (*kata to eikos e to anankaion*). The difference between a historian and a poet is not that one writes in prose and the other in verse. . . . The real difference is this, that one tells what happened and the other what might happen. For this reason poetry is something more scientific and serious than history, because poetry tends to give general truths while history gives particular facts. By a "general truth" I mean the sort of thing that a certain type of man will do or say either probably or necessarily. That is what poetry aims at in giving names to the characters. A "particular" fact is what Alcibiades did or what was done to him.[41]

History shows us what a particular individual did or what was done to him or her and tells the "truth"—meaning a real event in all its singularity. Poetry shows us what a certain type of person would normally do or say and tells what might well have taken place "probably or inevitably." The idea of probability that premodern classicism drew from Aristotle, Horace, and Plato stemmed from the intersection of two different elements. The first— empirical observation—unites the classical concept of probability to the modern one. By studying people's behavior we can formulate general laws that become sedimented in the discursive formations that serve us to classify characters, passions, and customs. In the culture of antiquity, these disciplines were primarily ethics and rhetoric. When Aristotle described the behavior of the young, the old, the man in his prime, the noble, the rich, and the powerful in book 2 of *Rhetoric* and in the *Nicomachean Ethics,* he made use of anthropological and sociological abstractions that we are still able to understand today, because they record empirical constants that have remained stable over time.[42] The second is foreign to modern common sense, because instead of coming from observation, it derives from normative ethics—from the idea that the task of poetry is to show things and people as they should be and not as they are. A noble hero must behave nobly: although we know from experience that the opposite occurs at times, the task of the poet is to portray the ideal essence of aristocratic characters and not their empirical imperfection. Conversely, the historian disregards the probable to tell the truth, which grants him license to describe

41. Aristotle, *Poetics* 9.1451a–1451b.
42. Aristotle, *Rhetoric* 2.12–17; *Nicomachean Ethics* 3 and 4 and passim.

life in all its contingent, imperfect, and centrifugal particularity.[43] As the keystone of classicist poetics between the second half of the sixteenth century and the first half of the eighteenth, the opposition between the universality of poetry and the particularity of history did not serve to distinguish works of fiction from works of historiography (the differences between the two genres are obvious). It primarily created a boundary inside the literature of invention, defining two different models of mimesis: the first was oriented to showing reality how it should be in its ideal perfection, while the second was oriented to showing reality as it truly is, in the contingency of its particular way of being. This opposition guided perception about narrative until the system established by premodern and early modern classicism dissolved during the Romantic period. We find it in Italian writers in the mid-sixteenth century[44] and in *Don Quixote*,[45] in French writers of the *âge classique*,[46] and in English literati of the mid-eighteenth century.[47] The critical vocabulary of Friedrich Schlegel and Gia-

43. René Bray, *La Formation de la doctrine classique en France* (Paris: Nizet, 1945), part 3, chap. 1; Marvin T. Herrick, *The Fusion of Horatian and Aristotelian Literary Criticism, 1531–1555* (Urbana: University of Illinois Press, 1946), chaps. 5 and 7; Bernard Weinberg, *A History of Literary Criticism in the Italian Renaissance* (Chicago: University of Chicago Press, 1961), passim; Gérard Genette, "Vraisemblance et motivation," in *Figures II* (Paris: Seuil, 1969), 71–99; Áron Kibédi Varga, "La Vraisemblance: problèmes de terminologie, problèmes de poétique," in *Critique et création littéraires en France au XVIIᵉ siècle* (Paris: CNRS, 1977), 325–332; Anne Duprat, *Vraisemblances: poétiques et théorie de la fiction, du Cinquecento à Jean Chapelain (1500–1670)* (Paris: Champion, 2009), 136ff., 327ff.

44. See Pigna, *I romanzi*, 93ff. and passim; Giraldi Cinzio, *Discorso sui romanzi*, 47ff., 88ff., and passim.

45. See Miguel de Cervantes, *Don Quijote de la Mancha* (1605–1615); English translation *Don Quixote de la Mancha*, trans. Charles Jarvis; edited with an introduction and notes by Edward C. Riley (Oxford: Oxford University Press, 2008).

46. See Pierre-Daniel Huet, *Traité de l'origine des romans*; English translation *The History of Romances*, trans. Stephen Lewis (London: J. Hooke, at the Flower-de-luce, and T. Caldecott, at the Sun; both against St. Dunstan's Church in Fleetstreet, 1715), 3.

47. See Henry Fielding, *The History of Tom Jones, a Foundling* (1749), ed. Fredson Bowers and Martin Carey Battestin, *Wesleyan Edition of the Complete Works of Henry Fielding* (Oxford: Oxford University Press, 1975), bk. 2, chap. 1, pp. 75ff. and bk. 8, chap. 1, p. 400; Samuel Johnson, *Rambler*, no. 4 (Saturday, March 31, 1750); also by Johnson, *Essays from the Rambler, Adventurer, and Idler*, ed. Walter Jackson Bate (New Haven, CT: Yale University Press, 1968), 14. Fielding defines the uniqueness of his work by appealing to the Aristotelian opposition between history and poetry: *Tom Jones* is a *history*, but it deals with a subject that has no unanimous testimonies or verifiable documentation. It is therefore forced to remain within the limits of the probable. Johnson maintains that the best novels should not pursue

como Leopardi still bears traces of this opposition.[48] The theory was used to impose order on the profusion of unorthodox narrative writings that were being gathered into one group under the artificial names *roman, romanzo, novel-and-romance,* and *novela.*

Symbolic Thresholds: 1670

If 1550 marks a first frontier, a second symbolic threshold can be seen to fall around 1670, for at least two reasons.

1. In 1670 Pierre-Daniel Huet published a *Lettre sur l'origine des romans* (Letter on the Origin of Novels) as a preface to *Zayde,* written by Madame de La Fayette and appearing under the name of Segrais. Revised and published a year later in the form of a treatise, and continuously rewritten until 1711, the *Traité de l'origine des romans* became the standard reference for anyone writing about the novel until at least the mid-eighteenth century.[49] While Italian theorists of the 1500s identified the *romanzo* with the chivalric poem, Huet broadened its historical framework. He did so almost despite himself: his treatise actually sought to restrict the field of legitimate writings and transform the Greek novel into the perfect example of what the genre should be. And yet, regardless of his intentions, Huet traced out a hybrid history. He wrote that Greek narratives are the standard, but recognized that the word *roman* derives from medieval narrative literature. He talked about the works of Heliodorus as a model, but also reflected

the imperfections of life, as do works of history, but depict life as it should be, exhibiting "the most perfect idea of virtue," as do works of poetry.

48. When Friedrich Schlegel writes that romantic poetry "is based entirely on a historical foundation," or that *The Decameron* "is almost entirely true history," what he means is that these works tell contingent stories about particular individuals rather than offering exemplary characters and plots drawn from myths or other literature. When Leopardi writes that his *Idylls* express "situations, affections, historic adventures of my soul," what he means is that these poems arise out of contingent biographical anecdotes, and not out of generic literary situations. The concept of "historical" that Schlegel and Leopardi refer to is still the classical notion deriving from Aristotle's *Poetics.* See Schlegel, *Dialogue on Poetry,* 100; Giacomo Leopardi, *Disegni letterari,* in *Prose e poesie,* vol. 2, *Prose,* ed. Rolando Damiani (Milan: Mondadori, 1988), 1218.

49. For more on the publication history of this work, see Camille Esmein, *Poétiques du roman: Scudéry, Huet, Du Plaisir et autres textes théoriques et critiques du XVIIᵉ siècle sur le genre romanesque* (Paris: Champion, 2004), 359ff.

on irregular works like Petronius's *Satyricon* and the courtly romance. In a word: Huet ultimately lumped together under the same name texts that were extremely diverse. What he treated as a single, unified thing would appear to be a confused, heterogeneous mass when grouped together under other categories. Later treatise writers repeated this same aggregating maneuver: from Gotthard Heidegger (*Mythoscopia romantica*, 1698), Lenglet du Fresnoy (*De l'usage des romans* [On the Use of Novels], 1734), and Blanckenburg (*Versuch über den Roman* [Essay on the Novel], 1774) to Clara Reeve (*The Progress of Romance*, 1785).

2. But 1670 marks a symbolic frontier for another, more important reason. Around this date an opposition began to circulate that would prove decisive in creating the novel as a genre. In response to a change in public taste, French writers began to distinguish between the *roman* and the *nouvelle*. The first term referred to the heroic Baroque novel, the second to a story of about a hundred or a hundred and fifty pages that, like Madame de La Fayette's *The Princesse de Clèves* (1678), told about the private, romantic affairs of characters, most of whom were aristocrats. In critical discussion, the meanings of the two words tended to multiply entropically;[50] however, taking into account the semantic chaos ensuing from all intellectual debates, it can be seen that the boundary line very often followed the Aristotelian opposition between poetry and history.[51] This critical schema is one that we come across continually: in Segrais's *Nouvelles françaises* (1656–1657);[52] in the preface to *Nouvelles galantes, comiques et*

---

50. Esmein-Sarrazin, *L'Essor du roman*, 18ff., 59ff.

51. Robin Howells, "Statut du romanesque: l'opposition roman/histoire dans la pratique signifiante de 1635 à 1785," in *Folies romanesques au siècle des Lumières*, ed. René Démoris and Henri Lafon (Paris: Desjonquères, 1998), 19–39.

52. The character Aurélie says: "We began to tell things as they are, and not how they should be; after all, it seems to me that this is the difference between the *roman* and the *nouvelle*: the *roman* writes things as dictated by literary decorum [*bienséance*] and as poets do; the *nouvelle* must stay somewhat closer to history and try to present the images of things as we see them ordinarily rather than how they are fashioned by our imagination." Jean Regnault de Segrais, *Les Nouvelles françaises, ou les Divertissements de la princesse Aurelie* (1656–1657), edited, introduced, and annotated by Roger Guichemerre, vol. 1 (Paris: Société des textes français modernes, 1990–1992), 99.

tragiques (1669) by Jean Donneau de Visé;[53] in the preface to *Les Annales galantes* (1670) by Madame de Villedieu;[54] in the preface to *Marie Stuart* (1674) by Boisguilbert;[55] in the *Illustre Parisienne* (1679) by Jean de Préchac;[56] in the most important seventeenth-century theory on the *nouvelle*, Du Plaisir's *Sentiments sur l'histoire* [Reflections on 'History'] (1683);[57] and in the preface to *Les Illustres Françaises* (1713) by Robert Challe.[58] The *roman* claims to follow the rules of Aristotelian probability and tells exemplary stories. The *nouvelle* follows the rules of the true within the limits permitted by good taste and presents itself as the history

53. "I do not doubt that in some of my *nouvelles* there are things that seem somewhat improbable; but the reader will reflect, if he might, on the fact that I am not a poet in this work but a historian. The poet must conform to probability and correct the truth, which is not probable. The historian, on the contrary, must not write anything untrue; and, assuming he is sure that what he tells is the truth, he need not concern himself about probability. Certainly, improbable things have often occurred: if not, we'd never see anything extraordinary or surprising happen. Being a faithful historian, I have not wanted to weigh in on incidents of this nature that I have come across, even though in many points, with two or three words, I could have made certain adventures more probable." Jean Donneau de Visé, *Les Nouvelles galantes, comiques et tragiques* (1669) (Geneva: Slatkine Reprints, 1979), preface, not paginated.

54. "The century boasts of so much subtlety and the license to write living plots has become so common [an allusion to *Nouvelles galantes, comiques et tragiques* by Donneau de Visé, which reported contemporary, often scandalous *faits divers*], that I felt I should forestall the public's errors with this note. I therefore declare that *Les Annales galantes* are historical truths, and I have marked the sources in the Table affixed for this purpose at the end of this first volume. These are not clever tales dressed up with real names. . . . They are faithful traits of General History." Madame de Villedieu, *Les Annales galantes* (1670) (Paris: Société des textes français modernes, 2004), 47–48 ("Avant propos").

55. Pierre le Pesant de Boisguilbert, *Marie Stuard, reine d'Écosse: nouvelle historique*, part 1 (Paris: C. Barbin, 1674), "Avis."

56. "Because what I write is a true history, I was obliged to take my heroine as I found her." Jean de Préchac, *L'Illustre Parisienne: histoire galante et veritable* (Paris: Chez la Veuve Olivier de Varennes, 1679), 2–3.

57. "Probability consists in saying only that which is morally credible. . . . The truth is not always probable, and yet he who writes a true history is not obliged to tone things down to make them believable. It is no guarantee of their probability, because they must be told as they happened and because they are known by many." Du Plaisir, *Sentiments sur les lettres et sur l'histoire, avec des scupules sur le style*, critical edition by Philippe Hourcade (Geneva: Droz, 1975), 46–47.

58. "If I had written fables, I would have been in control of the incidents, which I would have shaped as I pleased. But these are truths whose rules are completely contrary to those of *romans*." Robert Challe, *Les Illustres Françaises* (1713), new edition by Frédéric Deloffre and Jacques Cormier (Geneva: Droz, 1991), 4–5.

of a private life, according to a definition to which we will return. The *roman* was a "poetic" genre: it recounted the adventures of ideal heroes, set in times and spaces far removed from ordinary experience; its story line usually followed the *ordo artificialis,* and its archetypes were the Greek novel and pastoral narrative; its most recent expression was the heroic Baroque novel. The *nouvelle* tended instead to present itself as a "historical" narrative: it had a simple story line, and it recounted "particular actions of private individuals or those considered to be private,"[59] who were situated in an imperfect, contingent world, similar to the one experienced by readers.

In the French debate on *roman* and *nouvelle* this wider, metaphoric use of the categories of poetry and history that were common as early as the mid-sixteenth century became explicit. Indeed, the expression "true history" was used to define texts in which we find obviously invented episodes or characters, and in which expressions such as *nouvelle historique, nouvelle galante,* and *histoire véritable* are used as synonyms,[60] or about which the authors admit to having embellished the historical fact with fictional parts: "I confess that I have added a few embellishments to the simplicity of the history. . . . I have added some secret encounters and amorous conversations to the history. If they are not exactly those uttered by the characters, they are in any case what they should have said."[61]

A few decades later, the *nouvelle* was exported to Great Britain and the *roman-nouvelle* opposition generated the dichotomy between *romance* and *novel.*[62] The English opposition also initially bore the mark of the Aristotelian dialectic between history and poetry, as we see in reading the preface to *The Secret History of Queen Zarah* (1705) by Delarivier

---

59. Jean-Antoine de Charnes, *Conversations sur la critique de la Princesse de Clèves* (1679) (Tours: Publication du groupe d'étude du XVIIᵉ siècle de l'Université François-Rabelais, 1973), 135.

60. Esmein, "Le *tournant historique* comme construction théorique," §2.

61. Madame de Villedieu, *Les Annales galantes,* 48–49.

62. Williams, *Novel and Romance, 1700–1800.* William Congreve was probably the first to introduce the opposition between *novel* and *romance* in the preface to his *Incognita* (1692). See Irene Simon, "Early Theories of Prose Fiction: Congreve and Fielding," in *Imagined Worlds: Essays on Some English Novels and Novelists in Honour of John Butt,* ed. Maynard Mack and Ian Gregor (London: Methuen, 1968), 19.

Manley,[63] Defoe's preface to *Roxana* (1724),[64] or Fielding's *Tom Jones*.[65] The meanings of the terms *novel* and *romance* wavered greatly during the eighteenth century: the two categories overlapped and were confused for a long period of time. Only between the end of the eighteenth century and the beginning of the nineteenth did their respective spheres begin to gradually stabilize. An important contribution in this regard comes from the dialogue by Clara Reeve called *The Progress of Romance* (1785), in which the two words are used with the meanings they acquired in the nineteenth and twentieth centuries: *romances* tell adventurous, improbable stories about exceptional or unreal people; *novels* tell stories about relatively common people in relatively ordinary contexts:

> The Romance is an heroic fable, which treats of fabulous persons and things.—The Novel is a picture of real life and manners, and of the times in which it is written. The Romance in lofty and elevated language, describes what never happened nor is likely to happen.—The Novel gives a familiar relation of such things, as pass every day before our eyes, such as may happen to our friend, or to ourselves; and the perfection of it, is to represent every scene, in so easy and natural a manner, and to make them appear so probable, as to deceive us into a persuasion (at

63. "[The authors of Historical Novels] ought with great Care to observe the Probability of Truth, which consists in Saying nothing but what may Morally be believed. | For there are Truths that are not always probable; as for Example, 'tis an allowed Truth in the Roman History that Nero put his Mother to Death, but 'tis a Thing against all Reason and Probability that a Son shou'd embrue his Hand in the Blood of his own Mother. . . . He that writes a True History ought to place the Accidents as they Naturally happen, without endeavouring to sweeten them for to procure a greater Credit, because he is not obliged to answer for their Probability; but he that composes a History to his Fancy gives his Heroes what Characters he pleases; and places the Accidents as he thinks fit without believing he shall be contradicted by other Historians, therefore, he is obliged to Write nothing that is improbable." Delarivier Manley, *The Secret History of Queen Zarah, and the Zarazians*, in *The Selected Works of Delarivier Manley*, vol. 1, ed. Rachel Carnell (London: Pickering and Chatto, 2005), 86.

64. In the preface to *Roxana*, Defoe clarifies that "the Work is not a Story, but a History" founded in "Truth of Fact." See Daniel Defoe, *Roxana: The Fortunate Mistress* (1724), ed. John Mullan (Oxford: Oxford University Press, 1996), no page numbers.

65. In *Tom Jones*, Fielding says that he applied the method of the historian to private life. See Fielding, *The History of Tom Jones*, bk. 2, chap. 1, pp. 75ff.; bk. 8, chap. 1, pp. 395ff.

least while we are reading) that all is real, until we are affected by the joys or distresses, or the persons in the story, as if they were our own.[66]

The opposition shows that the genre of the novel is composed of two different narrative paradigms, but at the same time it indicates that these paradigms belong to a unified whole. In France the awareness that the two forms belonged to the same category never faded. This was the case even during the last decades of the seventeenth century when the supporters of the *nouvelle* quarreled ferociously with the supporters of the *roman;* or in the early decades of the eighteenth century, when writers preferred to avoid the term *roman* because it was considered to be discredited.[67] *Roman* and *nouvelle* always remained subgroups of the larger group called *roman* in the broad sense.[68] In Great Britain the opposition between *novels* and *romances* is rooted in the literary lexicon, but the uncertainty in tracing out a clear boundary is a sign that the two groups were perceived as a single class. It comes as no surprise that Clara Reeve, who also sharply distin-

---

66. Clara Reeve, *The Progress of Romance,* 2. vols (Colchester: Keymer, 1785), vol. 1, "Evening 7," 111.

67. Georges May, *Le Dilemme du roman au XVIIIe siècle: étude sur les rapports du roman et de la critique (1715–1761)* (New Haven, CT: Yale University Press; Paris: PUF, 1963), chap. 5; Jean Sgard, "Le Mot 'roman,'" in *Eighteenth-Century Fiction* 13, nos. 2–3 (2001): 181–195.

68. Not by chance, *nouvelles* were also called *romans* or *petits romans* during the last decades of the seventeenth century (see for example Pierre Bayle, *Nouvelles de la République des Lettres,* March 1686, in *Catalogue de livres nouveaux, accompagné de quelques remarques,* 2nd ed. [Amsterdam: H. Desbordes, 1686], 350–351), as well as in the 1730s (for example in Nicolas Lenglet du Fresnoy, *De l'usage des romans* [Amsterdam: Chez la Veuve de Poilras à la Vérité sans fard, 1734], 200–203). It must also be pointed out that eighteenth-century French poetics retained the idea of an internal division within the literary space of the novel. In *Mémoires et aventures d'un homme de qualité* Prévost calls *The Princesse de Clèves* a *roman,* but then compares "heroic novels [*romans*], like Cassandras, Cleopatra, the great Cyrus, Polexander" to "histoires amoureuses et nouvelles galantes (romantic histories and galant novels)" (Antoine François Prévost, *Mémoires et aventures d'un homme de qualité qui s'est retiré du monde,* ed. Pierre Berthiaume and Jean Sgard, in *Œuvres de Prévost,* vol. 1 [Grenoble: Presses Universitaires de Grenoble, 1978], 143). Lenglet du Fresnoy distinguishes the "Historiettes ou . . . nouvelles historiques [short histories or . . . historical *nouvelles*]" from "Romans réguliers [regular *romans*]," but interprets them as parts that have been separated from regular novels, to the extent of calling them "romans." The entry for "Roman" in the *Encyclopédie* unifies the genre, but breaks it down into the two distinct subgenres of the *roman* and the *nouvelle.*

guished the *novel* from the *romance,* considered them in reality to be two provinces belonging to the same narrative region.

Nouvelle and *roman, novel* and *romance* belong to the same literary space. Indeed: the birth of this dialectic is especially important because it indicates that, starting from a certain date, the two big narrative families deriving from *novellus-novus* and *romanice loqui* were perceived as different branches of a single genus. Today English-language literary criticism tends to straddle the opposition between *novel* and *romance* by referring to all fictional narratives as "novels." This practice brings English-language critical terminology into conformity with continental usage,[69] but in doing so it runs the risk of dissolving the last trace of a linguistic division that has a profound reason for being. The theoretical and classificatory use of the terms *novel* and *romance* to draw a boundary line inside the literary space of modern fiction is historically legitimate. Its foundation is perfectly solid. The border that it indicates is real. What converged in the *romance* and the *novel* between 1550 and 1800?

The Territory of the *Romance*

The kernels of the *romance* are the Greek novels, the pastoral narrative, and the chivalric narrative of the Middle Ages and the Renaissance. Genealogical kinships exist between these forms: the chivalric romance was likely influenced by Greek narrative through the mediation of Byzantine culture; the pastoral romance is a static, bucolic variant of the Hellenistic love and adventure novel; the heroic Baroque novel superimposes elements taken from the other two traditions onto the model of Heliodorus. But these works are united more by obvious typological similarities than by genetic relations: the events they tell about are exceptional states; the characters live in a world very different from the one experienced by human beings; the plots convey an image of what happens that is dominated by what Bakhtin called the "adventure-time."[70] A series of unexpected events temporarily diverts the characters' fates and generates a sequence of episodes, but it does not introduce any significant transformation into the heroes' outer or inner worlds; the protagonists never grow old, and their

---

69. See, for example, Doody, *The True Story of the Novel,* xvii, 16.
70. Bakhtin, "Forms of Time and of the Chronotope in the Novel," 237ff.

identity never changes; what happens is ruled by chance; the plot can be extended indefinitely and have continuations. The time and space surrounding the heroes are also indefinite and abstract, given that the former has no true historical or existential depth and the latter is multifaceted but generic: entrance into a different country involves only a change of scenery, but no encounter with another culture or another form of life. For these reasons, the romance of adventure is the intermediate stage between epic and romance. As in the epic poem, the characters act in a public dimension; but unlike what normally happens in the *epos,* they devote themselves to the private experiences of love and adventure.

At the beginning of the nineteenth century, having recognized a typological resemblance between these subgenres and a group of narrative forms that adopt a low register, Sir Walter Scott invented the category of the *comic romance.* The comic romance also tells stories about out-of-the-ordinary characters who have exceptional experiences in a very different world than the one inhabited by people like us, but it does so in a humble or low register. The beautiful and chaste youth of the Greek novels, the bucolic characters of the pastoral romance, and the knights of the courtly romance are replaced by penniless or ingenuous students, inexperienced young people who set off on voyages, thieves, and picaros. What remains unchanged is the idea that life is an adventure, a sequence of unforeseen events that transports the characters into unknown territories but that does not change their identity. Although the two traditions are situated at opposite points of the same literary space, they share this typological kinship. If the Greek novel, the pastoral romance, and the chivalric romance written in an elevated style represent the typical forms of the serious romance, then Petronius's *Satyricon,* Apuleius's *Golden Ass,* Lucian's *A True Story,* the low-register romances (Pulci's *Morgante,* Rabelais's *Gargantua and Pantagruel*), the parodies of serious romances, and the interpretation of the picaresque novel that took root starting from the seventeenth century mark the confines of the comic romance. While the success of the serious romance began to wane at the end of the seventeenth century, the comic romance was widely diffused in the eighteenth century, from Lesage to Smollett. *Tom Jones* can be read as the culmination of this tradition and, at the same time, as superseding it.

The Territory of the *Novel*

Novel can be used in a restricted historical sense to indicate a genre that arose in eighteenth-century England, or in a wider theoretical sense to indicate a narrative form that exists in many literatures and that eighteenth-century English literature consecrated. The most authoritative theory on this subgenre remains that of Ian Watt in *The Rise of the Novel* (1957). Watt's theory has exerted a great deal of influence, and its authority remains undisputed even today because it establishes with unparalleled lucidity the place that the *novel* occupied in the long-term history of European literature. Although many critics have attempted to reexamine its foundations over the past few decades,[71] his work has retained remarkable theoretical force.

For Watt, the two meanings of the word *novel* designate exactly the same thing. In his view, the English *novel* is the beginning of the *novel* as a form, and while it may be true that the genre extended out into every European literature between the second half of the eighteenth century and the beginning of the nineteenth, its original core developed in England with Defoe, Richardson, and Fielding. I believe that the basic framework of this interpretation still stands, but the historical and geographical picture it evokes is highly questionable. Let us examine the following idea, for example.

> The issue of individual identity is closely linked to the epistemological status of proper names because, in the words of Hobbes, "Proper names bring to mind one thing only; universals recall any one of many." As the verbal expression of the particular identity of each and every person, proper names have exactly the same function in the social life. In literature, however, it was only with the novel that this function of proper names became established.[72]

The *novel* is the genre of proper names: it tells stories about private persons who are located in a space and time similar to those we experience every day. The critical angle that Watt discovers is illuminating, but this is not how literary history really happened. It is not a matter of pedantically

---

71. See various authors, "Reconsidering the Rise of the Novel," special issue, *Eighteenth-Century Fiction* 12, nos. 2–3 (2000).

72. Watt, *The Rise of the Novel*, 18.

correcting a work that in many aspects remains unsurpassable; it is about understanding that Watt's interpretation grasps some crucial elements of the *novel*, but that the philosophy of literary history on which it is based suffers from insularity. We can retain the core of his interpretation and place it in a more plausible historical narrative. Long before English narrative made use of proper names, some genres of ancient Greek and Roman literature (the Old Comedy, iambus, the epigram, satire, and certain forms of subjective poetry) had already told stories about the lives of ordinary people. Furthermore, the *novel* did not suddenly appear in England during the eighteenth century. The first modern narrative form to tell about the contingency of proper names was not the eighteenth-century English *novel*. The medieval *exemplum,* the medieval and Renaissance *novella,* the Spanish picaresque narrative, and the French *nouvelle* of the second half of the seventeenth century told stories about private people. Andreuccio da Perugia, a horse broker who goes to Naples with five hundred gold florins in his purse hoping to close a good deal, or Lazarillo de Tormes, the son of a miller, have no less detailed identities and are no more vaguely situated than Robinson Crusoe, the son of a merchant of Bremen who immigrated to Hull. Certainly, the English *novel* represents a decisive moment in the history of the *novel* as a form because it expands the number of contingencies the texts are able to accommodate: what in *The Decameron* or in *Lazarillo* is conveyed with a few remarks occupies several pages in *Robinson Crusoe.* However, the grasp of particularities that eighteenth-century English narrative displays is nothing but the development of a trait already present in the *exemplum,* in the *novella,* in early picaresque narrative, in the *novela,* in the *nouvelle,* and in *mémoires,* all of which are genres full of proper names.

Therefore the literary space of the *novel* came prior to the English narrative of the eighteenth century. It comprises three literary families: the third-person *novella,* from its medieval archetypes to its seventeenth-century variations; the tradition of the sacred and profane biography; and first-person autobiographical writings (confessions, letters, epistolary novels, and *mémoires*). The three genealogies differ for morphological and historical reasons: while the *novella* and the biography are written in the third person, autobiographical-type works are written in the first person; while biographies and autobiographies tend to be long and their plots not very coherent, the *novella,* the *novela,* and the *nouvelle* tend to be short and have coherent plots. They do share a common characteristic, though: many of the texts that fall under the category of the *novel* present themselves as accounts of true histories or are told as if they were true. At the end of the seventeenth century, the *nouvelle* or the *histoire* written in third person can be confidently equated with the *mémoire* or the epistolary novel as "historical" forms opposed to the "poetry" of the *roman.*[73] However, the difference between a *mémoire* in first person and a *nouvelle historique* in third person follows the opposition typical of classical historiography between commentaries and "true histories," between the subjective narrative of the protagonist or of the witness, and the impartial, objective narrative written according to the rules of the art.[74] In any case, the two subgenres fall under the same category.

During the eighteenth century, as we have said, a fourth family joined up with the three original ones. This happened when it began to be admitted, without too many masks and without too many fears, that the *novel* was a fiction and not a "true history." At that point, the dialectic between historical genres and poetic genres no longer sufficed on its own to trace out the boundaries between the *novel* and the *romance.* The dialectic needed to be reworked, which Clara Reeve did. What distinguished the two forms was no longer the opposition between the true and the probable: it was the opposition between stories that are fictional but nevertheless "such as pass every day before our eyes" (Reeve) and stories that are fictional but improbable. It thus becomes possible to compare the *novel* to the genre that in the literature of antiquity and the classical period had the task of relating everyday life: *comedy.* After the flourishing of narrative texts that took place in France between the end of the 1720s and 1730s when Prévost and Marivaux were publishing their greatest works, the comparison between

---

73. Démoris, *Le Roman à la première personne,* 157ff. This is what happened, for example, in Madame de La Fayette's letter to Joseph-Marie de Lescheraine, in which she states that *The Princesse de Clèves* is not a *roman* but rather *des mémoires.* In fact, initially *mémoires* was supposed to appear in the title of the book. Madame de La Fayette, "Lettre à Lescheraine," April 13, 1678, in *Œuvres complètes,* ed., introduction, and notes by Roger Duchêne (Paris: Bourin, 1990), 622.

74. Fumaroli, "Les Mémoires du XVIIᵉ siècle au carrefour des genres en prose."

novels and comedies became a commonplace.[75] A few years later, we come across it again in the *Encyclopédie* under the entry for "Roman."[76]

> In the classical literary schema, comedy was "an imitation of life, a mirror of customs, and an image of the truth" (*imitatio vitae, speculum consuetudinis, imago veritatis*) according to a definition that Donatus attributed to Cicero[77] and that circulated widely from the sixteenth century on.[78] Starting in the eighteenth century, the *novel* appropriated these formulas and began to present itself as a mirror of life and customs. A significant slippage took place during this transition: for the culture of the ancient world, the New Comedy was a predominantly "poetic" genre focused on the ideographic representation of the typical, not on the detailed representation of the singular.[79] In the *novel* of the eighteenth century, however, the mimesis of customs took increasingly "historical" forms. At the same time some narrative forms with a comic tone, initially viewed as related to the tradition of the *romance*, entered into the territory of the *novel*. Fielding's *Tom Jones* played a decisive role in mixing up the categories. The work combines elements from different genres. The characters and the plot owed a great deal to the New Comedy, to the classicist comedy that was revived following the model of the New Comedy, and to the picaresque-type comic

75. May, *Le Dilemme du roman au XVIIIe siècle*, 112ff.

76. "Roman," in *Encyclopédie*, vol. 14 (Neuchâtel: Samuel Faulche, 1755), 342. The article was penned by Louis de Jaucourt.

77. Aelius Donatus, *Excerpta de comoedia*, in *Aeli Donati quod fertur commentum Terenti*, ed. Paul Wessner (Leipzig: Teubner, 1902), V, 1, 22.

78. See Herrick, *The Fusion of Horatian and Aristotelian Literary Criticism*.

79. According to Aristotle's formula, unlike the writers of iambics, comic playwrights construct their plots according to the probable and then add particular names taken at random: their characters are not singular individuals but human types (*Poetics* 9.1451b.11–15). This idea about comedies circulated widely during the time we are examining. In the mid-seventeenth century, for example, we find it cited literally in the "Advertissement aux lecteurs" that prefaces *Polyandre, Histoire comique* (1648) by Charles Sorel: "All of the characters named here can be taken as Chimeras or ideas, or rather as Characters or Tableaux of what is intended to be represented." It comes as no surprise that the *histoire comique* stands somewhere between the "poetic" and the "historical" genres: it is a comic romance in which the representation of reality is subjected to an obvious genre filter. See Charles Sorel, *Polyandre, Histoire comique* (Paris: Chez la Veuve Nicolas Cercy, 1648), "Advertissement aux lecteurs," no pagination.

romance. In the preface to *Joseph Andrews,* Fielding argues that his prose tales have the same relation to serious epic poems as comedy does to tragedy. He goes on to distinguish between intermediate comic literature, with which he associates himself, and burlesque literature. In doing so, he draws a potential boundary line between his works and romances that have a low, farcical tone.[80] On the other hand, Fielding—who deliberately recalls the Aristotelian distinction between history and poetry—includes himself among the tellers of *histories* and not *romances.*[81] His works introduced into the space of the *novel* a narrative form that came into being as comic romance and that was related to the genre of the comedy. They provide a different way of reading novels of the past, such as Lesage's *Gil Blas,* that in many respects were precursors of *Tom Jones.*

The territory of the *novel* is therefore extremely varied. Only between the end of the eighteenth century and the beginning of the nineteenth did the category become definitively stabilized. What unites the four families of texts that compose it is the interweaving between a theme and a form: telling "such things, as pass every day before our eyes" and doing so in a way that seems familiar[82]—that is, founded on common sense. The image of the world transmitted by the intersection of these four genealogies is very different from that conveyed by the tradition of the *romance.* The *novel* aspires to tell "things in the manner in which they occur in the ordinary course of the world."[83] The names its characters bear are plausible for individuals of their condition: they live in a measurable time; they move around in a defined space, through an environment subject to the same laws of probability that hold in ordinary experience; their status of reality is the same as what is expected of "our friend" or "ourselves."[84]

80. Henry Fielding, preface to *Joseph Andrews,* in the *Wesleyan Edition of the Complete Works of Henry Fielding,* 4ff.

81. Fielding, *The History of Tom Jones,* bk. 2, chap. 1 and bk. 8, chap. 1.

82. Reeve, *The Progress of Romance,* "Evening 7," 111.

83. Charnes, *Conversations sur la critique de la Princesse de Clèves,* 136.

84. Reeve, *The Progress of Romance,* "Evening 7," 111.

The Rise of the *Novel*

We have seen how the birth of the opposition between *roman* and *nou-velle,* and then between *romance* and *novel,* marked a decisive threshold in the unification of the novel. When the groups of texts that came from *romanice loqui* and *novellus-novus* converged, a struggle for literary hege-mony broke out. Beginning in the last decades of the seventeenth century, the debate on the *novel* and *romance* was relentlessly shot through with comparison, and little by little the second family gained importance and prestige over the first. Between 1670 and 1800 the power relations between the two genealogies changed: the *novel* gradually occupied the center of the literary space and became "the novel," in the emphatic sense, while the *romance* was pushed to the periphery of the system.

This is easily seen in the cultures that refer to the novel using words de-rived from *romanice loqui.* Huet's treatise speaks purely about narrative that developed from the Hellenistic and medieval models. How else could it be? In 1670 the word *roman* referred to the tradition of the *romance.* Instead, for those who were born between 1760 and 1780, and who wrote between the last years of the eighteenth century and the early years of the nineteenth—for the generation of Madame de Staël, Friedrich Schlegel, Sir Walter Scott, or Ugo Foscolo—the novel was above all the genre that spoke about relatively ordinary people while imitating the tech-niques of historiography. At the end of the eighteenth century, the *novel* far outweighed the *romance.*

> In France, Italy, and Germany, which is to say, for the literatures in which the term designating the genre derived from medieval romances, this trans-formation involved a kind of linguistic theft: the family of the *novella,* the *nouvelle, mémoires,* and the *novel* appropriated the words *roman* and *ro-manzo* and transformed their meaning. In 1800, Schlegel argued that Boc-caccio's *novelle,* having introduced into literature the "true history" of private cases, were essential for the birth of what the moderns called the novel.[85] Two years later, Madame de Staël, in the preface to *Delphine* (1802), diminished the role of the medieval works that lent their name to the genre. The *roman,* writes de Staël, is the only form that has allowed us

85. Schlegel, *Dialogue on Poetry,* 58.

to depict the passions of the heart and to tell the story of private lives. Unknown to the ancient Greek and Roman cultures, it emerged over the course of the Middle Ages, but in a much different form from the one it would subsequently take on. While medieval courtly narrative sought the wonder of adventure rather than the truth of feelings, *The Princesse de Clèves* combines the analysis of passion with the depiction of chivalric manners. The English novel of the eighteenth century perfects the possibilities that the genre bears with it.[86] Madame de Staël writes at the beginning of the nineteenth century, after Madame de La Fayette, Defoe, Marivaux, Prévost, Richardson, Fielding, Rousseau, Voltaire, Goethe, Burney, Laclos, Diderot, and Moritz. In her eyes, the courtly romance and other forms of *romance* do not signal a discontinuity comparable to the one introduced by *The Princesse de Clèves* or English fiction: the works that Madame de Staël considers to be masterpieces of the *roman* all belong to the tradition of the *novel*. A year later, in a review, Foscolo also condensed into a few pages the centuries-old history of narrative. In his judgement, the Italian *novelle* represent the medieval equivalent of the books that "we [moderns] call *romanzi*." In this case, too, what we are witnessing is a kind of linguistic theft. The true *romanzo* is the tradition of the *novel*:

> When Boccacci [*sic*], Sacchetti, Il Lasca, and Bandello wrote *novelle*, they portrayed the customs of their times, anecdotes about their governments, manners, festivities, languages, and clothing typical of their cities. Their books were similar to those we call *romanzi*, of which many recent and excellent ones are read in England, many in France, in Germany and in cultivated Europe. It comes as no surprise. . . . Writers of *romanzi* depict people's opinions, habits, and actions, so to speak, and physical appearances, where historians neither should nor can portray them because they cannot always see them. In short, history portrays nations and their forms, while the writer of *romanzi* portrays families and their affairs; history analyzes the mind of the few who govern, the writer of *romanzi* analyzes the heart of the many who serve.[87]

86. Madame de Staël, *Delphine* (1802), in *Œuvres littéraires,* vol. 2, ed. Lucia Omacini, notes by Simone Balayé (Paris: Champion, 2004), 9.

87. Ugo Foscolo, "Saggio di novelle di Luigi Sanvitale parmigiano" (1803), in *Scritti letterari e politici dal 1796 al 1808,* ed. Giovanni Gambarin, National Edition of the works of Ugo Foscolo, vol. 6 (Florence: Le Monnier, 1972), 263–264.

Between 1550 and 1800, then, a large literary space took form that comprised two different territories: "poetic" narrative and "historic" narrative, *romance* and *novel*. The two were species of the same genus and not separate forms. In the course of the eighteenth century, the tradition of the *novel* gained hegemony and pushed the *romance* to the outskirts of the system, but the system remained cohesive. What held the space of the novel together? Why did it happen that such different forms were viewed as belonging to a single genre?

CHAPTER THREE

The Novel and the Literature of the Ancien Régime

The Dialectic of Continuity and Change

For modern readers, texts that go by the name of novels are linked by their narrative form, a certain length, and the possibility they offer to tell stories about absolutely anything in any way whatsoever. For readers of the Ancien Régime, texts that were called successively *roman, romanzo, novela,* and *novel-and-romance* shared the narrative form, a certain length, and a total or partial rejection of the rules that governed literary writing in Europe between the second half of the sixteenth century and the second half of the eighteenth. If the first meaning of our genre resides in its narrative form, the second lies buried in this conflict. To talk about the novel, we have to first begin by reconstructing the apparatus of laws and habits to which the genre reacted in defining itself as a locus for potentially transgressive writings.

This backdrop, along with the characteristics of premodern and early modern aesthetics, forces us to think about the narrative of this period according to different mental schemas from the ones commonly adopted by modern culture. In the form that the history of literature took as it emerged out of the historicist culture of the nineteenth century, it tended consciously or unconsciously to imagine series of works and cultural periods in terms of a perpetual metamorphosis or a permanent revolution. This paradigm does not work, however, when attempting to interpret the literature of the Ancien Régime, because the disruptive elements are intertwined with an underlying layer of constants. What we see is a double movement. On the one hand, many of the new ways of telling stories that emerged between 1550 and 1800 were transferred from one nation to another and created discontinuities: the chivalric romance was hugely popular in the 1500s, only to decline in the next century; the rediscovery of Hellenistic novels in the mid-sixteenth century influenced the heroic Baroque novel; the short *novella* originating in Italy changed over the course of the 1600s, when the Spanish *novela* and then the French *nouvelle* created what were effectively two new subgenres; religious and secular letters, autobiographies, and the genre of the commentary influenced in various ways the first-person writings that were immensely popular beginning in the second half of the seventeenth century, thanks to the success of *mémoires* and epistolary novels. Through this current of invention, the ways of telling stories were transformed and a new paradigm was born. However, as visible as these changes are, in many ways the works written in this epoch remained bound together by a few common assumptions. The history of the European novel between the second half of the sixteenth century and the second half of the eighteenth can also be read as a closed system that shifted within stable premises: a nonexplicit movement of innovation coexisted alongside an explicit attachment to ancient structures of sense. In this chapter I will talk about the continuities that in many respects made the period between 1550 and 1800 a unified one. In Chapter 4 I will talk about the discontinuities that emerged little by little and that, at the end of a long and complicated process, caused these old structures to collapse.

A Cohesive Epoch

We must begin by acknowledging a distance. A systematic reading of the mass of prefaces and treatises accompanying the narrative fiction of this period makes it clear that between the mid-sixteenth century and the mid-eighteenth the reading and writing of stories involved habits and rules that were very different from the ones that later took root beginning in the second half of the eighteenth century. They took place at a faster or slower rhythm depending on the various national literatures: "most modern readers find it impossible to enjoy the narratives that early modern readers consumed obsessively."[1] Often theorists of the novel do not perceive this rift: those who study the narrative of the Ancien Régime view the distance as a basic premise that hardly calls for reflection, while those who study the genre as a whole tend to overlook the border dividing the epochs. This is because almost all theorists of the novel are trained on the narrative works of the past two centuries. For this reason they tend to read the works of the Ancien Régime in the light of the present, seeking to pinpoint the origin of forms that are recognized as familiar to the literature of the nineteenth, twentieth, and twenty-first centuries. Their attention is thus focused on the modernity of a dozen or so texts (*Gargantua et Pantagruel, Lazarillo, Don Quixote, The Portuguese Letters, The Princesse de Clèves, Gil Blas, Robinson Crusoe, Moll Flanders, The Life of Marianne, Pamela, Clarissa, Tom Jones, Tristram Shandy, The Sorrows of Young Werther, Dangerous Liaisons*, and a few others), neglecting both the undergrowth of works that are today considered minor and the assumptions that guided the writing and reading of narrative fiction in this period. This is why they end up unaware of the fact that the novels written between the mid-sixteenth century and the mid-eighteenth century obey a literary paradigm that differs in many ways from our own—a paradigm we have to reconstruct today as if it were a lost language.

But the theories, expectations, and concepts that informed the way narratives were conceived and judged between the mid-sixteenth and the mid-eighteenth century, in addition to being different from our own, also had a kinship. They maintained an extraordinary continuity for almost three centuries. Such a long period will of course present differences when examined up close. Every literature has its national history, and every subgenre has a different social readership. It would be naive to think that courtly readers or members of Italian academies in 1550 read chivalric poems the same way the Spanish pages described by Cervantes read *Don Quixote* in the early decades of the seventeenth century;[2] or that what the French aristocracy of 1678 sought in *The Princesse de Clèves* were the same things that the middle-class British public looked for in Fielding's works around

---

1. Terence Cave, "Suspense and the Pre-history of the Novel," *Revue de littérature comparée* 70, no. 4 (1996): 515.
2. Cervantes, *Don Quixote de la Mancha*, part 2, chap. 3.

1750. Although the differences are impossible to ignore, it is equally impossible to ignore the fact that the web of concepts, words, expectations, needs, *auctoritates,* and implicit or explicit rules with which narrative works were conceived and judged in Italy in 1550, in Spain in 1600, in France in 1670, in Germany in 1700, and in Great Britain in 1750 has a surprising internal unity to it. It has a tangible continuity with habits of very long duration and a tangible otherness compared to the paradigm that would take hold in the nineteenth and twentieth centuries. I will demonstrate this with an example.

In 1554 Giovan Battista Pigna published his treatise on *romanzi.* He wrote to legitimize the existence of a new narrative form and to explain its rules. What he meant by *romanzo* was the chivalrous tradition that in his judgment culminated in Ariosto's *Orlando Furioso.* He thought according to the schemas of the classicist literary theory that began to spread in Italy in the early 1500s. The canonical texts of ancient poetry had transmitted a set of mutually coherent, eternal precepts (Plato's *Republic,* Horace's *The Art of Poetry,* and especially Aristotle's *Poetics*), thus to discuss poetry meant either showing that a work conformed to these standards or using the *auctoritates* to establish rules for judging works that were unknown to the ancients. Texts that did not fit into the schemas drawn from the classics were considered imperfect. Pigna's reasoning is woven through with Aristotelian and Horatian topoi: the difference between history and poetry; the division between genres and high, middle, and low styles; the distinction between historical plots, which follow the *ordo naturalis,* and poetic plots, which begin in medias res; the idea that poetry should instruct and delight; the conviction that stories have or could have an allegorical meaning and that the hidden meaning explains the moral of the story.[3]

In 1670 Pierre Huet published the first version of his *Lettre sur l'origin des romans.* He begins by proposing a prescriptive definition: "We esteem nothing to be properly Romance but Fictions of Love Adventures, disposed into an Elegant Style in Prose; for the delight and instruction of the Reader."[4] They are called "fictions" to distinguish them from true histories, according to the opposition that Aristotle developed in the tenth chapter of his *Po-*

3. Pigna, *I romanzi,* 95.
4. Huet, *The History of Romances,* 3.

etics. They are written in "an elegant style" because they must follow the rules of poetry, by adopting a certain register and arranging the plot in accordance with the *ordo artificialis.* They must mix delight with instruction, as Horace dictates, transmitting morality under the veil of fiction and providing models for behavior.[5] Like Pigna, Huet also blends historical narrative with normative precepts; like Pigna, Huet also wants to teach us how to write proper novels and how to ennoble the genre by following the rules drawn from the poetics and models of antiquity.[6]

In 1742, in response to Richardson's *Pamela,* Henry Fielding published *Joseph Andrews.* In the preface, he claims to have invented a new genre and comments on his own discovery. Citing Aristotle, he writes that the epic is divided into tragedy and comedy: Homer gave us the models for both, but the exemplary work of the second family, *Margites,* has been lost. The epic can be written in verse or in prose, since meter, as Aristotle says, is not essential to the definition of poetry. A work like Fénelon's *Telemachus,* for example, differs from the *Odyssey* only because it is not in verse. This is precisely the reason that the new genre inaugurated by *Joseph Andrews* can be defined as a comic epic poem in prose, which differs from comedy as the serious epic does from tragedy. To describe his new genre, Fielding continues to use Aristotle's *Poetics* and its taxonomic categories. In reflecting on the difference between comedy and burlesque, calling on the principle that comedy exposes and rectifies foibles and vices, Fielding assumes that the purpose of stories is to serve as moral orthopedics.

I chose Pigna, Huet, and Fielding because they disseminated ideas destined to have significant effects, because they wrote centuries apart, because they lived in different national cultures, and because they addressed themselves to readers of different social extractions. They are not even talking about the same thing: what Pigna calls a *romanzo* is chivalric narrative in verse; Huet argues that proper novels are written in prose; Fielding's idea is a comic epic poem in prose, but what he has in mind is a literary genre that in many ways is opposite to what Huet had in mind. And yet their critical gestures are similar. They inherit the same general intention, which is half descriptive and half normative. They respond to the same need to

5. Ibid., 4–5.
6. Ibid., 144ff. and passim.

legitimize what ancient poetics would view as potentially unconventional narrative forms. They refer to the same *auctoritates,* the same vocabulary, and the same topics: Aristotle and Horace, the difference between history and poetry, the separation of styles, the poetics of *delectare et monere,* and the link between literature and moral precepts. Beneath the differences there can be glimpsed a continuity of medium duration—a shared web of theories, terms, habits, and commonplaces. At the end of the eighteenth century, avant-garde theoretical writings, those that anticipated ideas on narrative that would predominate only a short time later, moved in a completely different mental space. When we read Madame de Staël's *Essai sur les fictions* (1795) or Friedrich Schlegel's *Dialogue on Poetry* (1800), for example, no significant traces remain of the structures of sense that for Pigna, Huet, and Fielding formed the necessary background for any literary discourse. It is as if a completely new theoretical era had been ushered in.

We can make out the defining traits of the literary paradigms of long duration that confronted the novel during its formation by examining the fierce criticisms the genre received in institutional literary circles at least until the beginning of the nineteenth century, using them as a term of contrast. The hostility that accompanied the new genre for nearly three centuries is one of the most significant and symptomatic traits of its early modern history. Observed in retrospect, this atmosphere of mistrust serves as a sort of photographic negative: it shows the reversed image of the written and unwritten rules that the novel ran up against. Between the middle of the sixteenth century and the middle of the eighteenth, unconventional narrative texts were targeted by two relentless criticisms: they were accused of violating the laws of poetry and spreading immorality—of destroying good taste and corrupting morals.[7] By making explicit what remains implicit in these attacks, we discover the two main structures of sense with which our genre collided: *classicism* and *aesthetic Platonism* in its Christian version.

Classicism and the Separation of Styles

Premodern and early modern classicism was a relatively cohesive system of rules, models, habits, and topoi.[8] It took form with Italian humanism

---

7. On this dual accusation, see May, *Le Dilemme du roman au XVIIIᵉ siècle,* 4ff.

8. For more on the dialectic between unity and multiplicity in European classicism of the Ancien Régime, see various authors, *Un classicisme ou des classicismes?,* ed. Georges Fores-

and between the 1500s and the 1700s gradually spread in phases to France, Spain, Great Britain, and the German-speaking countries. The two and a half centuries during which this poetic established its hegemony over European literature were concurrent with the rise of the novel. Classicism became a unified force in the middle of the sixteenth century, when the normative reading of ancient aesthetics generated an apparatus of rules and models that was transmitted to the European literatures. One of the most conspicuous effects of this process was the dissemination of a critical lexicon. Pigna, Huet, and Fielding spoke three regional variations of the same language in different phases of its development. When the author of *Joseph Andrews* reflected on the difference between serious and comic epic poems, he continued to use a vocabulary that had emerged in the 1530s from the fusion of Aristotelian and Horatian poetics.[9]

It was partly thanks to classicism that the novel became a unified genre. What was shared by the works that contributed to shaping the new literary space was actually an absence: they lacked precedents in ancient literature and aesthetics because they could not be easily identified with the two forms of narrative known to classicism, the epic poem and historiography written according to the rules that also formed the basis for the construction of the classicist theory. The swarm of unconventional narrative texts thus made up an empty class. It was for this reason, too, that a common element became discernible in such diverse works, making it possible to group the unconventional writings under the same name.

But this distance from Greek and Latin models was not the only point of friction. Even more complicated and traumatic was the relationship that the new family of works entertained with the cornerstone of ancient poetics: the law of the separation of styles. One of the most important critical

---

tier and Jean-Pierre Néraudau (Pau: Publications de l'université de Pau, 1995), and Matteo Residori, "Classicismi e invenzioni," in *Letteratura europea*, ed. Piero Boitani and Massimo Fusillo (Turin: UTET, 2014).

9. Herrick, *The Fusion of Horatian and Aristotelian Literary Criticism, 1531–1555*. See also Bernard Weinberg, *A History of Literary Criticism in the Italian Renaissance*, 111ff.; Baxter Hathaway, *The Age of Criticism: The Late Renaissance in Italy* (Ithaca, NY: Cornell University Press, 1962); Antonio García Berrio, *Formación de la teoría literaria moderna: La tópica horaciana en Europa* (Madrid: Cupsa Editorial, 1977), 39ff.; Anne Duprat, "Morale et fiction en poétique: la combinaison des vraisemblances chez J. Chapelain," in "Morale et fiction aux XVIIᵉ et XVIIIᵉ siècles," special issue, *Revue des sciences humaines* 254, no. 2 (1999): 45–61; Brigitte Kappl, *Die Poetik des Aristoteles in der Dichtungstheorie des Cinquecento* (Berlin: De Gruyter, 2006), 15–29.

works of the twentieth century, *Mimesis* by Erich Auerbach, traces out a philosophy of Western literary history by following the transformations of this law. In Auerbach's view, the representation of reality in Greek and Latin literature is governed by a principle that acts as a habit or codified rule from one time to the next. We already find it in the *Iliad* and the *Odyssey*. The Homeric singers distinguished the narratable from the unnarratable in a hierarchical and classicist way: significant deeds are performed for the most part among the ruling and warrior class, while the other parts of society have a secondary, servile function.[10] During the fourth century BCE, this tendency gave rise to a sort of law. The first illustrious document to proclaim the separation of styles as a principle that was simultaneously descriptive and normative is the second chapter of Aristotle's *Poetics:*

> The things that representative artists represent are the actions of people, and if people are represented they are necessarily either superior [*spoudaious*] or inferior [*phaulous*], better or worse, than we are. (Differences in character you see derive from these categories, since it is by virtue [*arete*] or vice [*kakia*] that people are ethically distinct from each other.) So too with painters: Polygnotus portrayed better people, Pauson worse people, and Dionysius people just like us.[11]

The people that Aristotle called "better than we are," meaning the demigods or the aristocratic heroes of *epos* and tragedy, perform extraordinary feats or encounter exceptional misadventures that the poets represent in a serious, lofty style befitting the dignity of the deeds being represented. The people who are "worse than we are," meaning slaves or characters in comedies, perform ridiculous or trivial actions that the poets represent in a style suited to the subject matter. In Greek culture the hierarchy between people is sanctioned by criteria that are both social and moral: someone better than us possesses *arete* and is *spoudaios*, meaning "worthwhile," "serious," but also "noble"; someone worse than us is marked by a defect (*kakia*) or by a lack (*hamartema*) and is *phaulos,* meaning "trivial," "lightweight," or even "ignoble." Classical rhetoric gave a systematic order to Aristotle's cat-

10. Erich Auerbach, *Mimesis* (1946); English translation *Mimesis,* trans. Willard R. Trask (Princeton, NJ: Princeton University Press, 2003), 21.
11. Aristotle, *Poetics,* 2.1448a.1–5.

egories, by formulating a schema that grouped oratorical speeches and texts into three *genera elocutionis*—lowly or humble, medium or intermediate, and sublime—and linked them to the type of subject matter, according to a principle first formulated by Theophrastus. This idea, that each type of content has a natural form, is what inspired ancient rhetoric to strictly associate the qualities of the characters with the qualities of the story, the style, and the interest demanded of the reader. It did this by establishing a rule that mirrored the rigid social hierarchy, with only one possible exception, that of parody: a violation that overturned the rule without negating its value. The medieval *rota Vergilii* gives us a perfect illustration of these correspondences from a later period. Virgil's wheel condenses the genera of classical rhetoric into a unified schema, linking together the social class of the hero, the type of action represented, and the type of *ornatus*. This strict ordering principle allowed for styles to be alternated within the same speech, but not for them to be completely mixed up.[12]

While there may have been three genres of rhetoric, the ancient separation of styles (*Stiltrennung*) proved to be asymmetric and binary, because the boundaries between the humble and the intermediate were never entirely certain. Indeed, the low style could include the comic, the satiric, the playfully erotic, and the obscene, but also daily life, factual information, sketches, and trivia. The mime, the iambic, and the satire all belonged to the lowly genre as well, but so did the sections in a judicial oration that referred to private or money matters.[13] There is no doubt that Greek and Latin cultures reserved much less attention to people "like us" than what modern literature devotes to them, just as there is no doubt that a large portion of reality that today we judge worthy of serious, tragic, or problematic mimesis was confined to the domain of the comic or the intermediate style:

---

12. See Erich Auerbach, *Literatursprache und Publikum in der lateinischen Spätantike und im Mittelalter* (1958); English translation *Literary Language and Its Public in Late Latin Antiquity and in the Middle Ages*, trans. Ralph Manheim (Princeton, NJ: Princeton University Press, 1993), 43. The alternation of styles is widely used, for example, in the ancient novel, where it often happens that the story changes style as it adapts to the twists and turns of the plot. See Massimo Fusillo, *Il romanzo greco* (Venice: Marsilio, 1989), 20ff.

13. Auerbach, *Literary Language*, 37.

[For the rule of segregation of styles] everything commonly realistic (*alles gemein Realistische*), everything pertaining to everyday life must not be treated on any level except the comic, which admits no problematic probing (*ohne problematische Vertiefung*) . . . We are forced to conclude that there could be no serious literary treatment of everyday occupations and social classes—merchants, artisans, peasants, slaves—of everyday scenes and places—home, shop, field, store—of everyday customs and institutions—marriage, children, work, earning a living.[14]

According to the principles of the *Stiltrennung*, practices associated with private life, with the reproduction and production of life, with work, family, or domestic happiness, are only worthy to be treated with slapstick, satire, or, at most, in an intermediate style, exactly as they are handled in bucolic-pastoral literature or in the New Comedy. However, they may not be the theme of a completely serious work. Reading the *Poetics* in the light of the *Nicomachean Ethics*, we understand that people "like us" are those who live in the realm of common life, who perform activities that produce the well-being required to accede to the higher realms of public action and *theoresis*—but which grant no eminent virtue in themselves.

The *Stiltrennung* faded away with the end of paganism, the material crisis of the ancient culture, and the rise of a Christian literature inspired by the mix of styles that we find in the Bible, especially in the New Testament. These works ignored the ancient stylistic divisions and told about private life in a serious way. Creating humankind in his own image and likeness, incarnating himself in a mortal body to redeem humanity, surrounding himself with fishermen and carpenters, lepers and prostitutes, the Christian God gave a meaning to every aspect of reality inhabited by his creatures. Common places and objects, absolutely private aspects of the inner life, the imperfection of bodies, and all the aspects of the world that for classical art held no interest, or were worthy at most of comic interest, were redeemed by this new theological horizon, in which each individual had a universal significance and the divine manifested itself in everyday circumstances.[15]

14. Auerbach, *Mimesis*, 31.

15. Erich Auerbach, *Dante als Dichter der irdischen Welt* (1929); English translation *Dante: Poet of the Secular World*, trans. Ralph Manheim (Chicago: University of Chicago Press, 1961); Auerbach, *Mimesis*, chaps. 2, 3 and passim.

A new poetics of distinction arose in French courts of the twelfth century and spread through the success of chivalric narrative and the courtly form of life.[16] Although we cannot speak of a separation of styles in the strict sense, and although the influence of Greek and Roman models remained marginal, the overall effect of the medieval romances was similar to that created by the *Stiltrennung* of antiquity: an aristocratic class of representative characters had the right to serious mimesis, while the life of people like us remained shut off in a marginal background. Over time, the boundaries of what was dignified and undignified were redrawn: when the chivalric ideal was welcomed by citizen classes of bourgeois origin, nobility became widely interpreted as a quality of the soul and not of the blood. However, the idea that "nobility, greatness, and intrinsic values have nothing in common with everyday reality" remained unchanged.[17] The ancient type of separation of styles was revived with the fusion of Aristotelian and Horatian criticism in the mid-sixteenth century and became the basic premise of premodern and early modern European classicism until the second half of the eighteenth century. Although it was interpreted more or less rigidly depending on national cultures and literary fashions, in no other period of European history was the *Stiltrennung* applied with such severity. And if it is true that the classicist culture was balanced by authors and tendencies that maintained a bond with the Christian tradition of creaturely realism,[18] it is also true that the separation of styles permeated this period like a sort of transcendental structure, generating unbending, pervasive rules.

The *Stiltrennung* cast a hierarchical vision of society onto literature. To arrive at what remains implicit in Auerbach's theory, we can profitably juxtapose *Mimesis* to another philosophy of history, the one that we find presented in the works of Georges Dumézil. According to Dumézil, Indo-European societies preserve the trace of an original tripartite social division in their mythologies and value spheres: between a class that administers the religion, a class that holds sovereignty and military force, and a class that ensures the production and reproduction of life through labor, fertility,

16. Auerbach, *Mimesis*, chap. 6.
17. Ibid., 139.
18. Ibid., chaps. 11–12.

and family.[19] At the beginning of the eleventh century, Adalberon of Laon
named these groups *oratores, bellatores,* and *laboratores,* encapsulating the
schema in a memorable formula and passing it down to posterity. Dumézil's
theory has been the object of a debate that I lack the competence to weigh
in on; however, if we leave the field of philology and use a theory of this
sort for historical-philosophical purposes, these ideas shed light on the state
of affairs for which the *Stiltrennung* was the literary representation. The
tripartite separation of styles does not correspond at all to the threefold
division in the social realms: the boundaries are different, but the two systems highlight the same constant that runs deeply throughout European
history, namely, the subordinate role that the activities of *laboratores* played
for thousands of years in society and in the political unconscious of the
West. The *Stiltrennung* reflects an objective hierarchy: in ancient culture
just as in medieval culture, anything pertaining to the realm of work and
family did not deserve a serious, tragic, or problematic treatment. The extraordinary political force of Christianity also arose out of its ability to
overturn this scale of values. But leaving behind the pagan culture did not
suffice to put an end to the separation of styles and to the lower status of
laboratores. There were few periods of European history when Dumézil's
tripartite division of functions had such a presence and was so visible as
during the Ancien Régime. Similarly, in no other literary epoch was the
Stiltrennung so unyielding as during the centuries of premodern and early
modern classicism, when it acted as a sort of a priori crystallized in collective habits, influencing works in three ways.

1. The separation of styles imposed a hierarchy of *subject matters, styles,
and genres.* The stories of heroes, of great public figures, of mythological or legendary characters counted more than what happened to
common people; tragedy was more important than comedy; serious epic
was more important than comic epic. The hierarchy could be inverted
only if private stories were introduced into a frame that gave them a
hidden moral sense: for example, when they were used as *exempla* of
moral or theological truths. We find the same principle for the academic

19. An overview of this theory, developed over the course of multiple works and multiple
decades, can be found in Georges Dumézil, *Mythe et épopée I. L'idéologie des trois fonctions
dans les épopées des peuples indo-européens* (1968) (Paris: Gallimard, 1986).

painting of the early modern age and in its scale of genres. This placed public and distinguished entities at the top (scenes from sacred and profane history), assigned a lower rank to family and private subjects (portraits and genre scenes), and extended even less dignity to prehuman subjects (landscapes and still lifes). In 1679 Jean de Préchac published an *histoire galante et véritable,* entitled *L'Illustre Parisienne,* which begins like this:

> Everybody who has tried their hand at writing *romans* or *petites histori-ettes* has been particularly attached to giving their Heroes and Heroines a high birth; because it is certain that there is far more interest in the fate of a Prince than in that of an ordinary person.[20]

Préchac takes it for granted that the importance of a story is proportional to the characters' rank: the fate of a prince or a hero counts for more than the fate of an ordinary person. This idea was a basic assumption of European literature at least until the second half of the eighteenth century: even those who opposed it still moved in its shadow.

Few works more irritated classicist taste during the eighteenth century than Richardson's novels. They could not be dismissed as humorous, coarse, and vulgar stories, but at the same time they conflicted with dominant literary customs. In the prefatory writings to the second edition of *Pamela,* which came out in February 1741, the author shows that he is aware of the effect that his work has provoked. He knows that he is writing counter to the tastes of the literary elite, and to defend himself, he presents an epistolary dialogue between an anonymous "gentleman" and an anonymous admirer of *Pamela,* later revealed as the playwright Aaron Hill. Although the playwright expresses ideas that in certain respects are revolutionary, it is significant that he always takes for granted the existence of a strict hierarchy of subject matters:

> Who could have dreamt, he should find, under the modest Disguise of a *Novel,* all the *Soul* of Religion, Good-breeding, Discretion, Good-nature, Wit, Fancy, Fine Thought, and Morality?[21]

20. Préchac, *L'Illustre Parisienne,* 1.
21. Samuel Richardson, "Introduction to Pamela, Second Edition," in *The Pamela Controversy: Criticism and Adaptations of Samuel Richardson's "Pamela,"* vol. 1, ed. Thomas Keymer and Peter Sabor (London: Pickering and Chatto, 2001), 18.

[The author of *Pamela*] *moves* us, every where, with the Force of a TRAGEDY.[22]

These sorts of remarks run counter to an opposing, prevailing opinion that viewed the novel as a minor genre. According to this view, the story of a maid should be a comic subject, while at the top of the literary scale there should stand *epos* and tragedy, the genre to which Hill compares *Pamela*. In an even more eloquent passage, repeating a comment made by the gentleman who felt that some of the scenes in *Pamela* were too low, the playwright voices an idea that was in many respects revolutionary:

> I wonder indeed, what it is, that the Gentlemen, who talk of Low Scenes, wou'd desire should be understood by the Epithet? Nothing, properly speaking, is *low*, that suits well with the Place it is rais'd to.—The Passions of Nature are the same, in the *Lord*, and his *Coach-man*.[23]

This ethically and aesthetically provocative idea ("the passions of nature are the same in the *Lord* and his *Coach-man*") appears in the midst of a sentence that takes for granted that people have a natural place assigned by God. In the end, they will be judged for what they did on the basis of their respective ranks, as Pamela notes when commenting on Lady Davers's letter:

> This is a sad letter, my dear father and mother; and one may see how poor people are despised by the proud and rich! and yet we were all on a foot originally: . . . Surely these proud people never think what a short stage life is; and that, with all their vanity, a time is coming, when they shall be obliged to submit to be on a level with us: And true said the philosopher, when he looked upon the skull of a king, and that of a poor man, that he saw no difference between them. Besides, do they not know, that the richest of princes, and the poorest of beggars, are to have one great and tremendous Judge, at the last day; who will not distinguish between them according to their circumstances in life?—But, on the contrary, may make their condemnations the greater, as their neglected opportunities were the greater?[24]

---

22. Ibid., 19.
23. Ibid., 25.
24. Samuel Richardson, *Pamela: or, Virtue Rewarded*, edited with explanatory notes by Thomas Keymer and Alice Wakely (Oxford: Oxford University Press, 2001), part 2, p. 258.

For Hill, as for Richardson, it is still obvious that society is divided into ranks, and that each rank has a different weight: the a prioris of this discourse are still those of the Ancien Régime.

2. Implicit in this hierarchy is the conviction that the type of content, the type of style, the way of portraying the characters, the plot construction, and the value of the work must all correspond. In other words, the form does not express a personal way of seeing things, as the Romantic and modern conception of style would have it. Instead, it obeys public customs and ceremonial rules. At the core of the system lies the concept of *decorum,* the Ciceronian translation of *to prepon,* the term that Aristotle used to indicate the style appropriate to each character according to its social class, temperament, age, and gender.[25] In a long passage from *The Art of Poetry,* Horace strengthens this idea and formulates the concept of *convenientia;* in modern European languages *decorum* becomes *bienséance, decency,* and *decoro.* For the Italian theorists of the sixteenth century who picked up on this passage and commented on it, Horace had sought to establish a link among the status of the characters, the quality of their words, the quality of their actions, and the style of the composition. Noble heroes must think, act, and speak in accordance with their rank: a work that aspires to a high literary dignity cannot contain passages that are unsuitable for high genres. The same thing applies to the other classes of characters and texts.

Two of the major debates raised by narrative works in the early modern age took place in France after the appearance of *The Princesse de Clèves* and in Great Britain and France after the appearance of *Pamela.* In both, the corollaries of *Stiltrennung* were invoked incessantly. According to many commentators, the behavior of Madame de Clèves, especially in the episode when she confesses to her husband, is contrary to *bienséances;* in other words, to the manners that a princess of her rank should never abandon.[26] The letter prefacing the second edition of *Pamela* reports some of the criticisms that the novel had received and to which Richardson intended

25. Aristotle, *Rhetoric* 3.7.1–2; *Poetics,* 15.1454a.22–24. On *decorum* as a translation for *to propon,* see Cicero, *Orator* 21. In *The Art of Poetry* Horace talks about *convenientia* (lines 89–127). In literary sixteenth-century theory, *decorum* and *convenientia* overlapped: see Herrick, *The Fusion of Horatian and Aristotelian Literary Criticism,* chap. 5.

26. See Genette, "Vraisemblance et motivation," 71–99.

to respond. One of the most interesting regards the form. The objection is made that the style of Pamela's letters should have become higher as soon as the intentions of Mr. B became honorable, and especially after the marriage, because at that point the heroine "should be equal to the Rank she is rais'd to."[27] Many of the reactions to *Pamela* are marked by the *Stiltrennung*: it is difficult to accept a maid becoming a heroine; it is difficult to accept characters of aristocratic origin who adopt a vulgar *habitus*. These criticisms were especially frequent in France, because the French literary system adopted a particularly severe interpretation of the separation of styles: the reader was expressly invited to take an interest in characters of humble condition "with the promise that, in the end, the *paysan* would be *parvenu*, that he would rise to a condition capable of touching people of quality."[28]

3. The noble genres do not tell any kind of story whatsoever. Instead, they draw from a repertoire of events endowed with a meaning and a public value, backed by the great collective narratives that flowed through premodern and early modern European culture: mythology, ancient literature, sacred history, and epic communal stories. These are immediately readable events; they can be told again; they mean something to everyone; they are archetypes to which the narrative can always return.[29] Conversely, stories that do not belong to this repertoire must find a form of legitimization if they seek access to the serious style. From this perspective, the preface to *Robinson Crusoe* and the dialogue that occupies the second preface to *Julie, or The New Heloise* express a recurring problem in an era still marked by the separation of styles:

> If ever the Story of any private Man's Adventures in the World were worth making Publick, and were acceptable when Publish'd . . .[30]

---

27. Richardson, "Introduction to Pamela, Second Edition," 23.

28. May, *Le Dilemme du roman au XVIIIᵉ siècle* , 163ff.

29. See Jean Starobinski, "Fable et mythologie aux XVIIᵉ et XVIIIᵉ siècles dans la littérature et la réflexion théorique" (1981); English translation "Fable and Mythology from the 17th to 18th Centuries," in *Blessings in Disguise; or, The Morality of Evil*, trans. Arthur Goldhammer (Cambridge, UK: Polity Press; Cambridge, MA: Harvard University Press, 1993), 169–193.

30. Daniel Defoe, *Robinson Crusoe* (1719), ed. Michael Shinagel (New York: Norton, 1994), "The Preface," 3.

Events so natural, so simple that they are too much so; nothing unexpected; no dramatic surprises. Everything is foreseen well in advance; everything comes to pass as foreseen. Is it worth recording what anyone can see every day in his own home or in his neighbor's?[31]

Up until the second half of the eighteenth century, it was not obvious that stories about private, common individuals were worthy of public attention and problematic interest. Narrative democracy was achieved only during the past two centuries.

Aesthetic Platonism

While the separation of styles massively influenced literary writing between 1550 and 1800, the most formidable apparatus of criticism facing the texts that converged into the novel was moralistic and theoretical. Novelists were accused of spreading illicit behaviors, of neglecting important things to devote themselves to vain chimeras, of mixing truth with falsehood. The allegations appeared almost identical in texts belonging to different national cultures, and they emerged in substantially the same form between the sixteenth and eighteenth centuries. They were so widespread that it is difficult to find prefaces or treatises in which they do not appear, in more or less direct form, only to be denied or confirmed.[32] I cite some examples from different periods and national cultures.

In Italian debates on the narrative poem that developed in the middle of the sixteenth century, the heroes of *romanzi* were berated for roaming in search of love or adventure—a true hero should appear exemplary in all his behavior. Heroes should also pursue collective moral aims, like the characters in the ancient epics or in the modern-type Christian heroic poem.[33] Even the *romanzo* plot itself, punctuated by the centrifugal motion

31. Jean-Jacques Rousseau, *Julie ou la Nouvelle Héloïse* (1761); English translation *Julie, or The New Heloise*, trans. and annotated by Philip Stewart and Jean Vaché (Hanover, NH: University Press of New England, 1997), 8.

32. See Walter Siti, "Il romanzo sotto accusa" (2001); English translation *The Novel on Trial*, in *The Novel*, vol. 1, ed. Franco Moretti (Princeton, NJ: Princeton University Press, 2006), 94ff.

33. See Sergio Zatti, *L'ombra del Tasso. Epica e romanzo nel Cinquecento* (Milan: Bruno Mondadori, 1996), 14ff.; Stefano Jossa, *Rappresentazione e scrittura. La crisi della forme*

of adventures, was cause for suspicion because the narrative dispersion corresponded to the indulging in *regio dissimilitudinis* condemned by Saint Paul and Augustine.

The misgivings grew, of course, when the reality in which the characters wandered was steeped in fantastic elements, depicting a non-Christian, supernatural world suspended between vanity and idolatry. In addition, many *romanzi* talked about love—this choice of topic alone was enough to make the genre suspect in every European country, Catholic or Protestant, up to the second half of the eighteenth century. Teresa of Avila, in *The Book of My Life* (1562–1565), describes how her morals were damaged in her youth by reading books of chivalry.[34] Malón de Chaide begins *La conversión de la Magdalena* (1588) with a prologue in which he denounces the dangers of romances.[35] Georg Philipp Harsdörffer, in *Frauen-Zimmer Gespräch-Spiel* (1641), presents a sort of legal oration against tales of love (*Lustgedicht*), with an accusation and a response to the accusation. In 1667 Pierre Nicole ignited a polemic with Racine by rewriting what we read in the second, third, and tenth book of the *Republic,* using a lexicon that recalls Saint Paul, Augustine, Tertullian, and other Church Fathers.[36] In 1670, Huet devoted the last part of his treatise to the relationship between novels and morality.[37] In 1698 the Swiss Protestant pastor Gotthard Heidegger published a treatise on narrative fiction entitled *Mythoscopia romantica,* in which he methodically attacks the genre by calling on the *auctoritates* from whom the condemnation of the novel originally descended: Saint Paul, the Church Fathers, Seneca, some passages from the Scriptures and,

---

poetiche rinascimentali (1540–60) (Naples: Vivarium, 1996), 139ff.; by the same author, *La fondazione di un genere. Il poema eroico fra Ariosto e Tasso* (Florence: Carocci, 2002), 17, 115, and passim.

34. Teresa of Avila, *Libro de la vida* (1562–1565); English translation *The Book of My Life,* trans. Mirabai Starr (Boston: Shambhala Publications, 2007), chap. 2, 20.

35. Pedro Malón de Chaide, *La conversión de la Magdalena* (1588), ed. Félix García (Madrid: Espasa-Calpe, 1959), 24–25.

36. Pierre Nicole, *Traité de la comédie et autres pièces d'un procès du théâtre* (1667), ed. Laurent Thirouin (Paris: Champion, 1998), chap. 20 and following. The *Traité* was published for the first time in 1667; in 1675 Nicole included it, with numerous variations, in his *Essais de morale.*

37. "I know what they are accused for: They exhaust our Devotion, and inspire us with Irregular Passions, and corrupt our Manners." Huet, *The History of Romances,* 142–143.

ultimately, Plato.[38] In the debate on *novels* and *romances* that took place in eighteenth-century England, the idea that these genres can easily slide into immorality is a constant, so much so that it is easier to cite the texts where this commonplace does not appear. Even a relatively late, and in many respects new, theoretical work like *The Progress of Romance* by Clara Reeve ends with a long disquisition on the dangers of narrative fiction.[39]

Along with purely moral criticisms, others appeared that combined ethical and theoretical components. Because they told invented stories, novels exposed themselves to accusations of falsehood and futility. The interweaving of documentary truth with imagination that certain fictional forms presupposes, not to mention the very existence of a literature of invention, was long perceived as a problem during the early modern period, when the Reformation and the Council of Trent rekindled the ancient Platonic-Christian mistrust of poetry and fiction.[40] The translator's proem with which Amyot begins his version of Heliodorus, for example, starts by recalling Plato's condemnation of the lies of the poets.[41] In the second half of the seventeenth century, this religiously inspired mistrust joined forces with the suspicion that the new culture of pre-Enlightenment rationalism nurtured for the fictions of literature.[42] The issue of the credibility of *romances* and *novels* became more acute from the seventeenth century onward. During the same period, more and more witness accounts or instances of documentary evidence were exhibited in support of the claim that a novel

38. Gotthard Heidegger, *Mythoscopia romantica: Oder Discours von den so benanten Romans* (Zürich: David Gessner, 1698), chaps. 12, 36, 51, and passim.

39. Reeve, *The Progress of Romance*, vol. 2, "Evening 12," 77ff.

40. Adriano Prosperi, "Censurare le favole. Il protoromanzo e l'Europa cattolica," in *Il romanzo*, ed. Franco Moretti, vol. 1 (Turin: Einaudi, 2001), 71–106.

41. "As a great Philosopher [Plato] wisely warns wet-nurses not to indiscriminately tell their children all sorts of fairy tales for fear that their souls might become inebriated with madness from the outset, and that they might draw some vicious impression from them, so it seems to me that one might with good reason advise those who have reached the age of reason not to amuse themselves by reading without judgment all sorts of books, for fear that their minds might become accustomed little by little to loving lies and to feeding on vanities, in addition to the fact that it is a poor use of their time." Amyot, "Le Proësme du translateur," no page numbers.

42. See Francesco Orlando, *Illuminismo e retorica freudiana* (Turin: Einaudi, 1982).

told a true history.[43] In England, the phobia for poetic falsehood began to spread especially in Bunyan's time.[44] A few years later, in France, someone found it intolerable that invention and reality were intertwined as they were implicitly in a genre like the *nouvelle,* which sets private individuals steeped in fiction against a real historical background.[45] Gotthard Heidegger begins his *Mythoscopia romantica* by citing a passage from François Charpentier in which an attack is made on all romances and works that tell "masked lies."[46] This is the same accusation that Charles Gildon leveled against Defoe's *Robinson Crusoe* roughly twenty years later.[47] Vexation at the lies and *vanitas* of *novels* and *romances* frequently makes its appearance in eighteenth-century England. In 1751, three years after the publication of *Clarissa* and *Tom Jones,* Francis Coventry felt the need to explain why wise men, metaphysicians, men of science and learning, and politicians involved in the affairs of state should consider that the reading of novels is worthy of a serious man.[48] In 1767 a certain T. Row (a pseudonym for Samuel Pegge the elder) wrote to the *Gentleman's Magazine,* concerned because the young people of both sexes were wasting their time on *romances,* dissipating themselves in meaningless daydreams. He proposed obligating young people to engage in more useful readings, such as general history, English history, and natural history.[49]

The immediate cause of these accusations was the suspicious atmosphere toward the arts and anything fictional that the Reformation, the Counter-Reformation, and the pre-Enlightenment had introduced into European culture; but the deeper source lay much further back. Just as pre-

43. Arthur J. Tieje, "A Peculiar Phase of the Theory of Realism in Pre-Richardsonian Prose-Fiction," *Publications of the Modern Language Association of America* 28 (1913): 213–252.

44. Joseph Bunn Heidler, *The History, from 1700–1800, of English Criticism to Prose Fiction* (Urbana: University of Illinois, 1928); Beasley, *Novels of the 1740s,* 5ff.

45. Deloffre, *La Nouvelle en France à l'âge classique,* 57ff.

46. Heidegger, *Mythoscopia romantica,* chap. 62.

47. Charles Gildon, "From *An Epistle to Daniel Defoe,*" (1719) in Williams, *Novel and Romance,* 57–63.

48. Francis Coventry, "Dedication to *The History of Pompey the Little,*" in Williams, *Novel and Romance,* 176–179.

49. T. Row, "Evil Tendency of Reading Romances," *Gentleman's Magazine* 37 (December 1767); reprinted in Williams, *Novel and Romance,* 272–273.

modern and early modern classicism rested on the prior assumptions of the ancient *Stiltrennung,* similarly the moralistic and theoretical criticisms that novels received in these centuries revived a structure of sense of very long duration, a presupposition that for thousands of years had marked the reception of literature and mimesis in the West. What was this?

One of the most famous ideas that Hegel developed in his *Aesthetics* regards the *Vergangenheitscharakter,* the "past character" of art:

> Thought and reflection have spread their wings above fine art.... However all this may be, it is certainly the case that art no longer affords that satisfaction of spiritual needs which earlier ages and nations sought in it, and found in it alone.... The development of reflection in our life today has made it a need of ours, in relation both to our will and judgment, to cling to general considerations and to regulate the particular by them, with the result that universal forms, laws, duties, rights, maxims, prevail as determining reasons and are the chief regulator. In all these respects art, considered in its highest vocation, is and remains for us a thing of the past.[50]

According to Hegel, the spiritual needs of contemporary individuals are not entirely gratified by narratives, images, or music. When they want to know truth or form an idea of the totality, modern individuals do not rely on stories, sounds, or painting but rather enter the realm of the concept: they think. For the enlightened consciousness, the arts harbor a regressive, irrational, infantile, and magical element. Hegelian philosophy of history melded this transition with the advent of the Christian conception of truth as a supersensible, invisible entity. In point of fact, the first text of European culture that attached a "past character" to the mimetically transmitted image of the world preceded Christianity. It was Plato's *Republic* that initiated a way of conceiving, judging, disciplining, and underestimating the arts that would continue to produce effects until the second half of the eighteenth century. This is what we might call *aesthetic Platonism,* to use an expression coined by Marc Fumaroli.[51]

---

50. Hegel, *Aesthetics,* vol. 1, pp. 10–11.

51. See Marc Fumaroli, "La Querelle de la moralité du théâtre au XVIIᵉ siècle," *Bulletin de la société française de philosophie* 84, no. 3 (1990): 66; also by Fumaroli, "*Sacerdos sive rhetor, orator sive histrio:* rhétorique, théologie, et 'moralité du théâtre' en France de Corneille à Molière," in *Héros et orateurs: rhétorique et dramaturgie cornéliennes* (Geneva: Droz, 1990).

This attitude toward mimesis combines three forms of control.[52] The most radical is censorship: Socrates's character wants to expel most of the poets from the city, keeping only those who tell stories to the young that "bring the fairest lessons of virtue to their ears,"[53] "hymns to the gods and the praises of good men."[54] The poets who are allowed to remain behind are then subjected to another form of discipline, based on a normative aesthetic of an allegorical and moralistic type:

> "But if again someone should ask us to be specific and say what these compositions may be and what are the tales, what could we name?" And I replied, "Adeimantus, we are not poets, you and I at present, but founders of a state. And to founders it pertains to know the patterns (*typoi*) on which poets must compose their fables and from which their poems must not be allowed to deviate."[55]

The *Republic* fences off the figurative arts, confining them inside a peripheral cultural space. After censorship, what remains is divided into the opposite and complementary domains of amusement and instruction.[56] The first is a smaller territory that is separated from truth; the second partakes in truth only to the extent that it conveys to those who cannot access philosophy the *typoi* that the philosopher-founders of the ideal city grasp in pure form. In other words, as Panofsky writes: "For since Plato applied to the products of sculpture and painting the concept— utterly foreign to their nature—of cognitive truth (i.e., correspondence to the Ideas) as a measure of value, his philosophic system could have no

---

52. The concept of control (of the imaginary, mimesis, and narrative) was invented by Luiz Costa Lima. See especially his *O controle do imaginário* (1984; English translation *Control of the Imaginary: Reason and Imagination in Modern Times*, trans. Ronald W. Sousa [Minneapolis: University of Minnesota Press, 1988]), *Sociedade e Discurso Ficcional* (1986), and *O fingidor e o censor* (1988), now collected in *Trilogia do controle* (Rio de Janeiro: Topbooks, 2007); as well as the book Costa Lima wrote on the origin of the novel: *O controle do imaginário e a afirmaçao do romance* (São Paulo: Companhia das Letras, 2009). The remarks that follow take up the notion of control but develop it in a different direction.

53. Plato, *Republic* 2.378e.

54. Plato, *Republic* 10.607a.

55. Plato, *Republic* 2.378e–2.379a.

56. Plato, *Statesman* 288c.

room for an aesthetics of representational art as an intellectual realm *sui generis.*"[57]

The measures announced by Socrates's character to control the poets would prove to be more than an idle threat. Already in evidence before Plato's time, the dialectic set out in the *Republic* would become a topos of ancient poetry, medieval literary theory, and the classicist poetics that emerged during the humanist era and the Renaissance. In the first century BCE, Horace ensured its longevity by his memorable mottos: "Aut prodesse volunt aut delectare poëtae" (Poets aim either to benefit, or to amuse); "Omne tulit punctum, qui miscuit utile dulci | lectorem delectando pariterque monendo" (He has won every vote who has blended profit and pleasure, at once delighting and instructing the reader).[58] From one perspective, the literary field remained bound to instruction: "All Antiquity sees the poet as sage, teacher, educator,"[59] as a repository of moral, historical, and geographical knowledge, defender of the collective memory, propagator of *sententiae* and *exempla,* creator of allegorical tales, master of eloquence—just as when Homer was the cornerstone of public education in Greece. Yet, despite the survival of these topoi, the truths that the poets presented no longer had the same value of those that archaic Greek culture used to discover in the works of Homer. To fully understand this difference we must start from our time, adopt a form of retrospective estrangement, and allow the epochs to collide.

In the mid-1700s a discipline formed that reflected on the logic and content of truth in the arts: aesthetics. If the development of new, specialized fields is a sign of a physiological tendency of modern culture, the advent of this discursive region reflected a profound transformation in the basic frameworks of our culture. The main task that aesthetics has taken on during the two and a half centuries of its history is the production of arguments justifying the value of the arts in the face of other forms of knowledge. The most popular among these legitimizing discourses says that the arts, through their own languages, create an interpretation of reality that is different,

57. Erwin Panofsky, *Idea* (1924); English translation *Idea: A Concept in Art Theory,* trans. Joseph J. S. Peake (New York: Harper and Row, 1968), 4.

58. Horace, *Epistles* 2, lines 333, 343–344; English translation *Satires, Epistles, Ars Poetica,* trans. H. Rushton Fairclough (Cambridge, MA: Harvard University Press, 1942), 479.

59. Curtius, *European Literature and the Latin Middle Ages,* 203ff.

and in its own way more profound, than what knowledge arrives at when passing through the medium of reflection and abstract thought. In other words, the idea of truth to which aesthetics refers runs counter to the idea of truth implicit in philosophy, the natural sciences, or the human sciences. It thus becomes possible to claim what D. H. Lawrence writes in *Why the Novel Matters:* only a form of *mimesis*—in this case, the novel—really captures life, and nothing is important but life.

Mimesis was always vitally important in the ancient world, but for reasons different from those that have gained ground in recent centuries. It was admired for its ability to instruct and entertain, for its enormous psychagogical power, because it was able to convert the abstraction of concepts into the figurative force that classical rhetoric called *enargeia* or *evidentia*, generating emotion, pleasure, and persuasion. It was admired for its ability to preserve the memory of gods and mortals: ancient culture entrusted the memory of human actions to the two mimetic disciplines of history and poetry. But an argument like the one used by modern aesthetics to legitimize the learning power of art (mimesis preserves a primary knowledge, linked to particular life and untranslatable into the form of the concept) was unknown to classical culture. Up to the discursive transformation that took place between the sixth and fourth centuries BCE, poets were the rightful masters of truth; after the effects of this conflict had been felt, the relationship of mimesis to truth became problematic. Certainly, ancient culture continued to view poets as sages, and ancient writers continued to impart metaphysical, theological, political, moral, historical, scientific, and technical truths in the form of *sententiae, exempla,* and allegories, even perhaps retaining the invocation to the muses and appealing to the divine origin of art—but ever since knowledge acquired a conceptual form, the role of mimesis was irremediably transformed. Poetry transmits meanings because it contains or allegorizes ideas, and not because it preserves a type of knowledge that is refractory to concepts but essential to the understanding of life. It assumes a nobly pedagogic, educational, and ornamental function; it serves to disseminate, in figurative, pleasant, and memorable ways that are understandable to a wide audience, what other disciplines already know and express in ways that are appropriate to the thing-in-itself but which are elitist. It is vulnerable to the ethical and theoretical judgments of philosophy and theology. In response to Plato's criticisms, Isocrates expressed an opinion that ran throughout ancient pedagogy: poetry lies within the realm of knowledge because it serves as a propedeutics for philosophy.[60] Aristotle gave explicit expression to the idea that the forms of knowledge are arranged in a hierarchy culminating in the hard kernel of philosophy: that of metaphysics.[61] The Platonic and Aristotelian scale of ranking between games of truth proved to be decisive in the interpretation of Judeo-Christian sacred texts, which were read through the medium of a theology—a discourse charged with the task of explaining in the form of concepts what the sacred texts expressed in the form of stories and metaphors.[62] The Christian version of control over mimesis picked up on and emphasized the moralistic gaze immanent to aesthetic Platonism: poets and artists were asked to not indulge in the mimesis of imperfect contingency, unless the story of weakness and sin took place within an allegorical and exemplary framework. After the Protestant Reformation and the Catholic Counter-Reformation, the criticism that the Church Fathers directed against mimesis spread far and wide.

The idea that fables instruct and entertain was transmitted to the Middle Ages.[63] However, from late antiquity to the advent of Scholasticism, the perception of the boundaries between the fields of poetry and abstract thought dissolved because the material crisis of the ancient culture and ancient world reduced the number of available texts and diminished the intellectual specialization. For almost a thousand years, poets were also read as philosophical and scientific authorities, and the term *philosophia* served to designate all forms of knowledge: poetry, rhetoric, grammar, philology, engineering, the art of war.[64] Of course, there was no lack of opposing theories. A counter-discourse developed in the culture of medieval Platonism between the ninth and thirteenth centuries that gave new value to the knowledge transmitted by fables, symbols, myths, and

60. Curtius, *European Literature and the Latin Middle Ages*, 37.

61. Aristotle, *Metaphysics* 1.982b.17–19.

62. Henri de Lubac, *Éxégèse médiévale: les quatre sens de l'Écriture* (Paris: Aubier, 1959–1964); Pépin, *Mythe et allégorie: les origines grecques et les contestations judéo-chrétiennes*, 215ff; by the same author, *La Tradition de l'allégorie de Philon d'Alexandrie à Dante* (Paris: Études Augustiniennes, 1987).

63. Edgar de Bruyne, *Études d'esthétique médiévale* (1946), vol. 2 (Geneva: Slatkine Reprints, 1975), 313ff.

64. Curtius, *European Literature and the Latin Middle Ages*, 203ff.

images.[65] An interpretation of the doctrine of Ideas very distant from the original Platonic one was essential for legitimizing the figurative arts in the Renaissance,[66] and its effects endured until the Romantic period.[67] But these aesthetic alternatives did not ultimately break free from the logic of the allegory, and, most importantly, they never engendered a cultural transformation comparable to what led to the abandonment of the Platonic hierarchy, the Romantic consecration of art, and the birth of modern aesthetics.

A systematic reflection on the confines between disciplines arose in the twelfth century with the development of Scholasticism, the spread of universities, and the growing division of intellectual labor. In his commentary on Aristotle's *Metaphysics* and in his own *Summa theologiae*, Thomas Aquinas reestablished a rigid hierarchical relationship between the theoretical arts and poetry ("the least of all the sciences"), restoring the ancient scale of ranking.[68] Medieval literary theory justified its subject matter by continuing to use the arguments of ancient aesthetics and by adding a new discourse of legitimization—a discourse that was in the minority but important nonetheless, because it involved the Bible. We find this explained in an exemplary fashion in one of the most famous fourteenth-century defenses of poetry, Albertino Mussato's seventh epistle, which entwines Horace's ideas with a new type of argument, namely, the idea that it was the poets who heralded the divine. By virtue of its allegorical form and its content, writes Mussato, the Bible shows how poetry can become a second theology as well as a second philosophy.[69] In reality, one of the last poets to act as the legitimate guardian of a primary knowledge was Dante, and the appeal of his work derives partially from this anachronism. Already during early humanism there reappeared the practice of the allegorical commentary, which subordinated fictions to their exemplary hidden

---

65. Peter Dronke, *Fabula: Explorations into the Uses of Myth in Medieval Platonism* (Leiden: Brill, 1974), chap. 1 and passim.

66. Panofsky, *Idea*; Teresa Chevrolet, *L'Idée de fable: théories de la fiction poétique à la Renaissance* (Geneva: Droz, 2007), part 1, especially pp. 61ff.

67. Paolo Tortonese, *L'Œil de Platon et le regard romantique* (Paris: Kimé, 2006), 103ff.

68. Thomas Aquinas, *In duodecim libros Metaphysicorum Aristotelis expositio*, ed. M.-R. Cathala and Raimondo M. Spiazzi (Turin: Marietti, 1977), bk. 1, lesson 3, and *Summa theologicae* 1.1.9.

69. See Giorgio Ronconi, *Le origini delle dispute umanistiche sulla poesia (Mussato e Petrarca)* (Rome: Bulzoni, 1976), 17–59.

moral sense and made poetry an *ancilla philosophiae*—a handmaid to philosophy.[70]

Moralism and Allegory

But the most intense period of control over mimesis began after the Protestant Reformation and the Catholic Counter-Reformation, in the mid-sixteenth century. During this period, Christian aesthetic Platonism produced preventive censorship and a body of implicit or explicit rules that influenced the writing and reception of novels. The apparatus of rules was based on three principles.

1. In the first place, *a pedagogical and moralistic conception of art: mimesis* disseminates useful knowledge and virtuous schemas of behavior in addition to what Aristotle called *phronesis:* a changeable wisdom regarding human affairs, a capacity to understand life and to act prudently in particular circumstances.[71] The link between poetry, oratory, and instruction became especially tight after the classicism in the mid-sixteenth century became more rigid[72] and Horace's principle of *delectare et monere* became the most obsessively repeated topos in prefaces to novels through to the second half of the eighteenth century.[73] Reading Huet's treatise or looking at the way the education of girls is described in the works of Jane Austen a century and a half later, it is clear that novels were used to furnish models of behavior to women and young people. Indeed, the formula that best describes the influence of aesthetic Platonism comes from Huet: novels are "silent tutors."

---

70. See Anne Duprat and Françoise Lavocat, "La Bataille des fables: conditions de l'émergence d'une théorie de la fiction en Europe (XIVe–XVIIe siècles)," in *Fiction et cultures,* ed. Françoise Lavocat and Anne Duprat (Paris: SFLGC, 2010), 243–248.

71. Aristotle, *Nicomachean Ethics* 6.5, 6.8–13.

72. See Bray, *La Formation de la doctrine classique en France,* part 2, chap. 1; Marc Fumaroli, *L'Âge de l'éloquence: rhétorique et "res literaria" de la Renaissance au seuil de l'époque classique* (Geneva: Droz, 1980).

73. See Herrick, *The Fusion of Horatian and Aristotelian Literary Criticism,* chap. 4; García Berrio, *Formación de la teoría literaria moderna,* passim; Duprat, "Morale et fiction en poétique," 45ff.; Hunter, *Before Novels,* chap. 9.

2. This pedagogical element is united with *the tendency to read texts as allegories,* as illustrations of human types, as collections of maxims, eloquent phrases, and concepts.

> *Amadis of Gaul,* along with *Orlando Furioso,* was the most important chivalric romance of the sixteenth century. Translated into all the major European languages, it circulated widely and was reprinted countless times. In 1559 in France, extracts from *Amadis of Gaul* were used to create a *Trésor de tous les livres d'Amadis de Gaule.* The "treasure" contained speeches, letters, orations, objections, and maxims "useful for instructing the French nobility in eloquence, grace, virtue, and generosity."[74] A year later, in Italy, a new edition of Bandello's novels appeared with a title that speaks for itself: *First volume of the* Novelle *by Bandello, newly reprinted and corrected with diligence. With the addition of some moral meanings by Mr. Ascanio Centorio degli Ortensi composed for each novella.*[75] Universal precepts and norms were extracted from works that contained particular stories about particular individuals. We find the same approach two centuries later in England. The "Preface of the Editor" that introduces *Pamela* spells out the moral meanings implicit in the novel:
>
> > If to *divert and entertain,* and at the same time *instruct and improve* the minds of the youth of both sexes,
> >
> > If to inculcate religion and morality in so easy and agreeable a manner, as shall render them equally *delightful* and *profitable* to the *younger class* of readers, as well as worthy of the attention of persons of *maturer* years and understandings;
> >
> > If to set forth in the most exemplary lights, the *parental, the filial and the social* duties, and that from low to high life:
> >
> > If to paint vice in its proper colours, to make it *deservedly odious;* and to set virtue in its own amiable light, to make it truly *lovely,* . . .

74. So reads the title page of one of the numerous reprints: *Trésor de tous les livres d'Amadis de Gaule contenant les harangues, épîtres, concions, lettres missives, demandes, réponses, répliques, sentences, cartels, complaintes et autres choses plus excellentes, très utile pour instruire la noblesse française à l'éloquence, grâce, vertu et générosité* (Lyon: Rigaud et J.-A. Huguetan, 1605).

75. *Primo volume delle Novelle del Bandello, nuovamente ristampato e con diligenza corretto. Con una aggiunta d'alcuni sensi morali dal S. Ascanio Centorio de gli Hortensii, a ciascuna novella fatti* (Milan: Giovanni Antonio degli Antonii, 1560).

If these (embellished with a great variety of entertaining incidents) be laudable or worthy recommendations of any work, the Editor of the following Letters, which have their foundation in *truth* and *nature*, ventures to assert, that all these desirable ends are achieved in these sheets.[76]

Fifteen years after the publication of *Pamela*, in 1755, Richardson brought out *A Collection of the Moral and Instructive Sentiments, Maxims, Cautions, and Reflections, Contained in the Histories of Pamela and Clarissa, and Sir Charles Grandison*. We thus encounter two connected phenomena that are repeated in identical ways at a distance of two centuries and in different national cultures. The meaning of narrative works was subjected to moral control and transliterated into the medium of the concept[77]—a repetition of what had happened in Greece when the commentators began to pull allegories out of Homer's and Hesiod's tales.

3. The tendency toward allegory characteristic of aesthetic Platonism became entwined with classicist poetics, engendering *an idea of probability*

---

76. Richardson, *Pamela*, 3–4.

77. It could be objected that books of maxims taken from narrative or theater works continue to exist (for example, the publishing success of maxims taken from Oscar Wilde's plays), but this is a different phenomenon. The practice of prefacing and concluding novels, dramatic works, or films with explanations that transcribe "the moral of our story" into the form of ideas, as the narrator of Manzoni's *The Betrothed* would put it, or the very conviction that a story should have a moral that can be expressed in maxims and precepts, is completely foreign to the aesthetic horizon of the past few centuries. For modern readers, what a work of fiction "really means" is the subject of endless, conflicting interpretations. The first task of literary criticism is precisely this: to translate into ideas the image of the world that lies sedimented inside the works. And yet this happens with the awareness that the language of mimesis possesses a truth that is irreducible to the medium of the concept. For the past two centuries now, interpretation has been an interminable practice: to expect to extract a unique message from James Joyce's *Ulysses*, from Proust's *In Search of Lost Time*, or from Beckett's *Waiting for Godot* is considered a naive pretense. Instead, in 1550 or in 1750 it was normal for writers and readers of novels to condense the moral of the story into a maxim, or to present the works as *exempla*, allegories, or representations of vices and virtues. Although difficult to comprehend for a reader of today, these habits are crucial for understanding the way narrative was written and interpreted in the Ancien Régime. The decline of allegorism is one of the great historical thresholds separating this epoch from our contemporary literary era. What declined was not a mere intellectual exercise practiced by a few scholars but rather a psychology of writing and reading, a collective *habitus*. In this case, too, the literary culture of the Ancien Régime revived a form of the subjection of mimesis to the concept that descended from Plato. See Terence Cave, "Pour une pré-histoire du suspens," in *Pré-histoires* (Geneva: Droz, 1999), 138–139.

very different from the modern one, founded on a varying combination between empirical observation and what ought to be. Literary imitation does not have the task of portraying the particularities of lives and forms of life; rather, it exemplifies already known universal concepts. What determine universal actions and passions are the same principles that govern classicism and Christian aesthetic Platonism: a hierarchical vision of society (each character must think and act in accordance with its rank) and a pedagogical and censorious conception of mimesis (immorality must be banished even from effigies).

Allegorical probability establishes two forms of bonds between the singular event and its hidden moral sense that go in different directions but have the same substance. The first joins the general idea to the particular *exemplum,* such as when prefaces explain the meaning of the story; the second creates the opposite movement. While the modern statistical concept of probability leaves room for the exception qua exception, the concept of probability that reigned in this epoch attached a potentially universal meaning to every episode and to every character. If a god behaves immorally, then the author's intention was to say that all gods are immoral; if the Princesse de Clèves confesses her love for another man to her husband, then Madame de La Fayette violated probability, since it is not morally acceptable for a princess to behave this way;[78] if *Robinson Crusoe* shows us a sailor who is shipwrecked, then Defoe wanted to both dissuade all people from taking to the sea, and to destroy English prosperity, which depended to a great extent on trade.[79] Today we entrust narrative the task of showing the different modes of finitude in all their dispersion. The idea that novels should represent typical stories and characters is only one of many possible poetics; with equally good arguments you could defend a contrary poetic, open to the mimesis of the unusual. In the allegorical paradigm that Platonism and classicism contributed to creating, there was no space for centrifugal movements, for the exception qua exception. The anomalous event or character was the subject matter of "history," not "poetry."

European classicism developed innumerable variants of these sorts of concepts. Italian and French literary theory of the second half of the sixteenth century and the seventeenth century, for example, constructed its

---

78. Genette, "Vraisemblance et motivation," 74ff.
79. See Gildon, "From *An Epistle to Daniel Defoe*," 57–63.

vision of mimesis around an allegorical interpretation of plots and characters. But the influence of aesthetic Platonism lasted much longer: we find it again in the essay on romance fiction that Samuel Johnson published in *The Rambler* (1750), at the close of a decade that was decisive for the development of the English novel.[80] Evidently, the "new province of writing" opened up by Fielding and Richardson had not yet transformed the premodern idea of probability.

Moralistic Apparatuses, Poetic Justice, Exemplary Heroes

The moralistic imperative, the habit of devising plots and characters as allegories of something, and the influence of classicism explain some aspects of the fiction of this period that modern readers find very difficult to understand.

1. First and foremost, *an outpouring of explanations in dedicatory epistles, in prefaces, and in the titles of works.* Between the second half of the sixteenth century and the second half of the eighteenth century, most novels were accompanied by preambles explaining the meaning of the text. Allegory and moralism invaded the front matter:

> Les Douze Livres d'Astrée où, par plusieurs Histoires et sous personnes de Bergers et d'autres, sont déduits les effets de l'honneste amitié.[81]

> Vitae humanae proscenium, in quo sub persona Guzmanii Alfaracii virtutes et vitia, fraudes, cautiones, simplicitas, nequitia, divitiae, mendacitas, bona, mala, omnia denique quae hominibus cuiuscumque aetatis aut ordinis evenire solent aut possunt, graphice ad vivum repraesentantur omni aetatis et conditionis hominum tam instructioni quam delectationi dicata.[82]

---

80. "It is therefore not a sufficient vindication of a character, that it is drawn as it appears; for many characters ought never to be drawn. . . . In narratives where historical veracity has no place, I cannot discover why there should not be exhibited the most perfect idea of virtue." Samuel Johnson, *The Rambler*, no. 4 (Saturday, March 31, 1750), in Johnson, *Essays from the Rambler, Adventurer, and Idler*, 11.

81. This is the title of the first edition of Honoré D'Urfé's *Astrée* (Paris: T. Du Bray, 1607).

82. This is the title with which the first Latin edition of Mateo Alemán's *Guzmán de Alfarache* appeared (Coloniae Agrippinae, excudebat Petrus a Brachel, 1623).

The Fortunes and Misfortunes of the Famous Moll Flanders, etc., Who
was Born in NEWGATE, and during a Life of continu'd Variety for Three-
score Years, besides her Childhood, was Twelve Year a Whore, five times
a Wife (whereof once to her own brother) Twelve Year a Thief, Eight
Year a Transported Felon in Virginia, at last grew Rich, liv'd Honest,
and died a Penitent.[83]

Two-part titles, created to explain the *sensus* hidden in the *narratio,* proliferated using a method descended from the rhetoric of medieval *exempla,*
which were immensely popular, especially in the eighteenth century: *Pamela;*
or, Virtue Rewarded; Les Liaisons dangereuses, ou Lettres recueillies dans
une société et publiées pour l'instruction de quelques autres; Justine, ou les
Malheurs de la vertu.

2. Another effect of allegorism was the insistence that poetic rules placed
on the *unity of plot and characters*. It was an obsession that dominated the
Italian debate on the *romanzo* in the 1550s. The detractors of the genre
associated chivalric literature with the risk of multiplicity and accused
romanzi of telling stories about characters who dissipated themselves in
adventures unworthy of a hero. This was made evident by the polyhistoric,
dispersive structure of the plots, based on the technique of *entrelacement*.
The normative poetics of the *epos* instead demanded unity of action and
character: the story should be organized around a great collective undertaking and a great, exemplary hero; the characters' actions should be motivated by significant goals; they should not go astray, abandon themselves to
sinful passions, or, in any case, to passions that are irrelevant to the ethical
purpose for which they fight.[84] In addition to obeying the principles that
the Renaissance theoreticians drew from Aristotle, this centripetal tendency expressed a strong drive toward allegorism and the cultural ether of
the Counter-Reformation. If literature is to be judged using moral orthopedics as its criterion of value, a unitary story and an exemplary hero are
reassuring. The unitary story and exemplary hero allow the raw material

---

83. This is the title with which Defoe's *Moll Flanders* first appeared (London: Chetwood,
1722).

84. For a long-term history of the opposition between epic unity and romance multiplicity, see David Quint, *Epic and Empire: Politics and Generic Form from Virgil to Milton*
(Princeton, NJ: Princeton University Press, 1993), 31ff.

of tales (which is always potentially ambiguous and polysemic, because it is written in a language quite different from that of ideas) to be interpreted as the unequivocal *exemplum* of something. The obsession with unity continued throughout the epoch of Christian aesthetic Platonism and classicism. We find it everywhere: in the principles that a theoretician like Huet expounds in his treatise and in the topoi that Manley, wishing to legitimate herself as serious writer, sets out in the preface to *Queen Zarah*. Moralism and allegory exerted their influence on plots and on characters. The most marked effect was the tremendous success enjoyed by *poetic justice* between the 1500s and the 1700s. Few devices point so accurately to Christian aesthetic Platonism as this figure of *dispositio*. Poetic justice is a normative principle: it requires that the plot be constructed in such a way that by the end of the story vice is punished and virtue rewarded. Formulated for the first time in 1588 by Leonardo Salviati, poetic justice soon became a widespread norm. In 1677 Thomas Rymer gave a name to it and invented the expression *poetical justice*.[85] The rule is based on a passage from Aristotle's *Poetics*[86] and, more obliquely, on passages in which Plato distinguishes between fictions that are morally acceptable and those that are morally unacceptable depending on how the vices and virtues are presented.[87] Many works were interpreted in this light: the plots of the Greek novels became examples of poetic justice; the prefaces of the English novels (*Colonel Jack, Moll Flanders, Roxana, Pamela, Clarissa, Ferdinand Count Fathom*) methodically insist on punishing vice and rewarding virtue. The more immoral episodes were included in the text, the more poetic justice was invoked as guidance on how it was to be read, so that the display of immorality could be fit into a moralistic design.

If poetic justice acted on the plot, its counterpart in the representation of the heroes was the tendency to construct and interpret characters as *exempla,* and in particular as representations of vices and virtues. An appeal to the exemplary nature of the hero often appeared in sixteenth-century poetics of the epic poem and of the romance that sought to imitate the forms of the *epos*. For sixteenth-century literary theory, for example, the

---

85. See Wolfgang Zach, *Poetic Justice: Theorie und Geschichte einer literarischen Doktrin. Begriff-Idee-Komödienkonzeption* (Tübingen: Max Niemeyer Verlag, 1986), 8ff.

86. Aristotle, *Poetics* 13.1452b.34–1453a.7.

87. Plato, *Republic* 3.392b.

heroines and heroes of the Greek novel were ideal characters because, even in the most difficult or awkward of circumstances, they always (or almost always) preserved their virtue.[88] In many Baroque novels, but also in many eighteenth-century novels, the heroes embody an abstract universal, according to a process that Lydia Ginzburg defines as deductive:

> For centuries a kind of deductive principle prevailed in literature, whereby individual gestures and speech were characterized by an *ideal* relation to the situations in which they occurred. Whatever the circumstances, the literary hero's physical behavior followed the precepts of the given style.[89]

A technique of this sort is moralistic and classicist at the same time.[90] It serves to create models of virtuous behavior, especially when the characters belong to groups of people who must be disciplined through the reading of novels: women, young girls, and young boys. Pamela, Clarissa, and Julie may make mistakes, they may wander in the realm of imperfection, but in the end they never abandon the idea of virtue that they embody and to which they return: their inner life is rigid and composed of principles (Virtue, Courage, Ambition, Value, Liberality, Generosity, Vice, Honor). The plot of their destiny is the unfolding of a moral project.

An example of this approach is a device that modern readers struggle to understand, just like poetic justice. I call it *the hero's self-correction.* It occurs very frequently in first-person novels that describe themselves as true histories: the characters may find themselves in risqué situations or give in to temptations, but in the end they have to acknowledge their wrongdoing and reaffirm their personal morality. A similar practice descends from spiritual autobiographies and their great archetype, Augustine's *Confessions,* where the years spent in the *regio dissimilitudinis* of error are narrated from the point of view of someone who has repented and changed his way of living. But the technique is also widespread in narratives that are not spiritual autobiographies in the strict sense of the term. In Defoe's *Moll Flanders* and *Roxana,* or in Duclos's *Les Confessions du Comte de * * ***

---

88. See Pavel, *L'Art de l'éloignement: essai sur l'imagination classique* (Paris: Gallimard, 1996), and *La Pensée du roman,* 58ff.

89. Lydia Ginzburg, *On Psychological Prose,* trans. Judson Rosengrant (Princeton, NJ: Princeton University Press, 1991), 297ff.

90. See Herrick, *The Fusion of Horatian and Aristotelian Literary Criticism,* chap. 7; Pavel, *La Pensée du roman,* 142ff.

(1742), for example, we find the same device, although the proportion between the two parts is different: reflection on the years of error prevails by
far over the edifying passages. In Richardson's novels, on the other hand,
the hero's self-correction is applied in a more extremist fashion. Whenever
Pamela and Clarissa find themselves in indecent situations, they feel the
need to reaffirm their morality, and this almost always takes place in the
same letter in which the racy incident is being recounted.

A technique of this sort has no credibility in the eyes of modern readers,
who view the inner life as a set of changeable forces rather than embodied
ideas. Instead, the allegorical and moralistic paradigm legitimizes the hero's self-correction and in some way demands it. In reflecting on the image
of humankind and the world transmitted by Hellenistic novels and chivalric and pastoral romances, Thomas Pavel introduces a succinct concept
that can be fittingly applied to a wide variety of cases. In his opinion, the
regime of fiction adopted by these works is "ideographic" rather than
"inductive":[91] the stories and characters do not imitate the empirical reality
according to the criteria of probability that would be imposed in modern
times; rather, they act as allegories of an Idea established a priori. It is a
principle that applies to many novels written between the mid-sixteenth
century and the mid-eighteenth century: the heroes of the heroic Baroque
novel, for example, are models of moral exemplarity, far removed from any
empirical probability. Although finding themselves in the most difficult of
circumstances, Pamela and Clarissa remains models of virtue.[92]

Today we no longer ask our high-brow literature to perform this
ideographic task: our prevailing need is not for moral orthopedics but for
realism, however we might choose to define this term. This is one of the
reasons readers of our day tend to underestimate the importance that moralism and allegorism held between the sixteenth and the eighteenth centuries. For their part, nineteenth- and twentieth-century theories of the novel
pass over these phenomena, or read them with modern eyes, as if they
were superstructures added a posteriori as a way to pass on transgressive
material. There is undoubtedly some truth to this view, considering that
even the pornographic novelists of the 1700s, from John Cleland to the

91. Pavel, *La Pensée du roman*, 111ff.
92. Ibid., 145ff.

Marquis de Sade, represented themselves as creators of *exempla*. In the finale to *Memoirs of a Woman of Pleasure,* we read:

> If you do me then justice, you will esteem me perfectly consistent in the incense I burn to virtue. If I have painted vice in all its gayest colours, if I have deck'd it with flowers, it has been solely in order to make the worthier, solemner sacrifice of it to virtue.[93]

In the dedication "To libertines" that precedes *Philosophy in the Boudoir,* in the introductory matter to *Justine,* or in the first chapter of the *Nouvelle Justine,* we find a sort of upside-down moralism. The titles make no secret of it, for that matter (*Justine, ou les Malheurs de la vertu*):

> The aims of this fiction (which is not as fictional as some might think) are doubtless new. The ascendancy of Virtue over Vice, good rewarded and evil punished, such is the general trend of works of this nature. Shall we ever tire of reading them! But everywhere to represent Vice as triumphant and Virtue a victim of its attacks; to show a wretched girl wandering from one misfortune to another . . . with the sole aim of obtaining from all of this one of the most sublime moral lessons that humanity has ever been taught, was, I am sure you will agree, to reach this goal by a road seldom trodden before.[94]

> We shall give the public this history of the virtuous Justine to lend support to these systems (we no longer conceal it). It is essential for the fools to stop showering this ridiculous idol of virtue with praise, which until now has repaid them with nothing but ingratitude. . . . Without a doubt, it is terrible to have to depict, on the one hand, the horrific misadventures by which heaven plagues a sweet and sensitive woman who respects virtue to her utmost, and, on the other, the affluence that rains down on those who torment and mortify this same woman. But the man of letters, who is enough a philosopher to tell the truth, manages to overcome these unpleasantries.[95]

93. John Cleland, *Memoirs of a Woman of Pleasure,* vol. 2 (London: Fenton, 1749), 254.

94. Donatien Alphonse François de Sade, *Justine, ou les Malheurs de la vertu*; English translation *Justine, or The Misfortunes of Virtue,* trans. John Philips (Oxford: Oxford University Press, 2012).

95. Donatien Alphonse François de Sade, *La Nouvelle Justine,* in *Œuvres,* vol. 2, ed. Michel Delon (Paris: Gallimard, 1995), 129.

To dismiss these forms of reading and writing as cynical masquerades or as forms of irony would be tantamount to misunderstanding an epoch. Moral control and allegorism were two of the basic assumptions that governed mimesis and fiction during the early modern age: they formed the mental landscape, the aesthetic environment, inhabited by writers and readers of the time. Today we believe that an author's task is primarily to tell stories about the real world or about an invented world in a credible, compelling manner. The readers of the early modern era were inclined more than we are to submit characters and plots to an implicit or explicit moral judgment and to an implicit or explicit conceptual interpretation. This superegoic, allegorical need was part of their literary system, and it made its way into the text like a sort of second nature.

The Legitimization of the *Romance*

How were *romances* and *novels* defended from the accusations directed at them by classicism and Christian aesthetic Platonism? The arguments that writers used to justify their works clearly reveal that the genre arose out of two traditions: the lines of reasoning used for legitimization tend to follow different strategies depending on whether the work to be defended was "poetic" or "historic," whether it was a *romance* or a *novel*.

The romance of low style had no need to be ennobled. It could never be a serious genre, and it fit perfectly into the poetics of the separation of styles, occupying the place intended for works of this sort: farcical romances were a form of light entertainment; romances written in an intermediate comic tone employed the strategies invented for justifying the usefulness of comedy and presented themselves as a description of manners. Those who defended lofty-style romance from the accusation of violating the rules of the art used other strategies of legitimization.

The first consisted in presenting the high romance as the modern counterpart of the epic poem. This is an argument that passed from Italian treatises of the mid-sixteenth century to French treatises of the later seventeenth century. According to Giraldi, the first *romanzi*, the French medieval ones, arose "in place of the heroic compositions of the Greeks and Romans."[96] Pigna and Fornari sought to establish the rules of the chivalric poem by examining the rules of the *epos*. *Orlando Furioso* entered into the canon of modern classics partly because its supporters endeavored to present it as the sixteenth-century equivalent of the ancient heroic poem.[97]

As Aristotelianism became more unyielding over the course of the sixteenth century, it became harder and harder to defend the chivalric poem using an argument of this sort: clearly, the technique of *entrelacement* was not in keeping with the precepts derived from Aristotle's *Poetics* on the unity of plot. It did remain possible to interpret the Greek novel in the light of the epic poem, though. The difference depended more on the prestige that the ancient authors enjoyed, precisely because of their antiquity, more than it did on any formal criteria. Between the mid-sixteenth century and the seventeenth century, the *Aethiopica* became the model for the romance inspired by the rules for the epic.[98] This interpretation gained popularity mainly in France—in the nation that, despite having invented the courtly medieval romance, during the Renaissance lacked a work comparable to *Amadis* or *Orlando Furioso*. The canonization of Heliodorus was decisive for the birth of the heroic Baroque novel. In the first pages of *Ibrahim* (1641–1644), Scudéry writes that the modern *roman* must imitate the structure of the epic poem, as did Heliodorus, who followed the unity of action principle.[99] Huet used the same strategy to establish a normative poetics for the genre.[100]

The second line of reasoning used for legitimization was based on a classic Aristotelian argument. The Greek novels or chivalric romances, we are told, are poetic, not historical, texts; therefore they should be read as *exempla* of ideal behavior. *Orlando Furioso* is often subjected to this allegorical, ennobling interpretation.[101] Similar ways of conceiving romances

---

96. Giraldi Cinzio, *Discorsi dei romanzi*, 36.

97. Daniel Javitch, *Proclaiming a Classic: The Canonization of "Orlando Furioso"* (Princeton, NJ: Princeton University Press, 1991), 160ff.

98. See Giorgetto Giorgi, introduction to *Les Poétiques italiennes du "roman": Simon Fornari, Jean-Baptiste Giraldi Cinzio, Jean-Baptiste Pigna*, ed. by Giorgetto Giorgi (Paris: Champion, 2005); Esmein-Sarrazin, *L'Essor du roman*, 82ff.

99. Madame de Scudéry, *Ibrahim, ou l'Illustre Bassa* (Paris: Pour la Compagnie des Libraires du Palais, 1665), "Préface," no page numbers.

100. "I call those [Romances] Regular, which are composed after the Rules of an Heroic Poem." Huet, *The History of Romances*, 83.

101. See Javitch, *Proclaiming a Classic*, chap. 2, pp. 33ff.

spread widely across Europe during the seventeenth and eighteenth centuries. This is partly because the hermeneutic founded on hidden moral senses made it possible to respond to Platonic and Augustinian arguments against mimesis using the same philosophical assumptions, but arriving at different conclusions. If the purpose of good art is to represent reality as it should be and not as it is, then works that create a "poetic" world, a world that is therefore better than the imperfect one described by history, deserve to be defended. Stated with clarity in a passage in Francis Bacon's *Of the Proficience and Advancement of Learning* (1605, 1623),[102] this argument circulated in countless versions between the seventeenth and eighteenth centuries. We find it in texts that vary in period, genre, and style: in Barclay's *Argenis* (1621)[103] and Théophraste Renaudot's *Conférences du Bureau d'adresse* (1634–1641);[104] in the Abbé de Pure's dialogue *La Prétieuse* (1656)[105] and Huet's treatise;[106] in Charles Sorel[107] and Père Rapin;[108] and in the previ-

102. "The use of this *feigned history* hath been to give some shadow of satisfaction to the mind of man in those points wherein the nature of things doth deny it, the world being in proportion inferior to the soul; by reason whereof there is, agreeable to the spirit of man, a more ample greatness, a more exact goodness, and a more absolute variety, than can be found in the nature of things. Therefore, because the acts or events of *true history* have not that magnitude which satisfieth the mind of man, *poesy* feigneth acts and events greater and more heroical: because true history propoundeth the successes and issues of actions not so agreeable to the merits of virtue and vice, therefore poesy feigns them more just in retributions, and more according to revealed providence: because true history representeth actions and events more ordinary, and less interchanged, therefore poesy endueth them with more rareness, and more unexpected and alternative variations: so as it appeareth that poesy serveth and conferreth to magnamimity, morality, and to delectation." Francis Bacon, *Of the Proficience and Advancement of Learning: Divine and Human* (London: John W. Parker and Son, West Strand, 1852), 80–81.

103. John Barclay, *Argenis* (1621), ed. and trans. Mark Riley and Dorothy Pritchard Huber (Assen: Royal Van Gorcum/Tempe, AZ: Arizona Center for Medieval and Renaissance Studies, 2004), bk. 2, chap. 14, p. 336.

104. Thomas Renaudot, *Recueil général des questions traitées ès conférences du bureau d'adresse, sur toutes sortes de matières; par les plus beaux esprits de ce temps* (Lyon: Valançol, 1666), conférence 107, 2, pp. 107ff.

105. Michel de Pure, *La Prétieuse, ou le Mystère des ruelles* (1656), vol. 1, ed. Émile Magne (Paris: Droz, 1938), 138.

106. Huet, *The History of Romances*, 144ff.

107. Charles Sorel, *De la connoissance des bons livres, ou Examen de plusieurs auteurs* (1671), ed. Lucia Moretti Cenerini (Rome: Bulzoni, 1974), 82ff.

108. René Rapin, *Réflexions sur la Poétique d'Aristote et sur les ouvrages des poètes anciens et modernes* (Paris: François Muguet, 1674), 123.

ously cited passages from Lenglet Du Fresnoy and Samuel Johnson. In the last decades of the eighteenth century, Clara Reeve repeated the argument with a few variations.[109]

The Legitimization of the *Novel*

The defensive strategies for the texts that ended up as *novels* were completely different. While all the books that entered into the category of novel came under, or might have come under, the fire of the accusations we talked about in the preceding sections, there was a certain type of criticism that was addressed exclusively to "historical" narratives. The *romance* accentuated the poetical and exemplary nature of fiction, whereas *novelle, novelas, nouvelles,* and autobiographical or biographical writings described particularities: proper names, singular deeds, and potentially eccentric or immoral actions. To justify this exposure to contingency and imperfection, writers and critics attempted comparisons with the well-known genres of comedy and tragedy;[110] they especially drew on the arguments used by classical literature and Christian literature to defend the moral usefulness of history. However, there was an obvious asymmetry between ancient history and the works that converged into the *novel*: the former spoke of public figures, the latter of private individuals. This asymmetry did not exist in

109. Lenglet Du Fresnoy argues that the novel should occupy itself with moral exemplariness, honoring virtue, instilling respect for the integrity of princes, and rewarding wisdom, while history may also represent the world in its imperfection (Lenglet du Fresnoy, *De l'usage des romans*, vol. 1, chap. 3, pp. 204ff., especially 210–211, and then chap. 4). Resorting to the same arguments, Samuel Johnson recommends that where historical veracity has no place, the writers of narratives should show the most perfect idea of morality. At the end of *The Progress of Romance*, the character Euphrasia cites a sentence from *A Comparative View of the State and Faculties of Man with Those of the Animal World* by Gregory: "The *old Romances* produced more favorable moral effects than *modern Novels* because the former represented models of courage, truth, generosity, humanity, virtue, while the latter have begun to represent mankind as he is." Reeve, *The Progress of Romance*, vol. 2, "Evening 12," 86–87.

110. In the eighteenth century, as we have said, it was quite common to compare the tradition of the *novel* with comedy: both genres talked about private individuals; both described manners and, in theory, helped to improve them. In the same way, the *novella* or the *nouvelle* could be compared to tragedy, perhaps based on the fact that the latter, according to Aristotle, could employ historical characters. This comparison is implicit in the choice to call some of the novellas that circulated autonomously "tragic stories," or in the way the plots of *The Portuguese Letters* and *The Princesse de Clèves* were constructed, for example.

the Christian historiographical tradition, which instead attached an exemplary ethical value to what happened to all people. That is why the texts that converged in the territory of the *novel* sought to legitimize themselves by systematically resorting to arguments typical of spiritual autobiography, spiritual biography, and especially the *exemplum.*

In classical rhetoric, the *exemplum* is one of three avenues to oratorical persuasion, the other two being the *signum* and the *argumentum,* and it is presented as a statement of true facts even when the events being told are legendary.[111] The genre underwent crucial changes with the rise of Christian culture and then the crisis of the classical tradition in the high Middle Ages. While the authorities that the ancient *exemplum* drew on were the *mos maiorum,* or the great figures of the mythical or historical past, the medieval Christian *exemplum* referred primarily to sacred history and to stories about common people. Read as *narratio authentica* and set against the *narratio ficta* of the *fabulae,* it ended up including themes about daily life, which were otherwise considered unworthy of being written about.[112]

To legitimize picaresque novels, *novelle, novelas, nouvelles, mémoires,* and *novels,* writers appealed to the classical topos of the *historia magistra vitae* and developed it into the Christian form of the *exemplum.* Rooted in this line of reasoning is the idea that morality is conveyed better with anecdotes than with rules, especially when the interlocutors are young or simple people.[113] Seneca expressed this in a widely cited maxim: "Longum iter est per praecepta, breve et efficax per exempla (Teaching by precept is a long road, but brief and effective is the way by example)."[114] The original source of this kind of thinking, as we know, was the *Republic:* the

---

111. See Manfred Fuhrmann, "Das Exemplum in der antiken Rhetorik," in *Geschichte— Ereignis und Erzählung,* ed. Von Reinhart Koselleck and Wolf-Dieter Stempel (Munich: Fink, 1973), 449–452; Claude Bremond, Jacques le Goff, and Jean-Claude Schmitt, *L' "Exemplum"* (Turnhout: Brepols, 1982); Carlo Delcorno, *Exemplum e letteratura. Tra Medioevo e Rinascimento* (Bologna: Il Mulino, 1989).

112. Bremond, Le Goff, and Schmitt, *L' "Exemplum,"* chap. 3 and p. 79; Michel Zink, "Le temps du récit et la mise en scène du narrateur dans le fabliau et dans l'exemplum," in *La Nouvelle,* Actes du colloque international de Montréal, McGill University, October 14–16, 1982, ed. Michelangelo Picone, Giuseppe Di Stefano, and Pamela D. Stewart (Montreal: Plato Academic Press, 1983), 29; Delcorno, *Exemplum e letteratura,* 8.

113. See Plato, *Republic* 2.377a and following.

114. Seneca, *Moral Letters to Lucilius,* vol. 1, letter 6, 5.

poets who write hymns to the gods and eulogies to good men are performing a useful function, because mimesis is able to speak even to those who lack the intellectual resources to arrive at truth through abstract thought. In the 1600s and 1700s, ideas like these appeared frequently in prefaces to "historical" kinds of narrative works, in Spain as in Italy, in France as in Great Britain.[115] The more unbelievable the plot and the heroes were in Aristotelian terms, the more the work had the right to claim its historicity, and therefore its didactic usefulness: that which is strange, that which goes against "poetic" probability, is more likely to be true and useful.[116] The moral of the work, writes Defoe in the preface to *Moll Flanders,* justifies the "true" telling of some immoral acts.[117] The anonymous author of *The Finish'd Rake; or Gallantry in Perfection: Being the Genuine and Entertaining Adventures of a Young Gentleman of Fortune* (1733) writes that his adventures, remarkable but true, may serve as "a warning to deter other People from following my Example."[118]

A similar reasoning justifies the importance of private life: when it comes to imparting moral paradigms, the affairs of unknown people are just as effective as stories about famous heroes. In Segrais's *Nouvelles françaises,* the character of Alpanice argues that since one writes to instruct or to entertain, it is not necessary to tell stories about kings or emperors, as we find in romances. In the *Discours sur le roman* that opens *Theresa, histoire italienne* (1745), Baculard d'Arnaud writes that the works of Prévost, Marivaux, and Crébillon fascinate the reader because they talk about familiar topics that readers can identify with, and from which they can learn more than from reading history books.[119] In the preface to *Memoirs of the Life and Writings of Alexander Pope* (1745), William Ayre writes that the lives of private individuals provide examples of greatness and

---

115. See Hautcoeur Pérez-Espejo, *Parentés franco-espagnoles au XVIIe siècle,* 42; Albert N. Mancini, *Romanzi e romanzieri del Seicento* (Naples: Società editrice napoletana, 1981); May, *Le Dilemme du roman au XVIIIe siècle,* 106ff.; Hunter, *Before Novels,* 280ff.; McKeon, *The Origins of the English Novel, 1600–1740,* 47ff. and passim.

116. See McKeon, *The Origins of the English Novel,* 47ff., and Hunter, *Before Novels,* chap. 8.

117. Defoe, *Moll Flanders,* ed. Edward Kelly (New York: Norton, 1973), 3.

118. Anonymous, *The Finish'd Rake; or Gallantry in Perfection: Being the Genuine and Entertaining Adventures of a Young Gentleman of Fortune* (1733), in Williams, *Novel and Romance,* 86.

119. Cited in May, *Le Dilemme du roman au XVIIIe siècle,* 148–149.

power, just like the lives of princes, but they have the advantage of lending themselves better to imitation.[120] Once again, the source of this idea is the medieval rhetoric of the *exemplum,* which abolished the distinction between public events and private anecdotes, even privileging the latter because they stand closer to the world of those for whom the text is intended.[121]

The novel took the form it has today between 1550 and 1800, when a heterogeneous mass of narrative writings began to be grouped under the same name. The genre was perceived as a unified whole because the works that belonged to it took a narrative form and because they were partially or totally removed from the dominant paradigms. From the outset, the territory was divided into two parts: narratives of a poetic type were opposed to narratives of a historical type; what would come to be called *romance* was juxtaposed to what would come to be called *novel.* These two subgenres sought to justify themselves in the face of the official literature. Up to the second half of the eighteenth century, novelists still took into account, often to a great extent, devices deriving from Christian aesthetic Platonism and classicism. It is impossible to read the narrative of this period without perceiving its underlying dual schema. But to the elements of continuity there corresponded powerful elements of disruption: although the genre did not openly proclaim its originality in this period, texts that ended up in the *novel-and-romance* category introduced new and revolutionary ways of telling stories. In this chapter we have seen how these texts remained bound to the literary structures of the Ancien Régime. In Chapter 4 we will focus on a paradigm leap that the genre brought with it.

---

120. Cited in Hunter, *Before Novels,* 350.
121. Bremond, Le Goff, and Schmitt, *L'"Exemplum,"* 44.

CHAPTER FOUR

The Book of Particular Life

The *Romance* and Private Aims

During the eighteenth century and at the beginning of the nineteenth, many writers gradually lost sight of the threshold that the *romance* had introduced into the history of narrative fiction. When the *novel*'s dominance became established, the *romance* may not have seemed like a revolutionary genre because, fundamentally, like serious and comic epic poems, it talked about events and heroes that were removed from everyday life. One might think that the suspicion with which the chivalric romance, the Greek novel, or the Baroque novel were received between the middle of the sixteenth century and the end of the seventeenth was a passing phase—a temporary effect of aesthetic Platonism and the classicist, normative inflexibility that was destined to disappear. The truth is that this apparent continuity was precisely what concealed the signs of a new paradigm.

The genre most disruptive to the dominant literary system was the *serious romance*. Contrary to Bakhtin's theories, as long as the poetics of the separation of styles formed the backbone of European literature, the comic genres occupied a specific, minor position in the system of forms and did not present a problem for the prevailing canons. Its serious variant should not have profoundly shaken up the Christian and classicist structures of sense either, one might suppose, since the stories told by the subgenres belonging to this literary family were drawn from a canonized repertoire set in a distant, aristocratic past. But although they conflicted with the rules derived from Aristotle's *Poetics*, they did not threaten the separation of styles—

because the characters they told about were better than us. They thus confirmed the foundational principle of the *Stiltrennung*, namely, the belief that the noble, the great, and the important have nothing to do with common reality.[1] From a long-term perspective, then, what was the disruptive factor implicit in the Greek novel, the chivalric romance, and Baroque novels?

As we have seen, like a photographic negative, problems of legitimization bring into visibility the points of rupture that works introduce into a literary system. Even though the spectrum of criticisms launched against the serious romance was very wide, the traditions that converged into this genre were vulnerable to a few accusations that cut across the entire range: they corrupted manners, they had no precedents in the noble forms of classic literature, they violated the rules of ancient poetics, they invited readers to lose themselves in centrifugal adventures, and they praised a dangerous passion like love. When viewed from the flip side, each of these criticisms reveals a disruptive element.

However, among these evident innovations there circulated one that was more abstract, more subtle, and more important. To grasp it, we have to leave behind the centuries that witnessed the burgeoning polemic against the novel and observe the narrative fiction of the period from the position of those who wrote after the crisis of classicism, after the crisis of Christian Platonic aesthetics, and during the emergence of a new paradigm—like Madame de Staël or Friedrich Schlegel. Hegel belonged to this generation. In some of his lectures on aesthetics, he reflects on the place that chivalric romances occupied in the overall arc of European literature:

> The subject [of chivalry and chivalric romances] is only full of himself by being inherently infinite individuality; he does not need the importance or further concrete development of an inherently objective substantial content of interests, aims, and actions.[2]

> The actions achieved here [in chivalric romances], and the events, do not affect any national interests; on the contrary, they are the actions of individuals with the individual himself as such as their substance; this I have described already in dealing with romantic chivalry. It is true, consequently, that the individuals stand there on their own feet, free and

1. Auerbach, *Mimesis*, 139.
2. Hegel, *Aesthetics*, vol. 1, p. 553.

fully independent, and thus, within a surrounding world not yet consolidated into a prosaic organization, they form a new group of heroes who
nevertheless in their interests, whether fantastically religious or, in mundane matters, purely subjective and imaginary, lack that fundamental
realism which is the basis on which the Greek heroes fight either alone or
in company, and conquer and perish.[3]

Hegel reworks themes that circulated widely in the literary culture
during Goethe's time. The idea that the novel was concerned with the stories and passions of private individuals, overshadowing all the enthusiasm
for collective causes that motivated the actions of the heroes of the *epos,*
had already appeared in Friedrich von Blanckenburg.[4] The privilege granted
to the chivalric romance was also tied to a master narrative that was
popular in the culture of German idealism, which connected the birth of
modern subjectivity to the effect of Christianity.

We can accept the truth content of this passage without entering into its
historical and philosophical premises. The ability with which Hegel perceived
a number of fundamental evolutionary lines stems primarily from a posi-
tional advantage: whoever was born around 1770 was able to evaluate the
history of literary genres in the light of what narrative fiction had become
during the eighteenth century. Thanks to the historical perspective from
which he spoke, Hegel was able to establish a crucial point: the serious romance occupied a strategic place in the development of European literature
because its heroes were motivated by love and by the spirit of adventure
rather than by public aims. It was the first time that Western stories gave
so much weight to characters who were effectively driven by private aims
and passions. Hegel understood this partly because he knew something that
the theorists from the 1500s and 1600s could not have known: namely, that
"the actions of individuals," detached from any collective goal or hidden political meaning, would become the main subject matter of modern narrative
fiction.

The noble genres of the culture of antiquity, the *epos* and the tragedy,
tell stories whose plots are focused on supraindividual conflicts; their he-

3. Ibid., vol. 2, 1104–1105.
4. See Christian Friedrich von Blanckenburg, *Versuch über den Roman* (1774), ed. Von E.
Lämmert (Stuttgart: J. B. Metzlersche Berlagsbuchhandlung, 1965), 7ff.

roes are not just any private beings; their world is governed by collective goals and made universal by mythology or public history. Although some of the works ultimately focus on the internal conflicts of the heroes, as in Euripides or Virgil, the moral reality in which the characters move remains governed by a solid community ethos. In the classicist literary system, the mimesis of private persons who pursue private aims is relegated to the inherently lower genres of comedy and satire. The philosophy of history that fueled Hegel's work demanded that narrative individualism be attributed to the chivalric romance—in other words, to a form that came into being at the height of the Christian era. But if we leave aside this overarching vision, we realize that similar ideas also describe perfectly the Greek novel, whose characters are driven by private aims no different from those animating the characters of courtly literature. Unlike comedy and satire, the Greek novel and the medieval romance did not come into being marked to be minor genres: Greek novels tell stories about noble characters and have a serious register; medieval romances describe heroes who are in every way similar to those of the *chanson de geste*. The worlds of the *epos* and the serious romance are so close to each other that they sometimes overlap. In both cases, the characters are not just any individuals: the purpose of the recognition that furnishes the Hellenistic narrative plot with its telos is to show that the hero or heroine whose story the reader has been following is actually of noble birth. However, there was a slippage between the class of texts that belonged to the family of the *epos* and the class of texts that belonged to the family of the novel. This was the transition that Hegel emphasized: epic heroes pursue collective, significant aims, while the heroes of romance pursue private, trivial aims. Out of these theories there arose a topos of nineteenth-century literary criticism: the idea that the difference between epic and romance follows the same line that divides communal closure and individualistic opening, public and private, unity and variety. The comparison between the two genres that we find in Lukács's *The Theory of the Novel* or in Bakhtin's "Epic and Novel" are new interpretations of these issues, and a similar opposition, in multiple forms, still permeates contemporary critical discourse.

Chivalric romances, and before them, Greek novels, contained an individualistic, anarchic, dispersive, centrifugal element, rooted in the *regio dissimilitudinis*. They signaled a significant step in the representation of the private in literature not because they told stories about people like us, but because they told stories about public or semipublic people in the act of having private, irregular experiences of love and adventure. The fear aroused in classicism and Christian aesthetic Platonism by the variety of romances, by their wandering plots, by the anarchy of their passions, reflected this slippage. The potentially subversive innovation came into being through a blatant compromise, though, because the heroes of *romance* are "better than us." The same assumption on which the epic of antiquity and the *chanson de geste* were founded continued to hold for the Greek novel and the chivalric romance: the noble and the interesting had no relation with common reality.

This transformation is also perceptible in the way of understanding the opposition between the "poetic" narrative of the *romance* and the "historical" narrative of the *novel*. Until the second half of the seventeenth century, Hellenistic novels, courtly and pastoral romances, and Baroque novels could be read according to an ideographic principle: their characters and unrealistic plots were allegories of general and collective values. Nevertheless, if we take instead the general definition of *romance* that Clara Reeve proposed in 1785, then the signs of a turning point become perceptible: "The Romance is an heroic fable; . . . [it] describes what never happened nor is likely to happen."[5] For classicist aesthetics, a "poetic" composition talks about universals, "what could and would happen either probably or inevitably"; for Clara Reeve, the *romance* tells stories about "what never happened nor is likely to happen." At the end of the seventeenth century a narrative fiction could be interpreted as an *exemplum* of general ideas and values, shared and expressed according to a collective allegorical code; by the end of the eighteenth century, narrative that kept a distance from ordinary life appeared to be primarily a work of the subjective imagination. There are traces of the old interpretation in Reeve's dialogue,[6] but the tendency to attribute the *romance* to the personal imagination, to a taste for fabulous adventures, predominates. The new interpretation would prevail in the 1800s and 1900s. Like the *novel*, the understanding of the *romance* also veered toward the private.

5. Reeve, *The Progress of Romance*, vol. 1, "Evening 7," 111.
6. Ibid., "Evening 7" and passim.

Suspense, *Entrelacement,* and the Romanesque

The *romance* was also a new genre because in a subtle fashion it renewed the way stories were told. It was apparently far removed from common life, but furnished Western fictions with *Gestalten* that were capable of modeling and making interesting the *regio dissimilitudinis* and private passions. The archetypes of what is called Romanesque in the critical lexicon—the set of *peripeteia*, reversals, recognitions, projections of expectations, and twists of fate that captured the attention of readers, drawing them into the characters' stories—came into existence thanks to the serious romance.

The most conspicuous and widespread *Gestalt* was that of suspense. Amyot ennobled Heliodorus by comparing his work to epic poems: as it happens, the *Aethiopica* begins in medias res, exactly as the normative poetic rules of traditional *epos* demand. But Heliodorus's *ordo artificialis* is peculiar: the way he went about it, writes Amyot, causes our understanding to remain suspended (*l'entendement demeure suspendu*), producing a pleasurable effect on the reader.[7] At the beginning of the *Aethiopica,* some men armed as brigands are looking out onto the beach at the mouth of the Nile, discovering it to be strewn with dead and mutilated bodies. They see a vessel with no crew and no cargo on the shore; traces of the massacre are mixed with the remains of a feast that took place before the slaughter. In the midst of the bodies, a beautiful young woman sits on a rock, unscathed; at her feet lies a young man, equally beautiful and horribly wounded. The description does not explain the meaning of what the characters see: only in the fifth chapter will the reader be able to fully reconstruct the prior events leading up to this scene. While the beginnings in medias res of the *Iliad,* the *Odyssey,* and the *Aeneid* do not create protracted puzzles to be solved, the *ordo artificialis* of the *Aethiopica* keeps our attention suspended for many pages. Widely imitated beginning in the second half of the sixteenth century, this technique became a typical feature of the heroic Baroque novel.[8]

To define the effect created by the first pages of the *Aethiopica,* Amyot appealed to a formula put into circulation twenty years earlier by Marco Gerolamo Vida: in book 2 of the *Ars poetica* (1527) we read that the *incipit*

---

7. Amyot, "Le Proësme du translateur," no page numbers.
8. See Cave, "Suspense and the Pre-history of the Novel," 507–516.

in medias res has the power to *suspendere animos.*[9] We don't know if Vida was familiar with the *Aethiopica,* printed for the first time in Greek in Basel in 1536, but he certainly knew the technique of *sustentatio* described by Quintilian in the *Institutio Oratoria.*[10] And he surely knew the medieval technique of *entrelacement,* which alternately entwines and interrupts the characters' stories, usually at the point when the reader's curiosity is at its peak. Pigna observed that the story lines of chivalric romances wander just like their characters, keeping the reader's attention suspended.[11] While the concept of suspense is used today in a narrow sense to describe the effect of a few literary and film subgenres, in the mid-sixteenth century *suspendere animos* meant to inspire the kind of curiosity that would become normal for all novel readers from the eighteenth century on. What innovations are implicit in this writing technique?

First of all, the effect of suspense is difficult to create unless the person to whom the story is addressed has a synoptic view of the plot attainable only through the practice of reading. The informational delay of the *Aethiopica* or the virtuoso *entrelacement* of *Orlando Furioso* assumes a reader more than a listener. As Terence Cave remarks, "With the *Aethiopica* in Amyot's version, the age of the individual reader, the individual purchaser of discrete fictions, seems to have arrived."[12] Through the medium of the book and the spread of silent reading, the historic phase in which romances would be addressed to solitary individuals was nigh.[13]

In addition to assuming a new relationship between an isolated reader and heroes who pursue subjective aims, suspense introduces another disruptive factor. I will describe it in reference to the criticisms that Gotthard

---

9. Marco Girolamo Vida, *De arte poetica libri III* (Rome: L. Vincentium, 1527), bk. 2, lines 59–76.

10. Quintilian, *Institutio oratoria* 9.2.22. See Cave, "Pour une pré-histoire du suspens," 129–141.

11. Pigna, *I romanzi,* 49.

12. See Cave, "Suspense and the Pre-history of the Novel," 511.

13. See Walter Benjamin, "Der Erzähler. Betrachtungen zum Werk Nikolai Lesskows" (1936); English translation "The Storyteller: Reflections on the Works of Nicolai Leskov," in *Illuminations* (New York: Schocken Books, 2007), 83–110. On the relationship between the novel and the spread of silent reading, see Rosamaria Loretelli, *L'invenzione del romanzo. Dall'oralità alla lettura silenziosa* (Rome: Laterza, 2010), which locates the decisive turning point in the eighteenth century.

Heidegger launched in *Mythoscopia romantica,* directed against a certain way of reading fiction:

> Books of this type are constructed in such a way that they can't be read skipping from one spot to another; the entire *drama* has to be followed in its order. It is based on the uncontrolled human appetite for curiosity. The moment one starts (I'm talking about the simple-minded), one becomes greedy, one remains trapped in the net, one forgets about everything else only to reach the end of the book.[14]

In Gotthard Heidegger's view, narrative works should not arouse a form of illusion that leads to forgetting about everything; they should be read, instead, with the vigilance characteristic of readers who strive to grasp the hidden moral sense and to exercise their moral judgment on every page. This is a completely different habit of reading from what had been established over the previous two and a half centuries. Gotthard Heidegger asks what a certain action or a certain passion means when translated into its conceptual form, he submits plots and characters to a judgment, and he interprets works as *exempla.* In this extremist presentation, we find the trace of a common behavior that vanished. Until the second half of the eighteenth century, allegory was not an interpretive strategy for the learned: it was a *habitus,* a way of approaching texts that had become second nature. Suspense was the harbinger of new habits. Allegorical readers interpreted finite beings and their plots as signs of something else; they preferred a slow reading to allow the time to draw conclusions; they associated the meaning of the story with concepts and judgments, and they asked themselves: "What does this action mean?" "What general idea are the characters and story alluding to?" Readers who focus on suspense are immersed in the fictitious world created by the text. They identify with the heroes; they are intensely involved in their fates, and they ask themselves: "What are the past and future of this singular individual?" "What will become of him or her?" "How will it end?"[15] The polemic against the effects of the Greek novel and the chivalric romance was the sign that an aesthetic alternative to allegorism was beginning to emerge. Of course, identifying with the heroes of a story and suspense existed before this turning point, but these habits

14. Heidegger, *Mythoscopia romantica,* chap. 53.
15. Cave, "Pour une pré-histoire du suspens," 139.

were not the only ways of reading nor were they the most legitimate. More-over, the transition was not a sudden one, as becomes clear when we con-sider the strategies writers of *romances* and *novels* used while seeking to justify their works. Nevertheless, there was a clear direction. The readership of serious romances experimented with a form of reading, that, using Goethe's terms, would be called symbolic and not allegorical:

> There is a great difference whether a poet is looking for the particular that goes with the general, or sees the general in the particular. The first gives rise to allegory where the particular only counts as an example, an illustration of the particular; but the latter in fact constitutes the nature of poetry, expressing something particular without any thought of the general, and without indicating it. Now whoever has this living grasp of the particular is at the same time in possession of the general, without realizing it, or else only realizing it later on.[16]

It is significant that this reflection, published for the first time in the pe-riodical *Kunst und Altertum* in 1825, appeared at a time when modern literature was emancipating itself from moralism and the logic of the *ex-emplum.* Narrative fiction participated in this transformation, abandoning the web of codified hidden moral senses that until the second half of the eighteenth century had enveloped the stories of individuals, and directing readers' interest toward particular stories. At this stage in its history, the modern novel worked according to a symbolic logic, not an allegorical one. Allegorism would resurface only later, and in a very different form from the premodern one.

Heliodorus's suspense and *entrelacement* had another function as well, mirroring the one we have just discussed: they indicated a shift in narrative focus toward immanence, and at the same time provided the *Ge-stalten,* the schemata that enabled the stories of individuals inhabiting the immanence to become narratable. As long as the characters represent an idea, readers' interest (at least their intellectual interest) is guaranteed a priori, but when the characters signify only themselves, gaining the readers' interest becomes problematic. The difficulties we talked about in Chapter 3, which reached their mature expression in the preface to *Robinson Crusoe* or in the second preface to *The New Heloise,* now come to the fore: Why

---

16. Johann Wolfgang von Goethe, *Maximen und Reflexionen;* English translation *Maxims and Reflections,* trans. Elisabeth Stopp (London: Penguin Books, 1998), 34.

should we be concerned about the life of a simple, private person or about everyday things we can all see?

One of the ways to make the world of particular life more attractive is to resort to devices that captivate the reader. For a long period of time, the Western novel reused the techniques that the Greek novel and the courtly romance had made available. The technique of delaying information would be integrated into the architecture of the nineteenth-century realistic novel, constructed on a theatrical model. Take, for example, a scene that every Italian reader is familiar with:

> Two men were there, facing each other at the junction of the two paths. One sat astride the low wall, with one foot dangling over its outer surface, and the other resting on the solid ground of the track. His companion was standing slouched against the other wall, with his arms crossed over his chest. Their clothes, attitudes and what the curé could see of their faces at that distance left no doubt about what they were. Each of them wore a green hairnet, which hung down on his left shoulder, ending in a large tassel, while a huge quiff emerged from it in front to hang over his forehead. Each had long, pointed moustaches, a polished leather belt bearing two pistols, a small powder-horn hanging down on his chest like a pendant, a dagger the hilt of which stuck out of its special pocket in his wide and well-padded breeches, and a heavy sword with a great polished glittering guard composed of a network of narrow strips of bronze arranged in a sort of monogram. The first glance showed that they were members of the species known as bravoes.[17]

The appearance of the bravoes in *The Betrothed* is seen before it is understood. At the beginning of the twenty-first century we are rightly inclined to consider this mode of description typical of nineteenth-century realism and its pictorial-theatrical methods; nevertheless, the embryo of this technique remains the *Aethiopica*. Another legacy of Heliodorus is to be found in plots that play on the effect of delayed information. For example, only one-quarter of the way into the book does a reader of Balzac's *Père Goriot* (1835) understand what happened before the story starts—only then do we find out that, having been president of a section during the French Revolution, Goriot has

---

17. Alessandro Manzoni, *I promessi sposi* (1827, 1840–1842); English translation *The Betrothed*, trans. Bruce Penman (London: Penguin Classics, 1972), 28.

become an embarrassment to his daughters after the Restoration. Out of his love for them, he has decided to sacrifice himself.

The technique of *entrelacement* proved to be equally vital. In its simplest form, this device appears everywhere in the narrative tradition and modern cinema: it is used to create tension, interrupting the story at the moment of *Spannung* so as to leave readers anxious about the heroes' fates. However, *entrelacement* also lent itself to a less conspicuous but more structural use. It was an indispensable device for the nineteenth-century realistic novel and the modernist novel. It occupied a crucial place in the structure of individual texts, in the works of Scott as in Manzoni, in those of Tolstoy as in Hermann Broch. From Balzac on, it was used more extensively in the architecture of the great novelistic cycles. The first writer to apply this model of plot to the historical novel, Sir Walter Scott, explicitly acknowledged his debt to Ariosto:

> Like the digressive poet Ariosto, I find myself under the necessity of connecting the branches of my story.[18]

> The occasion of this interruption we can only explain by resuming the adventures of another set of our characters; for, like old Ariosto, we do not pique ourselves upon continuing uniformly to keep company with any one personage of our drama.[19]

There were intermediaries between Ariosto and Scott, the most important of which was *Tom Jones,* but the basic connection remains. The modern polyhistoric novel has a kinship with medieval *entrelacement,* based on a genealogy of some significance to which we will return.

The History of Private Lives

The center of gravity of European narrative was thus shifted by serious romance, which introduced heroes who fought for individual rather than collective aims, and concerned itself with the immanent destiny of people rather than with the universal meanings they were supposed to represent.

---

18. Sir Walter Scott, *The Heart of Mid-Lothian* (1818), vol. 2, ed. David Hewitt and Alison Lumsden (Edinburgh: Edinburgh University Press, 2004), chap. 3 [16], p. 143.

19. Sir Walter Scott, *Ivanhoe* (1820), vol. 2, ed. Graham Tulloch (Edinburgh: Edinburgh University Press, 1998), chap. 4 [17], p. 152. On the relationship between Scott and Ariosto, see Roberto Bigazzi, *Le risorse del romanzo* (Pisa: Nistri Lischi, 1996), 29ff.

However, this shift never fully manifested, because the characters of the *romance* were never like us. The transition became conspicuous only with the *novel* and its ordinary heroes.

Although mimesis is the discursive formation that expresses particular life in all its breadth and depth, ancient literature always kept its distance from pure particularity. Its detachment concerned both sides of this ontological dimension. In French they are combined into the double meaning of the word *particulier*—the equivalent of the English adjective *particular* and the term that signifies the condition of the private individual. The two planes are linked by a necessary dialectic: the more human life disappears from the sphere of public visibility, the more its degree of particularity increases.

The noble forms of Greek and Latin literature, *epos* and tragedy, tell stories about public characters (heroes, kings, mythological figures) and deeds that possess an evident general significance. For the rule of the separation of styles, everyday private life, the existence of people like us, is a topic reserved for the genres with a comic or intermediate register: the Old Comedy, the New Comedy, the iambic, the epigram, and satire. It is true that certain forms of the New Comedy and subjective poetry might employ serious registers. In this context, Pavel is right when he reproaches Auerbach for having associated under the same name of *Stiltrennung* the separation of styles in the proper sense and a corollary that should be treated separately. If we adopt the serious mimesis of private life as the sole criterion, then it could be said that Hellenistic novels and bucolic-pastoral literature preceded the realism of Balzac and Stendhal by nearly two thousand years. It could also be said that long before novels, plays, and modern poems, the New Comedy and Horatian-style lyric poetry recounted the private affairs of private individuals—in the intermediate or noble styles, but in any case in a serious tone.[20] What distinguishes the forms of noncomic mimesis of everyday life that we encounter in Greek and Latin literature from the forms that the realism of the past two centuries has made familiar to us is not so much the dignity of the register as the tendency to select the facts of reality through a filter that refines contingencies, idealizes details, and introduces the anarchy of the real into the laws of a literary genre. Up until a certain time, it seemed as if the conquest of a noncomic

20. See Pavel, *L'Art de l'eloignement*, 273–274.

tone in the representation of *particuliers* had caused a distance to be taken from their actual particularity. Ancient lyric, epigrammatic, or elegiac poetry was able to give voice to an I that spoke seriously about itself, but only on condition that the first person channeled the difference of its biography into the collective conventions of the chosen genre.[21] In the same way, the literary form that ancient poetics delegated to represent the variety of characters and manners in tones that might spill over the confines of the comic, namely, the New Comedy, brought particular life back to general, ahistorical types.[22]

While the classicism of the Ancien Régime had relegated serious story-telling about particular individuals to historiography, in the second half of the 1600s the idea spread that the tradition of the *novel* was a "history of private life": Charles Sorel used a similar formula with regard to *novelle, novelas,* and *nouvelles;* Charnes applied it to *The Princesse de Clèves.*[23] Seventy years later, this idea had become a topos and Fielding had transformed it into a principle of poetics.[24] Between the mid-sixteenth century and the mid-eighteenth, the aggregate of texts that would be called *novels* helped to introduce a multitude of private persons and accidental qualities into European culture. This was a conspicuous and revolutionary innovation, because it covered a relatively sparsely populated territory and because the discursive gap into which the *novel* fit was not confined solely to literature.

A Discursive Gap

For several centuries now our culture has possessed several types of conceptual knowledge that accurately map the region of particularity: historiography has opened itself to describing the private sphere; the "human sciences" analyze, classify, and record ways of being individuals; reflection

---

21. I have spoken about this more extensively in Guido Mazzoni, *Sulla poesia moderna* (Bologna: Il Mulino, 2005), 105ff.

22. Auerbach, *Mimesis,* 31.

23. Charles Sorel, *La Bibliothèque françoise: seconde édition revue et augmentée* (1667) (Geneva: Slatkine, 1970), 178ff.; Charnes, *Conversations sur la critique de la Princesse de Clèves.*

24. Fielding, *The History of Tom Jones,* bk. 2, chap. 1 and bk. 8, chap. 1.

on the forms of everyday life has become a central theme of contemporary philosophy. But although these disciplines have acquired tremendous importance over the past two hundred years, the region of particularity long occupied a smaller space in the official discourses of European culture. The gray area encompassed both history and philosophy. Classical historiography was divided by a clash between the model of Herodotus, focused on geography and ethnography, and the model of Thucydides, focused on reporting the great political events of his time.[25] That of Thucydides prevailed, and with it the conviction that the *res gestae* of public men were more important than the cultural history of peoples. One of the phenomena that cut across disciplines and changed modern philosophy is what Habermas called the positioning (*Situierung*) of reason in circumstances, the idea that a thought is not unconditional, but rather stems from forces external to it that are rooted in the social or instinctual life.[26] The "school of suspicion" arose out of this process: out of the conviction that consciousness is not what determines material conditions (or unconscious forces); rather, material conditions (or unconscious forces) determine consciousness, according to a schema of thought that attacks the foundations of Western metaphysics, starting from its most important assumption—that abstract thought can conquer truths that are independent from their circumstances. It is no coincidence that contemporary philosophical discourse has become more and more welcoming to other disciplines, such as the human sciences, which are founded on the opposite assumption—on the systematic positioning of thought. Another effect of these discursive formations is the analytical reflection on the changeability and multiplicity of life that they introduce into the sphere of conceptual knowledge: to situate people means to effectively replace the unitary, abstract subject of Western metaphysics with a plurality of different subjects (social classes, psychological types, cultural groups, genders), distinguished and described by the human sciences.

25. Arnaldo Momigliano, "Il posto di Erodoto nella storia della storiografia" (1958), in *La storiografia greca* (Turin: Einaudi, 1982), 138–155; also by Momigliano, *The Classical Foundations of Modern Historiography* (Berkeley: University of California Press, 1990), chap. 2.

26. Jürgen Habermas, *Nachmetaphysisches Denken. Philosophische Aufsätze* (1988); English translation *Postmetaphysical Thinking*, trans. William Mark Hohengarten (Cambridge, MA: MIT Press, 1993), 6ff. and chap. 3.

Until the early modern age, reflection on the plurality of forms of life was a peripheral topic for European philosophy, whose essential core was occupied with "things that are forever in the same state, without anything mixed in it."[27] Philosophers ignored the perpetual dislocation that history and geography have introduced into thought during the last few centuries. Even though reflection on characters and manners that Aristotle introduced with his *Rhetoric* and the *Nicomachean Ethics,* continued by Theophrastus with his *Characters,* was a decisive factor for the prehistory of contemporary human sciences,[28] this approach never had the weight that sociology, cultural anthropology, and ethnography acquired in the modern era. Only during the sixteenth century did European culture begin with renewed attention to concern itself with particular life. This was a profound, geological transformation that advanced slowly for more than two hundred years. It accompanied the birth of the novel; it changed the orography of the discursive space; it made its way through every discipline, reaching maturity with the development of the nineteenth-century "human sciences." However, its beginnings date back to the 1500s, when geographical discoveries and the first colonial empires changed the horizon of the known world, and when historiography recovered the model of Herodotus with its geographic and multicultural elements.[29] Humanistic philology had already introduced an early form of cultural anthropology, of ethnography, when it studied the Greek and Roman culture as a vanished world to be brought back to life using antiquarian methods.[30] Montaigne reflected at length on the psychology, manners, and protean changeability of particular life as well as on the rooting of thought in circumstances. His legacy intersected with the rediscovery of Theophrastus that took place between the end of the sixteenth century and the beginning of the seventeenth, with Casaubon's edition of *Characters* and the development of the "character" as a literary genre, inaugurating

---

27. Plato, *Philebus* 59b–c.

28. See Carnevali, "L'Observatoire des moeurs: les coutumes et les caractères, entre littérature et morale," 159–178; and by the same author, "Mimesis littéraire et connaissance morale: la tradition de l'éthopée,'" 291–322.

29. Momigliano, "Il posto di Erodoto nella storia della storiografia."

30. Claude Lévi-Strauss, "Les trois humanismes" (1956); English translation "Answers to Some Investigations (The Three Humanisms)," in *Structural Anthropology,* vol. 2, trans. Monique Layton (Chicago: University of Chicago Press, 1983), 271–287.

a tradition of thought that continued until the French moralists.[31] The birth of the novel as the history of the private individual and the early developmental stages of the European human sciences were contemporary phenomena.

But despite the emergence of conceptual forms of knowledge that reflect on the plurality of forms of life, for a long time the novel maintained an advantage in the mimesis of the particular. Up until 1890, writes Arnold Gehlen, the gap between the psychological fertility of narrative and the inflexibility of scientific psychology still appeared to be insurmountable.[32] Even if we tone down his opinion and adjust his dates, a similar observation can be extended to the rest of the human sciences. In 1800, to know "how people were bored in London, when to be bored was the fashion," Friedrich Schlegel could not count on a work of history that could stand up to comparison with the novels of Fanny Burney, or on the discipline that a few decades later Auguste Comte would call "sociology." Up until an indeterminate moment in the nineteenth century, with a chronology that varies from discipline to discipline, the gap between the mimetic accuracy of the novel and the descriptive poverty of the other forms of knowledge remained substantial. The authors of the first modern historical novels who at the beginning of the nineteenth century proclaimed the originality of their writing were not simply promoting themselves: when Scott, in the first pages of *Ivanhoe* (1820), wrote that historians have only cursorily dwelt on private life, or when Manzoni, in his *Discorso sur alcuni punti della storia longobardica in Italia* (Discussion on some points concerning the history of the Lombards in Italy) (1822), wrote that millions of ordinary people have spent their lives on the earth without a historian recording

---

31. Boyce, *The Theophrastan Character in England to 1642*, chap. 2; Smeed, *The Theophrastan "Character"*; Louis Van Delft, *Le Moraliste classique: essai de définition et de typologie* (Geneva: Droz, 1982); also by Van Delft: *Littérature et anthropologie: nature humaine et caractère à l'âge classique* (Paris: PUF, 1993), *Frammento e anatomia. Rivoluzione scientifica e creazione letteraria* (Bologna: Il Mulino, 2004), and *Les Spectateurs de la vie: généalogie du regard moraliste* (Quebec: Les Presses de l'Université Laval, 2005); Carnevali, "L'Observatoire des moeurs" and "Mimesis littéraire et connaissance morale."

32. Arnold Gehlen, *Die Seele im technischen Zeitalter: Sozialpsychologische Probleme in den industriellen Gesellschaft* (1957); English translation *Man in the Age of Technology*, trans. Patricia Lipscomb (New York: Columbia University Press, 1980), chap. 7.

their existence,[33] the two novelists were expressing opinions that many others in their epoch might have shared. A novelist of our times would not feel as confident in voicing these ideas. In the early decades of the nineteenth century, the region of human particularities could still seem unexplored, or badly explored; today it is saturated with discourses. Between the 1500s and the 1800s, the tradition of the *novel* filled a relatively empty space.

The first subgenre to occupy this territory was the medieval *novella:* in *The Decameron* we find "the first great, organic narrative representation of contemporary society."[34] While it is true that many Italian *novelle* remained confined within the boundaries of the comic, and therefore did not violate the traditional hierarchies, it is equally true that some texts went beyond the limits of the *Stiltrennung.* In the history of Lisabetta da Messina or in the "tragic histories" circulating autonomously between the sixteenth and seventeenth centuries, for example, the genre of the *novella* went beyond the separation of styles to recount the history of private lives in a serious manner. What made this rupture possible?

The first aspect to be considered is the dialectical relationship that *novelle, novelas,* and even *nouvelles* and the *conte philosophique* had with the genres of Christian allegorism. Up until the second half of the eighteenth century, as we have seen, the particular stories that the tradition of the *novel* told referred to a framework of ideas and ethical rules that transcended individual lives. We find them in titles, in frame tales, in prefaces, in the way of constructing characters and the plot, in the act of extracting the universal *sensus* from the *narratio* of the individual case. The balance between meaning and story changed over time: Boccaccio was an innovator partly because he extended the autonomy of the story to the detriment of the meaning. He did so by writing *novelle* that, thanks to the wealth of details and the autonomy of the characters, were able to describe bare peculiarities.[35] However, the narrative structures of *The Decameron* still remain

---

33. Alessandro Manzoni, *Discorso sur alcuni punti della storia longobardica in Italia* (1822), in *Tutte le opere,* vol. 3, *Opere morali e filosofiche,* ed. Alberto Chiari and Fausto Ghisalberti (Milan: Mondadori, 1963), chap. 2, pp. 194–211.

34. Vittore Branca, "Una chiave di lettura per il *Decameron,*" in Giovanni Boccaccio, *Decameron,* ed. Vittore Branca (Turin: Einaudi, 1987).

35. See Hans-Jörg Neuschäfer, *Boccaccio und der Beginn der Novelle* (Munich: Fink, 1969).

clearly linked to the rhetoric of the *exemplum,* which persists in the frame
tales, in the thematic organization of the material, in the titles of the stories, as well as in the habit of connecting the particular events to general
categories or maxims.

In addition to still depending on Christian allegorical rhetoric, the *novella* was also a short narrative form. In this case, the length of the story is
not a marginal aspect: for a long time, private life could be recounted only
if it was captured in a momentary state of exception. If discontinuity is inscribed in the logic of narrative insomuch as narrative is a language game,
all the more reason for this to be true for the *novella:* the *casus* that is its
raison d'être is explicitly or implicitly surrounded by a long period of time
devoid of significant events. According to Goethe, *die Novelle* tells the story
of an "unprecedented event."[36] It is a genre that, like classical historiography or modern event-based historiography, imagines reality as a static
surface interrupted by some ripples, which are then the only things worth
talking about.[37] The events recounted jut out from the expanse of life, to
use an expression by Ernesto De Martino;[38] they focus on the *res gestae*
that escape from the cyclic order. But because the ordinary existence of
common people does not jut out except in a few states of exception, novellas tend to be short. Hence, instead of telling about ordinary life, the
genre reports on the *casus*—the moment when ordinary life escapes from
repetition and acquires a story. As we shall see, the modern novel would
go beyond the limits of the *novella* to eventually narrate the entire destinies of people like us. In any case, private life began to enter the discursive
space in the West thanks to this genre. This was a crucial achievement, and
not for literature alone.

36. Johann Peter Eckermann, *Gespräche mit Goethe in den letzten Jahren seines Lebens,*
ed. Heinz Schlaffer (Munich: Carl Hanser, 1986), January 29, 1829, p. 203.

37. Fernand Braudel, "Histoire et sciences sociales: la longue durée" (1958); English
translation "History and the Social Sciences: The *Longue Durée,*" in *On History,* trans. Sarah
Matthews (Chicago: University of Chicago Press, 1982), 25–54.

38. "What is *history?* An event that 'juts out'; that reveals itself, that rises above routine,
and that in various ways also forces presence to rise above routine, to engage in a single
mental and practical behavior that is individual, completely adapted, and integrated." Ernesto
De Martino, "I fondamenti di una teoria del sacro," in *Storia e metastoria,* ed. Marcello Mas-
senzio (Lecce: Argo, 1995), 128–129.

The Pathos of Proximity

This shift in interest toward what lies close to us was accompanied by a new outlook on life and a new idea of beauty. Well before Friedrich Schlegel juxtaposed the "historical" subjects of Boccaccio to the mythical-legendary subjects of ancient poetry, the works that belonged to the tradition of the *novel* became filled with a commonplace that had already appeared in the rhetoric of the *exemplum*. One of the first to reintroduce it was Montaigne: "Even the life of Caesar is less exemplary for us than our own; a life whether imperial or plebeian is always a life affected by everything that can happen to a man."[39] For the purposes of moral reflection, all lives are equally worthy: the biography of an emperor is just as valuable as that of any other person. Observations of this kind proliferated at the end of the seventeenth century and into the eighteenth. There was growing acknowledgment that reading about people who are similar to us is more pleasurable; or it was argued that morality is better transmitted when stories tell about heroes with whom readers can identify:

> You certainly have been more amused listening to a story that unfolded in places you ordinarily frequent than to another in which all the events were located in other places. Nevertheless, many who do not know this secret offer you only the most faraway stories, which can never touch the heart so deeply, and they are mistaken thinking they are doing right by this, often disguising what has happened in our country and dressing it up in foreign costume.[40]

> The counselor said that nothing could be more diverting than our modern romances; that the French alone knew how to write good ones; however, that the Spaniards had a peculiar talent to compose little stories, which they called *novelas*, which are more useful and more probable patterns for us to follow than those imaginary heroes of antiquity.[41]

---

39. Michel de Montaigne, *Essais* (1580–1595); English translation *The Complete Essays*, trans. Michael A. Screech (London: Penguin, 1991), bk. 3, chap. 13, p. 1218

40. Charles Sorel, *Les Nouvelles françaises* (1623) (Geneva: Slatkine Reprints, 1972), 358–359.

41. Paul Scarron, *Le Roman comique* (1651–57); English translation *The Comic Romance of Monsieur Scarron*, trans. Oliver Goldsmith, 2 vols. (London: Printed for W. Griffin, in Catharine Street, Strand, 1775), 1:230–231.

How many adventures, resumed Alpanice, have we come to know about that, had they been written, would be anything but displeasing? ... [S]ince things are written either to entertain or to instruct, what need is there for all the examples that are offered to be of kings or emperors, as they are in all the *Romans?* Will a private individual who reads them perhaps model his deeds on those who have armies at their bidding?[42]

This commonplace abounds during the 1700s: stories about people like us are more instructive or more interesting than stories about the extraordinary heroes of antiquity:

The lives of private men, though they afford not examples that fill the mind with ideas of greatness and power like those of princes ..., yet are they such as are more open to common imitation.[43]

History is a relation of the most natural and important events: history therefore gratifies curiosity, but it does not often excite either terror or pity; nor is it so much alarmed at the migration of barbarians who mark their way with desolation, and fill the world with violence and rapine, as at the fury of a husband, who deceived into jealousy by false appearances, stabs a faithful and affectionate wife, kneeling at his feet, and pleading to be heard.[44]

The misfortune of those whose circumstances most resemble our own must naturally penetrate most deeply into our hearts, and if we pity kings, we pity them as human beings rather than as kings. Though their position often renders their misfortunes more important, it does not make them more interesting. Whole nations may be involved in them, but our sympathy requires an individual object, and a state is far too much an abstract conception to touch our feelings.[45]

The most applauded French *romans* generally represent only the illustrious actions of illustrious people; every detail of their private lives is forbidden; those who speak are heroes, beings who have neither our

42. Segrais, *Les Nouvelles françaises ou les Divertissements de la princesse Aurélie,* 21.

43. William Ayre, preface to *Memoirs of the Life and Writings of Alexander Pope* (1750), cited in Hunter, *Before Novels,* 350.

44. John Hawkesworth, in *The Adventurer,* no. 4 (Saturday, November 18, 1752), 20.

45. Gotthold Ephraim Lessing, *Hamburgische Dramaturgie* (1767); English translation *Hamburg Dramaturgy,* with a new introduction by Victor Lange, (New York: Dover, 1962), vol. 1, chap. 14, 38–39.

needs, our way of living, our vices, nor our virtues. . . . [In Richardson's *Clarissa*] we see a virtuous person, but who comes from our same conditions, suffer with an admirable purity and constancy. The misfortunes of an Ariane do not move me; those of the Princesse de Clèves move me only slightly. These heroes are too dissimilar from me; their misfortunes have no relationship with those that might move me. I feel that it is a fairy tale—and from that moment on it no longer moves me.[46]

The high and low, as they have the same faculties and the same senses, have no less similitude in their pains and pleasures. The sensations are the same in all, tho' produced by very different occasions. The prince feels the same pain when an invader seizes a province, as the farmer when a thief drives away his cow. Men thus equal in themselves will appear equal in honest and impartial biography; and those whom fortune or nature place at the greatest distance may afford instruction to each other.[47]

This author does not send blood flowing down the walls, he does not transport you to distant lands, he does not expose you to being eaten by savages, he does not confine himself with the secret haunts of debauchery, he never wanders off into the world of fantasy. The world we live in is his scene of action, his drama is anchored in truth, his people are as real as it is possible to be, his characters are taken from the world of society, his events belong to the customs of all civilized nations; the passions he portrays are those I feel within me.[48]

The pathos of proximity that fuels the new genres of modern literature is a sign. The *novel*, the *drama bourgeois*, and modern poetry attach the utmost importance to the experiences of individuals like us; the major forms of ancient and classicist literature are instead shot through by an equal and opposing pathos of distance. The *Stiltrennung*, as we have said, implies three things: that there is a hierarchy of subject matters; that the

---

46. Albrecht von Haller, review of *Clarissa* by Samuel Richardson, *Bibliothèque raisonnee des ouvrages des savans de l'Europe*, vol. 42 (January–March 1749), part 1, pp. 326–333.

47. Samuel Johnson, *Idler*, no. 84 (Saturday, November 24, 1759), in *The Yale Edition of the Works of Samuel Johnson*, vol. 2, *The Idler and The Adventurer*, ed. Walter Jackson Bate, John Marshall Bullitt, and Lawrence Fitzroy Powell (New Haven, CT: Yale University Press, 1963), 263.

48. Denis Diderot, *Éloge de Richardson* (1762); English translation "In Praise of Richardson," in *Selected Writings on Art and Literature*, trans. and with an introduction by Geoffrey Bremner (London: Penguin, 1994), 80–97; quote from p. 83.

register of the style must correspond to the rank of the subject matter; that the noble genres should tell stories about public heroes legitimated by communal history, sacred history, mythology, or legend. In *epos* and tragedy, the past and the repertoire are what counts; in modern poetry, theater, and novels, what counts are the present and close experiences. A prince who sees his province being invaded experiences the same pain as a farmer who sees his cow being stolen: the tradition of the *novel* explores these passions as if they were both of the utmost importance.

The Interesting

Along with the pathos of proximity, an aesthetic category that accompanied the development of the modern novel began to gain ground: the *interesting*. The concept took form in the debates that followed the appearance of *The Princesse de Clèves*. In the most radical pamphlet, Du Plaisir's *Sentiments sur l'histoire,* the concept appears in two crucial passages:

> We are hardly curious about unknown centuries and countries; contrariwise, we are curious about those that are scarcely foreign to us; and unquestionably, between two stories that are equally fashioned, one of which contains all the events that happened in France in recent centuries, and the other all the events that happened in Greece or during the first lineage of our kings, the latter will be infinitely less interesting.[49]

> The chief and natural goal of these types of works is to make known to us the fortunes of the characters (*acteurs*) or to spark our interest in them.[50]

In reality, all the remarks on the pathos of proximity we have cited thus far contain a similar idea, expressed implicitly or explicitly. In the mid-eighteenth century, the interesting became the law governing the new province of writing that Fielding claimed to have founded: "Nor do I doubt, while I make their interest the great rule of my writings, [my readers] will unanimously concur in supporting my dignity, and in rendering me all the honour I shall deserve or desire."[51]

---

49. Du Plaisir, *Sentiments sur les lettres et sur l'histoire, avec des scrupules sur le style,* 65.
50. Ibid., 64.
51. Fielding, *The History of Tom Jones,* 78.

Diderot was one of the first to transform the category into a topic of reflection.[52] At the end of the eighteenth century, the interesting had become a cornerstone of the Romantic aesthetic. In his essay *On the Study of Greek Poetry* (1797), Friedrich Schlegel sought to establish the general sense of the changes that European literature had undergone during the previous two centuries. He contrasted ancient poetry, which he says preserves a mythological core and pursues the ideal of eternal beauty, to modern poetry, which deals with historical themes and attempts to make itself interesting to the people who live in the present time, knowing that it might not speak with the same intensity to those who will live in the future.

While the task of reconstructing the history of the concept in all its eighteenth- and nineteenth-century ramifications is beyond me, I would like to reflect on its theoretical significance. The official literature of the Ancien Régime requires the knowledge of a tradition in order to be understood. A class of literary professionals or semiprofessionals kept alive the literature of an era two thousand years distant; they published editions of ancient texts and composed works inspired by Greek and Latin poetry. While the noble genres of the Ancien Régime rested on the past, the pathos of proximity and the concept of the interesting marked a rupture: some groups of writers and readers, partially or totally unconnected to the repertoires and rules, demanded a taste founded on the present, on contemporary topics, and on the effect the work produced in the here and now. This was a sign that the historicity of all things was penetrating into the domain of art, forever weakening classical faith in the eternity of canons.[53] The concept of the interesting contained the most violent attack ever launched against the idea of Beauty as conceived by Plato and as it had become incorporated into ancient poetry. Aesthetic value became subject to time and circumstances; shortly afterward, the ideas of the True and the Good would suffer the same fate. Historicist relativism entered into European culture by way of the artistic sphere.

52. See Peter Brooks, *The Melodramatic Imagination: Balzac, Henry James, Melodrama, and the Mode of Excess* (New Haven, CT: Yale University Press, 1976), 13.

53. Ibid.; and Giovanna Rosa, *Il patto narrativo. La fondazione della civiltà romanzesca in Italia* (Milan: Il Saggiatore, 2008), 24ff.

The Novel's Readership

So far I have avoided tackling the sociological theme, which is a recurring one in studies on the origin of the novel. A commonplace of literary theory links the development of the genre with the rise of a middle-class public. We know that the novel grew along with the increase in books and readers, but we also know that the new readers were in no way homogeneous. Each national literature has its own history. In the two countries that most contributed to the rise of the novel between the 1600s and the 1700s, France and England, the revived readership was a much bigger factor for England than it was for France:[54] in French literature the appearance of the aristocratic novel preceded the arrival of the bourgeois novel.[55] Furthermore, the subgenres making up the novel were addressed to different classes of readers. *Nouvelles* and *histoires secrètes,* for example, came into being in the aristocratic milieu during the time of Louis XIV: their subject matters (amorous intrigues in the world of the court), their form (lacking any extreme drops in register), their way of representing the interior life (marked by a psychology of Augustinian origin) would have been inconceivable outside of this society. This is the same group of readers that only a few decades earlier had been avidly reading heroic Baroque novels.[56] The novels of Richardson and Fielding, on the contrary, were also intended for the new readership created by the growth of literacy in England.[57] And yet, when

54. There is an enormous bibliography on the social composition of readers of novels, romances, and *romans* in France and England. The two best overviews, in my opinion, are by Hunter, *Before Novels,* chap. 3, and Esmein-Sarrazin, *L'Essor du roman,* passim. For Italy, the best source is by Alberto Cadioli, *La storia finta. Il romanzo e i suoi lettori nei dibattiti di primo Ottocento* (Milan: Il Saggiatore, 2001), "Introduzione."

55. See DiPiero, *Dangerous Truths and Criminal Passions,* chap. 1, "The Rise of Aristocratic Fiction," and passim. On the expansion of the French reading public during the late eighteenth century, see François Furet and Mona Ozouf, *Lire et écrire: l'alphabétisation des Français, de Calvin à Jules Ferry,* vol. 1 (Paris: Minuit, 1977), 46–57 and passim; Daniel Roche, *Le Peuple de Paris: essai sur la culture populaire au XVIIIe siècle* (1981) (Paris: Fayard, 1998), 271–320; Roger Chartier and Henri-Jean Martin, eds., *Historie de l'édition française,* vol. 2 (Paris: Promodis, 1984), 218–230, 402–429; Reinhard Wittmann, "Une révolution de la lecture à la fin du XVIIIe siècle," in *Histoire de la lecture dans le monde occidental,* ed. Giovanni Cavallo and Roger Chartier (Paris: Seuil, 1997), 331–364.

56. DiPiero, Introduction to *Dangerous Truths and Criminal Passions.*

57. Hunter, *Before Novels,* chap. 3.

we contextualize these highly diverse groups by locating them in the cultural spaces of their time, we come to realize that the readers of novels are linked by a homology of position. Ugo Foscolo pinpointed this with great clarity in 1803:

> History, eloquence, sublime tragedy and poetry, and the epic poem are commodities for this sort of men. Because they spend all their time communing with the writings of the ancients and reading about the affairs of past ages, they can only understand high literature and in a certain way they divorce themselves from their own times. . . . But *novelle* and *romanzi* were never written for men of letters, nor do these productions gain literary prestige except for their antiquity. This is why Boccaccio himself considered his least worthy production, which he says was written in a completely vulgar tongue, the very *Decameron* that is venerated by Italians as an example for all styles. . . . *Novelle* and *romanzi* are made for that large number of people who occupy the space between idiots and men of letters.[58]

The noble literary genres of the Ancien Régime were understandable as long as there existed an audience that valued traditional stories and the conventional forms. Although belonging to different social groups, readers of *novelle, novelas, nouvelles, mémoires, histoires,* or English *novels* of the early eighteenth century had no interest in the literary repertoire. They were interested in the present, or in a recent past that resembled the present. A princess who feels attracted to a man other than her husband and a merchant who is shipwrecked on a deserted island live in different worlds; but when we compare their stories to the adventures of Theagenes or Chariclea, we realize that the internal logics of their microcosms resemble each other: the adventures of Madame de Clèves and Robinson Crusoe still maintain a relationship with the reality principle on which private individuals base their lives, while those of Theagenes and Chariclea do not. Although their customs and cultures were extremely different, the readers of Madame de La Fayette and Defoe were attracted by fictional worlds that reminded them of their own lifeworlds. Expressed in the terms of art criticism, we might say that an ignorance of iconography is allowed for readers of novels: the text can be understood without knowledge of

---

58. Foscolo, "Saggio di novelle di Luigi Sanvitale parmigiano," 263–264.

the literary past. The readership of the new genre, wrote Foscolo, stood "between idiots and men of letters": these readers were educated but nonspecialists. They were equidistant from the mass of illiterate people and the narrow circle of those who continued to face backward toward the classicist past.

Another commonplace of literary sociology ties the development of the novel to a female readership. As we know, the novel was long associated with women: in the literary debates of the Ancien Régime, the association was so widespread that it became proverbial. There is some reality to this: a substantial portion of the texts that ended up in the genre of the novel (from medieval narrative to the epistolary narrative of the seventeenth century, from *The Decameron* to Jane Austen) was written, in actuality or in name, for women. In this case, too, what counts is the similarity of position in the social space: female readers were unfamiliar with the literary tradition or tended to ignore it, and they were relegated to living in the existential sphere that the new genre explored—that of private life. The bond between the novel and female readership is ideological before it is sociological.

Particular Life

We have seen how the rise of the novel, in the broad theoretical sense of the term, was part of a wider transformation between the 1500s and the 1700s that led European culture to pay renewed attention to forms of life and their historical, social, and geographical mutability. We have also seen that for a long time the novel maintained a sort of primacy in describing private life. This happened for two reasons: private life was the main subject of the novel; and the novel took advantage of the organic connection with the sphere of contingency that is immanent to narrative as a form. Plots tell about finite beings endowed with qualities that identify them (a proper name, a body, a character, manners), situated in an environment, and subject to change: beings whose own lives intersect with the lives of others through action, speech, thought, and passions until the imbalance that drives this mechanism is righted and the story reaches its end. Each one of the elements involved in the existential analytics implicit in a plot is potentially charged with multiplicity.

1. The novel is the genre of *proper names, stories, and personal destinies.* Thanks to the novel, the space that European culture dedicated to individuals experienced tremendous growth. The multiplicity of particulars spilled over into the internal structure of the works. A symptom of this process was the device of *entrelacement.* During the 1500s, as we have said, the call to unity of action became filled with hidden moral senses: it meant the possibility of interpreting mythos as an allegory for something else; it meant that, instead of the story being broken up and dispersed into streams of captivating, centrifugal stories, it was expected to remain faithful to a single, large undertaking with an exemplary status. The plots of chivalric romances went in the opposite direction, toward the dispersion of personal aims and destinies.[59] Picked up again by Fielding and then by Scott, *entrelacement* was transmitted to the historical and social novel of the nineteenth century.

But the proliferation of individuals also had a subjective side. In addition to multiplying the number of personal stories, the novel also increased the variety of consciousnesses who revealed their worlds through writing. This is what happened to humorous narrative of the eighteenth century: Friedrich Schlegel had this subgenre in mind when he defined the novel as "a more or less veiled confession of the author, the profit of his experience, the quintessence of his originality."[60] Humorous narrative had a critical role in Hegel's theory of modern art as well. One of the two lines of development that the *Aesthetics* foresaw in contemporary works (to show "the liberation of subjectivity, in accordance with its inner contingency"[61]) was perfectly expressed in works like *Tristram Shandy* or *Jacques the Fatalist.*

2. The second type of multiplicity explored by the novel regarded the *plurality of environments and forms of life.* The interest that noble genres from the culture of antiquity reserved for the variety of characters, manners, and contexts was very limited compared to what has occurred in the literature of recent centuries.[62] Tragedy enacts rituals taking place in a time and space divorced from contingency; the epic poem depicts conflicts between peoples

59. Quint, *Epic and Empire*, 31ff.
60. Schlegel, *Dialogue on Poetry*, 103.
61. Hegel, *Aesthetics*, vol.1, p. 608.
62. Auerbach, *Mimesis*, 319ff.

and cultures, but the specific difference between those peoples and cultures is never explored in depth. Instead, many of the subgenres that converged into the novel had a historical-ethnographic component, starting with Hellenistic narrative. At the beginning of the *Aethiopica,* the mysterious young woman and man who are found alive in the midst of a massacre are led by a group of brigands into the region of Bucolia, which is briefly described by the narrator:

> The whole tract, called by the Egyptians The Pasturage [Bucolia], is a sunken valley in which an influx from the overflow of the Nile forms a lake. The middle of this lake is of unfathomable depth; around the edges it shoals into a marsh. What shores are to the sea, marshes are to lakes. Here the brigands of Egypt maintain their existence. One lives on a bit of land that rises above the water, where he builds a hut; another spends his life aboard a boat, which serves at once as transportation and living quarters. On the boat the women work their wool and bear their babies. After the babies are weaned from their mother's milk they are fed on fish from the lake which are roasted in the sun. When the baby shows signs of creeping, they tie a thong to his ankle which permits him to go the length of the boat or of the hut. The string on his ankle is a novel kind of tutor.[63]

From here on, the movements of Theagenes and Chariclea are almost always accompanied by short descriptions of the places they visit. The regions that the characters pass through are not realistic, but what counts is the intellectual gesture: the narrator recognizes that traveling the world means encountering different forms of life. The Greek novel situates its main subject matter—the love and adventure plot—before a hazy but persistent historical, geographical, and ethnographic backdrop.

Arriving by its own route, the Italian *novella* also included this descriptive element in its structure. Some of the *novelle* in *The Decameron* dwell on differences between social classes: for example, in order for the story of Cisti the baker to be told, the social distance separating a rich baker from someone with the title of Messer must also be described, no matter how fledgling the attempt. Arriving by its own route as well, the Spanish picaresque novel also went into the details of social conditions:

---

63. Heliodorus, *An Ethiopian Romance,* translated with an introduction by Moses Hadas (Philadelphia: University of Pennsylvania Press, 1999), 6.

My father, God rest his soul, was in charge of a windmill on the river-bank. He worked for over fifteen years. My mother was pregnant with me, ready to give birth, and one night I came onto this world right there, so I can say I was truly born on the river.

Now when I was eight years old, my father was caught stealing from the sacks belonging to the mill. He was arrested and confessed, denying nothing. He was prosecuted and punished by law. . . . There was a campaign against the Moors in those years and my father took part in it, since he was already living away as part of the sentence. He went as a mule driver for a gentleman that went to the campaign. His life ended when he and this gentleman were killed.

My widowed mother, finding herself without a husband and without shelter, opted to approach some wealthy patrons and thus came to live in the city with one of them. She began to cook for certain students and to wash clothes for the stable boys of the Comendador of La Magdalena. So she hung about the stables.[64]

Cervantes was the first to combine the traditions of the Hellenistic novel, the comic romance, the *novella,* and the picaresque novel. His works describe forms of life: soldiers, literati, Turks, or actors in *Don Quixote* (1.38; 1.40; 2.11); gypsies in *The Little Gypsy Girl;* the Turks in *The Generous Lover;* basket-carriers in *Rinconete and Cortadillo;* soldiers in *The Licentiate Vidriera,* and so on. Sometimes the descriptions are quite detailed; at other times they create what in painterly terms would be called a sketch or a genre scene. Regardless of how successful he was in these attempts, Cervantes understood that a narrator could not ignore the fact that reality is divided into social circles—the segmentation of the world into worlds. Thanks to the Spanish picaresque novel and *novelas,* this sensibility was transmitted to the French *nouvelles* (*Les Illustres Françaises* by Challe, for example), to the English *novel,* and to the French *roman* of the eighteenth century.

3. The attention paid to *the multiplicity of sceneries and objects* was part of the interest in the variety of environments. This lingering over backgrounds and details is a recent phenomenon in the history of literature. Classicist poetics discouraged the descriptive forms that took root with the

---

64. *The Life of Lazarillo de Tormes, His Fortunes and Adversities,* trans. and ed. Ilan Stavans (New York: W. W. Norton, 2016), 5.

birth of the modern realistic novel. The reasons for this, in line with what we read in Aristotle, is that mimesis was intended as an imitation of people in action and not of the circumstances surrounding them. Furthermore, classic poetics forbade the writer to dwell on minutiae that did not directly contribute to plot development. Roland Barthes calls these details "reality effects."[65] What he means by this are purely contingent notations extraneous to the economy of the story line that, precisely because of their gratuitous contingency, seem to say to the reader, "The only reason we were included in the text is our empirical truth": *"we are the real."*[66]

However, extended reflection on the invention of this device started more than two centuries before Barthes. The first texts in praise of details can be found in a historical type of narrative that converged into the novel: in *Don Quixote,* for example, the narrator tells us that Cide Hamete Benengeli is a careful, accurate historian because he also dwells on inconsequential things.[67] But the event that triggered an out-and-out polemic on the topic was the French translation of *Pamela.* The English novel with the greatest wealth of detail clashed with the most classicist of European literary cultures. There may have been several reasons why Richardson did not appeal to the French, but one of those most mentioned was the abundance of minute details. The translation by Prévost, which simplified or cut passages that were loaded with details, is the symptom of a difference in taste. The Abbé Marquet, who contributed to the debate with his *Lettre sur Pamela* (1742), found certain descriptions to be long-winded. The episode in which Pamela leaves Mrs. Jervis, for example, contains a boring list that has "the air of an inventory."[68] Two decades later, Diderot overturned the arguments used by his fellow countrymen in reaction to *Pamela,* writing that the illusion of truth created by the works of Richardson arises precisely from the skill with which objects and surroundings are presented.[69] This is one of the first times that the reality effect was theorized. It would fall to the founder of the nineteenth-century historical novel,

65. Roland Barthes, "L'Effet de réel" (1968); English translation "The Reality Effect," in *The Rustle of Language,* trans. Richard Howard (New York: Hill and Wang, 1986), 141–148.

66. Ibid., 148.

67. Cervantes, *Don Quixote de la Mancha,* part 1, chap. 16.

68. Abbé Marquet, *Lettre sur Pamela* (London, 1742), 16.

69. Diderot, *Éloge de Richardson,* 133.

Scott, to illustrate the mimetic force of this device. He did so in essays dedicated, not by chance, to Defoe, Swift, and Richardson.[70] For Balzac, the most important inheritor of Scott, "details alone will henceforth determine the merit of works improperly called *romans*."[71]

4. The fourth form of variety our genre lays claim to is the realm of existence we usually locate *in interiore homine: the changing folds of the life that today we call psychic.*

The appearance of *The Princesse de Clèves* in 1678 was accompanied by a series of reactions that snowballed, generating one of the most important literary quarrels of the *âge classique*. Readers were struck by the skill with which Madame de La Fayette depicted passions:

> All the movements [of the heart] could not be better known or expressed more forcefully and with more delicacy. The way Madame de Clèves returns to herself, these anxieties, these divergent thoughts that shatter against each other, this difference we discover between what she is today and what she was yesterday are things that happen inside us every day, that everybody feels, but few are able to portray in the fashion we see here.[72]

Du Plaisir comes up with a sort of theory: in his opinion, anyone who reads books like *The Princesse de Clèves* admires the narrator not for his or her ability to devise plots, but rather for the keenness with which the movements of the heart are revealed—an intangible content that earlier literature had never represented with suitable words.[73] Four years later, in discussing Catherine Bernard in the literary magazine *Le Mercure galant*, Fontenelle writes that he appreciates novels not so much for their plots or for their capacity to create surprises as for their ability to pin down "cer-

---

70. Sir Walter Scott, "Life of Swift" (1814), "Works of Swift" (1814), "Clara Reeve" (1823), "Samuel Richardson" (1824), "Defoe" (1827), in *Sir Walter Scott on Novelists and Fiction*, 44, 154, 157, 172–173, 179.

71. Honoré de Balzac, "Scènes de la vie privée: notes de la première édition," in *La Comédie humaine*, edition published under the direction of Pierre-Georges Castex, vol. 1 (Paris: Gallimard, 1976), 1175.

72. Jean-Baptiste-Henri de Valincour, *Lettres à Madame la Marquise * * * sur le sujet de la Princesse de Clèves* (1678) (Tours: Publication du groupe d'étude du XVIIe siècle de l'Université François-Rabelais, 1972), 199–200.

73. Du Plaisir, *Sentiments sur les lettres et sur l'histoire*, 51.

tain movements of the heart that are almost imperceptible due to their delicacy," and, by way of example, he cites *The Princesse de Clèves.*[74]

In 1688, a few years after Du Plaisir and Fontenelle, Charles Perrault began to publish his *Parallèle des Anciens et des Modernes.* As we read in the *Parallèle,* some of the progress made by the moderns compared to the ancients involves knowledge of the passions. Our understanding of the interior life has grown on par with the gains made in physics, astronomy, or anatomy. The ideas that the ancients had on some topics were inaccurate: their astronomy was familiar with the planets but ignorant of the satellites; similarly, their knowledge of the heart included the main passions but remained unaware of the small upheavals that the moderns have discovered and which they now pour into treatises on morals, tragedies, works on eloquence, and novels.[75] Perrault's words recall those with which Descartes had inaugurated a new era of reflection on the interior life some forty years earlier. His treatise *The Passions of the Soul* (1649) begins by arguing that nothing more clearly demonstrates the defectiveness of the learning inherited from the ancients than what they wrote concerning the passions.[76]

According to Dorrit Cohn, there are three ways to represent the interior life in fiction: "psycho-narration" (the omniscient analysis of the thoughts of others), "quoted monologue" (the first-person, public expression of what individuals are thinking or feeling), and "narrated monologue" (free indirect discourse).[77] However, if we leave the domain of fiction and extend the taxonomy to all forms of Western discourse, it becomes clear that there are two main types: *psychological analysis* and *monologue.* What we say about the interior life issues from one of these primary forms: from the gesture of someone who, starting from the outside, analyzes the psyche of others; and from the gesture of someone who, starting from the inside, expresses, or presses out, his or her hidden life and injects it into the public medium of words. The literary and philosophical culture of antiquity—which

---

74. Cited in ibid.

75. Charles Perrault, *Parallèle des Anciens et des Modernes* (2nd ed., 1692–1697) (Geneva: Slatkine Reprints, 1979), 101.

76. René Descartes, *Les Passions de l'âme* (1649); English translation in Descartes, *The Passions of the Soul and Other Philosophical Writings,* trans. Michael Moriarty (Oxford: Oxford University Press, 2015).

77. Cohn, *Transparent Minds,* 11ff.

Descartes and Perrault speak about in the singular, opposing it to a new culture—possessed both these devices.

Classical psychological analysis arose out of the multiform intersection of two genealogies. First is the theory of the four humors and the four temperaments introduced by Hippocrates, developed by Galen, and popularized between the Middle Ages and the Renaissance through a schema of correspondences between the human world and the larger cosmos.[78] Second is theory of the characters and the passions introduced by Aristotle in his *Rhetoric* and the *Nicomachean Ethics,* developed by Theophrastus, established in classical rhetoric and Scholastic theology, and then revived between the end of the 1500s and the beginning of the 1600s thanks to Casaubon's edition of Theophrastus and the development of the "character" as a literary genre, first in England and then throughout Europe. These families were bound together by their theoretical gestures, both of which rested on cornerstones that appeared to be far from stable in the eyes of modern culture. We find an exemplary presentation of them in the main treatise on descriptive psychology produced by ancient culture: book 2 of Aristotle's *Rhetoric.* The most important assumption was the conviction that an order could be imposed on the magma of the interior life by identifying and giving names to the forces that perturb it: an approach already present in Homer and made systematic by classical ethics and oratory. The Greek and Latin science of the passions was developed in the context of rhetoric, as an instrument that was vital for understanding the audience; and in the domain of moral law, as the first stage of inner therapy that served as the foundation for the ancient ethics focused on the care of the self.[79] The practice of identifying interior movements was then transmitted to Christian theology.

This approach arose from the concept of *character,* from the belief that the variety of individuals and the variability of their interior life can be traced back to types: the *ethe* Aristotle talks about in his *Rhetoric* and the *Nicomachean Ethics,* the thirty types of Theophrastus, and the temperaments of Hippocrates and Galen. More so than *ethos,* the Greek word transmitted

78. Erich Schöner, *Das Viererschema in der antiken Humoralpathologie* (Wiesbaden: Franz Steiner Verlag, 1964); Owsei Temkin, *Galenism: Rise and Decline of a Medical Philosophy* (Ithaca, NY: Cornell University Press, 1973).

79. Michel Foucault, *L'Herméneutique du sujet: cours au Collège de France. 1981-82*; English translation The *Hermeneutics of the Subject: Lectures at the Collège de France, 1981–82,* trans. Graham Burchell, ed. Frédéric Gros (New York: Picador, 2003), 4ff.

to the modern European languages was *charakter*. It originated in *charassein*, "to imprint," and it carried with it the idea that character is a mark, an imprint, a mold.[80] Implicit in this concept is the other load-bearing structure of the ancient introspective edifice, namely, the idea that an individual's actions and speech must be consistent with the mark imprinted on his or her interior life. In classical poetry and classicist poetics, the necessary link between ethos and behavior was expressed by the concept of *convenientia*. It was on the basis of this principle that Aristotle criticized Euripides's Iphigenia and her inner crises.[81] On the same basis, Horace advised writers who wanted to invent new characters, unfettered by tradition, to represent them as consistent with themselves from beginning to end.[82] What resulted from this was a "fixist psychology,"[83] founded on the assumption that the magma of passions and thoughts actually stemmed from stable matrices—rendering idiosyncratic, anomalous details transient and unworthy of interest. In this anthropological schema, inner movements can be traced to stable passions ("wrath," "serenity," "friendship," "enmity," "fear"). People are not singular, private individuals who resist classification: they are *exempla* of a public, universal typology that repeats.[84]

Along with this fixist psychology, the ancient culture developed and transmitted forms of monologue. Interestingly enough, there immediately arose a division of labor: analyses specialized in outlining permanent traits, monologues in expressing interior conflicts. While the soliloquies of Homeric characters already show a divided psyche, in the monologues of Sophocles and Euripides inner conflict takes on a more articulated form. The tragic model influenced the epic genre, as we see in Medea's words in book 3 of the *Argonautica*, or in the words of Dido in book 4 of the *Aeneid*.[85] In Latin lyric poetry between the first century BCE and the first

---

80. Van Delft, *Littérature et anthropologie*, chap. 1.

81. Aristotle, *Poetics* 15.1454a.32.

82. Horace, *Epistles* 2.3, lines 125–127.

83. Van Delft, *Le Moraliste classique*, 149.

84. Ibid., 139ff.; Van Delft, *Littérature et anthropologie*, 26. See also Étienne Gilson, "La scolastique et l'esprit classique," in *Les Idées et les Lettres* (Paris: Vrin, 1955), 243–261; and Alexandre Cioranescu, *El Barroco, or el descubrimiento del drama* (La Laguna: Universidad de la Laguna, 1957), 330ff.

85. Jacqueline de Romilly, *"Patience, mon cœur!": l'essor de la psychologie dans la littérature grecque classique* (Paris: Les Belles Lettres, 1984); Scholes, Phelan, and Kellogg, *The Nature of Narrative*, chap. 5.

century CE, the modes of the passions that perturbed the soliloquies of division become increasingly intimate. While the forms tended toward greater specialization, ancient analyses and monologues remained bound together by one thing: their vocabulary, their syntax, and their point of intonation were designed to translate the magma of the interior life into ostentatiously public forms. The categories of classical psychological analysis are exterior and aggregative: they relate the differences between individuals and the multiplicity of internal movements to common matrices. But the same thing can be said about the forms of monologue, which arose from genres designed to be declaimed aloud in a public space, in front of a crowd of people (the audience of a tragedy, the listeners of an oration, the disciples of a teacher). The tragedies of Sophocles and Euripides, which were contemporary to the development of judicial rhetoric, imitated its forms; the soliloqui of Apollonius of Rhodes, Virgil, and Ovid tended to take the form of the dilemma. Even in the Christian era, when Augustine inaugurated a new idea of the interior life and a new genre, the style of his constructions remained externalized. The story about himself, which occupies a substantial part of the *Confessions,* is constructed as a speech, in the second person, with obvious rhetorical features: "to such an extent is the spirit of the Greek public square still alive in it."[86]

Although animated by currents in some respects running opposite to each other, the models of psychological analysis and monologue that the ancient culture transmitted to the classicism of the early modern age were therefore bound by a shared attitude: they both try to express to make external—the motions of the psyche, to put them into forms that a group of people gathered in a public space can see. To achieve this, they must make common what may not be common: the psychological analyses assign a single name to the forces that inhabit the interior life and a single character to a plurality of individuals; monologues express thoughts and passions in an audible form. Both analyses and monologues were influenced by externalized discursive formations like rhetoric and normative ethics. These are the grammars that Descartes and Perrault might have had in mind when they

---

86. See Bakhtin, "Discourse in the Novel," in *The Dialogic Imagination: Four Essays,* 259–422.

spoke of the ancient science of the passions and, in response, announced the creation of a new paradigm.

The first signs of the transformation preceded the treatise *The Passions of the Soul* by half a century and the *Parallel between the Ancients and the Moderns* by a century: they can already be found in Montaigne's *Essays*.[87] One of the main innovations was without doubt the weakening of *chara-kter*. In the previous few centuries, the unity of psychological molds and the correspondence between the interior life and actions had become a problem. This does not mean that they were systematically negated; it means that they were no longer obvious, or that they had become less obvious. A fixist psychology, which saw only the planets, was flanked by a psychology that also attempted to discern the satellites. This is why the tradition of the novel played an essential role in the creation of another way of representing the interior life. In France, the *nouvelle* and the narrative fiction of worldliness[88] created a language of psychological analysis akin to the Augustinian tradition and organic to the culture of the *moralistes*. In book 3 of *The Princesse de Clèves*, Madame de La Fayette describes how the Prince de Clèves reacts to his wife's confession and to the suspicion that his wife has expressed her feelings in public. For her part, Madame de Clèves begins to suspect that the person responsible for spreading certain rumors is actually the man she is in love with, the Duke of Nemours:

> M. de Clèves had exhausted all fortitude in supporting the misery of seeing a wife whom he adored swayed by her passion for another man. He had no further strength, and thought he should not even find it in circumstances which were so damaging to his honour and his good name [*gloire*]. He did not know what to think of his wife; he could not decide what conduct he should prescribe for her, or how he should conduct himself; on all sides, he could see only gulfs and precipices. At length, after a long period of fretting and perplexity, realizing that he had shortly to go to Spain, he resolved to do nothing that might fuel suspicion or knowledge of his wretched state. . . .

87. Van Delft, *Littérature et anthropologie*, 7ff.; Louis Van Delft, *Frammento e anatomia*, chap. 2.

88. The definition comes from Peter Brooks, *The Novel of Worldliness: Crébillon, Marivaux, Laclos, Stendhal* (Princeton, NJ: Princeton University Press, 1969).

[Mme. de Clèves] could not doubt that [the Duke of Nemours] had told the story to the Vidame de Chartres: he had admitted as much; nor could she doubt also, from the manner in which he had spoken of it, that he knew the matter concerned her. How could she forgive such imprudence, and what had become of the prince's unusual discretion, which she had found so appealing? "He was discreet," she thought, "so long as he believed in his misfortune; but one glimpse of happiness, however uncertain, put an end to discretion. He could not imagine himself to be loved, without wishing to let it be known. . . . I was wrong to imagine that any man could be found who was able to conceal something that flattered his reputation [*gloire*]. And yet it is for the sake of this man, whom I believed so different to other men, that I have become like others of my sex, when I am so far from resembling them.[89]

Using the psychology of the *moralistes*, Madame de La Fayette gives a name to the inner forces ("fortitude," "misery," "happiness," *gloire*, "honor") and establishes some laws of action ("He could not imagine himself to be loved, without wishing to let it be known"; "I was wrong to imagine that any man could be found who was able to conceal something that flattered his reputation"). Underlying these expressions we glimpse the tendency to bring the formlessness of the interior life back into a few defined molds, and a device of classical fixist psychology: the maxim. And yet these categories are not used to reduce the complexity of the psyche, but to take it apart and probe it: the inner movements are now fragmented, the I is crisscrossed by a multitude of small subterranean forces and counterforces, analysis is valued more than synthesis—the motion of the satellites prevails over that of the planets. In France this introspective model, as we shall see, passed through the centuries and wielded its effects in Madame de La Fayette and Saint-Simon, in Crébillon and Marivaux, in Rousseau and Laclos, in Constant and Stendhal, in Flaubert, Maupassant, and Proust.

In England, on the other hand, the works of Richardson created a new form of monologue. The letters and diaries that make up his novels give voice to speech caught in the immediacy of passion, before the phrases take

---

89. Madame de La Fayette, *La Princesse de Clèves* (1678); English translation *The Princesse de Clèves*, trans. Robin Buss (London: Penguin, 2004), 130–132.

on a fully public form. This unprecedented point of intonation is expressed in the fractured syntax and colloquial lexicon employed by Richardson's characters:

> But then, thinks I, how do I know what I may be able to do? I have withstood his Anger; but may I not relent at his Kindness?—How shall I stand that!—Well, I hope, thought I, by the same protecting Grace in which I will always confide!—But then, what has he promised?—Why he will make my poor Father and Mother's Life comfortable. O, said I to myself, that is a rich Thought; but let me not dwell upon it.[90]

First appearing with Ovid's *Heroides,* and then revived in the Renaissance Humanist era, the narrative use of the letter contributed largely to the development of a novelistic psychology with *The Portuguese Letters, Pamela, Clarissa, The New Heloise, The Sorrows of Young Werther,* and *Dangerous Liaisons.* Nothing so eloquently illustrates the passage from public to private in the expression of self as the history of this genre. If the antecedents of the *Heroides* were the rhetorical exercises associated with the genres of *suasoriae, ethopoeia,* and *prosopopoeia, Pamela* and *Clarissa* shortened the logical and chronological distances between states of mind and their expression: the psychological movements are presented in their initial disorder. While the literature of French origin tended toward psycho-narration and objectivizing analysis, Richardson tended toward monologue and subjective expressivism. The epistolary novel veered toward intimacy and multiplicity. In fact, it ended up eliminating all traces of an interlocutor: the letters were not written to make oneself understood in a pragmatic fashion, but to allow the complex landscape of the psyche to emerge. Little by little, the mediations to be found in real letters began to disappear, as did the mediations found in diary entries. From this perspective, we see that the twentieth-century extension of this type of form is *stream of consciousness:* "the supreme culmination of the formal trend that Richardson initiated— James Joyce's *Ulysses.*"[91]

---

90. Richardson, *Pamela,* letter 30, p. 85.

91. Watt, *The Rise of the Novel,* 206. See also Leon Edel, *The Psychological Novel, 1900–1950* (London: Rupert Hart-Davis, 1955), 27.

National Differences: France and England

The development of the novel thus coincided with the eruption of particularity: private stories, forms of life, backgrounds and things, the multiplicity of our egos. The overall sense of the transformation is clear, but the local movements were disconnected and followed different directions in line with the different national cultures. The decisive period in the development of the novel as an institution, the period between 1670 and 1800, also coincided with the development of a hierarchy between the literatures that formed the European narrative space. Encamped at the center of the territory stood the literatures of France and England, which exported texts and models to Europe at least until the first half of the twentieth century.[92] The two most influential cultures followed different paths from each other. Less tied to classicism, English narrative fiction embraced the mimesis of social classes, environments, and objects with a freedom unknown to its French counterpart. For a long time French narrative fiction remained tied to a small circle—the *monde*—composed of the aristocracy and the members of the upper middle class who identified with the ideal of *honnêteté*.[93] To tell a serious story about a merchant, a former prostitute, or a maid, to depict manners that fell outside the *bienséances,* to provide detailed descriptions of a big city street or a maidservant's room, to report a conversation in the vernacular taking place in a tavern was more difficult for the French *roman* than for the English novel. The effects of the *Stiltrennung* remained alive much longer in France. The difference comes sharply into view when we examine the criticisms launched against Fielding and Richardson be-

---

92. See Franco Moretti, *Atlante del romanzo europeo 1800–1900* (1997); English translation *Atlas of the European Novel, 1800–1900* (London: Verso, 1999), 171ff. Moretti identifies three circles: the core, a transitional area (the semi-periphery), and the periphery. The first is occupied by French and English narrative fiction; the second by countries whose cultures slide from the core to the periphery (Italy, Spain), or by countries whose fiction experienced a period of great international success for a limited period of time (Germany, Russia); the third one, by all the other national traditions. This landscape changed in the twentieth century with the development of colonial literatures, starting with American literature. On the dominance of the French and English novel, see also Margaret Cohen and Carolyn Dever, eds., *The Literary Channel: The Inter-National Invention of the Novel* (Princeton, NJ: Princeton University Press, 2002).

93. Brooks, *The Novel of Worldliness.*

tween 1740 and 1755.[94] French readers were simultaneously fascinated and frightened by the English authors. Certain of their behaviors and words were judged to be vulgar; the translators took it upon themselves to tone down and censor the texts.[95]

But while the eighteenth-century French authors stylized environments and languages much more than the English writers, French literature developed a vocabulary for introspection that had no equivalent in English-language literature. And while British writers described the multiplicity of the external world with a wealth of detail that the French writers would only achieve many decades later, the language of French psychological analysis strongly influenced European literature of the 1800s and 1900s, continuing to show its effects at least until Proust.[96] This asymmetry, too, stemmed from the relationship with the *monde*. The culture that developed in European court society, from Castiglione to the *moralistes*, engendered ways of thinking about themselves and about being in the midst of others that in the modern era would become hegemonic and disseminated to the masses. Some of the cultural infrastructures associated with the form of life that we inhabit did not arise out of the middle class world but out of court society. The most important of these was an anthropology founded on the idea that human beings are egocentric. A society that, in theory, still recognized shared rules and unquestionable universal values produced the first extended reflection on individualistic nonbelonging: "It was not only in the sphere of bourgeois-capitalist competition that the idea of egoism as a motive of human action was formed, but first of all in the competition at court, and from the latter came the first unveiled descriptions of the human affects in modern times. La Rochefoucauld's *Maxims* are one example."[97]

Philosophy inscribed this idea into its own languages with the political thought and anthropology of Machiavelli and Hobbes,[98] but the minute

94. See May, *Le Dilemme du roman au XVIIIᵉ siècle*, 163ff.

95. See Jacques Proust, "Les maîtres sont les maîtres," *Romanistische Zeitschrift für Literaturgeschichte* 1, no. 1 (1977): 145–172.

96. Norbert Elias, *Die höfische Gesellschaft* (1969), English translation *The Court Society*, trans. Edmund Jephcott (New York: Pantheon Books, 1983), 104ff.; also by Elias, *Über den Prozess der Zivilisation*, vol. 2 (1969), English translation *The Civilizing Process*, rev. ed., trans. Edmund Jephcott (Oxford: Blackwell, 2000), 401–2; Brooks, *The Novel of Worldliness*, chap. 2 and passim.

97. Elias, *The Court Society*, 105.

98. Leo Strauss, *Natural Right and History* (Chicago: University of Chicago Press, 1953).

analysis of *amour propre* was a product of the culture of France during the second half of the seventeenth century and the eighteenth. Philosophical thought on the inherent *worldliness* of human beings, in both senses of the word, arose out of this same environment.[99] Although religion continued to dominate the public sphere, and although society remained faithful to forms and institutions that postulated a continuity of collective values over time, there emerged the idea that the battles from which human beings derive meaning or futility, joy or sorrow, are waged in an entirely earthly dimension. This immanence was conceived as a network of inter-subjective relations that referred to a group, to a society. The *monde* was a restricted circle of people who shared the same values and struggle for prestige—to rise in the esteem of their superiors and peers—in a society that had transformed uncontrolled, physical violence into regulated, psychological violence.[100] In this world, where the rank of individuals depended on the judgment of others, the ability to control oneself, analyze oneself, and decipher others was a key resource.[101] The literature of the *moralistes* and Madame de La Fayette, the French novel of worldliness (Crébillon, Marivaux, Laclos), and the autobiographical writing of Rousseau all operate in this dimension, which they view as the medium of our being-in-the-world. For this reason they represent human beings in their ontological relationship with others. The language of introspection they refer to can come into existence only in a closed circle, held together by homogeneous values, composed of people who, living shoulder to shoulder in a regime of latent symbolic competition, are used to observing each other and being observed. The uniformity of the milieu was a necessary condition for the refinement of psychological analysis. Equally important was an autoptic tradition originating with Augustine that persisted in French

99. For more on *mondanité* as an integral component of French culture during the *âge classique* and the Enlightenment period, see Roland Barthes, "La Bruyère," (1963), English translation in *Critical Essays* (Evanston, IL: Northwestern University Press, 1972), 221–238; Brooks, *The Novel of Worldliness*; Antoine Lilti, *Le Monde des salons: sociabilité et mondanité à Paris au XVIIIe siècle* (Paris: Fayard, 2005); Barbara Carnevali, *Romanticismo e riconoscimento. Figure della coscienza in Rousseau* (Bologna: Il Mulino, 2004); also by Carnevali, "Salotti," *Storica* 33 (2005): 133–141, and "Società e riconoscimento," in *Illuminismo*, ed. Gianni Paganini and Edoardo Tortarolo (Turin: Bollati Boringhieri, 2008), 279–293.

100. Elias, *The Civilizing Process*, 397ff.

101. Elias, *The Court Society*, 104ff.; Elias, *The Civilizing Process*, 397ff.; Carnevali, *Romanticismo e riconoscimento*, passim.

culture throughout the seventeenth and eighteenth centuries.[102] This way of expressing the mimesis of the interior life was fully introduced into English narrative fiction only between the end of the 1700s and the beginning of the 1800s, with Fanny Burney and then with Jane Austen. The works of George Eliot and Henry James would be inconceivable outside of this current.

102. Brooks, *The Novel of Worldliness*, chap. 2; Philippe Seillier, *Port-Royal et la littérature. II. Le siècle de Saint-Augustin, La Rochefoucauld, Madame de Lafayette, Sacy, Racine* (Paris: Champion, 2000).

CHAPTER FIVE

The Birth of the Modern Novel

In the previous chapters we saw that the emergence of the novel was punctuated by three historical thresholds. The first occurred around 1550, when a large territory of heterogeneous and unconventional narrative writings began to form. Some of them originated in the ancient world and others in the Middle Ages. Slowly they converged into a single genre. Within this new territory, two distinct regions took shape that we are retrospectively entitled to call by the names they acquired in England over the course of the eighteenth century: *novel* and *romance*. A second threshold occurred around 1670. From that moment on, during a process lasting over a century, the two territories became better defined and, little by little, the *novel* became the novel par excellence. As a consequence, the *romance* was gradually relegated to a peripheral position, and a new focus on contingent forms of life was introduced into the discursive space of European culture. But for over a century this transformation was not perceived as a threshold. Up until the second half of the eighteenth century, writers and readers attempted to fit this novelty into the structures of sense that had governed early modern literature. It is almost as if this era were driven by two identical but opposing motions: a gradual shift toward the mimesis of contingency (the tradition of the *romance* lost ground in favor of the *novel*, while the *novel* specialized in the literary reproduction of particularities) was balanced by the survival of premodern structures that hindered the unfettered representation of particular life. Only around 1800 did these changes completely overthrow all the ancient structures to engender a third, decisive frontier. Many different aspects were affected by this transformation:

style, the attitude toward stories, and the place of the novel in the literary system.

Freedom from the Rules of Style

In the last decades of the seventeenth century, just when the pathos of proximity began to spread rapidly, prefaces and treaties became filled with a commonplace: novels, it was said, must be written in a plain, natural style similar to what is used in conversation. This topos was propagated everywhere: in Donneau de Visé's *Nouvelles galantes, comiques et tragiques* (1669)[1] and Manley's *The Secret History of Queen Zarah* (1705); in Challe's *Les Illustres Françaises* (1713)[2] and Richardson's *Pamela* (1740). It was to be found in the arguments that Charnes used to praise Madame de La Fayette in 1679[3] and in those William Owen used to recommend Fielding in 1751.[4] In the eighteenth century, comments of this sort were extremely common; by the nineteenth century, the "simple style" had become the backbone of nineteenth-century realism;[5] in the twentieth century, this supposed naturalness became problematic. When this happened, it became possible to understand the place that the poetics of plain writing had occupied in the history of narrative fiction.

In 1966, the collection *The Experimental Novel* came out in Italy. It presented essays by young critics and writers who, influenced by the French *nouveau roman*, avant-garde German fiction, and translations, discovered or rediscovered the avant-garde movements of the past and modernism. Today many of these essays strike us as extremist and reductionist because they flatten out the dialectic between continuity and discontinuity linking

---

1. "I beg those who may find the style of my *nouvelles* to be insufficiently turgid to remember that, since works of this type are nothing more than stories of things more familiar than lofty, the style must be as plain and as natural as that of a person of wit who is improvising a story." Donneau de Visé, *Les Nouvelles galantes, comiques et tragiques*, preface (no page numbers).

2. "I wrote in the way I would have spoken to my friends, in a purely natural and familiar style." Challe, *Les Illustres Françaises*, 4.

3. Charnes, *Conversations sur la critique de la Princesse de Clèves*, 280.

4. William Owen, "An Essay on the New Species of Writing Founded by Mr. Fielding" (1751), in Williams, *Novel and Romance*, 152.

5. On the concept of the simple style, see Enrico Testa, *Lo stile semplice: Discorso e romanzo* (Turin: Einaudi, 1997).

the novel of the late nineteenth century to the novel of the early twentieth century. In doing so, they emphasize the rupture and pass over the aspects that persisted. Moreover, unlike what happened in the great works of modernist fiction, the model of the novel they promoted ran the risk of losing any relationship with the lifeworld. And yet the unilateralism of their perspectives does bring into focus a sharply delineated view of the tradition that these writers sought to repudiate. Thanks to his extremism, Giorgio Manganelli was able to clearly establish the meaning of "the simple style" in the history of prose writing:

> The novel appeared in European literature just when the taste for and understanding of classical rhetoric was declining; that is, when the idea of the literary work as artifice entered into crisis. More specifically, the nineteenth-century explosion of the novel coincided with the defeat and disappearance of classical rhetoric.[6]

Until the development of the novel, European literary prose was governed by the rules of rhetoric: even the genre tasked with representing the particular—historiography—was *opus oratorium maxime*. The appeals to naturalness that we find scattered throughout prefaces and treatises between 1650 and 1800 allude instead to another idea of form. In principle, the simple style was a register codified by the rhetorical system originating in the ancient world, as authors with a solid classicist culture knew very well.[7] More generally, the *sermo humilis* was well suited to some of the great prose models that certain novelistic subgenres openly patterned themselves on, namely, *commentarii*, the classic archetype of *mémoires*, and epistles.[8] Similarly, many of those who looked to the conversation of *honnêtes gens* were aware of the fact that this practice followed a ritual governed by implicit habits and explicit rules that had been codified by a century and a half of treatises—from Castiglione to Guazzo to the French

---

6. Giorgio Manganelli, "Il romanzo" (1963), reprinted in *Il rumore sottile della prosa* (Milan: Adelphi, 1994), 58.

7. See, for example, Fielding, preface to *Joseph Andrews*, 4ff., or Monboddo, *The Origin and Progress of Language* (Edinburgh: Balfour, 1773–1792), vol. 3, part 2, bk. 4, chaps. 10 and 16.

8. See Fumaroli, "Genèse de l'épistolographie classique: rhétorique humaniste de la lettre, de Pétrarque à Juste Lipse."

literary circles of the *âge classique*.[9] But even if *mediocritas* was a code laid down by classicist writings, the significance of the call to naturalness of expression was unprecedented and went against tradition. Writers of novels were now making claims to a new model of prose, less regulated than what the rules of eloquence dictated, or in any case, one altogether more fluid and smooth. Those who were active in the subgenres that later converged into the territory of the *novel* were searching for an informal style—exactly what they were able to find in the stories of experience that arose outside the oratorical tradition.[10] The authors who wrote when rhetoric was losing or had already lost influence on narrative prose immediately grasped the significance of this process. Sir Walter Scott accurately identified this transition in an essay on Defoe:

> Defoe does not display much acquaintance with classic learning, neither does it appear that his attendance on the Newington [Green] seminary had led him deep into the study of ancient languages. His own language is genuine English, often simple even to vulgarity, but always so distinctly impressive, that its very vulgarity had . . . an efficacy in giving an air of truth or probability to the facts and sentiments it conveys.[11]

Scott understood that the explosion of the novel coincided with the decline of classical rhetoric: the novel carried European prose out of the age of eloquence. Its simple style was not the *sermo humilis* tradition of eloquence, but a prose of experience severed from rhetorical art, which, while appearing "simple even to vulgarity," was capable of making stories credible with a force that classical literature did not possess.

This transition included an even more macroscopic phenomenon. With the modern novel, prose became the ordinary medium of storytelling; the development of the genre was contemporary with a slow but progressive decline of narrative written in verse. Ever since ancient Greek culture had

9. See Peter Burke, *The Art of Conversation* (Cambridge: Polity Press, 1993); Marc Fumaroli, "Préface" to *L'Art de la conversation*, ed. Jacqueline Hellegouarc'h (Paris: Classiques Garnier, 1997), i–xxxix; Benedetta Craveri, *La civiltà della conversazione* (Milan: Adelphi, 2001).

10. See Sylvie Thorel-Cailleteau, "The Poetry of Mediocrity," in *The Novel*, vol. 2, *Forms and Themes*, ed. Franco Moretti (Princeton, NJ: Princeton University Press, 2007), 64ff.; and by the same author, *Splendeurs de la médiocrité: une idée du roman* (Geneva: Droz, 2008).

11. Scott, "Defoe," p. 165.

begun to rely solely on sentences that were not broken into separate lines for its discourses of truth, following in Anaximander's lead, versification became a trope—something different from the ordinary way of saying things. The notion that prose is the most linear way of expressing oneself is already implicit in the etymology of the words: *versus* is a "line," a "row," but also "that which faces backwards"; *oratio provorsa* (or, in its contracted form, *oratio prosa*) is "speech turned straight forward." The opposition between the two forms became an object of reflection in France in the thirteenth and fourteenth centuries, along with the idea that verse lies and only prose tells the truth.[12] The culture of modern rationalism would transform this way of thinking into a commonplace. During the French *âge classique,* writes Roland Barthes,

> prose and poetry are quantities, their difference can be measured; they are neither more nor less separated than two different numbers, contiguous like them, but dissimilar because of the very difference in their magnitudes. If I use the word prose for a minimal form of speech, the most economical vehicle for thought, and if I use the letters a, b, c for certain attributes of languages, which are useless but decorative, such as metre, rhyme or the ritual of images, all the linguistic surface will be accounted for in M. Jourdin's double equation:
>
> Poetry = Prose + a + b + c
> Prose = Poetry − a − b − c[13]

In Hegel's lectures on aesthetics, as we shall see more clearly in Chapter 6, he uses prose as a metaphor to indicate a social arrangement ("this world of prose and everyday") in which collective action is decided by suprapersonal entities (states and the mechanisms of civil society), while individuals act in a restricted sphere of private interests.[14] Abandoning verse for prose and abandoning oratorical prose for a simple style borrowed from the writings of experience are gestures that go together. Following the control that aesthetic Platonism and the separation of styles had imposed on representations, mimesis was transformed into an activity governed by public

12. Wlad Godzich and Jeffrey Kittay, *The Emergence of Prose: An Essay in Prosaics* (Minneapolis: University of Minnesota Press, 1987).

13. Roland Barthes, *Le Degré zéro de l'écriture* (1953); English translation *Writing Degree Zero,* trans. Annette Layers and Colin Smith (New York: Hill and Wang, 1977), 41.

14. On Hegel's use of prose as a metaphor, see Michel Pelad Ginsburg and Lorri G. Dandrea, "The Prose of the World," in Moretti, *The Novel,* 2:244–273.

rules. Implicit or explicit standards establish a ritual; the passage from verse to prose and the development of the simple style confirmed the rise of a nonritual mimesis. Stories told in verse strip life of its contingency;[15] the rules that regimented prose during the age of eloquence gave rise to the same effect. Only informal prose allows absolutely any story to be told in any way whatsoever.

Freedom from Allegory and Morality

Thanks to the novel, in the second half of the eighteenth century literature experienced particular life with a breadth and depth that would have been inconceivable two and a half centuries earlier: such a thing had been completely unknown to European culture. How was an innovation of this sort justified at the time? Until the end of the 1700s many novels continued to present themselves as exemplary stories, almost as if the genre were bringing to completion a line of development already discernible in the medieval *novella*: *narratio* expanded to the detriment of the *sensus,* the plots became more complicated and the characters less schematic, but the work continued to legitimize itself as an *exemplum.* Novel writers used a Christian structure of sense to justify their break with the ideographic poetics of classicism. By presenting their works as life stories intended for the education and salvation of their readers, they were able to recount the lives of people like us in a serious register, to linger on details, and to use a simple style. The events they told about were anomalous and eccentric, because ordinary life became worthy of description only when it broke free from seriality and was transformed into a *casus.* But eccentricity was a guarantee of realism, because in the Aristotelian and classicist sense of the term, the real is almost never probable.[16] On the other hand, this embracing of imperfection had a moral purpose: officially, stories that are improbable—but for this very reason true—were presented as *exempla* to be meditated on. In order to understand this dialectic, we need to avoid falling into two opposite traps. We must not think that the moralistic apparatuses were only a hypocritical conceit or the automatic prolongation of an outmoded habit. It is true that some eighteenth-century texts played with poetic jus-

---

15. See Lukács, *The Theory of the Novel,* 57.
16. McKeon, *The Origins of the English Novel, 1600–1740,* 47ff. and passim.

tice, with the exemplarity of the heroes, and with edifying prefaces: the pornographic novel is an unequivocal example of this. But it is equally true that a cultural institution does not remain alive for such a long period of time only from inertia or because it has become the butt of irony. If novels circulated until the end of the eighteenth century clad in moralistic armor, this means that to a certain extent moralism and allegorism were still a crucial part of the literary ether inhabited by writers and readers. On the other hand, we should not think that the premodern structures of sense remained unchanged. As we saw in Chapter 3, the pedagogical conception of art defended by Christian aesthetic Platonism engendered two families of precepts: the first disseminated a moral law through poetic justice and the creation of exemplary heroes; the second disseminated *phronesis,* the practical wisdom of human affairs. It was precisely by appealing to the usefulness of practical knowledge that certain eighteenth-century novels portrayed passions and manners without moralizing them, with the aim of teaching how to live. The preface to *Dangerous Liaisons* is quite clear on this point: Laclos presents the work as an *exemplum,* in line with the traditional approach, but he adds that his novel is especially useful because it reveals the means used by the depraved to corrupt the virtuous, and certainly not because it shows examples of virtue. *Phronesis* and the psychological-moral realism that followed from it were more important than poetic justice or the self-correction of the heroes:

> The usefulness of the work, which will be perhaps even more disputed, seems to me to be easier to establish. It seems to me at least that it is doing a service to society to unveil the strategies used by the immorals to corrupt the moral, and I believe these letters will make an effective contribution to this end. In them are also to be found the proof and the example of two important truths which one might suppose to be unacknowledged, seeing how little they are practised. One, that any woman who consents to receive into her circle of friends an unprincipled man ends up by becoming his victim; the other, that any mother who allows her daughter to confide in anyone but herself is at the very best lacking in prudence. Young people of both sexes might also learn from it that the friendship that immoral persons seem to grant them so easily is only ever a dangerous trap, and as fatal to their happiness as to their virtue. Moreover, it seems to me that the harm which may so often follow closely upon the benefits is greatly to be feared in this case and, far from advising young

people to read this book, I believe it is important to keep all such books out of their way. The age when this one may cease to be dangerous, and become useful, seems to me to have been very well understood, for her own sex, by a mother who is not only intelligent but also sensible. "I should believe," she told me, after reading the manuscript of this correspondence, "I was doing my daughter a great service if I gave it to her on her wedding day." If all mothers thought like that, I should congratulate myself on publishing it for ever more.[17]

Fifty years earlier, after repeating the moralistic arguments against the novel, Lenglet Du Fresnoy had dedicated a chapter of his treatise to the wisdom that the genre transmits when it illustrates the manners and dangers of the *monde* to readers, especially female ones.[18] This appeal to the practical value of the novel and the edifying rhetoric remained intertwined for a long time in eighteenth-century commentaries and were interpreted as two consequences of the same poetics. Nevertheless, they led in different directions. Emphasizing *phronesis* over normative ethics actually meant shifting the work's center of gravity toward the disenchanted analysis of human beings, diminishing the apparatuses of control to the benefit of moral realism. Until the second half of the eighteenth century, the novel lived off the dialectic between orthopedic devices and anarchic actions. Over the course of time it became increasingly clear that the interest did not lie in the transcendence of the *sensus* but in the immanence of the *narratio*. The story now expanded at the expense of the meaning and became increasingly uncontrollable. In some cases, the sham nature of the moralistic infrastructure was obvious. In order to grasp this transformation, we need not venture into eighteenth-century pornographic fiction: in the novels of a writer deeply influenced by puritanism, like Defoe, for example, the hidden moral sense did not prevent the represented world from brimming over with indecent actions. The erratic character who takes center stage and attracts readers started with *Lazarillo de Tormes*: edifying prefaces, poetic justice, and the self-correction of the hero did nothing to dim the allure of transgressive behavior.

17. Pierre Ambroise François Choderlos de Laclos, *Les Liaisons dangereuses* (1782); English translation *Dangerous Liaisons*, trans. Helen Constantine (London: Penguin, 2007), 6–7.

18. Lenglet Du Fresnoy, *De l'usage des romans*, chap. 6, especially pp. 291–292.

At the end of the eighteenth century, though, we witness a radical transformation: allegorism and moralism began to disappear from texts. This was not a sudden transition but a slow process that took many decades to complete. Moreover, the bipartite structure of the modern narrative space—divided between works created for specialists and those for a wider public—led to different escape velocities, because the novelists who wrote for middle- or lower-class readers never relinquished moral control. In France in the mid-nineteenth century, the literary field was split by a conflict between realistic art, founded on observation and intended for avant-garde readers, and idealizing art, founded on clear ethical oppositions and intended for a bourgeois public:[19] the major intellectuals of the generation born in the 1820s (Baudelaire, Flaubert, the Goncourt brothers, Taine) still battled fiercely against moralism. It took decades for vice and virtue to become chemical products like vitriol and sugar—the remark by Taine that Zola put as an epigraph to the second edition of *Thérèse Raquin* (1868) with the provocative aim of subverting the *doxa*. The change traveled at different speeds depending on the different national literatures. In Victorian England, and in English-language literatures in general, censorious stances were stronger than in France, especially in the sectors that formed the rear guard, those who addressed themselves to Protestant middle-class readers.[20] In 1884, Henry James published "The Art of Fiction" in response to an essay of the same name written by Walter Besant, in which there still resounds the "old evangelical hostility" toward the novel.[21]

The transformation was thus complex, gradual, and partially incomplete. Today, the elite public calls on literature to observe reality in a disenchanted, insightful way rather than expecting it to issue an ethical-normative judgment on characters or plots. Writers must "paint [the facts] as they are,"[22] as Balzac wrote in his introduction (1842) to *The Human*

---

19. See Pierre Bourdieu, *Les Règles de l'art* (1992, 1998); English translation *The Rules of Art: Genesis and Structure of the Literary Field,* trans. Susan Emanuel (Stanford, CA: Stanford University Press, 1996).

20. Richard Stang, *The Theory of the Novel in England, 1850–1870* (London: Routledge and Kegan Paul, 1959), 47ff.

21. Henry James, "The Art of Fiction" (1884), in *Literary Criticism: Essays on Literature, American Writers, English Writers* (New York: Library of America, 1984), 44–65.

22. Balzac, "Author's Introduction" to *The Human Comedy*, lxiv.

Comedy; the novelist must become "a registrar [*enregistreur*] of good and evil," even at the cost of "being stigmatized as immoral."[23] Today those who criticize Walter Siti, Michel Houellebecq, or Jonathan Littell with moralistic arguments position themselves in the intellectual rear guard. And yet, edifying and allegorical paradigms are still effective in arts intended for the masses, especially in movies and television. Sociological realism would be appreciated instead in literature or films intended for a restricted, sophisticated public: it would be considered an adult choice. The historical threshold when this metamorphosis began took form near the end of the eighteenth century: this is when moralism started to become a conservative gesture. What were the effects of this transformation?

Moralism, Empathy, and Observation

1. The first effect was the disappearance of the allegorical devices that governed mimesis, starting with poetic justice. *Dangerous Liaisons* was patently inspired by *The New Heloise;* the epigraph of the book quotes from the preface of the novel by Rousseau: "I have seen the morals of my times and I have published these letters." In 1802, forty-one years after *The New Heloise* and twenty years after the work of Laclos, Madame de Staël published *Delphine.* The unconventional behaviors of the characters, the unresolved conflict between principles and desires, the asymmetry between reciprocated love and adverse fate, the failures met by noble sentiments, and the tragic finale scandalized readers, who struggled to find a reassuring hidden moral sense in the work. What ensued from it was a rather harsh polemic, in which Benjamin Constant also participated. While reviewing *Delphine* in *The French Citizen,* after comparing the novel to *The New Heloise,* Constant defends Madame de Staël from accusations of immorality:

> Does the fact that virtue is shown to be superior to all seduction, to all the energy of the passions, to all the force of circumstances, not therefore aim at a moral intent? We would have wished for the virtue of Delphine and Léonce to be rewarded, for them to end up happy instead of arriving at the extremes of misfortune. The critics say that this means discouraging the practice of virtue.... Do these people not

23. Ibid., lviii

know perhaps that the way events occur is independent of virtue and vice, and that, as a result, there is no way to ensure one and the other the respective treatments they would seem to deserve? . . . It would be entirely possible, then, . . . that there is some morality in this *dangerous* work, unless one must conform to the dominant opinion and view all works as immoral in which philosophy and reason are not positively insulted.[24]

To demand that vice be punished and virtue rewarded is an insult to the intelligence, because we know that in the real world vice is not necessarily punished and virtue is not necessarily rewarded. The signs of a new narrative paradigm and a new idea of probability were beginning to emerge. For Constant, it was by now implicit that the task of the writer was primarily to show things as they are: respect for the reality principle was more important than moral orthopedics.

It would take many more decades to rid high-culture literature of poetic justice. There are two antithetical statements in the introduction to *The Human Comedy*, only pages away from each other. First Balzac writes that the novelist should tell the truth even at the cost of being called immoral; then he lets fall the idea that the plot of *The Human Comedy* punishes blameworthy actions, albeit in a covert way.[25] Four decades earlier, Madame de Staël was situated right in the midst of this process. Although the plot of *Delphine* did not reward virtue, the protagonists of the novel, Delphine and Léonce, embodied a moral principle, as Constant wrote in his reviews although poetic justice was dissolving, the tendency to create heroes who were packed and imbued with an idea did not disappear. But the transformation had already begun. Little by little the edifying characters tended to play more minor roles in the literature of the elite, as did poetic justice. Already by the end of the seventeenth century, French narrative fiction had created a new way of representing people, showing the cracks underlying the apparent unity of our egos. Constant would once again ally himself with this genealogy, which by then was also that of Madame de La Fayette, by writing *Adolphe*.

24. Benjamin Constant, "Compte rendu de *Delphine* de Madame de Staël," in *Œuvres complètes*, ed. Paul Delbouille, vol. 3, *Écrits littéraires* (Tübingen: Max Niemeyer, 1995), 932–936.

25. Balzac, "Author's Introduction" to *The Human Comedy*, lxiv and ff.

2. The second consequence was the disappearance of moralistic introductions. Eight years before *Dangerous Liaisons,* in 1774, there appeared the most famous of the works created under the influence that *The New Heloise* had exerted on European literature: *The Sorrows of Young Werther.* While *The New Heloise* came out enveloped in a massive, edifying armature, *Werther* appeared with brief prefatory remarks written in altogether new tones:

> I have diligently collected everything I have been able to discover concerning the story of poor Werther, and here present it to you in the knowledge that you will be grateful for it. You cannot deny your admiration and love for his spirit and character, nor your tears at his fate.
>
> And you, good soul, who feel a compulsive longing such as his, draw consolation from his sorrow, and let this little book be your friend whenever through fate or through your own fault you can find no closer companion.[26]

3. The preface to *Werther* is also significant because it shows that new moral attitudes toward stories and people were emerging. Vice and virtue, or what the work "means" in a conceptual form, stopped being crucial issues; novels no longer presented themselves as secondary texts that gave form to an *exemplum* of something already known, but rather as primary texts recounting experiences irreducible to a preexisting truth. Attention shifted from the transcendence of meanings to the immanence of finite beings, following a path similar to what was implicit in the birth of suspense. Richardson's readers had already experienced a previously unknown feeling of identification:

> I still remember the first time Richardson's work fell into my hands: I was in the country. How delightfully moved I was by the reading! With every moment I saw happiness growing shorter by the page. Soon I had the same feeling experienced by men who get on extremely well together, and having lived together for a long time, are about to separate. When it was finished, I suddenly felt that I was left alone.[27]

---

26. Johann Wolfgang von Goethe, *Die Leiden des jungen Werthers* (1774); English translation *The Sorrows of Young Werther,* trans. Michael Hulse (London: Penguin Classics, 1989), 23.

27. Diderot, "In Praise of Richardson," 84.

The aesthetic of identification subverted the habits that make an allegorical interpretation possible. Gotthard Heidegger, as we have seen, feared the "greedy" manners of those who immersed themselves in their books, thereby losing the detachment that made it possible to express an allegorical-moral judgment.[28] Instead, the first page of *Werther* programmatically invited readers to identify themselves with the sufferings of the characters.[29] Immanent in the mimesis of every period and location, this way of reading stories conquered a new place in the modern era. Its spread was parallel to the massive growth in solitary, silent reading that took place over the course of the eighteenth century.[30]

Today the aesthetics of empathy strike us as an obvious presupposition of the novel. According to a commonplace inscribed in the unconscious of readers who are our contemporaries, the main task of a writer is to create empathy with the heroes, regardless of moral judgments. An exemplary expression of a similar idea can be found in an interview with Orhan Pamuk:

> But the very strength of the art of the novel is that the writer identifies with the character he creates with such great intensity that no moral judgment should be passed on a character. The art of the novel is based on the unique capacity of human beings to identify with the Other.[31]

Compare this passage with a page out of *Tom Jones*. In the first chapter of book 7, in developing the topos of the world as theater, the narrator tries to imagine the reactions of the spectators to the episode concluding book 6:

---

28. Heidegger, *Mythoscopia romantica*, chap. 53.

29. See Hans Robert Jauss, "Rousseaus *Nouvelle Héloïse* und Goethes *Werther* im Horizontwandel zwischen französischer Aufklärung und deutschem Idealismus," in Jauss, *Ästhetische Erfahrung und literarische Hermeneutik* (Frankfurt am Main: Suhrkamp, 1982), 589–632; Anselm Haverkamp, "Illusion und Empathie: Die Struktur der teilnehmenden Lektüre in den *Leiden Werthers*," in *Erzählforschung*, ed. Eberhard Lämmert (Stuttgart: Metzler, 1983), 243–269.

30. See Loretelli, *L'invenzione del romanzo*, chap. 5 and passim.

31. Orhan Pamuk, interview with Paul Holdengraber, New York Public Library, September 17, 2007, http://www.nypl.org/audiovideo/orhan-pamuk-conversation-paul-holdengräber. Excerpts published in *New Perspectives Quarterly* 31, no. 2 (2014); available at http://www.digitalnpq.org/archive/2014_spring/index.html.

Let us examine this in one example; for instance, in the behaviour of the great audience on that scene which Nature was pleased to exhibit in the twelfth chapter of the preceding book, where she introduced Black George running away with the £500 from his friend and benefactor. Those who sat in the world's upper gallery treated that incident, I am well convinced, with their usual vociferation; and every term of scurrilous reproach was most probably vented on that occasion.

If we had descended to the next order of spectators, we should have found an equal degree of abhorrence, though less of noise and scurrility; yet here the good women gave Black George to the devil, and many of them expected every minute that the cloven-footed gentleman would fetch his own.

The pit, as usual, was no doubt divided; those who delight in heroic virtue and perfect character objected to the producing such instances of villany, without punishing them very severely for the sake of example. Some of the author's friends cryed, "Look'e, gentlemen, the man is a villain, but it is nature for all that." And all the young critics of the age . . . called it low, and fell a groaning.

As for the boxes, they behaved with their accustomed politeness. Most of them were attending to something else. Some of those few who regarded the scene at all, declared he was a bad kind of man; while others refused to give their opinion, till they had heard that of the best judges.[32]

Tom Jones describes a public that still considers a moral judgment about stories to be an essential, dominant part of the aesthetic experience. Most of the spectators depicted by Fielding do not ask themselves whether the scene was represented in such a way as to arouse an empathetic identification with the characters, but whether the characters' behavior was morally acceptable. Only the author's friends, who are probably also writers, resort to the realism argument ("Look'e, gentlemen, the man is a villain, but it is nature for all that"). Every page of *Tom Jones* is permeated by the idea that one must instruct while entertaining, so that the narrator continually makes use of his sense of humor to judge the characters and issue precepts: at certain points the density of these interjections creates true

---

32. Fielding, *The History of Tom Jones*, bk. 6, chap. 1, pp. 325–326.

moral *quaestiones*.[33] These kinds of digressions signal that Fielding is moving in a mental horizon quite different from that of Pamuk. And while it may be true that his words often take on an ironic tone, it is also true that problems which no longer concern us are never the object of irony. Ever since aesthetic Platonism began to exert its influence on narrative, it has been completely normal for stories and heroes to be evaluated in the light of normative ethics; only after the collapse of these a prioris did opinions like Pamuk's become conceivable.

Alongside an attitude of this sort, there soon appeared another that was different yet complementary. Both were already to be found in the tradition of the *novel*, but they gained strength during the eighteenth century. Works like *Pamela*, *Clarissa*, or *The New Heloise* owe their success to the capacity to arouse an identification extending beyond moral judgment. At the same time, the interest in *phronesis* that spread in many novels in the 1700s led to the development of a purely descriptive eye with regard to human imperfection. Influenced by this conception of narrative fiction, the novel underwent a metamorphosis that had previously taken place in moral philosophy. For centuries the science of the passions had kept a close bond with normative ethics, but starting in the second half of the 1500s, a new attitude developed:[34] Montaigne invented two notions that would prove to be decisive in the history of thought on the affects, those of "spectator of life" (*spectateur de la vie*) and "natural philosopher" (*naturaliste*);[35] Descartes sought to study the passions with a contemplative outlook borrowed from physics[36] Spinoza attacked those who disliked and derided the af

---

33. The massive presence of *quaestiones* is a basic feature of *Tom Jones*: every action of the characters is subject to the judgment of the narrator, the community, or the character itself. Throughout the novel, discussion is continuous. If we randomly open the work (to book 3, for example), we immediately find a series of moral problems: whether Tom, in wanting to help the gamekeeper's family, acted rightly or wrongly in selling the horse given to him by Mr. Allworthy (bk. 3, chaps. 8 and 9); whether young Master Blifil did well or badly in allowing Sophia's bird to escape (bk. 4, chaps. 3 and 4); whether Tom behaved properly or improperly toward Sophia (bk. 4, chap. 5).

34. See Remo Bodei, *Geometria delle passioni* (Milan: Feltrinelli, 1991); Denis Kambouchner, "Passions," in *Dictionnaire d'éthique et de philosophie morale*, ed. Monique Canto-Sperber (Paris: PUF, 2004), 1397–1404.

35. Montaigne, *The Complete* Essays, bk. 1, chap. 18, p. 81; bk. 1, chap. 26, p. 177–178; bk. 3, chap. 12, p.1197. See Van Delft, *Les Spectateurs de la vie: généalogie du regard moraliste*, 5ff.

36. Descartes, *The Passions of the Soul*.

fects instead of trying to understand them as if they were lines, surfaces, and bodies.[37] Little by little, a form of scientific distance emerged that would be called "anatomical" and, at the end of the eighteenth century, "analytical."[38] It was a slow process (the Pauline and Augustinian legacy remained alive for a long time), but it did make possible the works of the French *moralistes,* among others. Over the course of the eighteenth century, the narrators of fiction could proudly lay claim to the act of detached observation.

> The fact that the naturalist's stance was late to make its entrance into the world of the novel is not surprising, because it often happens that a genre with dubious legitimacy adopts more conservative ideas than those with a noble cultural genealogy. The transformation became visible in the metaphors that authors used to describe the act of storytelling, starting with the most celebrated one—the *mirror.* The image has a long history: it appears in book 10 of the *Republic,*[39] passes through two thousand years of history, and takes a crucial turn in the modern era. For classicist poetics, a work that mirrors the world reflects the ideas of things and not their mere sensible appearances. Starting in the nineteenth century, the image was used to express two different positions: to lay claim to contingency perceived by the senses, but also to emphasize that all visions of reality arise out of subjective mediation, since each mirror reflects things according to its own specific curvature.[40] Hence, in the modern era, the metaphor described the presumptions of realism as well as its contradictions.

37. Baruch Spinoza, *Ethica* (1677), preface to part 3, trans. Samuel Shirley, in *Complete Works* (Indianapolis: Hackett, 2002), 277–278.

38. Van Delft, *Littérature et anthropologie;* by the same author, *Frammento e anatomia: Rivoluzione scientifica e creazione letteraria,* chap. 1; Fernando Vidal, *Les sciences de l'âme XVIᵉ-XVIIIe siècle* (2006), English translation *The Sciences of the Soul : The Early Modern Origins of Psychology,* trans. Saskia Brown (Chicago: University of Chicago Press, 2011), chap. 1.

39. The first appearances are actually pre-Platonic: see Halliwell, *The Aesthetics of Mimesis,* 171.

40. Meyer H. Abrams, *The Mirror and the Lamp: Romantic Theory and the Critical Tradition* (Oxford: Oxford University Press, 1953). On the history of metaphor in the nineteenth century, see Peter Brooks, *Realist Vision* (New Haven, CT: Yale University Press, 2005), and Federico Bertoni, *Realismo e letteratura. Una storia possibile* (Turin: Einaudi, 2007), 90ff. and passim.

Nevertheless, even prior to illustrating the dilemmas of mimesis, when reference was made to the mirror, the aim was to proclaim a new attitude toward the represented world. One of the oldest and most famous versions of the metaphor is to be found in *The Red and the Black* (1830):

> A novel is a mirror, taking a walk down a big road. Sometimes you'll see nothing but blue skies; sometimes you'll see the muck in the mud piles along the road. And you'll accuse the highway where the mud is piled, or, more strongly still, the street inspector who leaves water wallowing in the roads, so the mud piles can come into being.[41]

Clearly, the original meaning of the image is ethical, not theoretical. In addition to asserting his faithfulness to the true, what Stendhal is intending to communicate through this visual image is the novelist's neutrality toward morality and the end of the era in which novels were silent tutors. Rather than teaching normative ethics, the narrator now limits himself or herself to observing. Two years after *The Red and the Black* appeared, George Sand published *Indiana* (1832). In the foreword we read:

> If, in the course of his task, he [the writer] has happened to express cries of pain wrung from his characters by the social unease which affects them; if he has not been afraid to record their aspirations towards a better life, let society be blamed for its inequalities and fate for its whims. The writer is only a mirror which reflects them, a machine which traces their outline, and he has nothing for which to apologize if the impressions are correct and the reflection is faithful.[42]

Once again, the metaphor of the mirror is used to assert autonomy from morality during a period when the French literary world was gripped by a debate between those who defended the premodern idea of the novel as a didactic genre and those who attributed other than ethical-normative purposes to the novelist.[43] During the nineteenth century the metaphor took on more complexity. In the preface to *Cromwell* (1827), Hugo talks about a mirror that concentrates into a flame what in reality appears as a set of

---

41. Stendhal, *Le Rouge et le Noir* (1830); English translation *The Red and the Black*, trans. Burton Raffel (New York: Random House, 2004), 342.

42. George Sand, *Indiana* (1832); English translation *Indiana*, trans. Sylvia Raphael, with an introduction by Naomi Schor (Oxford: Oxford University Press, 1994), 5.

43. See Marguerite Iknayan, *The Idea of the Novel in France: The Critical Reaction, 1815–1848* (Geneva: Droz-Minard, 1961), 93ff.

scattered rays. In *Adam Bede* (1859), George Eliot talks about a mirror that represents things as they are reflected in the mind of the author: the writer seeks to be faithful to reality but cannot be entirely objective.[44] The image illustrates the dialectic between the pretense of representing things as they are, and the awareness that every mimetic act reflects the world according to a particular curvature. But what this divided metaphorical world really has in common is the rejection of precepts in favor of observation, the birth of a new ethical attitude toward life and stories.

Parallel to the development of metaphors that signify neutrality toward morality, writers adopted the stance of the *spectator*.

In the ninth chapter of *Pride and Prejudice* (1813), when Elizabeth Bennett quotes a maxim on the differences between people, Bingley responds: "I did not know . . . that you were a studier of character."[45] A *studier of character*: the formula applies well to many of Austen's heroines—but it is clear that the author is also referring to herself. In the early nineteenth century, many novelists laid claim to this kind of outlook: the gesture of the observer recurs constantly in *The Human Comedy*;[46] when Mérimée asked Stendhal what his job was, he replied, "Observer of the human heart." The first reviews of Balzac and Stendhal return again and again to the novelty of this attitude: "[The author of *The Red and the Black*] is a cold observer, a cruel critic, an evil skeptic who is content to not believe in anything";[47] "[Balzac] observes with a rare insight and reproduces reality with precision";[48] "the sole object [of Stendhal's] thought was a science of observation."[49] Their contemporaries were immediately cognizant of the rupture entailed by this approach.[50] Interestingly enough, some

44. See Bertoni, *Realismo e letteratura*, 93.

45. Jane Austen, *Pride and Prejudice*, ed. Pat Rogers, in *The Cambridge Edition of the Works of Jane Austen* (Cambridge: Cambridge University Press, 2006), vol. 1, chap. 9, p. 47.

46. See Anne-Marie Baron, "Statut et fonctions de l'observateur balzacien," *L'Année balzacienne* 10 (1989): 301–316.

47. Jules Janin, "*Le Rouge et le Noir*," *Journal des débats*, December 26, 1830.

48. Eugène d'Izalguier, "*La Vieille Fille*," *Phalange*, November 20, 1836, 1, col. 434.

49. Auguste Bussière, "Poètes et romanciers modernes de la France XLVIII: Henri Beyle (M. de Stendhal)," *Revue des deux mondes* 1 (January 15, 1843): 254.

50. See Bernard Weinberg, *French Realism: The Critical Reaction, 1830–1870* (1937; repr., New York: Modern Language Association, 1937), chaps. 1 and 2.

times this perception of novelty was accompanied by moralistic criticisms: limiting oneself to watching meant failing to issue an ethical judgment— something that less audacious writers and readers in the first half of the nineteenth century considered a duty.[51] At least half a century before naturalism transformed the observer stance into a poetic principle, it spread among European novelists, taking its place alongside the stance of the tutor, which it gradually replaced. Narratives presented as parables written with the purpose of instructing and correcting gave way to narratives presented as "studies" or "documents" written in order to contemplate and comprehend.

4. As we saw in Chapter 3, in 1741 Aaron Hill pinpointed Richardson's novelty with a trenchant turn of phrase: "[The author of *Pamela*] moves us, every where, with the Force of a TRAGEDY"; the story of a maidservant is just as valuable as that of a queen. It was a revolutionary idea for many reasons. The most obvious is social: Richardson heralded the time in which every human being would gain what the Goncourt brothers, in the preface to *Germinie Lacerteux* (1865), would call a "right to the Novel."[52] The other reasons are less obvious but no less important. They concern the principles of interpretation of individual lives and lie at the deepest, archaeological level, so to speak.

It must first be said that Aaron Hill's reasoning was less revolutionary than it seems. In fact, it took its lead from the Christian logic of the *exemplum*: like all human beings, even maidservants are creatures of God, the battle between vice and virtue that must be fought inside them and around them has an absolute value. This is why "under the modest Disguise of a novel," *Pamela* contained "all the *Soul* of Religion." Richardson chose a heroine of low standing so that every female reader could feel potentially deserving of the reward that Pamela received for her virtue. The true revolution came a century later when the religious harmonics had faded out. In 1853, an essay by Louis Clément de Ris on Balzac presented ideas very close to those expounded by Aaron Hill:

51. Ibid.

52. Edmond de Goncourt and Jules de Goncourt, *Germinie Lacerteux* (1865), ed. Nadine Satiat (Paris: Flammarion, 1990), "Préface," 55.

[Balzac] understood and made it understood that the drama lay on the inside, not the outside, that he could find as much passion, rage, intoxication, and pain in the soul of a draper, a perfumer, a millionaire, a duchess, and a dandy as in that of a bandit or a page boy.[53]

Just as for Hill, "the Passions of Nature are the same, in the *Lord* and in his *Coach-man*," but the ultimate aim of the mimesis of the human world, officially, remained that of moral orthopedics. For Balzac and Clément de Ris, on the other hand, the passions were intriguing in their pure immanence: a perfumer was as worthy as a duchess because every life and interior landscape was becoming worthy of attention in itself, for no other reason. The scale of public values that allowed disparities between people to be created was less important than the subjective right to consider one's own life an absolute value.

The conceptual apparatuses constructed by the cultures of antiquity and Christianity to impose a hidden moral sense and order on the proliferation of the human world (allegorism, moralism, the hierarchy implied by the separation of styles, and the repertoire of events) dissolved. In their place there arose the pathos of proximity and a new interest in bare particular life. Two forms of transcendence were implied in classicism and Christian aesthetic Platonism: the transcendence of public stories from the past versus private stories from the present; and the transcendence of universal significance versus the immanence of singular events. While classicism took its stories from the great ancient literary and mythological repertoire, Christian aesthetic Platonism looked to absolute metaphysical and moral truths set out in the form of precepts or ideas. Both these structures of sense presupposed that the singular life was valuable as an *exemplum* of a universal, and that mimesis was an effective discursive formation for instruction and entertainment but secondary with respect to the truth. Beginning with the shift that took place between the end of the eighteenth century and the beginning of the nineteenth century, *individual stories broke free from the ancient hidden moral senses and laid claim to an inherent value, in their very contingency.* A culture of subjective nonbelonging, to tradition as well as to ideas, was beginning to take form. The contingent life proliferated far from any center and was interesting in itself, and for no other reason. While

53. Louis Clément de Ris, "Honoré de Balzac," in *Portraits à la plume* (Paris: Didier, 1853), 312–313.

it might be the object of empathy or analysis, it could not be read as the allegory of an already-known truth.

A New Conceptual Ether

The transformation in attitudes toward the kinds of stories being told and the rise of empathic or analytical observation were accompanied by a change in the categories through which authors and narrators interpreted reality. In Chapter 1 we saw how every story composed of words comes into being surrounded by a conceptual ether that allows the narrator to show the invisible dimensions implicit in the visible lives of people. One of the frontiers that narrative crossed over between the second half of the eighteenth century and the beginning of the nineteenth century involved precisely this ether.

In *Tom Jones,* perhaps the more important third-person novel of the eighteenth century, the narrator intervenes continuously by commenting on the story. Here is a typical observation:

> Molly was charmed with the first opportunity she ever had of showing her beauty to advantage; for though she could very well bear to contemplate herself in the glass, even when dressed in rags; and though she had in that dress conquered the heart of Jones, and perhaps of some others; yet she thought the addition of finery would much improve her charms, and extend her conquests.
>
> Molly, therefore, having dressed herself out in this sash, with a new laced cap, and some other ornaments which Tom had given her, repairs to church with her fan in her hand the very next Sunday. The great are deceived if they imagine they have appropriated ambition and vanity to themselves. These noble qualities flourish as notably in a country church and churchyard as in the drawing-room, or in the closet. Schemes have indeed been laid in the vestry which would hardly disgrace the conclave. Here is a ministry, and here is an opposition. Here are plots and circumventions, parties and factions, equal to those which are to be found in courts.
>
> Nor are the women here less practised in the highest feminine arts than their fair superiors in quality and fortune. Here are prudes and coquettes. Here are dressing and ogling, falsehood, envy, malice, scandal; in short, everything which is common to the most splendid assembly, or

politest circle. Let those of high life, therefore, no longer despise the ignorance of their inferiors; nor the vulgar any longer rail at the vices of
their betters.[54]

A few months before *Tom Jones,* Richardson published *Clarissa* (1748):

> The following History is given in a series of letters, written principally in
> a double yet separate correspondence;
>
> Between two young ladies of virtue and honour, bearing an inviolable
> friendship for each other, and writing not merely for amusement, but
> upon most *interesting* subjects; in which every private family, more or
> less, may find itself concerned: and,
>
> Between two gentlemen of free lives; one of them glorying in his tal-
> ents for stratagem and invention, and communicating to the other, in
> confidence, all the secret purposes of an intriguing head and resolute
> heart.[55]

Almost seventy years later, in 1814, this is how Sir Walter Scott presented the setting and background for the story told in *Waverley:*

> The ministry of George the First's time were prudently anxious to di-
> minish the phalanx of opposition. The Tory nobility, depending for their
> reflected lustre upon the sunshine of a court, had for some time been
> gradually reconciling themselves to the new dynasty. But the wealthy
> country gentlemen of England, a rank which retained, with much of an-
> cient manners and primitive integrity, a great proportion of obstinate and
> unyielding prejudice, stood aloof in haughty and sullen opposition, and
> cast many a look of mingled regret and hope to Bois le Due, Avignon,
> and Italy.[56]

What contemporaries admired in Scott's main disciple, Balzac, was the
novelty of his *préparation;* in other words, the parts in which the narrator
introduces the story's characters and setting.[57] Here is the *préparation* for
The Muse of the Department (1837):

---

54. Fielding, *The History of Tom Jones,* bk. 4, chap. 7, pp. 176–177.

55. Samuel Richardson, preface to *Clarissa, or The History of a Young Lady,* ed. Angus
Ross (London: Penguin, 1985), 35.

56. Sir Walter Scott, *Waverley; or, 'Tis Sixty Years Since,* ed. Claire Lamont (Oxford: Clarendon Press, 1981), chap. 2, p. 7.

57. Weinberg, *French Realism,* 53, 69.

The hill on which the houses of Sancerre are grouped is so far from the river that the little river-port of Saint-Thibault thrives on the life of Sancerre. There wine is shipped and oak staves are landed, with all the produce brought from the upper and lower Loire. At the period when this story begins the suspension bridges at Cosne and at Saint-Thibault were already built. Travelers from Paris to Sancerre by the southern road were no longer ferried across the river from Cosne to Saint-Thibault; and this of itself is enough to show that the great cross-shuffle of 1830 was a thing of the past, for the House of Orleans has always had a care for substantial improvements, though somewhat after the fashion of a husband who makes his wife presents out of her marriage portion.

Excepting that part of Sancerre which occupies the little plateau, the streets are more or less steep, and the town is surrounded by slopes known as the Great Ramparts, a name which shows that they are the highroads of the place.

Outside the ramparts lies a belt of vineyards. Wine forms the chief industry and the most important trade of the country, which yields several vintages of high-class wine full of aroma, and so nearly resembling the wines of Burgundy, that the vulgar palate is deceived. So Sancerre finds in the wineshops of Paris the quick market indispensable for liquor that will not keep for more than seven or eight years. . . . The town still bears much of its ancient aspect. . . . The citadel, a relic of military power and feudal times, stood one of the most terrible sieges of our religious wars. . . . The town of Sancerre, rich in its greater past, but widowed now of its military importance, is doomed to an even less glorious future, for the course of trade lies on the right bank of the Loire. . . . Sancerre, the pride of the left bank, numbers three thousand five hundred inhabitants at most, while at Cosne there are now more than six thousand. Within half a century the part played by these two towns standing opposite each other has been reversed. . . . Under such conditions, though there are the usual disadvantages of life in a small town, and each one lives under the officious eye which makes private life almost a public concern, on the other hand, the spirit of township—a sort of patriotism, which cannot indeed take the place of a love of home—flourishes triumphantly.[58]

---

58. Honoré de Balzac, *La Muse du département* (1837); English translation *The Muse of the Department*, trans. James Waring, in *The Works of Honoré de Balzac*, vol. 15 (Boston: Dana Estes, 1901), 224–225.

Clearly, there is a caesura between the time of Fielding and Richardson and that of Scott and Balzac. Fielding moves in a conceptual ether made of ahistorical notions, using an approach inherited from the New Comedy that presupposes a fixist conception of characters and manners ("the great" and "their inferiors," men and women, "prudes" and "coquettes"). Richardson is imbued with the same static categories that Fielding uses ("young ladies of virtue and honor," "gentlemen of free lives") and, officially at least, he writes with an explicit prescriptive intent. Instead, Scott and Balzac use concepts of a different type: they talk about social classes, they illustrate power relations, they describe commercial trends. The background events are explained using sociological, political, and economic categories: the Tory nobility and English gentlemen; the development and decline of the town of Sancerre in relation to the wine market and the trade flows along the Loire. They are set in a thoroughly historical dimension—in *Waverley*, the Jacobite Rebellion of 1745; in *The Muse of the Department*, 1830 in France.

One of the guiding ideas that provides the groundwork for the schema Auerbach presents in *Mimesis* is his thought on the historical frameworks to which texts refer. Every text presupposes a web of concepts that situates the particular stories told in each individual text within a general context. Arguing from a perspective of long duration, Auerbach identifies three of these frameworks. The first is the static, atemporal mode used by the classicist culture of antiquity to observe characters and manners, running from Theophrastus to La Bruyère: with this final branch of the genealogy in mind, perhaps, Auerbach calls it "moralistic."[59] The second is the theological framework that made Christian realism possible. In its most complex forms, this type of apparatus generated the frame encompassing Augustine's *Confessions*, which opens with a prayer to God and ends with a commentary on the book of Genesis, or the conceptual architecture that made Dante's journey possible by imposing an order on the afterlife. In its most common forms, this type can be seen in the sense of impermanence, vanity, and sin accompanying medieval stories on human life. The third frame of reference places particular people into a political, economic, and social totality that varies according to the times and places. Unknown to

---

59. Auerbach, *Mimesis*, 28; in the same book, see the appendix (pp. 559–574), "Epilegomena to *Mimesis*" (1953), p. 561.

ancient and Christian literature, this conceptual environment emerged in the modern era thanks to the realistic novels of the nineteenth century. Auerbach defines it as having "a sense of historical dynamics."

The vocabulary Fielding's narrator draws on to comment on events is "moralistic," in the sense that Auerbach gives to the word. Richardson's lexicon belongs to the same family as Christian realism and the poetics of the *exemplum*. Scott and Balzac, on the other hand, live and breathe in a new philosophical ether. A critical dividing line falls between the middle of the eighteenth century and the early nineteenth century, the same one that marks the dawning of modern human sciences. The conceptual ether of contemporary fiction writers who look to the tradition of the novel is largely composed of notions endowed with a sense of historical dynamics. In its banal and ordinary form, this philosophical vocabulary finds expression in the categories of common sense that we usually use to interpret life. We contemporaries link biographies to time and space on the basis of historical, sociological, psychological, and economic notions that have become sedimented in our outlook and in our *doxa:* these are the same ones the human sciences claim to transform into *episteme.* For us, Rastignac is neither the timeless Theophrastian Man of Petty Ambition nor a sinner to be set up as an *exemplum* of vice: he is a young man belonging to the provincial nobility who, like many of his peers living in France under the Restoration, threw himself into the competitive regime of modern civil society in order to work his way up in life. Most contemporary novelists still use this lexicon. If we were to cite three of the most significant works to appear in the past fifteen years, we might say that the conceptual language used to set the characters' stories within a universal context by Philip Roth in *American Pastoral* (1997), Michel Houellebecq in *Elementary Particles* (1998), and Jonathan Littell in *The Kindly Ones* (2006) belongs to the same strain as the one used by Scott and Balzac as well as by Jane Austen, Alessandro Manzoni, and Stendhal. The two centuries separating us from the early 1800s have changed the vocabulary by replacing certain words with others, but the fundamental grammar has remained the same.

The philosophical ether revealed by the sociohistorical novels of the early nineteenth century is not entirely lacking in precedents. Some eighteenth-century narratives focusing on *phronesis* anticipated the type of perspective that the realism of the next century would develop. However, this is primarily because in the novel of the seventeenth and eighteenth centuries, there was a tradition of analysis of the inner life that crossed completely unscathed over the dividing line we are describing. In 1830 Stendhal wrote an essay titled "Walter Scott and *The Princesse de Clèves.*"[60] In it, he contrasts two novelistic models that seemed feasible to him in his time: that of Madame de La Fayette, which privileges the meticulous description of the passions; and that of Scott, which privileges the meticulous description of the context. Officially, Stendhal liked the first and did not appreciate the second; in reality, he was influenced by Scott much more than he was willing to admit. The surface of their novels is completely different (Scott is wordy and systematic, Stendhal is quick and fragmented), but the logic that their works obey is in many respects the same: Stendhal, like Scott, locates the particular plot events within a general sociopolitical context; the period and place in which the characters are born and live are essential, determining structures. The heroes can rebel against the laws of the context, but they cannot ignore them, because their lives and destinies are always run through by the environment. A passage like the following one would never have been written had Scott not contributed to introducing historical dynamics into the novel:

> On 15 May 1796, General Bonaparte made his entry into Milan at the head of the youthful army which had just crossed the bridge at Lodi and let the world know that after all these centuries, Caesar and Alexander had a successor. The miracles of valour and of genius of which Italy was the witness within a few months reawoke a slumbering people; a week before the arrival of the French, the Milanese still saw them only as a bunch of brigands, used always to taking flight faced by the troops of His Imperial and Royal Majesty: that anyway was what a small newspaper the size of a human hand, printed on filthy paper, repeated to them three times a week. . . . An entire people realized, on 15 May 1796, that everything it had respected hitherto was supremely ridiculous and sometimes odious. The departure of the last Austrian regiment signalled the fall of the old ideas: to risk one's life became the fashion; they could see that in order to be happy after centuries of increasingly lukewarm sensations one needed to feel a genuine love of their homeland and go in quest of heroic deeds. They had been plunged into blackest night by the

60. Stendhal, "Walter Scott et la Princesse de Clèves" (1830), in *Mélanges de littérature,* vol. 3, ed. Henri Martineau (Paris: Le Divan, 1933).

continuation of the jealous despotism of Charles V and Philip II; their statues were thrown down and they suddenly found themselves flooded with light.[61]

The interesting part of Stendhal's essay is not, therefore, his attack against Scott, but his defense of Madame de La Fayette. In this case, Stendhal was right: the tradition born with *The Princesse de Clèves* was still alive in the first decades of the nineteenth century, and it contributed to creating introspective masterpieces like Constant's *Adolphe* and, as we have been saying, Stendhal's novels themselves. The two human sciences we encounter most often in the narrators' vocabularies are psychology and sociology: a division corresponding to the split rooted in modern common sense between the I and the world, between "character" and "manners." This threshold could easily be deconstructed using the methods of abstract thought and genealogical history, but the deconstruction would not eliminate the enduring presence of the opposition as well as its value as a symptom. Now: while the tradition of psychological analysis descending from Madame de La Fayette steadily converged into the lexicon of modern fiction, the sociological categories of eighteenth-century narrative were quite dissimilar from those that would prevail with the novel of the early nineteenth century. In other words, if modern narrative sociology is a recent invention, a part of modern narrative psychology arrived prior to the nineteenth century.

The Weight of Novels

The last aspect of the paradigm leap we are describing concerns the weight that the novel had in the literary system and, more generally, among games of truth. Between the end of the eighteenth century and the first half of the nineteenth, the status of the genre changed: "dans un roman frivole aisément tout s'excuse; / c'est assez qu'en courant la fiction amuse; / trop de rigueur serait hors de saison," wrote Boileau in *The Art of Poetry* (1674)[62] (in the historic translation by Soames and Dryden: "In a romance

---

61. Stendhal, *La Chartreuse de Parme* (1839, 1841); English translation *The Charterhouse of Parma*, trans. John Sturrock (London: Penguin Books, 2006), 7–8.

62. Nicolas Boileau, *L'Art poétique* (1674); English translation *The Art of Poetry*, trans. Sir William Soames, revised by Sir John Dryden (London, 1683), chant 3, lines 119–121.

those errors are excused: / There 'tis enough that, reading, we're amused: / Rules too severe would there be useless found"). Boileau gave expression to an opinion shared by almost all European classicist writers between the second half of the sixteenth century and the second half of the eighteenth: *novels* and *romances* were minor works; a serious man of letters might derive some amusement from reading them, but it would be absurd to judge them according the rules of the art or to put one's hopes for glory in them. Being foreign to the conventions prescribed by ancient poetry, they must not be taken too seriously; lacking distinguished ancestors, they are works of *entertainment* that will be swept away by time. This is the same attitude that intellectuals from the second half of the twentieth century had (and still have) when judging Hollywood movies and television shows.[63] One hundred and twenty years later, a writer who belonged to the same national culture as Boileau considered the novel to be "one of the most beautiful inventions of the human spirit" and one of the most useful to public morals.[64] For the avant-garde authors born between 1760 and 1780, for Madame de Staël as for Friedrich Schlegel, Novalis, Scott, or Foscolo, the novel was a legitimate and important art form.

The genre acquired prestige partly because the rise of the *novel* and the decline of the *romance* redefined its position. Boileau associated the term *roman* with heroic Baroque novels; Madame de Staël associated it with completely different texts. In the time separating Boileau's *Art of Poetry* (1674) from Madame de Staël's *Essay on Fictions* (1795), French *nouvelles,* the works of Prevost, Crébillon, Marivaux, Richardson, Fielding, Rousseau, Goethe, Diderot, Laclos, Moritz, and the *roman personnel* that began to spread at the end of the eighteenth century thanks to the influence of Rousseau and *The Sorrows of Young Werther* had demonstrated that the novel was no longer a minor genre. Similarly, Reitz's *Heimat* (1984–2004), Greenaway's *A TV Dante* (1989–1991), Von Trier's *Medea* (1988) and *The Kingdom* (1994), Lynch's *Twin Peaks* (1990–1991), and a number of American television series from the past thirty years, from *Hill Street Blues* (1981–1987) to *The Wire* (2002–2008) or *Mad Men* (2007–2015), made it

63. See Warner, *Licensing Entertainment*, 6; Siti, "The Novel on Trial," 94.

64. Madame de Staël, *Essai sur les fictions* (1795), in *Œuvres de jeunesse*, ed. John Isbell (Paris: Desjonquères, 1997), 146.

conceivable that the medium of television was capable of producing works of art and not only degraded forms of entertainment.

The metaphor of the novel as a book of life already began to appear in the first half of the eighteenth century. At the beginning, it did not have the weight that it would acquire between the eighteenth and nineteenth centuries, because it was a variant of the expressions used by ancient poetics to define comedy, as we saw in Chapter 2. In his introduction to *The Wanderings of the Heart and Mind* (1735–1738), Crébillon wrote:

> The novel [*roman*], so disdained by the judicious, and often with reason, is of all literary forms the one which could perhaps be made the most useful, if it were managed; if, instead of filling it with farfetched and obscure situations, and heroes whose characters and adventures are alike always incredible, we were to make it, like comedy, a picture of human life [*le tableau de la vie humaine*], in which we censured vice and folly.[65]

In the "Discours sur le roman" that opens *Theresa, histoire italienne* (1745) by Baculard d'Arnaud, we read that the *roman* provides a natural picture of society that is within everybody's reach. These expressions of praise were made possible by the transformation that the genre underwent when the *novel* prevailed over the *romance* and the old romance tales were pushed aside by "modern works":

> The *roman* is very different. I want to talk about these modern works, like *Cleveland*, *Les Mémoires d'un homme de qualité*, *Marianne*, *Le Paysan parvenu*, *Les Égarements du cœur*, *Les Confessions du comte de * * *,* and not those pitiful productions born of an impoverished imagination known by the name of tales [*fables*]. The novel thus represents man as he is, his virtues and vices. It is a natural picture of society [*tableau naturel de la société*] within everybody's reach. All readers can enjoy the pleasure of recognizing themselves, of discovering themselves in them; and as a consequence, the pleasure of being entertained and instructed at the same time, in a much better way than slogging through history books.[66]

---

65. Claude Crébillon, *Les Égarements du cœur et de l'esprit* (1735–1738); English translation *The Wayward Head and Heart*, trans. Barbara Bray (London: Oxford University Press 1963), xvi.

66. Cited in May, *Le Dilemme du roman au XVIIIᵉ siècle*, 148–149.

Four years later, in *Tom Jones,* the painting turned into a book: Fielding talks about the novel as a "doomsday-book of nature," a cadastre of human nature. But these formulations by Crébillon, Baculard d'Arnaud, and Fielding still show their kinship with the culture of classicism and aesthetic Platonism, either because they apply the canonical definition of comedy to the novel or because they continue to operate in a system of hierarchies within which the comedy and the novel, although garnering value, can never attain the symbolic weight of tragedy or epic poetry.

When Diderot published his "Éloge de Richardson" in 1762, his description of the novel included new emphases:

> O Richardson! I dare say that the most truthful history is full of lies and that your novel is full of truths. History depicts only a few individuals, while you depict the human race. History attributes to a few individuals things they have neither said nor done; everything you attribute to human beings, they have said and done. History encompasses only one portion of time, only one point on the surface of the globe; you encompass all places and all times. The model from which you copy is the human heart, which was, is, and will always be the same. If we submitted the best historian to a harsh critique, would he be able to stand up to it as you have? From this point of view, I dare say that history is often a bad novel, and that the novel, as you have made it, is a good history.[67]

A year earlier *The New Heloise* had appeared, meeting with as much success as *Pamela.* It is not unlikely that Diderot wrote the *Éloge de Richardson* partly to restore the Englishman's stature, diminishing Rousseau's role.[68] But even if this were the case, the writers Diderot implicitly compares were divided by a crucial sociological difference. Although he was indebted to Richardson, the author of *The New Heloise* occupied a very different position in the contemporary literary field from the one occupied by the author of *Pamela:* in 1740 Richardson was a printer with no reputation whatsoever; in 1761 Rousseau had already written the *Discourse on the Arts and Sciences* and the *Discourse on the Origin of Inequality;* the following year he would publish the *Social Contract.* Although notorious for being somewhat of a bizarre person, he was nonetheless one

67. Diderot, "In Praise of Richardson," 90.
68. Brooks, *The Novel of Worldliness,* 163ff.

of the most talked-about philosophers of his time. In his *Conversation about Novels* that prefaces the new editions of *The New Heloise*, Rousseau refers to novels using the expression "tableaux of humankind" *(tableaux de l'humanité)*.[69]

The passage from *Pamela* to *The New Heloise* also shows that, starting in the 1760s, the novel was attracting a growing number of educated men of letters. *The Sorrows of Young Werther,* the book that gave rise to a social phenomenon in the 1770s comparable to the one caused in 1740 by the printer Samuel Richardson, was the work of a writer with a solid classicist culture. We begin to see the same dialectic that runs through our genre today: one portion of the novel is aimed at readers of average or low education, another at highly educated and specialized readers. It may happen that some of the works from the second type are also successful with the broader public, but the dividing line remains. Between the second half of the eighteenth century and the beginning of the nineteenth, there arose "pride in the novel,"[70] the awareness that this art form can impart truths about life and the world that escape philosophy, science, and religion. The first traces of a now modern, postclassicist use of the book metaphor are to be found in German aesthetics during the last half of the eighteenth century, especially in Blanckenburg's *Versuch über den Roman* (1774).[71] At the end of the eighteenth century, when Novalis wrote that the novel is a life in the form of a book,[72] the image now meant what it would for D. H. Lawrence in 1925. In Italian literature, one of the decisive symbolic events was the choice Manzoni made around 1821 to stop writing tragedies in order to devote himself instead to the first draft of *The Betrothed*. He rejected a traditional literary genre to make a high-culture use of a new, popular form.[73]

Certainly, the number and variety of works that went by the name of novels, as well as the dual literary regime divided between an elite public and the general readership, enveloped the genre in an air of suspicion even

69. Rousseau, *Julie, or The New Heloise,* 8.

70. Siti, "L'orgoglio del romanzo."

71. Blanckenburg, *Versuch über den Roman,* xv.

72. "Ein Roman ist ein *Leben,* als Buch." Novalis, *Teplitzer Fragmente,* in *Das philosophisch-theoretische Werk,* ed. Hans-Joachim Mähl (Munich: Carl Hanser, 1978), 388.

73. See Daniela Brogi, *Il genere proscritto. Manzoni dalla tragedia al romanzo* (Pisa: Giardini, 2005).

after 1800. The process leading to legitimacy was long, tortuous, and strati-
fied. For a large part of the nineteenth century, the novel continued to
receive criticism even within the predominant European narrative traditions. In France, the controversy about its prestige, value, and place in the
history of literature still raged during the Romantic period. Important
writers had dedicated themselves to the novel, but the production of entertainment and the well-established critical topoi slowed its widespread
acceptance. The debate was resolved around 1830, when the birth of the
French social novel was accompanied by a critical discourse presenting
the works of Stendhal and Balzac as the intellectual redemption of a
form that until then had been intended for entertainment.[74] Although
useful for purposes of self-promotion, this idea was actually controversial,
because, while the reputation of the French novel was still being con-
tested, the genre had already been dignified by authors like Rousseau,
Diderot, Madame de Staël, Chateaubriand, and Constant.[75] Interestingly
enough, in a review appearing in 1832 in the *Revue de Paris,* the choice
to abandon tragedy in favor of the novel is described as typical of the
latest generation of writers: "Only a few years ago, young people fresh out
of secondary schools wanted to write a tragedy, if they didn't already have
one in hand. . . . Now that tragedy is dead . . . , every high-school student
begins with a novel, and as we've seen, many learned writers also end
with one."[76]

The text that symbolically enshrined the consecration of the genre in
France was Balzac's 1842 introduction to *The Human Comedy.* Here
Balzac presents the novel as a noble form of knowledge, as a game of truth
rivaling philosophy, history, and the sciences. The novelist will be the zo-
ologist of the human species, the historian of manners, the historian of the
human heart, a competitor to civil status. The novelist will rediscover the
spirit of laws fallen into disuse and explain the life of peoples. He or she will
primarily search for causes and principles,[77] laying claim to the intellectual
gesture that had defined philosophy starting from the opening pages of
Aristotle's *Metaphysics.* Balzac's view was not an isolated case: in French

74. Margaret Cohen also reconstructs this discourse in *The Sentimental Education of the
Novel* (Princeton, NJ: Princeton University Press, 1999).

75. See Iknayan, *The Idea of the Novel in France,* chap. 3.

76. Review of *Sous les tilleuls* by Alphonse Karr, in *Revue de Paris* 4, no. 41 (1832): 128.

77. Balzac, "Author's Introduction" to *The Human Comedy.*

literary debates of the 1830s, sparked by the attacks Nisard launched against the genre around 1833, many people treated the novel as an important form of knowledge about life.[78] The traditionalist fringes of the literary field remained wary, however: until at least the middle of the nineteenth century, the French novel continued to be targeted by moralistic attacks from the medical establishment, the Church, and the conservative press.[79]

In Britain, Scott was a decisive author for many reasons, starting with the fact that he turned to the novel after having already secured a reputation as a poet. This is how a reviewer of *Waverley* commented on this choice in the *Critical Review:* "Why a poet of established fame should dwindle into a scribbler of novels, we cannot tell."[80] In addition to choosing a genre still considered to be risky, through his essays the author of *Waverley* consigned it to the history of literature by constructing a critical discourse around the eighteenth-century novel, treating as a cultural institution what many, until then, had considered a form of entertainment.[81] British debates on the value of the novel extended beyond the mid-nineteenth century. In the essay "Criticism in Relation to Novels" (1865), George Henry Lewes writes that "although the fame of a great novelist is only something less than the fame of a great poet, and the reputation of a clever novelist is far superior to that of a respectable poet," there remains something condescending in the way critics talk about the novel, suggesting that, in spite of everything, the genre was still a minor, facile form.[82] As the nineteenth century progressed, those who attacked the novel found themselves in the rear guard more often than not: the new genre could still be criticized, but its legitimacy was continually gaining ground.[83]

78. See Iknayan, *The Idea of the Novel in France*, 64ff., and Judith Lyon-Caen, *La Lecture et la Vie: les usages du roman au temps de Balzac* (Paris: Tallandier, 2006), 50ff.

79. See Lyon-Caen, *La Lecture et la Vie*, 56ff.

80. Cited in James T. Hillhouse, *The Waverley Novels and Their Critics* (Minneapolis: University of Minnesota Press, 1936), 76.

81. Brown, *Institutions of the English Novel*, 176ff.

82. George Henry Lewes, "Criticism in Relation to Novels," *Fortnightly Review* 3 (December 15, 1865–February 1, 1866): 352.

83. Stang, *The Theory of the Novel in England*, 3–46.

If we wanted to identify a threshold in this slow transformation that took place in different layers, lasting almost a century, we would have to choose the year 1800. The date serves as a frontier both because it marks the midpoint between the time in which some avant-garde writers, such as Rousseau and Goethe, began to devote themselves to the novel, and the moment in which the rise of the genre became a *fait accompli;* also because it indicates the symbolic boundary starting from which the new form displayed its revolutionary character. We have seen that the early modern history of the novel is the history of a dialectic: some of its elements conflicted with classicism and Christian aesthetic Platonism, while others were completely permeated with them. For a long time, writers and critics sought legitimacy by accentuating the continuous aspect. Friedrich Schlegel was the first to openly insist on the breach that the novel introduced into European literary history. Many writers of his generation followed suit. Born between two paradigms, Madame de Staël, Friedrich Schlegel, Novalis, Scott, and Foscolo clearly perceived this historic threshold. The literature that continued to operate within the structures of sense derived from classicist and Platonic sources possessed a ritual system of forms and content; the new literature entered into the domain of particularity and proliferated without rules. One might have thought that the metamorphosis began with the advent of Christianity or the Middle Ages, according to a historical-philosophical schema popular in the culture of German idealism; the first signs of rupture might have been identified in Dante or Shakespeare. But in the end, the genre that contributed to broadening the mimesis of particularity more than any other, and to writing the inner and outer history of private life, was unquestionably the novel.[84]

84. Friedrich Schlegel uses the word *Roman* in a narrow sense and in a broad sense, in the first case to indicate the genre we are examining, and in the second to indicate "every romantic book," such as Dante's *Divine Comedy* or the works of Shakespeare. This juxtaposition contains a condensed philosophy of history: according to Schlegel, the search for the individual, the characteristic, the interesting singularity that the novel makes manifest, already came to light in Dante or Shakespeare. See fragments V, 76, 86, 359 in Friedrich Schlegel, *Fragmente zur Poesie und Literatur*, part 1, ed. Hans Eichner (Munich: Paderborn; Zürich: F. Schöningh Thomas-Verlag, 1981); see also his *Dialogue on Poetry*, 72.

The Expansion of the Narratable World

We have seen the two-thousand-year-old structures of sense that the novel dissolved; we must now speak about the structures that came into being during the new era. The first a priori of modern mimesis is its theoretical lack of rituality—its virtual absence of constraints. The literature of the past two centuries can represent anything in any way whatsoever: ahead of their time, Schlegel's theories describe processes that attained complete form only over the course of the nineteenth and twentieth centuries. The direct consequence of this transformation was an enormous expansion of the narratable world. This broadening took place along three directions: the first two correspond to "the liberation of subjectivity, in accordance with its inner contingency" (individual imagination, autobiography, introspection); the third to "the imitation of external objectivity in all its contingent shapes"[85] (stories about the external world or "realism").

1. The English gothic novel and the narrative fiction of German Romanticism expanded the territory of mimesis to imaginary universes that lay very distant from common sense. They ushered in the modern period of fantastic literature and created a new form of romance. Out of this there arose a tradition that would traverse the entire nineteenth century: from the *gothic novel* to Hoffmann, from Potocki to Mary Shelley, from Edgar Allan Poe to Nerval and Théophile Gautier, from Bram Stoker to Wilkie Collins. It was also practiced by the authors of novels who, starting from the 1830s, would be called "realistic": from Balzac and Flaubert to Maupassant and Henry James. As heir to the premodern romance, the new unreal literature no longer sought legitimacy by claiming to describe the world according to the poetic order of the idea, namely, according to a public exemplarity given as an a priori, but rather as a creation of the subjective imagination. On the other hand, it also took up some of the descriptive traits that the eighteenth- and nineteenth-century novel had developed to create a reality effect. In this way it revived the conception of the supernatural by rooting fantastic tales in the concreteness of the sensible and the everyday.

85. Hegel, *Aesthetics*, vol. 1, p. 533.

2. During the same years, a new type of autobiographical narrative developed that at the beginning of the twentieth century Joachim Merlant would call the *roman personnel*.[86] It brought together the autobiographical tradition descending from Rousseau's *Confessions* with the novel-diary that arose out of the transformations that *The New Heloise* and *The Sorrows of Young Werther* introduced into the epistolary genre.[87] This is the group of texts best corresponding to Schlegel's idea that many novels are actually, more or less covertly, confessions of the author.[88] Moreover, the *roman personnel* expanded during the same period that Schlegel was writing his theory of the novel: Foscolo's *The Last Letters of Jacopo Ortis* (1798–1817), Chateaubriand's *Atala* (1801) and *René* (1802), Madame de Staël's *Delphine* (1802) and *Corinne* (1807), Senancour's *Obermann* (1804), Madame de Krüdener's *Valérie* (1804), and Constant's *Adolphe* (1816) came out only a few years earlier or later than the *Dialogue on Poetry* and the *Athenaeum Fragments*. While fantastic literature multiplied imaginary worlds, the *roman personnel* collected together confessions from the author or sentimental stories, ushering into narrative fiction the multiform contingency of personal life—the accidentality of private biography.

3. During the nineteenth century, the novel appropriated the objective variety of life with a breadth of vision unknown to previous fiction. In 1795 Madame de Staël attested to the persistence of a topos with a centuries-old history: at the end of the eighteenth century, writes the author of the *Essay on Fictions,* the novel is still considered a genre in which one speaks of love. To make use of the possibilities implicit in this literary form, she suggests, we should instead talk about all the passions, even those of adulthood: ambition, pride, avarice, vanity. This sort of tableau of the inner life, writes de Staël, already exists in works of history; but while historiography is limited to recounting the events of public figures, the novel talks about private persons like us and therefore has a truly universal value.[89] In 1795, this program was still largely hypothetical, because

---

86. See Joachim Merlant, *Le Roman personnel de Rousseau à Fromentin* (1905) (Geneva: Slatkine, 1978).

87. On the transformation of the epistolary novel into the eighteenth-century novel-diary, see Rousset, "Une forme littéraire: le roman par lettres."

88. Schlegel, *Dialogue on Poetry*, 103.

89. Madame de Staël, *Essai sur les fictions*, 146.

at the end of the eighteenth century the novel was still perceived by many as a genre whose staple was love stories;[90] about half a century later, when Balzac proposed to describe every class, every character, every custom of contemporary France, like a Buffon of the social life,[91] the program set out in the *Essay on Fictions* received a sort of symbolic crowning. *The Human Comedy* fully accomplished a process that began with the German *Bildungsroman* and the *roman personnel*, and continued with Jane Austen and the historical novels of Scott and Stendhal. What Balzac says about the innovations introduced by Scott into the history of narrative fiction can be interpreted in this light: "The biggest criticism that has been made about him is that he gave love a secondary role. . . . Envy, hatred, false zeal, superstition, and fanaticism are the passions that come naturally into his frame because of the importance and nature of the subject."[92]

A few decades later, the project of *The Human Comedy*—the utopia of a fictional cycle mimicking the totality of social life—consecrated a literary genre that openly defied the other language games, presenting itself as the most important discursive formation of humankind, as the true book of life. It was the first time this had happened in such explicit terms.

We have seen that a revolutionary expansion of forms of life embedded in the narrative had already taken place between the last decades of the seventeenth century and the second half of the eighteenth. This was when the novel shifted interest to stories about private people, when works were invaded by a new mass of characters and things, and when heroes and actions that the classicist literary system had confined to the comic register became the object of serious and problematic storytelling. But if we look at the overall picture of the eighteenth-century novel from the perspective of 1850, the year of Balzac's death, it can clearly be seen that between *The Human Comedy* and the narrative fiction of the eighteenth century there falls another threshold. Expanding the narratable world did not mean just making all its subject matters available; it also meant incorpo-

90. See Cohen, *The Sentimental Education of the Novel*, 3ff.

91. Balzac, "Author's Introduction" to *The Human Comedy*, lv.

92. Honoré de Balzac, "Les Eaux de Saint-Ronan par Sir Walter Scott" (1824), in *Œuvres diverses*, vol. 2, ed. Roland Chollet, René Guise, and Christiane Guise (Paris: Gallimard, 1996), 107.

rating subject matters that the novel had not possessed until then and which acquired a crucial value for the readers of the new epoch. The possibility of telling stories about anything in any way whatsoever is the first characteristic of modern narrative; the second involves the appropriation of these new types of content. What were these all about?

The Middle Station of Life

At the beginning of *Robinson Crusoe,* the father of the protagonist has an important talk with his son. Robinson would like to be a sailor; his father would prefer him to study law and achieve a good position in life. Mr. Crusoe is a merchant from Bremen who emigrated to Hull—the English habit of mispronouncing words transformed his family surname from Kreutznaer to Crusoe. Thanks to his business, Mr. Kreutznaer accumulates a modest fortune: he retires from work, moves to York, and marries. Robinson is his third son: the first, an officer in the infantry, died fighting against the Spaniards in Dunkirk; Robinson knows nothing about the second. Mr. Kreutznaer, now afflicted with gout, is very concerned about the fate of his youngest son.

> He called me one morning into his chamber, where he was confined by the gout, and expostulated very warmly with me upon this subject. He asked me what reasons, more than a mere wandering inclination, I had for leaving my father's house and my native country, where I might be well introduced, and had a prospect of raising my fortune by application and industry, with a life of ease and pleasure. He told me it was men of desperate fortunes on one hand, or of aspiring, superior fortunes on the other, who went abroad upon adventures, to rise by enterprise, and make themselves famous in undertakings of a nature out of the common road; that these things were all either too far above me or too far below me; that mine was the middle state, or what might be called the upper station of low life, which he had found, by long experience, was the best state in the world, the most suited to human happiness, not exposed to the miseries and hardships, the labour and sufferings of the mechanic part of mankind, and not embarrassed with the pride, luxury, ambition, and envy of the upper part of mankind.[93]

93. Defoe, *Robinson Crusoe,* 4–5.

This passage is fundamental to the history of the novel.[94] Faced with a son who seeks adventure, Robinson's father lays out the advantages of the *middle state* or, as he calls it a few lines later, the *middle station of life:* a comfortable fate, with no adventures, miseries, or vicissitudes, with everything needed to attain private happiness, to go "silently and smoothly through the world, and comfortably out of it."[95]

A hidden, literary moral sense could be picked up in Mr. Kreutznaer's words. "Undertakings of a nature out of the common road" also provided the primary material for narrative fiction written up to this point: when Robinson's father talks about the instability that awaits those of aspiring, superior fortunes or those of desperate fortunes, he is also tracing out a history of epic art. The heroes of *epos* or serious romance are men of aspiring, superior fortunes who go abroad in search of adventure; the heroes of comic romance are men of desperate fortune who suffer the upheavals of fate. For those who judge these lives from the perspective of the middle class, the deeds of knights and the wanderings of picaros appear equally alien.

The notion of the *middle station of life* emerged out of the interweaving of three different strands. First, the *medietas* of social conditions, of belonging to a class that is neither too rich nor too poor. Second, the *medietas* of experiences: while "men of desperate fortunes or of aspiring superior fortunes" go in search of adventure, men of the middle state remain in the world of bourgeois normalcy and pursue private happiness through quiet, industrious lives. Finally, the rootedness in a stable, limiting environment: adventures presuppose an abstract, dynamic world where anything can happen; Robinson's father is surrounded by an orderly, regular reality, consisting of mechanisms, duties, work, family, money, and repetition. Circumstances have little effect on epic heroes, on the heroes of chivalric romance, or on picaros: the environment remains extraneous to the text, or it is presented as a vague backdrop to the adventures, not as an a priori that determines individual lives. Mr. Kreutznaer, however, enters into the text marked by a place and a date of birth, by a family status and a social

---

94. See Gianni Celati, *Finzioni occidentali* (Turin: Einaudi, 1975), 29–30. On mediocrity as the specific sphere of the modern novel, see also Thorel-Cailleteau, *Splendeurs de la médiocrité.*

95. Defoe, *Robinson Crusoe*, 10.

class: the world, for him, is a regulated and predictable horizon, a milieu that weighs on people's destinies, making them predictable in their turn. At the same time that Robinson's father is explaining the existential model of the Puritan middle class between the seventeenth and eighteenth centuries, he is also describing the future: the middle state exists in every culture, but the modern era extended, consolidated, and transformed it into a project of life, thanks to the new ethics of bourgeois normalcy focused on work and family. This is the sphere that Charles Taylor, unwittingly using an expression that recurred often in prefaces and reviews of English novels, called *ordinary life*.[96] The culture of antiquity had always neglected ordinary life—what free men share with animals and slaves—subordinating it to political action, to the contemplative life, or to the search for wisdom. With the advent of bourgeois society, work and family became what they had never been in previous cultures: absolute reasons for living.[97] And yet *Robinson Crusoe* does not tell the story of Mr. Kreutznaer's middle state: instead, it gives an account of the "strange surprizing adventures" of his son, as the book title announces, because in order to capture readers' interest, Defoe still needed to transcend *medietas*. Three-quarters of a century later, Goethe's *Wilhelm Meister's Apprenticeship* (1795–1796) also talked about everyday life—it was one of the first novels to do so.[98] However, the architrave that holds up the novelistic edifice is not the destiny of Werner, the merchant, but that of Wilhelm, the artist. In reflecting on his relationship with Mariane, Wilhelm realizes that the reason the girl is so important to him is because she can save him from the "stifling, draggle-tailed middle-class existence."[99] Compared to *Robinson Crusoe*, the middle station of life has gained ground to become the backdrop against which everyone's stories stand out in relief. But the fulcrum of the narrative discontinuity is, once again, a special character: bourgeois existence is not interesting.[100]

96. Charles Taylor, *Sources of the Self: The Making of the Modern Identity* (Cambridge, MA: Harvard University Press, 1992), 23–25 and part 3, "The Affirmation of Ordinary Life," 211–304.

97. Ibid., 211ff.

98. Franco Moretti, "Prefazione 1999," in *Il romanzo di formazione* (1986, 1999); English translation "Preface: Twenty Years Later," in *The Way of the World*, trans. Alberto Sbragia (London: Verso, 2000).

99. Goethe, *Wilhelm Meister's Apprenticeship*, bk. 1, chap. 9, p. 16.

100. See Moretti, "Preface: Twenty Years Later."

About thirty-five years later, however, Balzac embarked on the project of *The Human Comedy,* which made every life seem charged with interest and conflicts, even those of people similar in every respect to Robinson's father. Only a few years after Balzac's death, Flaubert could have described Kreutznaer's existence in all its banality, while Tolstoy and George Eliot could have imparted relative truths about it, juxtaposing it to the parallel movement of other people, each enclosed inside his or her own limited world, each locked into the unseeing movement of the whole. Another threshold thus lies between *Robinson Crusoe* and the nineteenth century.

The Serious Mimesis of Everyday Life

The philosophy of literary history that Auerbach puts forward in *Mimesis* culminates in the nineteenth century with the rise of an entirely modern way of telling stories. As we have said, Auerbach identifies two mimetic models that go back thousands of years: the first, of classical origin, is informed by a hierarchical and "moralistic" vision of life; the second, of Judeo-Christian origin, comes from an egalitarian and theological vision. At the end of a process beginning in the sixteenth century and culminating only with the realistic novel of the nineteenth century, both these paradigms were replaced by a third form of mimesis. This form was also egalitarian, but independent of the theological model and entirely immanent: it destroyed the hierarchy between classes, types of actions, and styles, and made it possible to tell about the ordinary life of common people in a serious way. Auerbach defines it in a number of ways: "modern tragic realism based on the contemporary";[101] "the serious realism of modern times [that] cannot represent man otherwise than as embedded in a total reality, political, social, and economic, which is concrete and constantly evolving—as is the case today in any novel or film";[102] "atmospheric realism" (*atmosphärische Realistik*) associated with atmospheric historicism.[103] But the clearest, most detailed account is the following:

101. Auerbach, *Mimesis,* 458.
102. Ibid., 463.
103. Ibid., 491.

The serious treatment of everyday reality, the rise of more extensive and socially inferior human groups to the position of subject matter for problematic-existential representation (*problematisch-existentieller Darstellung*), on the one hand; on the other, the embedding of random persons and events in the general course of contemporary history, the fluid historical background (*Hintergrund*)—these, we believe, are the foundations of modern realism.[104]

This definition is the best because it includes the two elements that make up modern realism. We have already talked about the second definition: at the beginning of the nineteenth century, novels endowed themselves with a new conceptual ether and set their stories against a backdrop consisting of ideas with a sense of historical dynamics. The first definition is a new way of expressing what Auerbach called *das Alltägliche,* the everyday, which he usually associates with the adjectives *ernst, problematisch, tragisch* (serious, problematic, tragic). Sometimes he also uses *existentiell:* in the "Epilegomena to *Mimesis,*" Auerbach writes that he had initially thought about calling the set of themes and forms subsequently designated as "a mixture of seriousness and the everyday" "existential realism," but in the end he was reluctant to use such a modern expression for a phenomenon whose earliest forms dated back to the distant past.[105]

What is the "everyday" for Auerbach? The most explicit passage in *Mimesis* is the following: "There could be no serious literary treatment [in antiquity] of everyday occupations and social classes—merchants, artisans, peasants, slaves—of everyday scenes and places—home, shop, field, store—of everyday customs and institutions—marriage, children, work, earning a living."[106] The "everyday" thus refers to a social condition (the middle and lower classes) and to a sphere of experience, fenced in by the institutional practices of common life (work and family), understood in a broader sense as well (the search for one's place in the world through career or marriage), and located in a historical context. What these various areas had in common was a form of censorship: due to the rule of the separation of styles they would have been unworthy of tragic or problematic interest. It must be added that *Alltägliche,* in Auerbach, is not necessarily tied to uneventfulness,

104. Ibid.
105. Auerbach, "Epilegomena to *Mimesis,*" 560.
106. Auerbach, *Mimesis,* 31.

to average everydayness dominated by repetition: the first writers who felt called on to represent the new tendency were Stendhal and Balzac, whose *ernste Nachahmung des Alltäglichen* (serious imitation of the everyday) arose out of exceptional states, out of adventures in the everyday. It was not a category, therefore, that described the flatness of ordinary life.

Aristotle's *people like us,* Defoe's *middle station of life,* Auerbach's *Alltägliche,* and Taylor's *ordinary life* are linked by a family resemblance. The bond of this kinship is their referral to the same form of life—a form that exists in all cultures, but that only modern bourgeois culture transformed into an ethical and existential ideal. For the first time in European history, certain experiences gained the right to serious, tragic, and problematic mimesis, taking center stage on the literary scene. While the overall direction of the transformation might be clear, when the transition took place is not. A debate at a distance on this issue divides Auerbach from some of his commentators. While the author of *Mimesis* attaches a decisive role to the French social novel of the early nineteenth century, Ian Watt attributes it to the works of Richardson,[107] and Francisco Rico to *Lazarillo* and *Guzman*—to the Spanish picaresque novels written before the subgenre of the picaresque slid into the comic.[108] Uncertainty on this topic is inevitable because the concepts around which *Mimesis* is constructed maintain an intentional air of vagueness, because the transformation was a systemic process lasting centuries, punctuated by phases that varied depending on the national literatures, and because Auerbach's *Alltägliche,* like the *middle station of life,* is a composite notion that weaves together various aspects. Where should the break be situated in a process that, like all great historical metamorphoses, developed slowly?

Let us consider some of the major texts in the rise of the novel. *Lazarillo* seems to be partly unaffected by the *Stiltrennung*: the work can be viewed as having a serious and problematic intent; the character comes from the lower stratum of society. However, the entire story line is programmatically adventurous, and it disregards the institutional normalcy of everyday life. *The Princesse de Clèves* admirably reduces the number of exceptional

107. Watt, *The Rise of the Novel.*

108. Rico, *The Spanish Picaresque Novel and the Point of View,* 126ff. See also by the same author, "Realtà e realismo," paper delivered at the conference "Auerbach's *Mimesis:* A Critical Assessment 60 Years Later," held in Pisa at the Scuola Normale Superiore, March 16, 2007.

states and tells of an intimate conflict almost completely devoid of melodramatic theatricality and adventure. Although the characters are aristocrats, they act like private persons rather than members of a class that has, or may have, a public function. Still, there is no mixing of styles and classes, and the story remains confined to a social circle that does not engage in work and has no practical responsibilities except to safeguard its honor and reputation. During the eighteenth century, the forms of narrative fiction describing heroes theoretically like us were the autobiographies of private people, whether real or fictitious, the epistolary novel, and the comic romance. The form most closely linked to premodern literature is the latter, which described particularity in many of its aspects. It also produced works like *Tom Jones,* in which the legacy of the *Stiltrennung* can still be felt due to the strong presence of the comic-intermediate register and the "moralistic" categories. The other eighteenth-century subgenres I have mentioned went beyond the separation of styles, but lacked the characteristics required to seriously represent the ordinary life. The characters who won the right to the memoir and autobiography, the heroes of Defoe, Marivaux, or Prévost, might come from the middle state or pass through it in one stage of their lives, but the experiences and adventures they encountered lie outside work- and family-related spheres. The same holds for the protagonists of the epistolary novel, a genre that describes the exceptional state induced by love but only marginally takes into account the institutional and prosaic aspects of this passion. Even when the heroines are maidservants or come from a middle-class environment, the passions and adventures they are led into maintain a certain distance from the mechanics of the common life. Pamela and Clarissa want to preserve their honor and must do so: this is the link between their personal history and society as an institutional order. Nevertheless, it is sufficient to compare this substrate with the lingering portrayals of the practical consequences of Lydia's love for Wickham in *Pride and Prejudice* in order to understand the sense and direction of this metamorphosis.

Auerbach's critics are right to point out that some elements of the seriousness of the everyday appeared before the nineteenth century. However, it was only in the 1800s that novels began to construct plots in which the middle station of life was described, without resorting to exceptional states. What is still missing in the works of Defoe but appears in various forms in the works of Austen, Balzac, Flaubert, Tolstoy, and George Eliot, is a serious, profound lingering on a sphere of reality that the modern world transformed into the symbolic center of every life.

The World of Prose

Theories of the novel of the past two centuries can be grouped into two large families. So far we have looked extensively at the one descending from the works of Friedrich Schlegel and culminating in the works of Bakhtin. The second takes its lead from the thoughts developed by Hegel in his *Aesthetics*. His ideas on the novel profoundly influenced twentieth-century criticism: Lukács, for example, had them in mind both before and after his adherence to Marxism.[109] The *Aesthetics* left an equally visible trace in the literary history produced by Auerbach.

For Hegel, the essential characteristic of the genre was not the creation of subjective worlds, polyphony, or the protean capacity to narrate anything in any way whatsoever, but rather the relationship the novel entertains with a historic period of the objective spirit: the "world of prose and everyday." Hegel describes it by comparing it with the "heroic age" that made *epos* and tragedy possible.[110] Epic and tragic actions have a universal meaning because they construct or symbolize collective destinies. They evoke an epoch in which institutions have not yet hardened into suprapersonal mechanisms and the deeds of a single individual can have a cosmic-historical significance, as they do in the *Iliad*, when the fight between Achilles and Hector decides the fate of two peoples in a public duel. Instead, the "prose of the world" arises when collective destinies are decided by states, laws, and institutions, and when individual action has a limited value:

> In the world of today the individual subject may of course act of himself in this or that matter, but still every individual, wherever he may twist or turn, belongs to an established social order and does not appear himself

---

109. The difference between *epos* and the novel as it is presented in *The Theory of the Novel*, for example, derives from Hegelian theory: the epic hero acts as the representative of a community in a world whose values still have a major significance; the acts of the novelistic hero are motivated by private aims, by "demons" (i.e., by exiled, unrecognized gods), and in a world ruled by mechanisms and conventions; see Lukács, *The Theory of the Novel*, chap. 3.

110. Hegel, *Aesthetics*, vol. 1, pp. 179ff.

as the independent, total, and at the same time individual living embodi-
ment of this society, but only as a restricted member of it. He acts, therefore, also as only involved in it, and interest in such a figure, like the
content of its aims and activity, is unendingly particular.[111]

The prose of the everyday is the condition of typical life in modern society, where collective decisions are made by state policy, relations between
people are governed by the law, and division of labor funnels people into
specializations, separates the microcosms, and makes each individual a limited subject, closed up inside a restricted circle of particular interests. As
the "modern bourgeois epic," the novel describes this condition: it tells the
stories of individuals who pursue their private aims in the midst of other
individuals who pursue other private aims, moving in a predictable reality
that is desacralized and organized according to the mechanisms of the state
and civil society.

The "world of prose and everyday" completes the family resemblance
we mentioned earlier, since it is the most acute way of conceiving the historical phase that supports people like us, the existence of *laboratores*.
There is a clear relationship between the *middle station of life* and the
world of prose: they are two ways of thinking about the same form of
life—a form in which the space for heroic action and adventure has been
narrowed and people exist as isolated and situated individuals, provided
with a date of birth, a place of birth, a job, and a family status. Hegel's
conception also brings together the two elements Auerbach identifies in
modern realism: the serious mimesis of people like us, and the presence of
a universal background with a sense of historical dynamics. In such a
world, individual paths are conditioned by suprapersonal forces: to tell the
story of a private matter also means telling about the collective circumstances surrounding it.

The first structures of sense underpinning the modern narrative space—its
virtual anarchy—corresponds perfectly to the theories of Schlegel and
Bakhtin. For an illustration of this, just browse the spines of novels stacked
on a bookstore shelf: there are all sorts. But if we based our understanding
on this a priori, we would get a distorted image: the ways of writing novels

---

111. Ibid., vol. 1, p. 194.

over the past two centuries are theoretically limitless, but they do not all lie on the same plane. *The reason the novel has proved to be such an important game of truth is not solely and primarily because of its capacity to tell any story in any way whatsoever. More important than this generic flexibility was the dawning of a specific mimetic mode that did not exist before a certain date and that became a deciding factor for the representation of the modern world. The novel became important mainly because it told serious stories about the lives of people like us in the middle station of life—private individuals immersed in the prose of the everyday who, thanks to the bourgeois form of life, became a class that earned the right to serious mimesis and the capacity to impose its values as absolute.* While Schlegel's and Bakhtin's theories describe the general morphology of the modern narrative space, the dominant form appears to be Hegelian and Auerbachian. This idea clashes with some of the critical topoi of our time and begs for two clarifications.

Center and Periphery

1. The capacity to represent the world of prose in a problematic way did not coincide with the realistic novel of the nineteenth century. The phenomenon must not be confused with its origin: the serious mimesis of everyday life emerged in the course of the 1800s, but it extended into new forms during the 1900s, maintaining a central position in the field of modern fiction. We must not think about a restricted poetics, but about an expansive structure of sense that took the place of classicism and Christian aesthetic Platonism, that lives in the long duration, and, like the a prioris it replaced, is traversed by a dialectic between continuity and change. One of the most fundamental parts of the historical schema of *Mimesis* is precisely this interweaving between persistence and transformations. In some respects, the modernist novels Auerbach discusses subvert the architecture of the nineteenth-century novel; in other respects, though, they prolong its legacy, to the extent that they remain bound to the same fundamental premise—the serious mimesis of everyday life placed against a background that possesses a sense of historical dynamics. What unites Flaubert to Proust, *War and Peace* to *Ulysses*, or, to stay with texts commented on in *Mimesis*, Stendhal to Virginia Woolf, is existential realism. When regarded from the perspective of over two thousand years, these highly diverse works are

united by a way of representing reality that occurred only episodically until the turning point we are discussing. They tell the stories of people like us in a serious way and situate their characters in the world using historical and dynamic concepts. Neither of these possibilities existed before a certain date. The themes of the stories can be the great twists of fate, as in Balzac, Stendhal, Flaubert, and Zola; or they can be apparently insignificant ones that count only for those who experience them, as in Proust or Virginia Woolf. The milieu can be the subject of sociological probing, as in Balzac or Zola; it can remain in the background, as in Woolf; or it can affect the intimate behavior of characters, as in Proust—but it always exists as a basic assumption, as does the seriousness of the everyday.

2. "Center" and "periphery" are not aesthetic or quantitative categories: they do not measure the spread or value of the works, but the hegemony of tendencies. Compared to the *romance,* the *novel* was most likely a numerically minor genre in all epochs of history.[112] There is no doubt that a considerable portion of the novels or stories that occupy a prominent position in the literary canon of the past two centuries disregard existential realism or engage with it only marginally: the masterpieces of Poe and Stevenson, Kafka and Beckett, Guimarães Rosa and García Márquez, Pynchon and Bolaño have no direct relationship with the seriousness of the everyday. But narrative modes that reject or circumscribe existential realism continue to define themselves in relation to this tradition—a clear sign that the problematic mimesis of ordinary life occupies the center of modern narrative space. When Breton opposes surrealism to nineteenth-century realism,[113] when Valéry accuses the novel of presenting an ordinary, superficial vision of the world,[114] when Alejo Carpentier opposes magic realism to "the return of

---

112. This is what can be deduced from several quantitative studies on novels published during the period of the rise of the novel. See Peter Garside, James Raven, and Rainer Schöwerling, eds., *The English Novel, 1770–1829: A Biographical Survey of Prose Fiction Published in the British Isles* (Oxford: Oxford University Press, 2000); John Austin, "USA 1780–1850," in Moretti, *The Novel,* 1:455–465.

113. André Breton, *Manifeste du surréalisme* (1924); English translation *Manifesto of Surrealism,* in Breton, *Manifestos of Surrealism,* trans. Richard Seaver and Helen R. Lane (Ann Arbor: University of Michigan Press, 1969), 6–7.

114. Paul Valéry, "Mauvaises pensées et autres" (1942), in *Œuvres,* vol. 2, ed. Jean Hytier (Paris: Gallimard, 1993), 802.

the real,"[115] when Robbe-Grillet opposes the *nouveau roman* to twentieth-century novelists who continue to write like Stendhal or Balzac,[116] or when John Barth theorizes the ironic reuse of the realistic novel,[117] the poetics embodying the normalcy of the novel—the virtual center of the literary genre—is always the one that tries to describe the world of prose in a serious way.

Narrative Democracy

The problematic mimesis of the middle station of life brings to fulfillment the attention for particular life that is immanent in the novel as a form: in this sense, the seriousness of the everyday is the culmination of a process that passes through the history of the novel. The primary meaning embedded in the modern novel as a discursive formation is *the conquest of particularities of any kind or, in other words, the entrance of democracy into literature.* The genre of the novel is the literary equivalent of the declaration of human rights: the Goncourt brothers used a similar terminology when they credited themselves for having extended "a right to the Novel" to everyone, even to the underclasses. This literary form has become one of the most important games of truth in the modern era primarily because it recounts the life of people like us in a serious, problematic, and, on occasion, tragic way. The core of its literary space is occupied by works that remain true to this project.

In addition to the social hierarchy, the transformation also affected forms of experience. The possibility of giving a serious account of work, the family, or the struggle to find a place in the world of prose represented a decisive conquest in the history of culture. Up until the birth of existential realism, illustrious narrative was focused on the heroic actions of epic poetry, on the adventures of the romance, on unprecedented events that were the topic of novellas and *exempla,* on love as a pure state of exception, and not as a state of exception within an institutional context. After

---

115. A. Carpentier, *El reino de este mundo,* in *Obras completas,* vol. 2 (Mexico City: Siglo Veintiuno editores, 1983), "Prólogo," 13ff.

116. Alain Robbe-Grillet, *Pour un nouveau roman* (1963); English translation *For a New Novel* (Evanston, IL: Northwestern University Press, 1992).

117. John Barth, "The Literature of Exhaustion" (1967), in *The Friday Book: Essays and Other Non-fiction* (New York: G. P. Putnam's Sons, 1984), 63–79.

the birth of existential realism, the choice fell on the social classes and on the spheres of experience that were the least suitable, in principle, for anomalies. The everyday, in this sense, represents the heart of the private condition. It is the life that barely juts out: it is particular existence in its pure being-there. In the twentieth century there emerged the mimetic utopia we find expressed in *The Encyclopedia of the Dead* by Danilo Kiš: *the utopia of universal narratability.* The simple existence, now free from hierarchies (the separation of styles), from ethical control (moralism), and from universal meanings (allegory), staked its claim to absolute attention.

To draw an overarching map of our territory, to grasp an image of the whole, we must follow the historical morphology of this ridge. Although the serious mimesis of everyday life did not coincide with the realistic novel of the nineteenth century, the core of modern narrative space did emerge, for the first time, precisely with the nineteenth-century realistic novel. It is from here that we must begin.

CHAPTER SIX

The Nineteenth-Century Paradigm

Abstractions

The "nineteenth-century novel" (or the "realistic nineteenth-century novel")
is more than anything else an abstraction: first, because a substantial
portion of the narrative fiction written during the 1800s shunned any pretense to realism; second, because there are wide divergences between
works labeled as realistic; and third, because the texts viewed as true to
reality by nineteenth-century culture were judged as implausible by
later literary periods. I will use this stereotype as if it had invisible quotation marks around it, and to refer to the subject at hand, I will use the
more specific and less ambiguous expression "the nineteenth-century
paradigm."

Nevertheless, it would be naive to stop at deconstructing commonplaces.
Shared topoi never appear by chance—they take form whenever a collective
intellectual subject seeks a concise expression to indicate a field of possibilities
that appears cohesive and unique when compared to other fields emerging
before or after it. Every *doxa* is a clue, a symptom: the fact that it exists is
more meaningful than the vagueness of its referent. Interestingly enough,
the stereotype we are discussing actually appeared during the twentieth
century, when third-person, realistic fiction had begun to be perceived as
the archetype of the "classic," "traditional" novel.

This process is especially easy to perceive in national literatures with a
solid nineteenth-century narrative tradition. By the beginning of the

1900s in France and England, the nineteenth-century novel had already become the archetype of the classic novel—an opinion shared equally by those who supported the model and those who were critical of it. During the debate that developed in France in the 1920s, nineteenth-century realism from Balzac to the naturalists was explicitly or implicitly considered to be the canonical form of the novel.[1] In his *Manifesto of Surrealism* (1924), for example, André Breton cites Paul Valéry's invention, the parody of nineteenth-century, third-person narrative fiction ("la marquise sortit à cinq heures" [the marquise went out at five]) and scoffs at a descriptive passage from Dostoevsky's *Crime and Punishment*. Clearly, if a writer as revolutionary as Dostoevsky was in many ways can come to represent the norm to be demolished, then when viewed from the perspective of the historical avant-gardes, differences internal to the model count for little.[2] During the same years in England, the essays of Virginia Woolf drew a sharp dividing line between "Edwardian" writers, the last heirs of nineteenth-century forms, and "Georgian" writers, whom she considered to be fully modernist.[3] The direct targets of this attack were H. G. Wells, Arnold Bennett, and John Galsworthy; the more distant quarry was "the entire tradition of the novel as it had crystallized in nineteenth-century British fiction."[4] In 1921 Percy Lubbock published *The Craft of Fiction*.[5] To his eyes as well, realistic narrative fiction of the 1800s—especially works written in the third person (Balzac, Dickens, Thackeray, Flaubert, Turgenev, Dostoevsky, Tolstoy, and Maupassant)—appears to be a relatively uniform set that established the canonic devices of the classic novel. These tools were refined and fully implemented by Henry James.

The family resemblance that Valéry, Breton, Woolf, and Lubbock implicitly refer to took root in the critical discourse. During the following decades it influenced the first histories of the twentieth-century novel, such

---

1. Michel Raimond, *La Crise du roman, des lendemains du Naturalisme aux années vingt* (Paris: Corti, 1966), 15, 162ff., 179.

2. Breton, "Manifesto of Surrealism," 6–7.

3. Woolf, "Modern Fiction," 157–165; by the same author, "Mr. Bennett and Mrs. Brown" (1923) and "Character in Fiction" (1924), in *The Essays of Virginia Woolf*, vol. 3, *1919–1924*, ed. Andrew McNeillie (London: Hogarth Press, 1988), 384–389, 420–438.

4. See Baruch Hochman, *The Test of Character: From the Victorian Novel to the Modern* (London: Associated University Presses, 1983), 11.

5. Percy Lubbock, *The Craft of Fiction* (London: Jonathan Cape, 1921).

as the one Joseph Warren Beach published in 1932.[6] It also left its mark on the first critical studies on the relationship between nineteenth- and twentieth-century narrative fiction, such as the ideas we find in *Axel's Castle* (1931) by Edmund Wilson or in the essays that Giacomo Debenedetti wrote between the 1920s and 1940s, from his first articles on Proust (1925–1927) to *Personaggi e destino* (Characters and Fate) (1947). Three decades later, during the second phase of the twentieth-century avant-garde, we find the same interpretation in Michel Raimond's *La Crise du roman* (The Crisis of the Novel) (1966), which traces the history of French narrative fiction between 1890 and 1930.[7] *La barriera del naturalismo* (The Barrier of Naturalism) (1964) by Renato Barilli applies a similar schema to Italian narrative fiction.[8]

Realisms

What exactly is the family resemblance behind this stereotype? Jules François Félix Husson, known as Champfleury, was one of the first theorists of the poetics that began in the 1830s to acquire the name "realism." Between 1853 and 1857 he published his main critical works and sketched out an overarching map of the narrative fiction of his time. As he saw it, writers who wanted to talk about reality had two avenues: they could either tell their story through inner analysis, as in Constant's *Adolphe,* or they could study others through objective observation, as in Balzac's novels.[9] The expansion of the narratable world that took place at the beginning of the nineteenth century moved in three directions: toward the fantastic, toward the autobiographical-introspective, and toward the mimesis of the common world. The first of these territories, which was programmatically alien to the ambition of describing the shared reality, created a new form of romance. The other two differed in the ways Champfleury described: the *roman personnel,* egocentric and usually written in the first person, and the social novel, outwardly focused and usually written in the third person,

6. Joseph Warren Beach, *The Twentieth Century Novel: Studies in Technique* (New York: Century, 1932).

7. Raimond, *La Crise du roman.*

8. Renato Barilli, *La barriera del naturalismo* (Milan: Mursia, 1964).

9. On Champfleury's theories, see Émile Bouvier, *La Bataille réaliste (1844–1857)* (1913) (Geneva: Slatkine, 1973), 304ff.

were what gave form to existential realism. The border separating them corresponded to a difference between narrative situations: at the beginning of the 1800s, the third person was associated with the need to describe in an objective fashion how people made their way in the world,[10] while the first person was associated with introspection. Stendhal states this clearly in *The Life of Henry Brulard:* "It is true one might write using the third person: *he* went, *he* said. Yes, but how to take account of the inner movements of the soul?"[11]

This was not a rigid division: there certainly exist novels written in the third person that are highly egocentric (Novalis's *Henry of Ofterdingen,* for example) and narratives in the first person that illustrate the relationship between private stories and public histories (Chateaubriand's *Memoirs from beyond the Tomb,* for example). Moreover, the third-person novel is undoubtedly capable of introspection. The works of Jane Austen and Stendhal represent the movements of the psyche with extraordinary clarity. In 1827, when *The Betrothed* appeared in print, Italian literature had never seen anything comparable to the analytical force and wealth of detail contained in the chapters on the story of Gertrude or on the conversion of the Unnamed. However, in the system of genres as it was conceived in this epoch, the division of roles was very clear: the first person was relied on to express the interior life; the third person was used for objective accounts.[12]

Between the late eighteenth century and the beginning of the nineteenth, the opposition between "I" and "he/she"—the timeless foundation of every narrative situation—took on new features. First of all, the narrators we find in the *Bildungsroman* and in historical and sociohistorical novels are clearly distinguishable from the narrators European literature had been familiar with until then: they employ a serious tone (not a comic-intermediate register, as in *Don Quixote* or *Tom Jones*), and they make use of historical and social concepts (not "moralistic" ones, as in comic romances, *novelle,* and *novelas*). The premodern third person that comes closest to the

10. See Weinberg, *French Realism,* passim, and Bouvier, *La Bataille réaliste,* 301ff.

11. Stendhal, *Vie de Henry Brulard;* English translation *The Life of Henry Brulard,* trans. John Sturrock (New York: New York Review of Books, 2002), 7. On the bond between the first person and introspection at the beginning of the nineteenth century, see Rousset, "Une forme littéraire: le roman par lettres," 73.

12. Cohn, *Transparent Minds,* 21.

nineteenth-century third person is the narrator in *The Princesse de Clèves.*
This is because Madame de La Fayette uses a serious, problematic, and,
when necessary, tragic tone, and because she shifts the focus from the visible
to the invisible—from public action to hidden motives—anticipating a literary gesture that the nineteenth-century paradigm would make its own.[13]
The difference is that the source of the events in the novels by Madame de
La Fayette resides *in interiore homine*—in other words, in the dialectic
between the satellites and planets that the Augustinian psychology of the
narrator deciphers and captures—while the nineteenth-century third person
further shifts causes into the new territories opened up by sociology and
modern historicism, namely, the *moment* and the *milieu,* the time and
place by which human beings are conditioned.

In addition to fostering the rise of a new kind of narrator, the nineteenth-
century novel split the division of labor between first and third persons in
a new way from the past. From the sixteenth century to the last decades of
the eighteenth century, the objective, public lives of heroes who came from
the lower or middle strata of society were mostly depicted in the first
person: Lazarillo, Guzmán, Robinson Crusoe, Moll Flanders, Roxana,
Marianne, Pamela, and Clarissa say "I." The novel of manners written in a
noncomic tone almost always had an autobiographical slant. During the
last decades of the eighteenth century, after Rousseau's *Confessions* and
Goethe's *The Sorrows of Young Werther,* the structure of first-person
narrative fiction changed, at least in works written for the elite. Instead
of heroes from humble or middle class origins who tell about their ad
ventures in the world, we now have characters with complicated inner
lives who tell inward-looking stories in which psychology and analysis
of the self and others are more important than public events. Twentieth-
century literary criticism came up with a concise name for these figures:
intellectual heroes.[14] A personage similar to the one already present in
the theater (Shakespeare's Hamlet, Molière's Alceste) now found a home
in the novel. The archetype is probably Saint-Preux in *The New Heloise,*

13. On the shift of focus from the outside to the inside, see Jean Rousset, "*La Princesse de
Clèves,*" in *Forme et signification.*

14. Albert Thibaudet, "Le Roman de l'intellectuel" (1921), in *Réflexions sur le roman*
(Paris: Gallimard, 1938), 138–145; Victor Brombert, *The Intellectual Hero: Studies in the
French Novel, 1880–1955* (Philadelphia: Lippincott, 1961); Alfonso Berardinelli, "L'eroe che
pensa: Amleto, Alceste, Andrej," in *L'eroe che pensa* (Turin: Einaudi, 1997), 173–202.

but the new figure became especially popular with the *roman personnel* of the late eighteenth and early nineteenth centuries. This took place during a process that coincided with the internal transformation of a great first-person narrative tradition: the epistolary novel. After *The Sorrows of Young Werther* had altered the form of the genre, fiction based on letters gradually lost the recipient that the messages were addressed to, at least in theory, and morphed into the private diary. Thus, between the end of the eighteenth and the first decades of the nineteenth centuries, the autobiographical novel specialized in the mimesis of the interior life, while the third-person novel specialized in the mimesis of the exterior life, individual destinies, manners, and large-scale public conflicts. Both occupy a central place in the modern literary space, although the second is the most prominent. This can be explained partly because a significant portion of contemporary narrative fiction today is still structured around the framework that descended from this model; and partly because the renewal of themes and forms that took place over the past hundred and fifty years has often been defined, perhaps polemically, in relation to this literary paradigm.

The ideal type of the "realistic nineteenth-century novel" thus refers primarily to narrative fiction written in the third person: in this regard, the critical *doxa* that predominated at the beginning of the twentieth century was right. However, it missed the mark on another fundamental point: contrary to the topos that arose in the age of the avant-gardes and modernism, the "nineteenth-century novel" was not a uniform entity. Two widely divergent literary periods can be distinguished within it. The first lasted until about 1850: the works of Austen, Scott, Manzoni, Balzac, Stendhal, and Dickens, although separated by differences, are united by several devices that the criticism of the twentieth century would identify as "nineteenth-century." At midcentury a new phase began. The crucial generation was the one born between the late 1810s and the early 1820s, which counts among its members George Eliot (1819), Dostoevsky (1821), Flaubert (1821), and Tolstoy (1828). The historical function of these writers was instrumental and dialectical: on the one hand, they reused the "nineteenth-century" structures that had appeared in the first half of the century; on the other, they subjected these forms to an internal critique that foreshadowed modernist novels. Reuse and critique often coexist within the same text. The "nineteenth-century paradigm" primarily describes novels written in the first half of the century: in the second half, this model was interwoven with forms heralding a new literary epoch.

The Frameworks of the Nineteenth-Century Paradigm

As an ideal type and family resemblance, the nineteenth-century paradigm is held together by a thematic choice (the seriousness of the everyday, existential realism) and by three technical devices.

1. Its stylistic foundation is the utopia of *transparent writing.* The novel from 1650 to 1800 had patiently developed the concept of a natural style. At the beginning of the nineteenth century, the metaphor of the mirror began to be used to illustrate a certain idea of mimesis. The image alluded to the relationship that writing sought to entertain with reality—the illusion of a distortion-free mimesis.

2. The second cornerstone is *a new type of narrator:* detached from the story being told, omniscient and objective like a historian, commentating on the plot, but at the same time intent on creating a world that seems real and autonomous, putting the protagonists on center stage and directing interest toward them. This double movement corresponds to the stylistic devices that the nineteenth-century paradigm perfected and transmitted to later literature. First and foremost, there is the narrative aorist or preterit tense, the verbal time of mimetic illusion. Although it already existed, the use of the simple past in narrative fiction was refined in the 1800s:[15] Valéry's parody, quoted by Breton in order to ridicule the traditional novel ("la marquise *sortit* à cinq heures"), alluded, among other things, to the nineteenth-century patina that the preterit tense brings with it. Second, there is the use of concepts with a sense of historical dynamics to comment on events. In their sophisticated version, these categories appeal to con-

---

15. The nature of the preterit narrative is a classic theme of nineteenth-century theoretical reflection on narrative fiction, starting from the essays by Benveniste and Weinrich. See Émile Benveniste, "Les relations de temps dans le verbe français" (1959); English translation "The Correlations of Tense in the French Verb," in *Problems in General Linguistics,* trans. Mary Elizabeth Meek (Coral Gables, FL: University of Miami Press, 1978), 205–216; Harald Weinrich, *Tempus: Besprochene und erzählte Welt* (Stuttgart: W. Kohlhammer, 1964).

temporary human sciences and, in their popularized version, to the common sense that established itself over the past two centuries.

3. The third foundation is *the bond that the new narrative model entertained with the arts of the public sphere: painting and especially theater.* The nineteenth-century paradigm was inspired by the dramatic form: this is something Scott and Balzac theorized about openly. Talking about himself in the third person in the self-penned review of his *Tales of My Landlord* that appeared in the *Quarterly Review,* Scott explains the principles of the technique:

> He has avoided the common language of narrative, and thrown his story, as much as possible, into a dramatic shape. In many cases this has added greatly to the effect, by keeping both the actors and action continually before the reader, and placing him, in some measure, in the situation of the audience at a theatre, who are compelled to gather the meaning of the scene from what the *dramatis personae* say to each other, and not from any explanation addressed immediately to themselves.[16]

Vanity was not the sole reason that Scott had a hard time naming his precursors:[17] the novel of the eighteenth century was inspired in some ways by the theater arts, but no eighteenth-century author had ever perfected such a technique. Balzac immediately grasped the innovation: "Sir Walter Scott rarely used narrative forms. It was through lively, dramatic dialog that he established the personality of his characters."[18]

Around 1830, Balzac's reflections on Scott were transformed into a principle of poetics. One of the decisive documents in this process was his review of the historical novel *Samuel Bernard et Jacques Borgarelly* by Rey-Dussueil. Balzac criticizes it heavily: he writes that Rey-Dussueil lacks a sense of history and that the parts of the plot are not linked together in such a way as to produce a dramatic effect ("the author must choose between writing history or creating a drama. A novel is a written tragedy or

---

16. Sir Walter Scott, "Tales of My Landlord" (1817), in *Sir Walter Scott on Novelists and Fiction,* 170.

17. The only precedent that he manages to cite is a passage in the *History of the Church of Scotland* by Defoe. See Scott, "Tales of My Landlord," 177.

18. Balzac, "Les Eaux de Saint-Ronan par Sir Walter Scott" (1824), 107.

comedy").[19] From that moment on, Sir Walter Scott became the technical model for Balzac that all contemporary novelists were expected to follow, while the theatrical form became the essential architectural element of *The Human Comedy*.[20]

How does nineteenth-century theatricality work? Let us take chapter 7 of *Ivanhoe*, where Scott tells the story of the tournament of Ashby-de-la-Zouch. The passage opens by presenting the historical scene that encompasses the particular events: the conditions in England, Richard the Lionheart's absence, Prince John's plots to usurp the throne, the anarchy created by the nobles and the bands of outlaws who defied feudal law. Then we pass on to the local scene. The narrator talks about the tournament—an event that gathers nobles and common people around a single, grand, symbolic spectacle. For several pages, the physical location where the episode takes place is described, then the description is interrupted to make way for the first scene. It describes a dispute over who will occupy the best seat at the lists. An old Norman, poor but noble, insults the Jew Isaac, the father of Rebecca.

> "Dog of an unbeliever!" said an old man, whose threadbare tunic bore witness to his poverty, as his sword, and dagger, and golden chain intimated his pretensions to rank—"whelp of a she-wolf! darest though press upon a Christian, and a Norman gentleman of the blood of Montdidier?"
>
> This rough expostulation was addressed to no other than our acquaintance Isaac, who, richly and even magnificently dressed in a gabardine, ornamented with lace and lined with fur, was endeavouring to make place in the foremost row.[21]

The reader of narrative fiction is placed in the position of spectator: we watch a scene unfold in front of us, described as if it were being seen for the first time. In principle, the identity of the person who insults Isaac is already known to the narrator, but the narrator presents the character as if he were a stranger to be identified on the basis of physical and social signs.

19. Honoré de Balzac, *Samuel Bernard et Jacques Borgarelly: histoire du temps de Louis XIV par Rey-Dussueil*, in *Œuvres diverses*, vol. 2, 692.

20. Elena Del Panta, "Balzac e la poetica del romanzo drammatico," *Rivista di Letterature moderne e comparate* 57, no. 4 (October–December 2004): 451–476.

21. Scott, *Ivanhoe*, chap. 7, p. 69.

An informational delay of this sort recalls the incipit of the *Aethiopica,* but the effect of suspense that Scott creates is peculiar, because it transposes into written narrative what happens in the theater. At the beginning of a play the spectators reconstruct a general sense of the story by interpreting the decor, costumes, gestures, and words they see and hear after the curtain draws open—hence the importance of the sense of sight and its verbal equivalent: description. This is the aspect that Italo Calvino stresses when he reflects on the outdated impression that some parts of nineteenth-century novels make on twentieth-century readers:

> There is a history of visibility in the novel—of the novel as the art of making persons and things *visible*—which coincides with some of the phases of the history of the novel itself, though not with all of them. From Madame de Lafayette to Benjamin Constant the novel explores the human mind with prodigious accuracy, but these pages are like closed shutters which prevent anything else from being seen. Visibility in the novel begins with Stendhal and Balzac, and reaches in Flaubert the ideal rapport between words and image (supreme economy with maximum effect). The crisis of visibility in the novel will begin about half a century later, coinciding with the advent of the cinema.[22]

In reality, the twentieth century did not lose "visibility" (Calvino's narrative work alone is enough to prove this point), but it was freed from a certain type of visibility, one that was implicit in the theatrical model. What became anachronistic for the expectations of a modern reader is a passage like the following:

> [Lucia] saw a curiously shaped window, covered by two heavy, close-barred gratings, with a hand's breadth interval between them, beyond which stood a nun. She looked about twenty-five years old, and the first impression was one of beauty—a flawed beauty, however, which had lost its bloom and was almost ready to fall into decay. The black veil which was stretched across the top of her head fell on either side of her face, clear of her cheeks; under a veil a band of the whitest linen covered half her forehead, which was equally white in its different way. A second, pleated band framed her face, ending under chin in a wimple, which hung

---

22. Italo Calvino, "Gustave Flaubert, *Trois contes*" (1980); English translation "Gustave Flaubert, *Trois contes*" (1980), in *Why Read the Classics?* (New York: Vintage Books, Random House, 2000), 151–153; quote from p. 152.

down a little over her chest, covering the top of her black dress. That snowy forehead often wrinkled in an apparently painful spasm, and then her black eyebrows twitched rapidly together. Her eyes were very black. Sometimes they stared intently into your face, with arrogant inquiry; sometimes their gaze was rapidly lowered, as if in search of somewhere to hide. There were moments when an acute observer might have detected in them an appeal for affection, understanding and compassion; others when he might think he saw in them the instantaneous revelation of an inveterate, suppressed hatred, something strangely threatening and ferocious. Sometimes her eyes remained motionless, staring at nothing: one observer might have thought her possessed by a proud and slothful indifference, while another might suspect the affliction of a hidden sorrow, a preoccupation of long standing which had more power over her mind than the objects around her.

These things made no impression on the two women, who knew little of the difference between one nun and another; and the Father Superior, who had seen her a number of times before, was already accustomed, like many others, to something strange in her appearance and manner.[23]

Manzoni presents the Nun of Monza with a long description that continues for another half page. A reader of today would most likely consider such a slow, painterly, and theatrical use of sight as old-fashioned and "nineteenth-centuryish." It is imbued with the convictions of physiognomy: that the inside should always be reflected on the outside, that signs are always meaningful, that the moral history of the character seeps out into the expression of the eyes or into the wrinkles of the forehead. Above all, the description is not from the point of view of the characters involved ("These things made no impression on the two women, who knew little of the difference between one nun and another"), but from the point of view of an external, "acute observer" who behaves, in effect, as if he or she were watching a play and trying to decipher the identity of a new character who had just appeared on the stage. The visual models condensed in the aesthetic unconscious of educated readers today appeal to a different visibility: one that is photographic and cinematographic in nature, quicker, more allusive, and more fragmented.

23. Manzoni, *The Betrothed*, 170–171.

Another characteristic element of this paradigm is the general structure that the plot takes. A narrative text can structure the relationship between narrative time and story time using the movements of ellipsis, scene, summary, and pause.[24] In the first situation, *ellipsis,* story time proceeds but nothing is recorded in the narrative; in the second, *scene,* narrative time coincides with story time; in the third, *summary,* stories taking place over a long period of time are compressed into a few lines of narrative; in the fourth, *pause,* story time comes to a halt while the narrator pauses to describe or reflect. According to the logic of the theatrical model, the essential events of the plot (turning points, recognitions, reversals) take place in the form of a scene, or "before the reader," as Scott puts it. The essential aspect is contained in the characters' words and actions, which generate a progressive motion that advances the action forward until the moment of *Spannung.* Summaries serve to reconstruct the previous events and create a bridge between one dramatic episode and another. The descriptions of the characters and the background precede and frame the events, forming something like the two wings of a theater: one consists of invisible entities, historical, social, psychological, and economic forces; the other of visible entities, objects, and environments. The first chapter of *The Betrothed,* for example, opens by describing the second of these wings, namely, the location where the episode takes place. Although the official identity of the character is immediately revealed, Don Abbondio is described through the signs he conveys and the actions he performs; the same thing happens with the bravoes. Later, when they appear on stage, the narrator opens up the other wing, disclosing the historical-social background of the episode taking place on the main stage, and reports on the history of Lombardy in 1628. The story of the characters is presented before the reader flanked by two contexts.

The Figurative Novel and Its Theatrical Model

The dialectic between scenes taking place on stage and those in the wings profoundly affected the early nineteenth-century novel. The success of Scott

---

24. I am using the terminology of Gérard Genette, *Figures III* (1972); English translation *Narrative Discourse: An Essay in Method*, trans. Jane E. Lewin (Ithaca, NY: Cornell University Press, 1980), 86ff.

contributed to disseminating it into European literature; Balzac embraced it and amplified its success. The theatrical model emerged primarily thanks to realistic novels, but it was also transmitted in texts belonging to the romance tradition: we find it, in whole or in part, in the works of Poe and Stevenson. What is implicit in this technique?

1. The first element is an inherent *extroversion*. In developing ideas that date back to Goethe and Schiller's correspondence on the differences between epic and drama, Peter Szondi reflects on the importance that "intersubjective action in the present tense" holds for classical theatrical forms. What he means by this are the actions that take place in real time on the stage and that bind one human being to other human beings,[25] as if the motives for decisions were contained in visible actions and audible speeches. In the same way, the movements occurring *in interiore homine*, the thoughts and passions, are presented out loud in an oratorical or confessionary form. The theater lives in the public sphere and in the dimension of appearances: it displays the region of being manifest to the senses, as does painting. It is no coincidence that the nineteenth-century paradigm drew inspiration from both these arts. The juxtaposition is not new: *ut pictura poësis* belongs to classicist poetics; the lexicon of eighteenth-century theater criticism employed figurative terms;[26] the use of pictorial terms to describe the tasks and techniques of the novel was shared by many eighteenth-century prefaces. However, nineteenth-century narrative fiction interwove figurative and theater vocabulary in a systematic, technical way. Phrases like "At the same time, two additional personages appeared on the scene"[27] or "Brigitte had the satisfaction of seeing her table surrounded by the principal personages of this drama"[28] became fixed formulas.

The nineteenth-century paradigm focuses on intersubjective action in the present tense, just like the theater. The essential aspect concerns public

25. Szondi, *Theory of the Modern Drama*, 9ff.

26. Consider the way Diderot used the notion of the *tableau* in the first of his *Entretiens sur Le fils naturel* (see Denis Diderot, "Dorval et moi, ou Entretiens sur *Le fils naturel*" (1757), in *Œuvres complètes,* vol. 3 [Paris: Le Club français du Livre, 1970], 115–210).

27. Scott, *Ivanhoe*, vol. 1, chap. 40, p. 362.

28. Honoré de Balzac, *Les Petits Bourgeois;* English translation *The Middle Classes,* trans. Clara Bell, in *The Works of Honoré de Balzac* (Boston: Dana Estes, 1901), vol. 14, part 2, 95.

relationships between people, and it is composed of massive entities, both visible and audible: scenes, actions, gestures, speeches. Although some of the early nineteenth-century novels already contained the first examples of the essayistic and introspective techniques that flourished in psychological novels and modern novel-essays between the second half of the nineteenth century and the first half of the twentieth, the narratives by Austen, Scott, Manzoni, Balzac, and Stendhal were read primarily for what was happening in the public space. The passages filled with historical, sociological, and philosophical observations or intimate analysis, although extended and refined, never became the symbolic center of the text as they did in Henry James, Woolf, Musil, and Proust. The invisible and the inaudible counted for less than the visible and the audible, which were full of interesting, macroscopic things: twists of fate, personal victories or defeats, questions of happiness and unhappiness, matters of life and death.

This desire to believe that the intersubjective public life contains engaging content may seem anachronistic today. The transformations the novel went through after the crisis of the nineteenth-century paradigm have accustomed us to believing that the deeds of people like us are almost always insignificant when they are reproduced without estrangement. Moreover, the daily life of modern individuals is disciplined and often dominated by repetition, work, boredom, and banality. The art of the visible that took the place of theater—namely, film—possesses devices to make stories meaningful that superimpose the subjective filters of the framing, editing, and soundtrack on top of events that take place in the public sphere. The characters in contemporary novels spend much less time on stage than nineteenth-century characters did, as was also the case, for that matter, before the theatrical model gained its hegemony over third-person narrative fiction: in *The Princesse de Clèves* (1678) by Madame de La Fayette or in *The Elementary Particles* (1998) by Michel Houellebecq, the scenes are much shorter and there are fewer of them than in *Waverley, The Betrothed, The Red and the Black*, or *Lost Illusions*. This does not mean that they do not exist or that they are not important: far from it. The episode in which Madame de Clèves confesses to her husband her love for another man, or the episode in which Christiane breaks her back in a swinger club, signal peaks of intensity in these two plots. But these dense spaces are surrounded by moments during which the intersubjective action in the present tense is restricted to summaries, passed over in silence because it lacks interest, or made the object of a nonfictional interpretation, as in Houellebecq. To find a theatrical density comparable to that of nineteenth-century novels we have to look in the subgenres of the contemporary romance: crime novels, noir fiction, or the fantastic.

2. Along with the conviction that what is essential in life happens in the public sphere, the theater model is also based on *a principle of order* that was destined to vanish from the later novel. I will describe it borrowing from the words of Jean Rousset. Speaking about *Madame Bovary,* Rousset called Flaubert "the first of the nonfigurative writers of the modern novel." In other words, Flaubert was the first writer to have shifted interest from the story line to the style or to the character's introspective moments, stacking up, one after another, fifty pages devoid of movement, action, and drama.[29] We will come back to these ideas: for now my interest lies in the concept proposed by Rousset. What is a figurative novel?

It is revealing to reflect on a semantic drift: the concept originated in painting, but what it refers to came out of the crisis of the theatrical model. Flaubert is a nonfigurative writer, above all, because he shifts interest from the plot to the way of presenting it. He draws our attention to the contents deposited in the style and in those great moments of suspension when anti-theatrical, stagnating stretches of inaction and boredom are permitted to emerge from the encounter between the words of the narrator and those of the character.[30] This semantic slippage is justified: theater and painting are both arts of appearance; the metaphoric references to one or the other in the critical vocabulary of the nineteenth-century narrators overlap. The twists and turns taken by the category invented by Rousset are also worth contemplating: a novel is "figurative" not particularly because it recalls painting as such, but because it recalls a certain type of painting. But what is figurative in an art made of words, an art in which, speaking literally, figuration can never be avoided, seeing as words are always semantic? The notion points to the existence of a hierarchy: painting is figurative when it captures the cloud of details that fill up our visual field around a center consisting of "figures." These figures coincide in reality with the entities that in Strawson's view populate the world imagined by naive realism:

29. Jean Rousset, "*Madame Bovary* ou le livre sur rien," in *Forme et signification,* 111.
30. Ibid., 132–133.

things and people. The nineteenth-century criticisms of the "traditional" novel insisted on this aspect. To describe it, we can start with plot analysis.

Constructing a story means putting events into a hierarchy. In applying and developing the ideas of Roland Barthes, Seymour Chatman breaks plots down into "kernels" and "satellites."[31] Kernels indicate twists of fate, the changes that lead the plot in a certain direction; satellites are minor episodes that enrich the story without changing its course. While the romance of adventure is constructed almost exclusively out of kernels ("les coups de théâtre"), the nineteenth-century realistic novel multiplies the satellites, the backdrop, and the "fillers."[32] What ends up in the background are both the two presentations of the wings between which the action takes place on center stage, and deviations from the main story. But if it is true that the nineteenth-century novel multiplies the fillers, it is equally true that these never blur the hierarchy between the essential and the contingent, because the focus of the narrative remains concentrated on the fate of the protagonists, namely, on "figures" that the figurative novel puts in the foreground. The cloud of marginal actions taking place next to the main events and the circumstances that affect the story line remain on the edges of the picture; in the center we find the major, objective turning points that alter the lives of the characters. Starting from the second half of the century, as I will explain, this model of the plot dissolved little by little, and novels appeared in which satellites eclipse kernels, details replace major events, and reflections on the circumstances accompany the story, transforming the novel into a novel-essay.

3. Another figurative element is the connection between the parts of the story. Chatman distinguishes between motivated and unmotivated elements,

---

31. Seymour Chatman, *Story and Discourse: Narrative Structure in Fiction and Film* (Ithaca, NY: Cornell University Press, 1978), 53–56. Chatman reworks and modifies the distinction between *noyau* and *catalyse* proposed by Roland Barthes, which is indebted in its turn to the distinction that Boris Tomashevsky made between dynamic and static motifs. But the first extended reflection on this internal dialectic of plots is perhaps to be found in the pages Goethe dedicates to the opposition between *forward striding, backward striding,* and *retarding* motives in his correspondence with Schiller. See Goethe and Schiller, "On Epic and Dramatic Poetry," 380ff.

32. See Franco Moretti, *The Way of the World,* 233ff.; and by the same author, "The Serious Century," in *The Novel,* 1:364–400.

between the developments of the plot that depend on a cause and those that depend on chance. In common language, and in the analysis of stories, what we call chance has a double face. On the one hand, it designates the coincidences that join up the lives of the protagonists, reinforcing their bonds. In *Père Goriot,* for example, Rastignac discovers he is living in the same pension as the father of a woman he just met at a dance; by chance, Vautrin and Victorine Taillefer also live in the same place. These types of coincidences help to concentrate the dramatic events, as if the world were not extraneous to the destinies of the individuals who are the focus of the narrative, but instead cooperated through the medium of chance encounters to draw out the characters' passions and the intersubjective relationships that bind them.

There does exist another type of chance, though. In the third chapter of the second part of *A Sentimental Education,* Frédéric Moreau discovers that Madame Arnoux is away from the city alone, without her husband, in the town where Arnoux's factory is located.[33] Frédéric skips an appointment with Dambreuse to take advantage of the opportunity to declare his love to her. In the one-page story of the trip, Flaubert's paratactic writing style becomes charged with an expectant atmosphere. Then Frédéric arrives at Creil, sees a large factory, asks the woman at the gate to visit the establishment, and discovers that Arnoux's factory is not in Creil. He sets off again, extending his journey, until he finally finds the right town. He goes into the Arnouxes' house without making a sound. Madame Arnoux is surprised and frightened; Frédéric's sudden appearance makes her cry out, and she realizes that she is poorly dressed. She goes back into the house to change her clothes and then takes Frédéric to see the factory. In describing the machinery, she says things that Frédéric finds grotesque. Every time the conversation seems to be becoming more intimate, the noise, the workers, and the presence of Sénécal prevent anything from happening. A movement originating from inside and directed toward an objective (Frédéric wants to declare himself) conflicts with a swarm of small, random events that block his impulse. Indifferent to the aims of the protagonist, reality acts as an inert background that follows a logic of its own: Madame Arnoux does

---

33. Gustave Flaubert, *L'Éducation sentimentale* (1869); English translation *A Sentimental Education,* trans. Douglas Parmée (Oxford: Oxford University Press, 1989), part 2, chap. 3, pp. 209ff.

not expect to receive a visit; Sénécal obtusely performs his job; the factory is a factory. In *Père Goriot*, chance creates an anthropocentric world; in *A Sentimental Education*, chance transcends individual desires: the first is statistically unlikely; the second is statistically common. In the theatrical plots of the nineteenth-century paradigm, the first type of chance is very popular, and the second plays a marginal role. Stories are held together by a solid substrate of motivated events, or seemingly random events that in the overall economy of the text are ultimately revealed to be motivated and anthropocentric. Casual, time-wasting encounters, contingent details, and trivial, gratuitous facts do not invade the text as they would later in modernist narrative.

If we were to cross the critical categories that define the relationships between the events of a story, we might come up with a new opposition between *centripetal plots* and *centrifugal plots*. The archetype of the centripetal *mythos* is the typical form of modern drama, which uses only a few elements (the characters on the stage), establishes strong bonds of cause and effect, limits digressions, and tends toward the denouement. The archetype of the centrifugal *mythos* is the journey without destination, which uses a virtually unlimited number of elements (everything the traveler can meet on his or her way), welcomes digressions, and may resolve itself in unexpected ways. Between the two forms there are an infinite number of intermediary ones, of course. The classic structure of the *Bildungsroman*, what we find illustrated perfectly in *Wilhelm Meister's Apprenticeship*, is the hero's journey in the world—a journey that in Goethe's novel follows steps that are necessary and connected, so connected, in fact, that they turn out to be part of a scheme organized by the Society of the Tower. Behind the centrifugal motion on the surface, the plots of Austen, Scott, Manzoni, and Balzac (Stendhal is a special case) always reveal an underlying centripetal motion. The *mythos* remains cohesive: it expands to show the multiplicity of the real or to depict the background, but it then establishes a link between the parties through ordered sequences based on cause-and-effect relationships and tends toward the motivated resolution of conflicts. These are interweavings in the strong sense of the term: the strands of human actions, woven together, make up a whole that has a precise logic and proceeds toward a telos.

One of the harshest attacks ever launched against the nineteenth-century paradigm is contained in Alain Robbe-Grillet's *For a New Novel* (1963). It is an interesting text, both because it helped to define the narrative aesthetics of the twentieth-century neo-avant-gardes, and because the author describes the armature of the model that he intends to demolish in such a brutally simplistic way that it becomes insightful for precisely this reason. One of the "obsolete notions" that *For a New Novel* attacks is what Robbe-Grillet calls "story."[34] A good novelist, say traditional critics, knows how to tell a story, how to create thrilling, dramatic climaxes and denouements, while the avant-garde novelists, writes Robbe-Grillet, do not possess the shortsightedness ("the foreshortening of the mind's perspective," as Robert Musil would have put it) required to construct a device of this sort. With its bluntly defined categories, *For a New Novel* provides a good picture of the infrastructure of the nineteenth-century paradigm: the essential element of the construction is a hierarchical plot organized around a few major public events—the "story."

4. The same order connecting the parts of the *mythos*—the same hierarchy between foreground and background, private matters and public backdrop, narrative kernels and satellites, motivated and unmotivated elements—also governs the way the nineteenth-century paradigm represents things and environments. Breton attacked traditional narrative fiction by citing a description by Dostoevsky that might have appeared in any realistic nineteenth-century novel:

> The little room into which the young man was shown was covered with yellow wallpaper: there were geraniums and muslin curtains in the windows; the setting sun cast a harsh light over all this . . . the room contained nothing special. The furniture, of yellow wood, was all very old. A sofa with a tall back turned down, an oval table facing the sofa, a dressing table and a mirror propped up in the recess, a few chairs along the walls, two or three prints of no value representing some German girls with birds in their hands—this is what the furnishings amounted to.[35]

34. Robbe-Grillet, *For a New Novel*, 29ff.

35. Fyodor Dostoyevsky, *Crime et Châtiment*, French translation by Victor Dérely, cited by Breton in "Manifeste du surréalisme" (André Breton, *Œuvres complètes*, vol. 1, ed. M. Bonnet [Paris: Gallimard, 1988, 314]): "La petite pièce dans laquelle le jeune homme fut introduit était tapissée de papier jaune: il y avait des géraniums et des rideaux de mousseline aux fenêtres; le soleil couchant jetait sur tout cela une lumière crue. . . . La chambre ne renfermait rien de particulier. Les meubles, en bois jaune, étaient tous très vieux. Un divan avec

According to Breton, the passage that we have read is nothing but "su-perimposed images taken from some stock catalogue," "postcards," "a schoolboy description." More simply, Dostoevsky follows a principle of order that Breton judges to be uninteresting. In broadening the scope of possibilities, the literature of the twentieth century showed that many things can be included in the description of a room. This is because environments exist in the medium of the subjective perception, and because a place can be described according to criteria of objectivity that are very different from those applied during the nineteenth century. Based on these differences of scale, Perec created a theory of perception as an alternative to the one that became crystallized in the nineteenth-century plot. Dostoevsky's narrator, like Scott's or Balzac's, does not show everything observable in the room, but limits himself to the details that are meaningful in relation to the human conflict that will fill up that space. On the one hand, not wishing to project the inner life onto the outer, the narrator wants to be objective; on the other hand, the environment is described so as to illustrate the disposition of the person who lives there and to prepare for the event that will take place, creating a theatrical wing for the next scene.

5. A similar ordering principle governs how the protagonists are described. As we saw in Chapter 4, early readers of *The Princesse de Clèves* were struck by the new psychology that the novel unveiled: Madame de La Fayette described the minor upheavals of the interior life with unprecedented analytical capacity. Ten years after the *The Princesse de Clèves,* in defining the difference between the ancient and the modern "sciences of the heart," Charles Perrault used a metaphor from astronomy. While the ancients knew only about the planets, the moderns also know about the satellites; in the same way, while the ancient science of the heart was acquainted only with the grand passions of the soul, the moderns also know about the mass of small affects that revolve around them. The novel is one of the genres that, in Perrault's estimation, allows the astronomical complexity of the interior life to be revealed.[36] Three centuries after the *Parallèle des anciens*

un grand dossier renversé, une table de forme ovale vis-à-vis du divan, une toilette et une glace adossées au trumeau, des chaises le long des murs, deux ou trois gravures sans valeur qui représentaient des demoiselles allemandes avec des oiseaux dans les mains—voilà à quoi se réduisait l'ameublement." Translated into English from the French version by Derély.

36. Perrault, *Parallèle des Anciens et des Modernes,* 101.

et des modernes, Chatman uses a similar metaphor (kernels and satellites) to describe plots.

In addition to the story, the other "obsolete notion" attacked by Robbe-Grillet is that of "character." According to traditional criticism, a novelist is known for the characters he or she creates: Balzac gave us Père Goriot; Dostoevsky created the Karamazovs. The concept grew out of the encounter between a proper name and a psychological continuity, between a sign that identifies individuals and a principle of predictability that distinguishes the essential features of an individual from contingent ones. Robbe-Grillet identifies a real phenomenon: some early nineteenth-century novelists are experts in recounting the psychological satellites orbiting the planets (Austen, Manzoni, and Stendhal have remarkable introspective talent), but their protagonists, like those of Scott or Balzac, maintain a *charakter,* an imprint, an internal coherence that is preserved over time and expressed in the hierarchy between the dominant psychology and the minor passions. "The currents of life can appear to lift him up, roll him over, cast him down," wrote Breton; "he will still belong to this *readymade* human type."[37] Stendhal was a precursor of the psychology that dissolves the character, but his characters almost always stay united, which is to say, they "are subject to the comments and appraisals—which are more or less successful—made by that author," as Breton put it. Immediately afterwards he adds that "where we really find them again is at the point at which Stendhal has lost them."[38] Sometimes Stendhal loses his characters, allowing them to behave unpredictably and anticipating what will happen twenty-five years after his death in the novels of Dostoevsky. Between the second half of the nineteenth century and the age of modernism, the preformed human type became complicated: it fragmented, became the subject of lengthy analysis, or dissolved. In some respects Stendhal was a precursor of this process. But if we leave his novels aside and consider the ideal type of the nineteenth-century novel, it can be seen that the complication of the interior life never dissolved the principle of unity by which we associate an internal hierarchy and a psychological coherence with every proper name. In the first half of the nineteenth century, the *charakter* was still cohesive.

37. André Breton, *Manifesto of Surrealism,* 8.
38. Ibid., 9.

The Discovery of the Environment

The primary significance of figurative and theatrical novels is an interest in the life of people like us considered in its public dimension, since mimesis is organized according to an order that places the visible actions of individuals at the center of the world. However, this same anthropocentric device opens up another plane of reality—one that is revealed in the way characters are presented and in the historically dynamic wings that surround individuals. Let us take a closer look at this.

We have seen that starting from the end of the seventeenth century, the tradition of the novel was partly legitimized by casting itself as the history of private life. We also saw that the birth of the modern novel coincided with increased attention on the part of European culture to forms of particular life. This transformation, so important in itself, worked its way through historiography, philology, and moral philosophy to join forces with an even more extensive metamorphosis. Between the 1500s and the 1800s, during the period when the process of the disenchantment of the world began, an ontological model gathered momentum in common sense and in discursive formations that imagined the relationship between individuals and the totality according to an *environmental paradigm*. This served as a hidden backbone to very different discursive corpora: philosophical systems, scientific systems, mimetic forms, and forms of thought. Its essential points already existed, but starting in the sixteenth century they were disseminated with a new pervasiveness. Another entire book would be required to reconstruct its history, its internal logic, and its variants. We can find traces of the environmental paradigm in pictorial perspective and in the ontology that made possible modern physics, in modern historicism and in Darwinism, in the existential analytic that Heidegger developed in *Being and Time,* and in systems theory.

According to this way of thinking, the human is a being rooted in a local world that transcends and determines individuals through external circumstances and circumstances introjected into the intimate disposition that gives form to individual lives (*ethos, hexis, habitus,* customs, manners). The foundations of this ontology are ancient: they date back to Greek thought on *to periechon,* on "what surrounds" human beings,[39] and to the notions

---

39. Leo Spitzer, "Milieu and Ambiance," in *Essays in Historical Semantics* (New York: Vanni, 1947), 180ff.

of *ethos* and *charakter,* which we talked about in previous chapters. The idea that the air, the sky, the climate, the cosmic environment, and manners have an influence on the human being, acting within and all around individuals, is a concept prevalent in many periods of Greek culture: in Anaximenes as in Hippocrates, in Herodotus as in Polybius.[40] *Ethos* is a central concept in Aristotle's thought on the human world. Thanks to the rhetorical tradition and Theophrastus, the representation of *charakter* became a literary genre.

The analysis of dispositions and circumstances met with renewed popularity between the sixteenth century and the early nineteenth, in the Renaissance theory of celestial influences and in the rediscovery of Herodotus, in Bodin and in Montaigne, in La Bruyère and in Montesquieu, in Vico and in the philosophy of history of German idealism, becoming a central theme of European culture. Modern localism and historicism reinterpreted *to periechon,* redefining the category of significant circumstances, while the secularization process reinterpreted the framework of forces, redefining the factors that were believed to determine human actions. During the 1600s the theory of celestial influences and astrology lost scientific credibility; over the 1700s, theories that emphasized natural influences lost ground to theories that insisted on cultural influences (manners, institutions). While for Bodin and Montesquieu the physical environment still held great weight, for the philosophies of history coming out of German idealism it occupied a minor role.

One of the discursive formations that contributed most to the rise of the environmental paradigm is modern narrative fiction, because at all times the form of the story makes visible the bond between a given individual and the world to which he or she belongs, acting on him or her as a set of external circumstances and introjected dispositions. The first author to emblematically proclaim pride in the novel, Balzac, insisted precisely on this point: narrative fiction can make understood what it means to be born in a certain place at a certain time. Philosophy had never gone into specifics regarding the relationship between individuals and the environment; historiography had confined its examination to the tradition descending from Herodotus, which for a long time remained secondary. Having stated that Madame de Rênal was "one of those provincial women one might very

40. Ibid., 180.

well take for stupid, for the first fifteen days that one knew her,"[41] because they have no experience of life, the novel then shows us, in the concrete circumstances of an existence, what it means to be one of those French provincial women who lived around 1830 without having any experience of life. Situation by situation, it shows us how such a person speaks, behaves, thinks, dresses, loves, and hates. The discipline that Comte would subsequently call "sociology" was capable of doing this only decades later.

In addition to creating a model that provided a detailed representation of the relationship between individuals and the world, novelists invented the words that gave a name to the ways *to periechon* is imagined by the modern form of life. In *Wilhelm Meister's Apprenticeship,* Goethe describes the interaction between characters and microcosms using the concept of *Kreis*, circle, which would become common in German sociology between the end of the nineteenth and the beginning of the twentieth centuries; Jane Austen talks about *spheres* in which individuals find themselves immersed;[42] Comte and Balzac began to apply the concept of *milieu* to the human world.[43]

During the same years when Scott's model of the novel was making its way throughout Europe, Hegel was reflecting on the epic as a form and developed the notion that we commented on in Chapter 1. What is specific to narrative fiction is its ability to illustrate the dialectic between personal destinies and the force of circumstances. Hegel would likely never have thought about the epic in this form if the novel of the eighteenth century and the first decades of the nineteenth had not been devoting more attention

41. Stendhal, *The Red and the Black*, 35.

42. Austen, *Pride and Prejudice*, vol. 3, chap. 14 (orig. chap. 56), p. 395.

43. Originally coming from the discipline of mechanics, *milieu* was introduced into French biology between the second half of the eighteenth century and the beginning of the nineteenth. Initially the word *milieu* was synonymous with the concept of fluid with which Newton had attempted to explain action at a distance between bodies. Although the term continued to have a mechanical meaning in the *Encyclopédie*, Lamarck introduced it into the lexicon of biology through the mediation of Buffon. Comte used the notion of *milieu* in his *Course in Positive Philosophy* (1838) to explain the behavior of all bodies, including that of human beings. Four years later, Balzac used the same concept in his introduction to *The Human Comedy*. See Spitzer, "Milieu and Ambiance"; Georges Canguilhem, *La Connaissance de la vie* (2nd ed., 1965); English translation *Knowledge of Life*, trans. Stefanos Geroulanos and Daniela Ginsburg (Brooklyn, NY: Fordham University Press, 2008).

to the environment and to introjected dispositions. By doing so, it made explicit a characteristic that is implicit in narrative as a language game, but much less clearly discernible in the ancient epic. But why was it that interest in *to periechon* and in the *habitus* of the characters became systematic only with the novel?

Dependent Individuals

It was actually Hegel who reflected on this metamorphosis in his lectures on aesthetics. The heroes of *epos* and tragedy, he writes, are independent and universal. They are independent because their action is a *primum:* it does not tautologically express a web of habits, a law, or an order from previous times, but creates new states of things. They are universal because their action conveys collective values:[44] they are subject to finitude (they have a body, they live in space and time, and they must die), but they are unaware of the limits that nonheroic individuals are subject to, walled up in the world of prose. Nonheroic individuals are instead dependent and particular. They are dependent because they are rooted: they exist in a given culture, in an environment, in a network of pre-individual forces that influence them and define them. More than anything, when compared to the animal world, the world of human beings multiplies dependencies, since people are unconsciously infused with the objective spirit— the culture to which they belong—and they stay alive by participating in the fabric of social life and its web of interdependencies.[45] Nonheroic individuals are particular because the person who exists in the age of prose is only an accidental fragment of the whole: his or her actions do not decide the destiny of a community; at most they determine a small, private matter of happiness or unhappiness. During the heroic age, a few extraordinary individuals acted in the name of the entire community; in the prose world, each person acts for personal aims, and life is governed by habits, laws, and institutions that give an exclusively particular significance to the actions of individuals:

44. Hegel, *Aesthetics*, vol. 1, pp. 179ff.
45. Ibid., p. 193ff.

The individual as he appears in this world of prose and everyday is not active out of the entirety of his own self and his resources, and he is intelligible not from himself, but from something else. For the individual man stands in dependence on external influences, laws, political institutions, civil relationships, which he just finds confronting him, and he must bow to them.[46]

The assembly of Homeric heroes presupposes an organic, communitarian society whose history is marked by great sovereign deeds; the heroes of modern novels move in a fragmented, controlled society whose history is marked by conflicts between states or by suprapersonal, economic rationales. Out of this arises the dialectic without resolution in which contemporary human beings find themselves enmeshed. The triumph of prose represents a remarkable achievement for universal history: where once the few were free to act with absolute autonomy, now there is the certainty of the law; where once individuals were absorbed into the collectivity, now they have the right to subjective freedom, to pursue purely personal interests, and to seek out private happiness.[47] But the increase in security, guarantees, and equality and the rise of a small sphere of autonomy entail a restricted range of possible experiences and an objective impoverishment of individual actions. The latter have a purely particular value and appear to be conditioned by the web of bonds, both introjected and external, that shape people's identities and destinies.

The impersonal and invisible forces affecting individuals internally and externally matter as little to the heroes of epic or tragedy as do the particularities of character, manners, and the environment. Interest in the middle station of life coincided with added attention to the chains of dependencies binding individuals to the objective spirit and to the force of circumstances, thereby limiting their sovereignty. Mr. Kreutznaer enters the narrative endowed with a *milieu* (his social class) and a *moment* (his place and date of birth). These a prioris act as identity-making sentinels, designating the system of coordinates that define and erect boundaries around what

---

46. Ibid., 149.
47. Georg Wilhelm Friedrich Hegel, *Grundlinien der Philosophie des Rechts* (1820–1821); English translation *Outlines of the Philosophy of Right*, trans. T. M. Knox (Oxford: Oxford University Press, 1967), §124, pp. 122–123.

a person can say or do. That is why the serious mimesis of the everyday presupposes the development of a backdrop designed according to the categories that modern human beings use to probe *to periechon*. The novel conceives of the relationship between the individual and the whole in a different way from the genres of ancient literature: it is more environmental and atmospheric;[48] it has a less anthropocentric structure than tragedy and *epos,* because it takes away a part of individuals' sovereignty over themselves and assigns it to the context.

During the eighteenth century, as we know, there were efforts to legitimize the novel by comparing it to the comedy. This was based on the fact that both genres represented the *consuetudo,* the *ethos,* and *moeurs.* Along with the idea that the novel is the history of private life, there spread the notion of a "novel of manners." But eighteenth-century narrative fiction, just like the comedy, defined manners primarily based on a philosophical vocabulary of a moralistic type, in the sense Auerbach gives to this adjective. Instead, the nineteenth-century novel conceived of circumstances according to a vocabulary that possessed a sense of historical dynamics. Out of this new conceptual ether, crystallized into themes and forms, an image of the world emerged. The center of the reality created by the text is occupied by people like us, and they find themselves caught up in interesting stories; around them there opens a totality that acts as double theater wings, made of nature and culture. A model of this sort brings together two opposite movements: an anthropocentric gesture originating in the theater that places the relationships between the characters in the fore ground; and the call to a new transcendence, a secularized, localized, and historicized transcendence that precedes, traverses, and conditions individuals. The two movements coexist without colliding. Balzac is the most theatrical of the nineteenth-century writers, and his everyday heroes have the stature of the great personages of tragedy and melodrama, but the edifice of *The Human Comedy* also includes the *Analytical Studies,* namely, some of the finest examples of the modern novel-essay. These two different structural choices evaluate the weight of individuals in the world in opposing ways and run throughout the same work: the first grants people

48. José Ortega y Gasset, *Ideas sobre la novela,* in *Obras completas* (Madrid: Alianza Editorial-Revista de West, 1983), 186ff.

sovereignty over their lives; the second shifts the location of ultimate causes outside the human sphere, deprives individuals of their autonomy, and submits them to a bluntly ethnological gaze. This divide is internal to the nineteenth-century paradigm: Balzac, the author who makes the most use of theatrical devices to stage massive, absolute conflicts in ordinary contexts, is also the writer who on several occasions assigns himself the task of revealing the "reasons"—the universal, invisible "principles"—that lie hidden in the particular actions of individuals.[49] Although it may be true that a division of this sort is inherent in the nineteenth-century novel, it must be added that in the narrative of the first half of the nineteenth century the two movements are always arranged in a hierarchy. The opposition is used to indicate the representative and universal value of the events being described, and not to stage a massive collision between people and the totality: individual actions come before supraindividual powers; the reader's interest stays focused on individual lives; the narration remains anthropocentric.

The Melodramatic Model

Thus far we have talked about the nineteenth-century model as an ideal type. Now we need to account for differences between the texts that compose it. To construct a map of the possibilities, I will begin with a problem that is crucial in all attempts to write serious stories of ordinary life. The task of making everyday life interesting is a difficult one, because the actions of private, common people always run the risk of lapsing into routine and tautology. Finitude is always varied and always the same, since it is composed of so many differences that when viewed from a distance prove to be ontologically indistinguishable, closed up in themselves, and identical in their diversity. On the first page of *Père Goriot*, Balzac wonders whether the story he is about to tell will be understandable outside Paris:

> Will anyone understand it outside Paris? That is open to doubt. The special features of this scene, full of local colour and observations, can only be appreciated in the area lying between the heights of Montmartre and

49. Balzac, "Author's Introduction" to *The Human Comedy*, lviii-lix.

the hills of Montrouge, in that illustrious valley of flaking plasterwork and gutters black with mud; a valley full of suffering that is real, and of joy that is often false, where life is so hectic that it takes something quite extraordinary to produce feelings that last.[50]

Since the stories that stir the world of the novel enter into life burdened by contingency, they run the risk of signifying only themselves. Over the course of the nineteenth century, a sense of this limit appears often and manifests in many ways: in the awareness that the vicissitudes of private individuals closed within the sphere of their own personal desires might be irrelevant ("Could there be a slenderer, more insignificant thread in human history than this consciousness of a girl, busy with her small inferences of the way in which she could make her life pleasant?"[51]); or in the awareness that individuals, in the end, all resemble each other ("she had had, like anyone else, her love story"[52]). How does each novel try to make everyday life interesting? What disruption does the novel bring to life in the endless expanse of ordinary life, forever different and forever the same? By tracing out the internal differences in the ideal type of the nineteenth-century novel, the answers to these questions allow a map to be created.

In the first half of the 1800s, the serious mimesis of daily life appeared primarily *in a melodramatic form.* Between the late eighteenth century and the beginning of the nineteenth, what was called "melodrama" in French theater was a popular genre composed of sensational incidents, violent conflicts, and pivotal scenes. Initially, the texts had musical parts, as in the Italian genre of the same name; the music later disappeared. The genre was related to the *drame bourgeois,* whose features it exaggerated,[53] and to the gothic novels of Walpole, Radcliffe, and Lewis, some of whose techniques and atmospheres it inherited.[54] It had a direct influence on the French novel

50. Honoré de Balzac, *Le Père Goriot* (1835); English translation *Père Goriot,* trans. A. J. Krailsheimer (Oxford: Oxford University Press, 2009), 1.

51. George Eliot, *Daniel Deronda,* ed. Graham Handley, vol. 2 (Oxford: Clarendon Press, 1984), chap. 11, p. 109.

52. Gustave Flaubert, "Un Coeur simple," in *Trois contes* (1877); English translation "A Simple Heart," in *Three Tales,* trans. A. J. Krailsheimer (Oxford: Oxford University Press, 1999), 4.

53. Brooks, *The Melodramatic Imagination,* chap. 4.

54. Christopher Prendergast, *Balzac: Fiction and Melodrama* (London: Edward Arnold, 1978), 3–6.

of the early nineteenth century: on Balzac, Eugene Sue, Dumas the Elder, and, generally, on the whole tradition of the *roman feuilleton* from the 1830s and 1840s.

But even before its direct influence, melodrama was important as a striking example of a way of representing reality that is implicit to theater as a form.[55] This approach arose conspicuously out of the plays of the late eighteenth century and met with considerable success in the nineteenth-century novel with writers who aimed at the general public (Sue, Dumas), with writers who used popular expedients to create ambitious works (Scott, Manzoni, Balzac, Stendhal, Dickens, Hugo), with a writer who defies categorization, like Dostoevsky, and with a markedly highbrow writer like Henry James.[56] Similar approaches spread everywhere in the literature of the early nineteenth century. Melodrama survived the disciplining of the novel advocated by naturalism as well as by modernism and the avant-garde: the works of Zola and Conrad would be unimaginable without devices dating back to this mimetic mode. In the second half of the twentieth century, works like Pasternak's *Doctor Zhivago* or Elsa Morante's *History* picked up on melodramatic techniques. Contemporary popular fiction, midcult fiction, and mainstream film are still based on the melodrama as well as on the romance. How does this form work?

Melodrama is the histrionic expression of theatricality that pervaded the nineteenth-century paradigm, because it heightens scenic devices, starting with the way human action in the present tense is represented. The public sphere becomes the site of clashes between universal forces embodied in individuals (good and evil, innocence and wickedness, adherence to ethical constraints and personal ambition, class warfare); the conflicts are often underpinned by the primary human bonds between the adversaries (fathers against sons, brothers against brothers, friends against friends). Melodrama magnifies and turns outward: the protagonists are statuesque and grandiose; the characters publicly express their inner life and behave unrestrainedly; passions are expressed through eloquent signs, poses, and confessions; the plot is dense, packed, crafted around stylistic gestures that are clear and centripetal, full of momentous confrontations and pivotal

55. Eric Bentley, *The Life of Drama* (1964) (New York: Atheneum, 1975), 157, 215ff.
56. Brooks, *The Melodramatic Imagination,* chap. 6 and "Conclusion"; Prendergast, *Balzac,* 10–15.

scenes. Coincidences and recognitions abound, as if the world and chance collaborated in weaving the characters' destinies. In every domain of the text, the planets crush the satellites: the protagonists are governed by a dominant passion, character is always expressed in action, and the action has no centrifugal movements—those arising from the segments of our divided self, from changes of mind and trivial contingent facts. There are nothing but unequivocal and defining gestures.

> Let us take a novel like *Père Goriot,* which is well suited as a sample text. This is partly because it offers a good intermediate model rather than an extreme example of melodrama such as *Scenes from a Courtesan's Life.* The plot is punctuated by centripetal chance (Rastignac, Goriot, Vautrin, and Victorine are all staying, by chance, at the same pension; by chance, the person that Rastignac meets at the first ball he attends is Goriot's daughter; by chance, Bianchon names Death-Dodger in front of Vautrin, and just at that moment, by chance, the police come into the pension and reveal that Vautrin is Death-Dodger). Conflicts are framed in absolute terms (duty to family versus personal interest) and amplified (Vautrin is the "Bonaparte of thieves"; Goriot is the "Christ of fatherhood"). The characters' pasts hide "mysteries" and "secrets." The story line is constructed theatrically: conflicts arise and resolve in big, pivotal scenes; the background noise of contingency never interrupts the dramatic action; the characters confess openly in front of strangers, like Vautrin, Madame de Nucingen, and Goriot before Rastignac. Gestures and words are always associated with the im prints of character and dominant passions that animate the protagonists. There is a necessary link between inside and outside, between the life of the psyche and physical features: when Rastignac speaks well of Goriot's daughter, whom he met at a ball, Goriot's face is happy; when Vautrin observes that Goriot's daughter is indebted to Gobseck, Goriot's face becomes sad. Moods, thoughts, and meanings are expressed in eloquent poses and didactic judgments ("a father hiding himself to see his daughters! I have given them my whole life and they won't give me just one hour today!"[57]). The characters compose pictorial-theatrical tableaux ("at that moment Vautrin came in very quietly, and looked at the picture of these two young

57. Balzac, *Père Goriot,* 247.

people in the lamplight, which seemed to play on them caressingly"[58]). Everything is anthropocentric, externalized, and magnified.

The Significance of the Melodramatic Novel

Long before it was named by Peter Brooks ("the melodramatic imagination"), this mimetic mode had been unintentionally described by György Lukács in the 1930s and 1940s. Lukács's essays occupy a special place in thought on nineteenth-century narrative fiction, because they define the internal mechanisms of the nineteenth-century novel with unparalleled critical force. And yet, they tie this description to a normative aesthetic that quickly became anachronistic in the second half of the twentieth century, when the political and philosophical foundations on which they were based no longer had a place in our horizon. Lukács offers a plausible reconstruction of the history of the nineteenth-century novel, but he also takes a stance in support of a specific mimetic model, juxtaposing the work of Scott and Balzac to that of Flaubert and Zola. Lukács takes his start from the problem of realism: How does one put the profound dynamics of modern life into narrative form? How is one to represent a world in which the distance between particular lives and the great universal forces has become so disproportionally big?

Genuine realism, he believes, should not be limited to reproducing average everydayness by describing a slice of life chosen at random or on the basis of a statistical average. Rather, it must be able to show "the typical": in any given narrative scene it must be able to embody the major collective conflicts that lie behind small, private disputes. In ordinary life we do not usually experience this *symbolon* of universal and particular that manifests in the typical situation: "In day-by-day existence, major contradictions are obscured in a whir of petty, disparate accidental events; they are exposed only when purified and intensified to such an extreme that their potential consequences are exposed and are readily perceived."[59] In other words, authentic realism does not arise from a direct mimetic gesture, but from an

---

58. Ibid., 170.

59. György Lukács, "Die intellektuelle Physiognomie des künstlerischen Gestalten" (1936); English translation "The Intellectual Physiognomy in Characterization," in *Writer and Critic and Other Essays*, trans. Arthur Kahn (Lincoln, NB: iUniverse.com, 2005), 149–188; quote from p. 158.

intellectual construction. While keeping stories in an everyday context, the great realist writer invents special situations and heroes with which he or she gives a plastic and tangible form to the forces at work in a society and in an epoch. This effect is achieved by working on the plot and characters. The plot has to condense, exacerbate, and bring to the stage conflicts that do not normally take a public form; the characters have to plausibly embody large collective entities (social classes, for example, or historical dynamics). Compared to ordinary life, the typical is a state of exception:

> It is obvious that an old French peasant in 1844 would not have used such words as these. And yet, the whole character and everything Balzac puts into his mouth are absolutely true to life, precisely because they go beyond the limits of a pedestrian copying of reality. All that Balzac does is to express on its potentially highest level what a peasant of the Fourchon type would dimly feel but would not be able to express clearly.[60]

> The success of great writers in creating typical characters and typical situations requires far more than accurate observation of everyday reality. Profound understanding of life is never restricted to the observation of everyday existence. The writer first defines the basic issues and movements of his time and then invents characters and situations not to be found in ordinary life, possessing capacities and propensities which when intensified illuminate the complex dialectic of the major contradictions, motive forces and tendencies of an era.[61]

Incorporating concepts from Hegel and Marx, the normative aesthetics of Lukács interpret and legitimize the techniques that Scott and Balzac took from the theater of their time. In effect, the theory of the typical was the first attempt to describe the melodramatic imagination. The foundational idea of this system is that by making actions and characters more wooden and larger than life, as they appear in a certain type of theater, universals can assume a finite, human form: "every really great drama expresses . . . an *affirmation of life*";[62] "melodramatic rhetoric implicitly insists that the world can be equal

---

60. György Lukács, "Balzac: *Les Paysans*" (1934); English translation "Balzac: *The Peasants*," in *Studies in European Realism*, trans. Edith Bone (London: Hillway, 1950), 42.

61. Lukács, "The Intellectual Physiognomy in Characterization," 149–189; quote from p. 158.

62. György Lukács, *The Historical Novel* (1937) (Lincoln: University of Nebraska Press, 1983), 122.

to our most feverish expectations about it . . . , that reality properly represented will never fail to live up to our phantasmatic demands upon it."[63] For a poetics of this sort the main problem of the modern realistic novel—to make everyday life interesting—is solved a priori, since it is taken for granted that cosmic, historical forces lie hidden in average, ordinary life, waiting to be expressed by the intellectual construction of the typical.

Why melodrama? What made this device possible? Brooks interprets the melodramatic imagination as the modern, secularized remnant of a sacred myth telling the story of the clash between the universal powers of good and evil.[64] Lukács instead interprets the development of the novel using categories drawn from the philosophy of history that the young Marx produced, drawing particularly on Marx's theory of the role of the bourgeoisie, the class that most of the nineteenth-century novelists belonged to and wrote for. According to this grand narrative, the bourgeoisie and its culture played a revolutionary role between 1789 and 1848, acting as the vanguard of historical progress. Even when bourgeois writers express moderate views, as Scott does, or are openly conservative, as in the case of Balzac, they are described as regarding history with interest and engagement. Moreover, between 1789 and 1814 the peoples of Europe went through more transformations than they had experienced in previous centuries. This metamorphosis bolstered an idea that eighteenth-century historicism had helped to spread—the belief that the fate of individual lives depends on history, that great, changeable, collective life in which they are immersed. "It was the French Revolution, the revolutionary wars and the rise and fall of Napoleon, which for the first time made history a *mass experience,* and moreover on a European scale."[65] The process continued even after the restoration of 1814, showing its effects in 1830, and more broadly in the social and economic changes Europe underwent in the early decades of the nineteenth century, especially in France and England. Until the middle of the nineteenth century, bourgeois intellectuals viewed history as a form of objective transcendence, acting around and within personal lives. Circumstances changed abruptly in 1848 when a new revolutionary class—the proletariat—loomed on the political scene as the vanguard of progress. In

---

63. Brooks, *The Melodramatic Imagination,* 40.
64. Ibid., 32ff. and passim.
65. Lukács, *The Historical Novel,* 23.

the face of this social turmoil, the bourgeoisie became a conservative force. This change was transferred into the cultural sphere and provoked distrust or disinterest in public life on the part of middle-class intellectuals. The literature reflects this change: while Scott and Balzac were experts at showing how the great collective history manifested itself in minor private histories, the forms of realism that developed in the second half of the nineteenth century lost the sense of the typical and divorced individual lives from collective processes.

The interpretations put forward by Lukács and Brooks diverge widely because the theories they draw from are incommensurately different, but their approaches resemble each other through a stylistic trait, a gesture. They both devote a great deal of space to analyzing plots and characters, but in the end, between the detailed readings and the general explanations there lies a gap. The general explanation derives from a philosophy of history that preceded the literature and has no relationship with the logic of the works being studied. Let us examine the same process but starting from a different point.

During the eighteenth century, painting underwent a metamorphosis similar to the one that transformed the literary sphere. A new public had emerged that was a stranger to the rules of classicist and academic painting, incapable of deciphering traditional iconography, and interested in everyday subjects. The first result of this transformation was the birth of an art devoid of eloquence, depicting characters engaged in their activities, as Chardin did.[66] But later, after a few decades, the painters of everyday life wound up reincorporating the theatrical, oratorical, and sentimental pathos that was typical of historical or religious painting. The pictorial approach that Greuze took, for example, was similar in many respects to that of Chardin, but with completely different results: by showing ostentatious, mannered gestures, his domestic scenes created the pictorial counterpart of melodrama. There is a sociological explanation for this development. Because the viewers of these works were not schooled in iconography, they had to understand the meaning of a painting purely on the basis of what they saw; for this reason the image had to clearly communicate the meaning

---

66. Michael Fried, *Absorption and Theatricality: Painting and Beholder in the Age of Diderot* (Chicago: University of Chicago Press, 1980), chap. 1.

of the scene, with no semantic fuzziness.[67] Greuze emphasizes the theatricality of gestures in part because the subjects he paints are bourgeois. While the meaning of conventional paintings is guaranteed by tradition and by the social hierarchy embedded in it, everyday environments and characters are potentially devoid of value. Until they are infused with meaning by art, they signify only themselves: instead of great scenes of sacred or profane history, they offer trivial anecdotes about unknown people. Eloquence and theatricality serve to cover this void: the intent is to show that the great universal passions, with their grandiloquent gestures, occur even in ordinary contexts. The melodramatic model works the same way: rather than being a remnant of sacred myth, melodrama is a vestige of tragedy, from which it inherits its techniques and tones. But while histories and tragic heroes are grand and important by definition, the stories and protagonists of a novel are not. To hide this lacuna, melodrama creates a pathetic-sentimental version of the noble genres, shifting interest from the objective importance of the stories to the subjective intensity of the passions. The aim is to show that the protagonists' feelings are universal, in spite of the work describing or portraying people in private situations. To this end, novelists and painters exaggerated gestures and intensified their tones. But the question remains why they came to think that this genre was suited to represent everyday life.

Melodrama transported the anthropocentrism of tragedy and epic—the idea that the struggles internal to a small group of individuals have a collective meaning—to the world inhabited by average or middle-class characters: it transferred the mimetic mechanisms that held sway in the heroic age to the age of prose. But while tradition, public history, and mythology justified the status of the *epos* and tragedy, the novel could not rely on this legitimacy. The idea that Père Goriot's vicissitudes are valuable took hold at a certain point in literary history for several reasons. On the one hand, this is because the private lives of ordinary people had acquired an absolute value and commanded unbounded attention. Melodrama expresses in its histrionic fashion the typically modern idea that private life is the only absolute and that its conflicts deserve to be told with unbounded passion. It is no coincidence that the genre has maintained its hegemony in mainstream literature and film for the past two centuries. On the other hand,

67. Ibid., chaps. 1 and 2.

this is because in some historical periods, institutions and manners are affected by sudden changes that disrupt the everyday existence of people like us, normally governed by repetition. Everyday life becomes transformed along with the great collective changes: during times like these, anthropocentric narrative forms seem more plausible. From this perspective, Lukács's theory may be valid even beyond the scope of its legitimizing philosophy. Between the French Revolution and the first half of the nineteenth century, history became an experience lived by the European masses: in periods of such turmoil and change, personal life can become the place of interesting collective conflicts, or at least it becomes easier to believe that this is the case. These decades coincided with the growth of the melodramatic novel.

The *Romance* in the *Novel*, Special Characters

During the early 1800s, the novel that would be called "realistic" made everyday life especially narratable because it introduced an element of *romance* into the world of the *novel*. In addition to taking a melodramatic form, the exceptional state was able to take on a more canonically adventurous appearance. The theatrical system of *The Betrothed* is constructed around the staging of obvious oppositions,[68] and a melodramatic structure is easily discernible in many episodes, but the primary disruption, the one holding up the armature of the text, comes prior to this theatricality and is genuinely romantic: in rewriting the topos of the innocent heroine kidnapped by an evil character, Manzoni constructs a novel based on an adventure from Greek romance. Even Stendhal's novels have no dearth of melodramatic features, but the current of romance is entrusted to the singular personality of the main characters who challenge other people's opinions, escape social conventions, indulge themselves in anarchic behavior, create the unexpected, and, in doing so, introduce the *romance* into the *novel*.[69] Boredom is unknown in Scott and Balzac: every one of their pages affirms life, as if the world would never disappoint us. Manzoni and Stendhal, on the other hand, are more than familiar with the repetition of existence

68. Ezio Raimondi, *Il romanzo senza idillio: Saggio sui "Promessi sposi"* (Turin: Einaudi, 1974), 249–307.

69. Christopher Prendergast, *The Order of Mimesis: Balzac, Stendhal, Nerval and Flaubert* (Cambridge: Cambridge University Press, 1986), chap. 4.

and the average stagnation of ordinary lives. This comes through in their descriptions of life in Verrières or the prosaic existence that Renzo and Lucia fall back into once their adventures have come to an end. Still, ordinary uneventfulness does not yet approach the anguished mire that twentieth-century narrators will long to escape from. This is because the novels of Stendhal and Manzoni focus on disruptions produced by exceptional events, and because the world of prose makes room for romantic adventures and characters who, following their demons at any cost, break the social order and generate unpredictable stories.

While Robinson Crusoe's father juxtaposed the middle station to actions out of the ordinary, for the novel of the early 1800s, daily life was animated by grandiose disruptions. But not all the works that contributed to forming the nineteenth-century paradigm expressed this image of the world. Wilhelm Meister, for example, shares the opinion of Mr. Kreutznaer and views bourgeois existence as uninteresting for narrative purposes. Goethe responds accordingly. The lives of people like Albert or Werner form the background of his novels, but the core is composed of characters who stand on the side of middle-class normality: the intellectual hero, the sensitive hero, the hero who develops his inner life by refining his thoughts and deepening his passions. Not by chance, the two most influential novels by Goethe (*The Sorrows of Young Werther* and *Wilhelm Meister's Apprenticeship*), which provided the archetypes for the two genres flanking the realism of the nineteenth century, namely, the *roman personnel* and the artist novel, do not feature average protagonists.

The Novel of Personal Destinies

Like Goethe, like Manzoni, and like Stendhal, Jane Austen knew that the private lives of people like us are almost always repetitive and conventional. What makes everyday life representable is not the special quality of the characters or the eruption of the romantic but a new way of conceiving the prose of the world. Austen cut down the number of potentially narratable stories: her books focus on a single human figure (a young woman of marriageable age), on a single social class (the gentry), and on a single situation (marriage). Other stories and ways of being enter into the plot but solely as a reflection of this primary core. Austen is interested exclusively, or almost exclusively, in a single period of life: the few months or few years when the heroines of her novels become adults, making a good marriage or a bad one. This time of life is cut across by a momentous disruption, while on either side there extends the prose of couples already formed, individual destinies already sealed and, therefore, unworthy of being told. A restriction of this sort could be interpreted as a limit.

In reality, Austen discovers a crucial aspect of the modern form of life: she discovers that our lives take on interest every time desire collides with reality and that the aftermath of the confrontation seals our destiny, deciding our happiness or unhappiness. She discovers that this collision has universal value, because the pursuit of private happiness (or of its disenchanted variant, "tranquility"[70]) is the only shared god still alive, the only thing that really matters for modern individuals. The content of this pursuit can be varied ("I wish as well as everybody else to be perfectly happy; but like everybody else it must be in my own way," says Edward in Sense and Sensibility[71]); nevertheless, the one value behind everybody's pursuit is that of achieving a balance. By focusing on a limited situation, Austen creates what we might call the *novel of personal destinies*. Eighteenth-century precedents do exist (the *Bildungsroman*, the *marriage novel*, and, more generally, narrative fiction telling the story of a young woman's entrance into society, as in the works of Fanny Burney, a writer who was very important to Austen), but Austen further normalizes exceptional states. The novel of personal destinies has a Christian archetype (the spiritual autobiography), only now it is situated in a secular, earthly horizon. Instead of saving one's soul, the goal is to achieve happiness in this world.

The first consequence of this shift affects the internal structure of the text. "Jane Austen is antimelodrama":[72] she has no need to exaggerate to add interest to the everyday situations she talks about. Although her works have a strong theatrical component—the characters seek meaning in their lives by acting in the public sphere—Austen's theatricality always, or almost always, skirts around the topoi of romance. This difference resides

70. Jane Austen, *Sense and Sensibility,* ed. Edward Copeland, in *The Cambridge Edition of the Works of Jane Austen,* (Cambridge: Cambridge University Press, 2006), vol. 2, chap. 1 (orig. chap. 23), p. 160.

71. Ibid., vol. 1, chap. 17, p. 105.

72. Giuseppe Tomasi di Lampedusa, *Letteratura inglese,* in *Opere,* ed. Nicoletta Polo (Milan: Mondadori, 1995), 982.

less in the structural and stylistic elements than in the type of interest the stories seek to arouse. The plots and characters do not have an immediate, universal hidden sense: they do not embody human types (the girl of marriageable age, the proud gentleman), historical forces (a class or segment of society), or cosmic powers (good and evil). Not even the universals cited by some of the titles (*Pride and Prejudice, Sense and Sensibility*) are so important that they transform the protagonists into allegorical figures and the stories into *exempla*. Austen knows that particular lives are dependent on circumstances and that they bear the imprint of character: she expertly describes the class differences within the confined social sphere to which the characters belong. Also, all her novels are built around a difference in status or conditions that marriage will overcome. And yet, a fracture is opened up between the particular and the universal. Suprapersonal forces are never embodied in individuals: particular events are influenced by circumstances, but they remain in the sphere of average everydayness and do not become typical, in the sense Lukács gives to this term. Elinor Dashwood, Marianne Dashwood, and Darcy are not allegories of Sense, Sensibility, and Pride: the text does not try to give an exemplary hidden moral sense to their character or actions, except in the choice of titles. The fulcrum of the novels, the reason the reader feels joy or pain, is the struggle for earthly happiness that each of them experiences. We are not interested in discerning Good Sense in Elinor or Pride in Darcy: what we are interested in knowing is whether Elinor or Darcy will ultimately succeed in reconciling desire and reality and achieving a life that meets their expectations. Also, observations on the circumstances make very brief appearances in the text, and only when they serve to explain the paths that individuals take: Austen's desire is not to demonstrate causes but to recount the destinies of her characters. The latter signify first and foremost themselves: *no universal transcends the subjective pursuit of happiness or tranquility.* True, the narrator expresses judgments and evaluates single-mindedly and unabashedly. If a personage is defined as slow-witted, his character is established objectively, with no polyphonic or perspectival games; and yet selfishness and stupidity are not sins, but ways of being, forms of life. Moreover, there is a strong sense of nuance: the characters are not entirely good or bad, or always good and always bad. The same rejection of melodrama can be found in the way the plot and episodes are constructed: the love between the main characters is offset by misunderstandings, chance, and circumstances. The awareness that social life is dominated by conventions prevents or damps down pivotal scenes.

A Map of the Nineteenth-Century Paradigm

We can therefore draw a map of the nineteenth-century paradigm by considering the ways narrative interest in everyday life is conceived. At the center of the spectrum, writers who rely on the melodramatic mode reveal absolute conflicts in the private lives of people like us, ones that can be made universal, significant, and typical by the presence of a historical backdrop. For Scott, Balzac or Dickens, the problem of making life interesting does not exist, because it is solved a priori: the utopia of universal narratability arose thanks to this poetics. Then there are the novelists who, while sensing the boredom of daily life, introduce an element of romance into the prose of the world: the kidnapping that disrupts the otherwise quiet and repetitive life of Renzo and Lucia or the singular actions of Stendhal's demonic characters serve this purpose. At the edges of the spectrum lie those who seek narrative interest in characters immersed in a prosaic context but who do not have prosaic lives or thoughts: the intellectual hero, the sensitive hero, the artist.

Jane Austen represents a later position. Her novels unearth an element of perpetual fascination in ordinary life: the clash between desire and reality, and the personal destinies that arise out of this collision, turn every life into a potential subject for a novel. Although Austen's works might appear to be limited, they contain another utopia of universal narratability, founded on the conviction that all human beings, even the most common, are faced with interesting conflicts during certain periods of their lives. This happens when objective turning points determine one's place in the world, fixing the relations between what one wants to be and what one becomes, laying the foundations for happiness or unhappiness, or, more modestly, tranquility or preoccupation. The historical-philosophical importance of Jane Austen's work is comparable to the weight literary histories have given for some time now to her contemporary, Sir Walter Scott. Prior to these writers, the common life could be the subject of a story only if it contained an adventure or a melodramatic conflict. Also, the novel contained a strong element of romance, following an approach that prolonged the Aristotelian-based poetics of historical narratives and the poetics of the *novella* as a story of unprecedented events. Austen tells instead about private disruptions that, however irrelevant or insignificant they may be in the eyes of others, are crucial to the individuals undergoing them. She was born in an era when particular individuals attributed an absolute, untranscendable meaning to the most minor events that concerned their private, earthly happiness. The epoch had arrived when nothing was important but life.

CHAPTER SEVEN

The Transition to Modernism

The Second Phase of Nineteenth-Century Realism

The symbolic weight that the nineteenth-century paradigm carried in the history of the novel became perceptible once its importance began to fade. In Chapter 6 we saw how the culture of modernism and the avant-garde movements cemented the ideal type, relegating the novel of the nineteenth century to the past and defining itself as its antithesis. In the 1930s and 1940s, György Lukács created a different narrative. The English edition of his *Studies in European Realism* (1950) opens with two questions: Is the classic nineteenth-century novel Balzac or Flaubert? Does the modern novel culminate in the works of Thomas Mann or in those of Gide, Proust, and Joyce? To answer these questions, continues Lukács, we need a new philosophy of literary history.[1] His theory dates the crisis of the nineteenth-century realistic model to an earlier time, identifying the first signs of dissolution in the works of Flaubert, the Goncourt brothers, Zola, and Maupassant. According to this schema, the authentic tradition of realism survived in the second half of the nineteenth century almost exclusively in the Russian novel, specifically in the work of Tolstoy.

While many aspects of this interpretation have become debatable (the importance of 1848, for example, and the idea that Tolstoy and Mann are the continuators of Balzac) and the normative poetics that sustain it are indefensible, Lukács's studies still offer historical insights that I find to be enlightening and irrefutable. The most important one is the following:

1. György Lukács, preface to *Studies in European Realism*, p. 2.

The novel of the nineteenth century is not a uniform entity. Nineteenth-century realism went through two phases, linked together by a dialectical relationship of continuities and ruptures. On the one hand, the works written after 1850 preserve and refine the devices of the nineteenth-century paradigm, especially the theater model, generating a new phase of realism that in many respects was more "realistic," or closer to the assumptions on which this poetics was based; on the other hand, they abandon the assumptions and forms of that model. This twofold movement is often present in a single text. The generation born between the late 1810s and late 1820s—that of George Eliot, Dostoevsky, Flaubert, and Tolstoy—was decisive in this regard: in their greatest works, the schemas of the nineteenth-century paradigm coexist alongside structures that prelude modernism. The same ambiguity permeates the works written by later generations. To gain a sense of this tangled imbrication of schemas, consider a list of novels published around 1890: Édouard Dujardin's *Les lauriers sont coupés* (1887), Pérez Galdós's *Fortunata y Jacinta* (1887), Maupassant's *Pierre and Jean* (1887–1888), Bourget's *The Disciple* (1889), Oscar Wilde's *The Portrait of Dorian Gray* (1891), Thomas Hardy's *Tess of the d'Urbervilles* (1891), Stephen Crane's *The Red Badge of Courage* (1894–1895), and Theodor Fontane's *Effi Briest* (1894–1895). The same overlapping is present in Italian literature: in a matter of a few years, we find Dossi's *Gli amori* (1887), Verga's *Mastro Don Gesualdo* (1889), D'Annunzio's *Pleasure* (1889), Gualdo's *Decadenza* (1892), Svevo's *Una Vita* (1892) and *Senility* (1898), and De Roberto's *The Viceroys* (1894). These decades offer a smorgasbord: works that reflect the nineteenth century in its prime and others in which naturalism opens into experimentation; novels of the decadent aesthete and the first example of interior monologue. The epochal eclecticism of this period recalls what took hold during the last decades of the twentieth century. The transition to modernism thus began in the second half of the nineteenth century; in 1890 the transformation was already perceptible; around 1910 new schemas prevailed and modernism entered into its mature phase.[2]

2. I use the term *modernism* in the sense it has in English-speaking literatures: it refers to the family resemblance shared by some of the most important novels that came out during the first four decades of the twentieth century. Over time, the concept of modernism gradually entered into the lexicons of the other European literatures. In the case of Italy, see the collected essays in Luca Somigli and Mario Moroni, eds., *Italian Modernism* (Toronto: University of

Realism without Melodrama

What distinguishes the first phase of nineteenth-century realism from the second? If we wanted to rewrite Lukács's insights using a different conceptual framework, we might say that while up to a certain date the European literary system considered the coexistence of realism and melodrama, or realism and romance, to be normal, in the second half of the century an overlap of this sort was viewed as a problem. During the period when Sue's *The Mysteries of Paris* (1842–1843) came out, it was praised as an example of realism.[3] *Les Miserables* (1862), published five years after the book edition of *Madame Bovary* (1857) and three years before *Germinie Lacerteux* (1865), was destined for quite a different critical reception: in a collection of essays entitled *Les Romanciers naturalistes,* in which Zola reconstructs the history of French realism, the works of Hugo are now viewed as the example of what a naturalist writer should not do. The most important successor of the melodramatic novel in the second half of the nineteenth century, Dostoevsky, worked with narrative structures inherited from Balzac and Dickens, from Sue, and from the tradition of the *roman feuilleton.* However, while in the 1830s and 1840s Balzac was at once the most important melodramatic author and the most influential realist of his era, between the 1870s and the 1880s Dostoevsky was forced to use the preface to *The Brothers Karamazov* to defend himself against the accusation that his characters were unrealistic and exaggerated:

> To me [Alexei Karamazov] is noteworthy, but I decidedly doubt that I shall succeed in proving it to the reader. . . . [H]e is a strange man, even an odd one. But strangeness and oddity will sooner harm than justify any

Toronto Press, 2004), and especially the entire book by Raffaele Donnarumma, *Gadda modernista* (Pisa: ETS, 2006), which interprets the Italian novel of the early twentieth century in the light of this category. The Anglophone usage of the concept of modernism makes a reappearance in studies by Loredana Di Martino, "Modernism/Postmodernism: Rethinking the Canon through Gadda," *Edinburgh Journal of Gadda Studies* 5 (2007), http://www.gadda.ed .ac.uk/Pages/journal/issue5/articles/dimartinocanon05.php. See also Riccardo Castellana, *Parole cose persone. Il realismo modernista di Tozzi* (Rome-Pisa: Fabrizio Serra, 2009); and by the same author, "Realismo modernista: Un'idea del romanzo italiano, 1915–1925," in *Italianistica* 39, no. 1 (2010): 23–45; and Valentino Baldi, *Reale invisibile Mimesi e interiorità nella narrativa di Pirandello e Gadda* (Venice: Marsilio, 2010).

3. See Lyon-Caen, *La Lecture et la Vie,* chap. 2.

claim to attention, especially when everyone is striving to unite particulars and find at least some general sense in the general senselessness.
Whereas an odd man is most often a particular and isolated case. Is that
not so? . . . For not only is an odd man "not always" a particular and
isolated case, but, on the contrary, it sometimes happens that it is precisely he, perhaps, who bears within himself the heart of the whole, while
the other people of his epoch have all for some reason been torn away
from it for a time by some kind of flooding wind.[4]

In the second half of the nineteenth century, Goncourt's imperative to
"tuer le romanesque" was a principle shared explicitly or implicitly by
most writers who saw themselves as part of the project of describing everyday
life in a serious way, and not only by the naturalists. From this perspective,
Tolstoy or George Eliot is much more stringent than Zola in eliminating
melodrama and romance. But what possibilities remained for writers who
attempted to limit unusual events yet at the same time were looking for
interesting material in the lives of people like us?

1. The most common device for sparking narrative interest in a novel is *the
strategic, local use of mechanisms deriving from melodrama and romance.*
Even the most theoretically rigorous of naturalist writers, for example,
maintain a problematic relationship with what they reject. The poetics of
Edmond de Goncourt and Zola often run contrary to their novels, in which
melodrama or romance make a regular appearance or are replaced by new
ways for generating exceptional disruptions: characters marked by a pa-
thology that makes them *ipso facto* romance-like; stories that take place
in downtrodden, working-class settings, where unconventionality or adventure appear to be a natural product of the environment.[5]

The most significant works from this point of view are by Zola. Consider
the novel that made him famous, *L'Assommoir* (1877). The characters display their passions with eloquent gestures: Gervaise weeps while describing the poverty of the house where she lives, quarrels theatrically with

4. Fyodor Dostoevsky, *Brat'ya Karamazovy* (1879–1880); English translation *The
Brothers Karamazov*, trans. Richard Pevear and Larissa Volokonsky (New York: Farrar,
Straus and Giroux, 1990), 3.

5. See Pierluigi Pellini, *In una casa di vetro. Generi e temi del naturalismo europeo* (Florence: Le Monnier, 2004), 89ff. and passim.

Lantier, then comes to blows with Virginie in the washhouse. Zola may think that this unfettered physicality is typical of the working-class environment; the fact remains that the general stylistic result is very similar to the gestures of melodrama. Furthermore, the Paris of the Goutte-d'or is described following a rhetoric of amplification: everything is immense or steeped in tragedy, from the "uninterrupted stream of men, animals and carts," "the endless procession of labourers," "slaughterhouses," "blood-stained aprons," and "the crude smell of slaughtered animals" to "the vast pit of Paris."[6] Some characters seem to come straight out of the world of Dickens: for example Lalie, the girl who raises her siblings after the death of her mother and dies from her alcoholic father's ill treatment. Chance meetings always intervene at the crucial turning points in the plot: Gervaise first finds Virginie and then Lantier; she loses everything she owns on the same day as Mother Coupeau's funeral; and finally, at her lowest moment, when she is driven to prostitution by hunger, in the "immensity of Paris," by chance she first comes across Old Bru and then Goujet.[7]

This ambiguity is hardly confined to naturalistic novels: the story of *War and Peace*, for example, involves masses of people and vast spaces, but the main characters always find each other, generating a continuous series of improbable meetings that advance the story line. Even more clearly, the realism of *Middlemarch* rests on romance-like narrative turning points: Featherstone's will, the sudden return of Raffles, Bulstrode's murky past. These pure forms of centripetal chance survive in the work of two writers who created some of the most mature, most humanely disenchanted examples of the serious mimesis of everyday life. Romance was never completely eradicated.

2. Another form of the romance's survival in a literary context that in theory rejected it is the *fait divers*. The prehistory of this form dates back to before the 1800s: rhetorical collections of cases, popular tales of memorabilia, marvelous events that provided the material for novellas were based on the same diegetic mechanism that came to be called *fait divers* during

---

6. Émile Zola, *L'Assommoir*; English translation *L'Assommoir*, trans. Margaret Mauldon (Oxford: Oxford University Press, 2009), chap. 1.
    7. Ibid., chap. 12, p. 114.

the nineteenth century.[8] Until the modern era, as we have seen, the irruption of private history into the narrative space was made possible by states of exception. With the development of the novel, disruptions of the everyday became introduced into a discourse that sought to be believable. Because it violated the statistical norm, the *fait divers* had to legitimate its anomalous nature by appealing to the authority of the real, like historiography according to Aristotle's *Poetics,* or like modern journalistic news stories.[9] Although *The Red and the Black* had earlier drawn its subject matter from a "little true fact" taken up by the press, the poetics of the *fait divers* became popular mainly in the era of naturalism, because it allowed aspects of the romance to be maintained while providing a rational justification for it. In the second half of the nineteenth century, from Flaubert to Chekhov, writers began to reflect on the repetitive, antinarrative, serial nature of ordinary life. The *fait divers* presented itself as an occasional, temporary, realistic interruption of everyday life—as the extension of *casus* into an era that, by regulating life, made the existence of people like us unnarratable.

3. Nonmelodramatic, nonromance-like narrative disruptions can be created through the device of the *tranche de vie.* In the fifth chapter of *L'Assommoir,* in about thirty pages Zola describes what it is like to work in a laundry.[10] After witnessing numerous fights, a courtship, a wedding, a birth, and the fall of Gervaise's husband from the roof, the reader is led to believe that this passage, like previous ones, should end with a pivotal scene or a twist of fate. But nothing happens: Zola limits himself to describing life in a laundry, the minor incidents that punctuate the flat expanse of the everyday. All his novels contain episodes of this type. To illustrate the difference between two models of realism, in "Narrate or Describe?" Lukács contrasts an episode taken from *Nana* (1880), set in a hippodrome, to the horse race during which Anna Karenina publicly demonstrates her love and suffering for Vronsky—a slice of life and the crucial turning point in a great

8. See Maurice Lever, *Canards sanglants: naissance du fait divers* (Paris: Fayard, 1993), and Philip Church, "Introduction: Fait divers et littérature," *Romantisme* 27, no. 97 (1997): 7–15.

9. See Clotilde Bertoni, *Letteratura e giornalismo* (Rome: Carocci, 2009), 28ff.

10. Zola, *L'Assommoir,* chap. 5, pp. 126ff.

novel of personal destinies.[11] Thanks to this device, Zola was the first novelist capable of describing work, an activity that, until then, had been talked about from a skewed perspective and only under special conditions (*Robinson Crusoe*); or it had been used as a backdrop, as a scenario for adventure stories. While Zola used this sort of expedient to make trivial, normal actions interesting, Flaubert, the author who invented this technique, gave the *tranche de vie* a dysphoric function. He used it to describe the great empty spaces of a daily life marked by the repetition of existence:

> But this, this life of hers was as cold as an attic that looks north; and boredom, quiet as the spider, was spinning its web in the shadowy places of her heart. She remembered the prize-giving days at the convent, when she went up on to the platform to receive her little crowns. With her hair in plaits, her white dress and her prunella shoes showing, she did look pretty, and the gentlemen, as she made her way back to her seat, would lean over to pay her compliments; the yard was full of carriages, people were saying goodbye to her from their windows, the music-master was waving as he passed by, carrying his violin case. How far away it was! So very far away!
>
> She called Djali, held her between her knees, stroked her long delicate head and told her:
>
> —Come on, kiss missy. Not a care in the world, have you?
>
> Then, gazing at the elegant creature's melancholy expression as it slowly gave a yawn, she was moved; and, comparing it to herself, she spoke aloud to it, as if consoling one of the afflicted.
>
> Now and again there came gusts of wind, sea-breezes sweeping right across the flat lands of Caux, bringing to inland fields the distant salt freshness. There was a whistling down among the rushes, a rustling and a fluttering in the beech-leaves; and the tree-tops, swaying to and fro, kept up their immense murmuring. Emma drew her shawl around her shoulders and got to her feet.
>
> In the avenue, a dim green light filtered down through the leaves on to the smooth moss that crackled softly beneath her feet. The sun was setting; the sky was red between the branches, and the row of tree-trunks looked just like a brown colonnade against a golden background; seized

11. György Lukács, "Erzählen oder beschreiben?" (1936); English translation "Narrate or Describe?" in *Writer and Critic and Other Essays*, 110–113.

with fear, she called Djali, hurried back to Tostes along the main road, slumped into an armchair, and spoke not a word all evening.[12]

Boredom and work are related: they express the stuff out of which ordinary days are made when life is subject to discipline or emptied.

4. Zola, as we have said, uses the *tranche de vie* for dysphoric purposes. He does this by observing episodes of everyday life as if he were seeing them for the first time, with the freshness of someone who has yet to experience repetition. In doing so, Zola resorts to another way of making everyday life narratable in the era when romance had become a problem: the device of *estrangement*. This technique arose out of the culture of ancient stoicism, reappearing every time the members of an intellectual elite develop the feeling that they do not belong to the culture, institutions, and common sense of their time.[13] But if we go beyond the limited genre that Montesquieu's *Persian Letters* (1721) inaugurated (the story of one's own culture told from the perspective of a foreigner), the intensive appearance of estrangement in European fiction actually came later than 1850 and took place following two lines of development.

Omniscient narrators began to tell their story using categories of judgment and stylistic forms that differed from those that would be adopted by common sense. An extreme example of this approach is Flaubert's style, with its uncompromising, paratactic syntax and his unusual use of verb tenses:

> The regular troops had made themselves scarce and the post was now defended only by the Municipal Guards. A wave of attackers boldly made towards the front steps; they were mown down; others followed; the door shuddered under the resounding blows of iron bars; the guards stood firm. But a barouche stuffed with hay and blazing like some giant torch was dragged up against the walls; firewood, straw and a cask of spirits were hastily tipped on. The fire darted along the stones; the

---

12. Gustave Flaubert, *Madame Bovary* (1856–1857); English translation *Madame Bovary*, trans. Geoffrey Wall (London: Penguin, 2003), part 1, chap. 7, pp. 42–43.

13. Carlo Ginzburg, "Straniamento: Preistoria di un procedimento letterario," in Ginzburg, *Occhiacci di legno: Nove riflessioni sulla distanza* (1998); English translation "Making It Strange: The Prehistory of a Literary Device," in *Wooden Eyes: Nine Reflections on Distance*, trans. Martin Ryle and Kate Soper (New York: Columbia University Press, 2001), 1–25.

building started puffing out smoke like a huge solfatara; enormous flames roared out between the pillars of the balustrade on the flat roof. National Guardsmen had occupied the first floor of the Palais-Royal and shots were coming from every window in the square; bullets whistled through the air and the water from the burst fountain mingled with the pools of blood on the ground; people were sliding about in the mud on pieces of clothing, military caps and weapons. Frédéric felt something soft underneath his foot: it was the hand of a sergeant in a grey greatcoat lying face down in the gutter. Fresh groups of workers were arriving all the time, urging the fighters on. The firing was intensifying. The wine merchants had opened their shops and people kept breaking off for a smoke and a pint of beer before going back to fight. A stray dog was howling. This made people laugh.[14]

The accumulation of sentences (stacked in a list with no final or causal connections) and the way everything is jumbled together (the taverns open during the shooting, the dead, the stray dog that makes people laugh) destroy any hierarchy of meaning. We could read in it the ideal continuation of the war stories that we encounter in the work of Stendhal, a writer who did not inspire Flaubert's enthusiasm. The difference is that in *Madame Bovary,* in *A Sentimental Education,* or in *A Simple Heart,* this technique invades every page no matter what the topic, not only those related to the war. The paratactic syntax and the use of the background imperfect communicate the idea that what happens is a mass of disorganized and uncontrollable minor events:

> Then, keen to get to know, at long last, that vague, indefinable will-o'-the-wisp, "society," he [Frédéric] wrote to the Dambreuses enquiring if he might call on them. Madame Dambreuse replied inviting him for the following day.
>
> It was her "at home" day. There were carriages standing in the courtyard. Two flunkeys hurried out from the glass porch and a third was waiting at the top of the steps to lead him into the house.
>
> Frédéric went through the entrance hall, another room, and then a large drawing-room with high windows and a monumental mantelpiece, on which stood a globe-shaped clock and a pair of porcelain vases of monstrous proportions from which two clusters of sconces were

14. Flaubert, *A Sentimental Education,* part 3, chap. 1, 312–313.

sprouting like two golden bushes. On the wall were paintings in the style of Ribera; the tapestry door-curtains were heavy and majestic and the furniture—the tables, consoles and armchairs—all in Empire style, had something so imposing and diplomatic about them that, in spite of himself, Frédéric had to smile. Finally he reached an apartment, oval in shape, panelled in rosewood, crammed with exquisite pieces of furniture, and lit by one single plate-glass window looking out on to a garden. Madame Dambreuse was sitting beside the fire with a dozen people grouped round her. She showed no surprise at not having seen him for so long and with a friendly nod invited him to sit down.

As [Frédéric] came in, they were singing the praises of the eloquent sermons of Father Coeur. Then, in reference to a theft committed by a footman, they bemoaned the immorality of servants. There was an endless stream of gossip: that old Sommery woman had a cold, Mademoiselle Turvisot was getting married, the Montcharrons wouldn't be back in town before the end of February, nor would the Bretancourts, people were staying on in the country later these days. The opulence of the surroundings seemed to emphasize the futility of the conversation; but what was being said was less stupid than the pointless, desultory and dreary way in which it was being spoken.[15]

The other great novelist who made substantial, systematic use of estrangement during the same decades was Tolstoy. In his major works, episodes, things, and environments are described while suspending the cognitive and value categories that should make them meaningful.[16] A random look through *War and Peace* easily turns up passages of this sort, not only in the major turning-point episodes, but in the minor secondary episodes as well. The Hussar Nikolai Rostov, in his first war experience, is encamped with his squadron waiting to fight with the French. He meets some Austrian farmers who are looking after the Russians' horses. To overcome the barrier of distance between human beings who belong to different cultures and classes, and who will probably not see each other again, they exchange small talk in order to socialize. He shouts, "Long live the Austrians, long live the Russians, long live Tsar Alexander, and long live the whole world!"

---

15. Ibid., part 2, chap. 2, pp. 141–142.

16. Victor Shklovsky, "Iskusstvo kak priem" (1917); English translation "Art as Device," in *Theory of Prose*, trans. Benjamin Sher (Normal, IL: Dalkey Archive Press, Illinois State University, 1998), 1–14.

But the warmth that the people involved in the scene work so hard to create is swept aside by the alienating gaze of the narrator:

> Rostov himself, like the German, waved his peaked cap above his head and, laughing, shouted: *"Und vivat die ganze Welt!"* Though there was no particular reason for rejoicing either for the German, who was cleaning his cowshed, or for Rostov, who had gone for hay with his section, the two men looked at each other with happy delight and brotherly love, shook their heads as a sign of mutual love, and smiling, went their way—the German to the cowshed, and Rostov to the cottage he occupied with Denisov.[17]

The other line of development takes the route of adopting a different point of view from that of the author. This approach is also characteristic of Tolstoy,[18] but it was European naturalism that really embraced it. In some of his novels, Zola allows the story to be narrated by the voice of characters who belong to the milieu being described, and who consider obvious things that the readers and the writer view as out of the ordinary. Verga also works with a similar approach when he employs a narrator who tells the story according to the common sense that prevails in the community of people to which the characters belong, assuming a point of view that the author and readers can only view as strange and backward.[19]

5. But the most important form of realism without melodrama is the *novel of personal destinies*. If the varieties of narrative that tell serious stories about the lives of people like us are distinguished by the way they make everyday life interesting, then, regardless of their obvious differences, the works of writers like Flaubert, George Eliot, and Tolstoy seem to be united by a common element. *Madame Bovary, War and Peace, A Sentimental Education, Middlemarch,* and *Anna Karenina* do not attract us by the novelty of the plot twists, the singularity of the characters, or the representa-

---

17. Leo Tolstoy, *Vojna i mir* (1865–1869); English translation *War and Peace* (1865–1869), trans. Richard Pevear and Larissa Volokhonsky (New York: Vintage Books, 2007), bk. 1, part 2, chap. 4, p. 128.

18. The text Shklovsky uses to present the technique of estrangement in Tolstoy is the story "Cholstomer," in which the narrative is performed by a horse. Shklovsky, "Art as Device."

19. See Guido Baldi, *L'artificio della regressione. Tecnica narrativa e ideologia nel Verga verista* (Naples: Liguori, 1980).

tive, typical value of the plots. While the melodramatic novel inflates particular stories to fill them with universal meanings, and the *novel* that contains elements of *romance* introduces adventures into the repetition of existence, these works reduce the number of states of exception and focus on the moments in which a life, interacting and conflicting with other lives, takes on a particular form and creates or submits to its fate. The novel of personal destinies arose out of the conviction that all existences can become interesting any time the desires of an individual—the potentials that make up the framework of its possibilities—collide with reality and are narrowed down to one. Each of us is familiar with these zones of density: the moments, hours, or days charged with public events that decide who we will become and if we will be happy or unhappy. There is no need for the actions to be externally anomalous: a space for narrative interest opens up every time a life crosses over a threshold that shapes it. Disruptions are marked by uncommon events (the experience of war), but also by completely common ones (a personal development, the choice or acceptance of a job, the success or failure of a marriage, the birth of a child). Whether the twists of fate are exceptional or predictable is ultimately incidental: what is important is that they are possibilities inherent in the life of people like us. The attention to the destiny of individuals counts more than the aura of romance in the stories. In *War and Peace, Middlemarch,* or *Anna Karenina,* every scene is told from the perspective of the characters' destiny and, page after page, the narrator traces out their arcs and reflects on what they have become. In *Madame Bovary* and *A Sentimental Education,* the existential turning points occur in the midst of the daily uneventfulness, inside the cloud of pointless actions. And yet this narrative filled with boredom, with existential waste, or with small contingencies is made tragic precisely by the fact that, ultimately, we are witnessing the passing of a life: a myriad of desires and possibilities is becoming something— something limited.

Although every novel founded on empathetic identification with the protagonists is ultimately a novel of personal destinies, this subgenre attained its maturity during the nineteenth century. Descended from the German *Bildungsroman,* it was perfected by the novels of Jane Austen, which focus extensively on the slow metamorphoses of ordinary life. The great writers of the generation born between the late 1810s and the late 1820s achieved a sort of synthesis between Austen's model and that of

Scott and Balzac. The experiences that Flaubert, Eliot, and Tolstoy describe cover many aspects of the human experience, as is the case in Balzac, but the plots focus on common activities, as in Austen's works. The stories are embedded in a complex historical and sociological framework, as in Balzac, but the intention of the novel is to follow the trajectories of a few individuals, and not to describe an epoch or a milieu. This is precisely why the work takes the implicit or explicit form of an existential scale—a scale that is always latent in the type of attention the narrator gives to the protagonists, and that becomes evident in certain passages: for example, in the last two chapters of *A Sentimental Education,* in the conclusion to *Middlemarch,* or at the times Tolstoy's characters who wonder about the meaning of life (Andrei Bolkonsky, Pierre Bezukhov, Konstantin Levin) reflect on what they have become.

During the last two decades of the nineteenth century, the structure of the novel of personal destinies was taken up by writers who subscribed to different poetics. Many naturalistic works actually tell the history of an individual. The novels of Hardy or those of Fontane follow the biographies of the protagonists. Symptomatically, a decade apart, Maupassant and Svevo published works entitled *Une vie* (1883) and *Una vita* (1892).[20] The early masterpiece by Henry James, *Portrait of a Lady* (1881), tells what Isabel Archer finally does with herself:

> But what was she going to do with herself? This question was irregular, for with most women one had no occasion to ask it. Most women did with themselves nothing at all; they waited, in attitudes more or less gracefully passive, for a man to come that way and furnish them with a destiny.[21]

Often, the writer weaves a few personal trajectories into a polyhistorical narrative (*War and Peace, Middlemarch, Anna Karenina*), perhaps in the form of the family novel. As an ethical unit and collective person, the family form allows singular lives to be bound in a natural way to the collective events, telling the story of how the first community cell becomes transformed.

---

20. Seventeen years after Svevo's *Una vita,* Gertrude Stein published *Three Lives* (1909).

21. Henry James, *Portrait of a Lady,* in *Novels, 1881–1886,* ed. William T. Stafford (New York: Library of America, 1985), chap. 7, p. 254.

As we noted about Jane Austen at the end of Chapter 6, the emergence of this type of novel was a decisive event in the history of Western narrative: its existence signaled the arrival of the epoch in which nothing is important but life. To attract the interest of the reader, a melodramatic conflict or a romance-like event is no longer necessary because, potentially, every individual now has an infinite value. But this process has a dialectical consequence that allows aspects implicit in the logic of the novel as a genre to emerge—aspects only the novel of personal destinies illuminates fully. When we focus on the lives of people like us, regardless of the collective significance of the desires that people fight for, we also devalue the values that transcend individuals and their pursuit of happiness (or tranquility). If each person is an epicenter of absolute meaning, then each person is potentially entitled to a legitimate point of view. The relativism and perspectivism that lie implicit in the genre of the novel are fully revealed in these types of narratives.

The novel of personal destinies brings two other important changes with it. The first is the emergence of a *new way of viewing time*. For the protagonists in narratives constructed on this basis, the time granted to a life is the only good that individuals possess, which is precisely why its passage becomes an issue. Of course, this theme is not without precedents: the Christian spiritual autobiography, for example, or the topos of the fleeting nature of life, so dear to ancient lyric poetry. However, never before had the problem of time entered so glaringly into narrative fiction. The eighteenth century is full of novels structured as biographies or autobiographies, in other words, as books in which the characters necessarily age, but rarely is the attention focused starkly on the flow of time, on the desire to not die unfulfilled. Usually the narrative focus falls on adventures that the protagonists face or on the problem of vice and virtue, but not on life and time as the single dimension of finite existence. The same thing can be said about Scott, Manzoni, Balzac, Stendhal, and Dickens: in their novels there are no passages to be found that bear resemblance to the endings of *A Sentimental Education* or *Middlemarch*—sections in which the reader's attention is captured not by fanciful stories but by a reflection on what Frédéric Moreau and Deslauriers, Dorothea Brooke, and Lydgate have managed to do with themselves. When the interest is concentrated on the characters' destiny, the use of life becomes a theme as well as a problem, and it takes on an emotional charge: hope or regret, expectation or anguish.

Only after this step is taken does it become possible to imagine an entire book in search of lost time. The final ending of *The Betrothed*, after the story has come to a conclusion, when we are told what happens to the characters, might vaguely resemble these; the endings of Jane Austen's novels offer a more solid precedent, but even they are still weak. Perhaps the text that best anticipates the perception of time for which the novel of personal destinies will become its vehicle is Chateaubriand's *Memoirs from Beyond the Tomb*, with its sense of universal impermanence.

The second change concerns how the relationship between private and collective matters is viewed. While the characters of Scott and Balzac embody universal historical forces, according to the principle of the typical described by Lukács, in novels of personal destinies the connection between small stories and the larger history is purely mechanical rather than organic. As in the novels of Jane Austen, works such as *A Sentimental Education, War and Peace,* and *Middlemarch* accept the separation between public and private spheres as a given. Singular existences live inside their bubbles of subjective meaning; when they are touched by historical events, a bond of pure exteriority is established between their little stories and the larger course of the world. The life of Frédéric Moreau is shattered by the revolutions of 1848, but he passes through the conflicts as if his life were detached from the collective events: "The wounded falling all around him and the dead lying on the ground didn't seem really dead or wounded. It was like being at a show."[22] The characters in *War and Peace* are swept away by major historical events, but this larger history seems to be separated from their essential concerns by a sort of ontological barrier:

> In 1808 the emperor Alexander went to Erfurt for a new meeting with the emperor Napoleon, and there was much talk in Petersburg high society about the grandeur of this solemn meeting.
>
> In 1809 the closeness of the two rulers of the world, as Napoleon and Alexander were called, had reached the point that, when Napoleon declared war on Austria that year, a Russian corps went abroad to assist their former enemy. . . .
>
> Life meanwhile, people's real life with its essential concerns of health, illness, work, rest, with its concerns of thought, learning, poetry, music,

22. Flaubert, *A Sentimental Education,* part 3, chap. 1, 312.

love, friendship, hatred, passions, went on as always, independently and outside of any political closeness of enmity with Napoleon Bonaparte and outside all possible reforms.[23]

From the second half of the nineteenth century onward, for the Western form of life it has become difficult to rediscover an organic relationship between private and global destinies. This can occur only on days or in years when history and politics go back to being an experience lived by the masses, namely, in states of exception. The norm is the world described by Tocqueville: private individuals enclosed inside personal spheres of meaning who regard world destinies with detachment, delegate their political participation, and submit to major historical upheavals as if they were uncontrollable, external events.

Historical Stations

Seeking to abolish or at least rein in melodrama and romance, the second phase of realism moved decisively away from the trends that prevailed in the first half of the nineteenth century. Nevertheless, some of the assumptions crucial to the nineteenth-century paradigm continued to be adopted: the inner and outer worlds preserved their order and hierarchy; the essential resided in actions and public speeches. Then, starting from the 1890s, the pace of innovation became faster and in the first decades of the twentieth century led to the turning point of modernism and the avant-gardes. The crisis of the nineteenth-century model thus took place in stages: between 1850 and 1890, a mix of completion and disintegration appeared in works by the same authors; starting from the 1890s, the rupture started to predominate; then around 1910, "human character changed,"[24] art lost its obviousness,[25] and the epoch of full-fledged modernism began. But the changes that transformed the face of the novel between 1910 and 1940 did

23. Tolstoy, *War and Peace*, bk. 2, part 3, chap. 1, p. 418.
24. "On or about December 1910, human character changed. . . . The change was not sudden and definite. . . . But a change there was, nevertheless; and since one must be arbitrary, let us date it about the year 1910." Woolf, "Character in Fiction," 421.
25. Theodor W. Adorno, *Ästhetische Theorie* (1970); English translation *Aesthetic Theory*, trans. Robert Hullot-Kentor (London: Athlone Press, 1977), 1.

not appear out of nowhere: they almost always arose out of processes that had already come forth, sometimes in conspicuous forms, during the late nineteenth century.

We must therefore imagine three historical phases bound together by a dialectical relationship of continuity and rupture. I will mark these confines using round figures that are deliberately vague:[26] the first extends from 1800 to 1850, the second from 1850 to 1900, and the third from 1900 to 1940. During the first, the nineteenth-century paradigm emerged; during the second, the paradigm began to transform into something else; during the third, the themes and technical solutions of modernist fiction fully developed and became predominant. There were overlaps between the three periods, and hybridizations continued. The most important element of continuity is the following: *before and after the crisis of the nineteenth-century novel, the stream of innovations rested on a substrate that remained unchanged, because the serious mimesis of the everyday and the existence of a backdrop with a sense of historical dynamics remained central to the European literary system.* For many of the great authors born between the 1870s and the 1880s—for Proust, Woolf, Forster, or Lawrence—the task of the novel was still that of telling about the existence of people like us, and not of creating fantastic worlds, stylistic games, metaliterature, *écriture*, or pure lies. The critical vocabulary that dominated during the years of modernism was very different from the critical lexicon used by the avant-garde movements of the 1950s and 1960s to justify their works. The basic reason was that, although conceived in different terms, a majority of modernist novelists remained faithful to the same project we find in the critical writings of the authors who were born around 1840 (Zola, James), and even before that in the critical writings of Balzac or Stendhal: to properly, realistically, represent everyday life. The intentions of the modernist authors swarm

---

26. There are two ways to demarcate the symbolic thresholds: one is to make use of emblematic years, distinguished by the appearance of major works or major events in world history; the second is to rely on generic thresholds. I opt for the latter solution, partly because each national culture has its own internal chronology and milestones, and partly because symbolic transformations are slow, extended processes, not sudden and discrete. The system of culture maintains partial autonomy with respect to political and social history: the latter can be quick and traumatic; the former is largely inert and sticky. Even the most traumatic crises, even world wars, take years to transform artistic approaches. Brusque changes are unknown to the collective imagination.

with appeals to "life." So the criticism that Proust and Woolf directed against the realism coming before them starts from a typically realistic literary project: the naturalists and the "Edwardians" are accused of not properly describing ordinary experience.[27] In English-speaking culture, the dialectical relationship between the literatures of the nineteenth and twentieth centuries is made explicit by F. R. Leavis, who connects modernist realism to the nineteenth-century novel through the concept of the *great tradition,* drawing an ideal continuity between Jane Austen, George Eliot, Henry James, and Joseph Conrad.[28]

What radically changed was the way of understanding life. A vivid grasp of this transition can be had by reading the essays of Virginia Woolf. One of the most important is "Modern Fiction," which came out in an early version in 1919 under the title "Modern Novels," and in its definitive version in 1925, as part of the collection *The Common Reader.* Woolf defines her own poetics in contrast to Bennett, Wells, and Galsworthy:

> Is life like this [as Bennett imagines it]? Must novels be like this? . . .
>
> Examine for a moment an ordinary mind on an ordinary day. The mind receives a myriad impressions—trivial, fantastic, evanescent, or engraved with the sharpness of steel. . . . Life is not a series of gig lights symmetrically arranged; life is a luminous halo, a semi-transparent envelope surrounding us from the beginning of consciousness to the end. Is it not the task of the novelist to convey this varying, this unknown and uncircumscribed spirit, whatever aberration or complexity it may display, with as little mixture of the alien and external as possible? We are not pleading merely for courage and sincerity; we are suggesting that the proper stuff of fiction is a little other than custom would have us believe it.[29]

Woolf explains a perceptual transformation, a gestaltic change. The modernists linger on the swarm of minute impressions, on unconscious and preconscious movements that run through a common mind on a common day, and they consider important some ontological levels that Edwardian writers did not comprehend or did not value. In other words, the modernist

27. Proust, *Finding Time Again,* 111ff.; Woolf, "Mr. Bennett and Mrs. Brown," 384–389.

28. See Niels Buch-Jepsen, "Arrière-garde et le modernisme en Angleterre: Leavis et la grande tradition de la rupture," in *Les Arrière-gardes au XXe siècle: l'autre face de la modernité esthétique,* ed. William Marx (Paris: Puf, 2004), 195–202.

29. Woolf, "Modern Fiction," 160–161.

novel changed the order of the discourse by changing the criteria separating the significant from the insignificant, the foreground from the background, the essential from the accidental. But while this transition may be clear, the persistence of a common element is equally so: the modernists were pursuing the same aim as the realists of the nineteenth century and their continuers—they wanted to properly represent life.[30] The relationship between the "nineteenth-century novel" and the "twentieth-century novel" (to use two unpolished and typically nineteenth-century critical concepts) is therefore dialectical: it is made of continuity and rupture. In fact, the narrative transformations that produced their most radical results between 1910 and 1930 were announced and prepared during the second half of the nineteenth century. The change affected the cornerstones of the novelistic edifice: narrators, plots, and characters.

New Narrators

According to the nineteenth-century paradigm, the narrator organizes, interprets, and controls. But, despite being ontologically above the characters, the narrator does not reduce them to mere satellites of his or her discourse. He or she is aware that the reader wants primarily to follow the stories of the individuals and not the comments of the narrating voice. The latter has the task of setting the characters in the milieu: he or she knows more than they do, but cannot crush their truths and their words under the weight of his or her own. Starting in the mid-nineteenth century, this equilibrium tipped in two opposite directions.

1. In some cases, the figure of the narrator became muted. Two of the most important writers from the generation born between the late 1810s and the late 1820s—Flaubert and Dostoevsky—created narrative voices quite distinct from those of the early nineteenth century. Flaubert cut the number of the narrator's opinions and comments down to as few as possible; Dostoevsky granted his characters their freedom, allowing what they said to be just as valuable as the narrator's words, creating a polyphonic effect.[31]

---

30. "The novelist is . . . terribly exposed to life." See Woolf, "Life and the Novelist," 400.

31. Mikhail Bakhtin, *Problemy poetiki Dostoevskogo* (1963); *Problems of Dostoevsky's Poetics*, trans. Carol Emerson (Minneapolis: University of Minnesota Press, 2003).

The same transformation can be seen in the works of the great writers born in the 1840s. In the novels of Zola, the narrator hides behind free indirect discourse, and the story is advanced by the interweaving of the characters' voices. Acting out of a completely different poetics, Henry James constructs his texts on the foundations of the dramatic method and a restricted point of view. In the initial phase of his work, the texts take on a theatrical form: he leaves the characters in the foreground and avoids casting an overly analytical light on the protagonists' psyche, but the narrator retains the prerogative of omniscience. In James's last phase, which began in 1897 with *The Spoils of Poynton* and *What Maisie Knew,* the narrator disappears to make room for the limited point of view of the characters, and, with no commentary, the novel resolves in a dramatic presentation of the partial, confused way that states of mind rise to the surface. This movement from an omniscience claiming to be objective to the narrowness of subjective points of view became common in the age of modernism.

The change in the literary *doxa* can be measured by comparing two essays written at a distance of sixty years that examine the attitude a narrator should take toward the story. One of the most important writings of Zola collected together in *Les Romanciers naturalistes* (The Naturalist Novelists) (1881) is dedicated to Stendhal.[32] What makes the essay especially interesting is its contradictions: Zola would like to turn Stendhal into a precursor of naturalism, but he cannot overlook the fact that the author of *The Red and the Black* simply fails to fit this role. In resuming a distinction typical of his critical lexicon, Zola places Stendhal among the "psychologists" rather than the "physiologists": in other words, he belongs to those who are interested in the mechanisms of the interior life, an approach characteristic of the French narrative tradition, but who ignore the role of the body and environments. Stendhal perpetuates the "abstract man" of the eighteenth century; in contrast, the naturalist novelists reveal the influence that the instincts and the outside world exert on personal destinies. Zola is not overly fond of Stendhal, partly because the psyches of characters like Julien Sorel, Madame de Rênal, and Mathilde de La Môle are too twisted

32. Émile Zola, "Stendhal," in Zola, *Les Romanciers naturalistes,* in *Œuvres complètes,* ed. Henri Mitterrand, vol. 10, *La Critique naturaliste* (1881) (Paris: Nouveau Monde, 2004), 478–502.

in his eyes ("life is simpler"), and because Stendhal systematically ignores the milieu. Zola focuses on one of the most beautiful chapters in *The Red and the Black,* the one in which Julien Sorel forces himself to take Madame de Rênal's hand:

> It is a small, silent drama of great power, and Stendhal has beautifully analyzed the states of mind of the two characters. Now, the milieu never appears, not once. We could be anywhere and under any conditions whatsoever: as long as it was dark, the scene would stay the same. Considering the tension created by his desire, I understand perfectly well that Julien is not affected by his milieu. He sees nothing, hears nothing, feels nothing: he just wants to take the hand of Madame de Rênal and hold it in his own. But Madame de Rênal, on the contrary, should be experiencing all the exterior influences. Give this episode to a writer for whom *mileux* exist and he will welcome the night into the surrender of this woman, with its smells, voices, and soft sensual pleasures. And this writer will be on the side of truth; the picture will be more complete.[33]

When he says that the novelist's task is to describe objective circumstances, Zola illustrates one of his poetic principles, but also a way of conceiving narrative fiction that was common among writers and readers in 1881: from Scott to Tolstoy, many eighteenth-century novelists believed that environments needed to be described and took this for granted.

Almost sixty years later, when the golden age of the modernist novel was drawing to a close, Sartre wrote one of his first essays on poetics, "M. François Mauriac and Freedom" (1939). The argument he puts forward goes against what Zola had defended in his essay on Stendhal. Sartre's view is that novelists must avoid transcending the subjective world of their protagonists. They must follow the good example of Conrad, who uses multiple and partial narrators, and not the bad example of Mauriac, who observes, controls, and judges the characters from a unitary, superior point of view:

> M. Mauriac is omniscient for everything relating to his little world. . . . It's time to say: God is not an artist. . . . I maintain . . . that [Mauriac] has no right to make these absolute judgments. A novel is an action related from

33. Ibid., 485.

various points of view. . . . The introduction of absolute truth or of God's standpoint constitutes a twofold error of technique: To begin with, it presupposes a purely contemplative narrator, withdrawn from the action. . . . And besides, the absolute is non-temporal. If you pitch the narrative in the absolute, the string of duration snaps; and the novel disappears before your eyes: All that remains is a dull truth, *sub specie aeternitatis*.[34]

This is a statement of poetics arising from the philosophy of freedom and choice that Sartre was developing during the years between his *Sketch for a Theory of the Emotions* (1939) and *Being and Nothing* (1943), but it is also the textual crystallization of a cultural atmosphere, like Zola's essay on Stendhal. In the early decades of the twentieth century, some of the structures and attitudes typical of the nineteenth century—such as the omniscient narrator and descriptions of the milieu—had lost prestige, becoming unacceptable or ideologically suspect. According to the new literary *doxa*, the only possible realism was one that abandoned a panoramic gaze, a superior transcendence, and accepted the finitude of individual points of view as an inviolable limit for all discourses on the world. After 1945, thanks to the influence of Sartre's literary theory, the concept of "subjective realism" became widely accepted by French literary critics. The concept is both descriptive and normative at the same time: as a principle of poetics, it enjoins novelists to not judge or observe the consciences of the characters from on high, in the light of future consequences; as a principle of literary history, it made it possible to rewrite the entire trajectory of the novel, making Stendhal a precursor of modernist subjectivism.[35]

2. Between the 1850s and the 1930s, then, "nineteenth-century" omniscience was attacked, but during exactly the same years the figure of the

---

34. Jean-Paul Sartre, "M. François Mauriac et la liberté" (1939); English translation "M. François Mauriac and Freedom" (1939), in *Literary and Philosophical Essays*, trans. Annette Michelson (New York: Collier Books, 1962), 15–16.

35. In 1954, Georges Blin published *Stendhal et les problèmes du roman*. In his view, the author of *The Red and the Black* initiated subjective realism, founded on restricted points of view and on the knowledge that individuals are inside reality and not above it. Very often the type of gaze Stendhal's narrator casts on the outside world takes the form of our daily lived experience: it is fragmentary, crossed by lines of force, deformed by our own interests and passions, centered on our self. See Georges Blin, *Stendhal et les problèmes du roman* (Paris: Corti, 1954), 107ff., 149ff.

narrator morphed in the opposite direction. In addition to being the era of restricted points of view, modernism is also the period of the *novel-essay,* that is, works in which narrative voices think, judge, and shift the balance of narrative interest from the story to the meaning of the story. The scaffolding of *In Search of Lost Time* and *The Man without Qualities* is composed of ideas; Hermann Broch inserts an actual essay into the last volume of *The Sleepwalkers;* first-person narrators like Mattia Pascal, Malte Laurids Brigge, or Zeno Cosini slip continuously from telling the story to reflecting on what it means.

The modern novel-essay has a long prehistory, punctuated by thresholds. When classicism and Christian aesthetic Platonism permeated the Western literary space, many texts belonging to the family of the novel were surrounded by allegorical infrastructures expressed in the form of the concept. However, there is an unsurmountable divide separating these apparatuses of ideas and those that have surrounded the novel over the past two centuries. The premodern conceptual atmosphere assumes that the universals are common knowledge, it treats the story line as an *exemplum,* and it uses "moralistic" categories. The modern conceptual atmosphere does not assume that there are any commonly known universals, it does not treat the story as an *exemplum,* and it uses categories that are sensitive to historical dynamics. From this perspective, the genealogy of the novel-essay can be seen to have undergone an early, crucial transformation at the beginning of the nineteenth century. Still, it rarely happens in the nineteenth-century novel that the weight of the ideas crushes the autonomy of the characters: concepts are used to create the backstage universals that surround the stories, but not to shift attention to theories. In most cases, a good balance is achieved: the narrator presents the historical, sociological, psychological, and anthropological forces that make the story understandable, but without deflecting the reader's interest from the story to the narrator's ideas.

The modern novel-essay came into existence when the center of gravity of the work shifted increasingly toward abstract thought. The first signs of this second historic frontier occurred early on: the last section of *The Human Comedy,* entitled *Analytical Studies,* is composed of essays. However, the real turning point occurred decades later, in the works of Tolstoy and Dostoevsky. At the beginning of the third book of *War and Peace,* the narrator interrupts the plot and introduces a reflection on the philosophy of history that grows as the novel progresses, eventually occupying the entire ending. The contemporary readership viewed this gesture as transgressing their reading codes. For his part, Tolstoy felt that the narrative form no longer had the capacity on its own to contain the truth about life, hence, his choice to slash the narrative canvas with a conceptual knife, superimposing the transcendence of ideas on the immanence of particular stories. Dostoevsky includes abstract thought in many ways. He allows a first-person narrator to mix autobiography and thought (*Notes from Underground*), he introduces apologues into the narrative plot ("The Legend of the Grand Inquisitor" in *The Brothers Karamazov*), but, more than anything, he transforms the theatrical conflicts that give form to his novels into conflicts between ideas. Thus, while Tolstoy strengthens the philosophical authority of the narrator, Dostoevsky multiplies the thinking voices. Still, no matter how divergent the works of these writers may be, they do have a common effect: they intensify the impression that stories are no longer adequate to talk about what is essential in life, and that, to do so, we must turn to ideas.

Nevertheless, there is another way to thicken mediation without using concepts: by employing *style*. It was Flaubert who initiated this new possibility. His readers were struck by the filtering effect his writing created. According to the author, when the subject matter of a novel or short story is the lives of common people (*Madame Bovary, A Sentimental Education, A Simple Heart*), it is up to the beauty of the form to redeem the misery of ordinary life—the "nothingness" of what is being written about.[36] Many twentieth-century readers have interpreted these ideas in the light of subsequent literary history, as if Flaubert's words were a prelude to the novel of uneventfulness that would become popular in the modernist era. In reality, the story of *Madame Bovary,* like those of *A Sentimental Education* and *A Simple Heart,* is rocked by events: Flaubert knows how to talk about the empty spaces of boredom, but the plots hinge on upsets and twists of fate. When Flaubert talks about "nothingness," he is not referring to a lack of peripeteia. Rather, he is expressing an opinion on the intrinsic value of the subject matter: his words betray

36. Gustave Flaubert, Letter to Louise Colet, August 8, 1846; Letter to Louise Colet, January 16, 1852, in *The Letters of Gustave Flaubert: 1830–1857,* trans. Francis Steegmuller (Cambridge, MA: Belknap Press of Harvard University Press, 1980), 50, 154.

the persistence of the background fallout from the *Stiltrennung*, the fossilized remnant of a classicist hierarchy that persisted into the Romantic era. This was transferred into the idea that certain topics are intrinsically less noble than others, and that, precisely for this reason, they need to be redeemed by means of the form. In comparison to the historical scenes Flaubert would go on to recount in *Salammbô* and *The Temptation of Saint Anthony*, the provincial story of *Madame Bovary* is a topic devoid of intrinsic greatness, a worthless subject. Even though the topic does not lend itself to beauty on its own merits, the book manages to stay on its feet thanks to style.

The difference between *Madame Bovary, A Sentimental Education, A Simple Heart*, and the practices of realistic narrative fiction is the fact that in these works the style *can be seen*. In theory, the novels of Flaubert—with their impersonality, their focus on the outer world, and their wealth of details—should embody the nineteenth-century ideal of transparent writing; in actuality, the style is superimposed on the story like an opaque filter that renews our perception of things[37] through its distancing effect. This is achieved by his relentless use of paratactic syntax and his extensive, peculiar use of the background imperfect, his transformation of things into agents of action, his destruction of causal and final links, which are replaced by temporal connections that align events without explaining them or subordinating them to a telos. The overall effect is the creation of a world in which lives pass "without the characters taking any active part so to speak in the action."[38] In addition to containing an unwitting memory of the *Stiltrennung*, these theories on books that are about nothing point to a shift in the balance: they indicate that the interest has moved from the story in itself to the way of telling it. While Flaubert's impersonal narrator may have given up on an explicit ideological role, apparently weakening his own mediation, he actually gives an ideological role to his writing that is implicit, judging the world much more continuously and pervasively than would a traditional, omniscient narrator. It is thanks to style that the

---

37. Marcel Proust, "À propos du 'style' de Flaubert" (1920); English translation "On Flaubert's 'Style,'" in *Against Sainte-Beuve and Other Essays*, trans. John Sturrock (London: Penguin Books, 1988), 261.

38. Ibid., 265.

novelist becomes truly "like God in creation—invisible and all-powerful; he should be everywhere felt, but nowhere seen."[39]

New Plots

The transformations in literary forms during the second half of the nineteenth century shook up the nineteenth-century plot model; during the modernist era, it would be repudiated by almost all the avant-garde writers. The novelists born between 1810 and 1850 had a decisive role in this change, but the most revolutionary of all was once again Flaubert: his works dissolve theatrical plots from within, retaining their armature but loosening the joints. Flaubert went about demolishing the cornerstones of nineteenth-century story lines: the causal connection between the parts and the hierarchy between the scenes. His novels have large, disconnected areas, no-man's-lands occupied by a plethora of small, centrifugal actions. This motion permeates every aspect of the text, from the individual episodes to the structure of the work. Random details shoot up in the middle of scenes, blocking the main action or ignoring it completely, while the plot tends to shatter into fragments.

> Consider an episode like the wedding of Madame Bovary, which occupies the entire fourth chapter of the first part of the novel.[40] Although what is being described is a turning point in the characters' lives, the events are presented in a long summary with no scene, held together by the list form: the arrival of the guests, their carriages and unbelievable clothes, the plethora of haphazard or ridiculous details, the idle chatter, the menu, the wedding-cake kitsch, the grogginess from all the food, and the pranks and obscene jokes of the relatives. A classic dramatic episode is inundated by a sequence of trivial, chaotic events and matters. Everything piles up and life seems to unfold in a perpetual background. Page after page, nothing happens: the crucial events are steeped in a swampy humus composed of repetition, false movements, and diverging actions. By creating a new dialectic between connection and disconnection, Flaubert disrupted the theatrical

---

39. Flaubert, Letter to Mademoiselle Leroyer de Chantepie, March 18, 1857, in *The Letters of Gustave Flaubert*.

40. Flaubert, *Madame Bovary*, part 1, chap. 4, pp. 25–30.

type of narrative logic[41] and, both directly and indirectly, had a decisive effect on naturalism and modernism.

But Flaubert is not the only author of the second half of the nineteenth century to contribute to the disintegration of plots. Many of the chapters in *War and Peace* or in *Anna Karenina*, for example, hinge on a central action that develops on the public stage, as in the classic nineteenth-century paradigm, but the narrative flow is continually interrupted by small secondary events, by impressions and perceptions that have no relationship to the main episode.

> The war scenes of *War and Peace* provide a clear example of this technique. Consider the scene where Tolstoy describes Nikolai Rostov's baptism of fire, the battle of the bridge on the Enns River.[42] At the beginning, the episode is described from the point of view of some Russian officers who are watching the shooting through a telescope while eating pastries as they sojourn at a castle: comments about the war are superimposed on their comments about the food. In the next scene, the Russian troops crowd helplessly on the bridge, mixing with the fleeing civilians while the French artillery fire on them as if they were in a shooting range. Prince Nesvicky, who has come down on horseback into the line of fire, is stuck in the crowd about the bridge. In addition to fearing for his own life and for the safety of the troops, he has time to watch the waves of the Enns River as they break against the bridge pillars, the details of the soldiers' uniforms, the feet moving in the mud transported onto the wooden floor planks, and the minor conflicts that explode between the people crammed on the bridge. In the following episode, the narrator multiplies the digressive details: soldiers who make obscene comments about the peasants, hussars who want to show off, misunderstandings between the Russian officers, the disorientation of Nikolai Rostov, the web of chaotic microevents that occur in this sort of situation. The main, centripetal action is interrupted continuously by centrifugal movements: life and the world are broad,

---

41. See Luca Pietromarchi, "Flaubert, le Parche e il filo del romanzo," in *La trama nel romanzo del '900*, ed. Luca Pietromarchi (Rome: Bulzoni, 2002), 41–58.
42. Tolstoy, *War and Peace*, bk. 1, part 2, chaps. 6–8, pp. 137–149.

frayed, and complex, and they transcend single individuals and their illusion of being in the foreground.

The same dialectic is found in more ordinary scenes. When Tolstoy's
characters have to confront the crises that decide their fates, the main action is almost always interrupted by secondary events that distract their
attention. In the first chapters of *Anna Karenina*, Stepan Oblonsky must
deal with the scandal caused by his infidelity, but this does not prevent him
from taking care of his correspondence and reading the newspapers.[43]
When Karenin needs to decide which public form to give his relations with
his wife after her relationship with Vronsky has become obvious, the anguish of making this choice is mixed with the reading of a book about the
Iguvine Tablets and the problem of land irrigation in Zaraysk Province.[44]
The scene does lead to a conclusion (in a "nineteenth-century" way, we
might say), but in the meantime the linearity of the plot has been disrupted
and the satellites have made the system much richer and more complicated.

Another significant change relates to endings. "Mimetic poetry . . . imitates human beings acting under compulsion or voluntarily, and as a result
of their actions supposing themselves to have fared well or ill and in all
this feeling either grief or joy," we read in the *Republic* (10.603c): the re-
solving of tension into an unambiguous outcome, whether good or bad,
seems to be inscribed in the transcendental form of narrative. Excluding
the tradition of the humorous romance, until the second half of the nineteenth century nearly all stories had clear endings. But already at the beginning of the nineteenth century, Jane Austen had introduced unusual secondary endings alongside the primary ones. In her novels, the outcomes of
the main stories are always happy and predictable, and conflict is resolved
once and for all without any semantic or emotional qualities. The outcomes of the secondary stories can be hazy and uncertain: the characters
choose or are forced into compromise solutions and end up finding themselves neither completely happy nor completely unhappy, like Charlotte
Lucas in *Pride and Prejudice*. The finale of *The Betrothed* also exudes edgi-
ness: Renzo and Lucia's life is first disturbed by slander from their neigh-
bors, but then it calms down, becoming "the most peaceful, happy and

43. Tolstoy, *Anna Karenina*, 1–8.
44. Ibid., part 3, chap. 14, pp. 283–286.

enviable of lives." But the narrator adds: "So much so that if I told you about it you would be bored to death."[45] The novel that began with the revolutionary intention of telling the stories of ordinary people, "mechanical folk and of but small account,"[46] closes by noting that the life of mechanical folk is narratable only when it is disturbed by an unpleasant, romance-like incident, after which there is only the repetition of existence—quiet but prosaic, and unnarratable.[47]

In the literature of the late nineteenth century, the rejection of a clear ending became a common solution: *Madame Bovary* and *War and Peace, A Sentimental Education* and *Middlemarch, Anna Karenina,* and many of the novels of Zola, *Mastro Don Gesualdo,* and *Effi Briest* all avoid ostentatiously concluding at the point of *Spannung.* In one way or another, they convey the idea that there is no such thing as absolute events, because the world, other people, the impersonal connection of things are unaware of personal stories. There is no episode that can put a stop to becoming, no action that can set itself up as culminating and tragic; reality is not anthropocentric; the commonplace by which "life goes on" conceals the iron law governing the human condition.

Another kind of denouement that the narrative of the late 1800s experimented with and transmitted to modernist literature is the quick, open-ended, or cursory ending. The precursor of this technique was Stendhal. In the second half of the century, the process of stripping denouements of their canonical structure intensified, anticipating the solutions of the early twentieth century. Virginia Woolf admired Chekhov's inconclusive, random endings, viewing them as closer to the life of the classically nineteenth-century closing, sealed by the sort of absolute facts that reality does not normally offer. The structure of Chekhov's stories shows that in the unpredictable web of events, human beings have no privileged status and that things happen as they happen, randomly, in a mediocre fashion:

---

45. Manzoni, *The Betrothed,* 719.
46. Ibid., foreword.
47. Ibid., chap. 38, pp. 719–20. On the ending of *The Betrothed,* see Ezio Raimondi, *Il romanzo senza idillio: Saggio sui "Promessi sposi"* (Turin: Einaudi, 1974), 185ff., 219ff., and passim, and Daniela Brogi, "Concludere per ricominciare: 'I promessi sposi,' XXXVIII," in *Per Romano Luperini,* ed. Pietro Cataldi (Palermo: Palumbo, 2010), 123–148.

[Chekhov] is aware that modern life is full of nondescript melancholy, of discomfort, of queer relationships which beget emotions that are half-ludicrous and yet painful and that an inconclusive ending for all these impulses is much more usual than anything extreme. He knows all this as we know it, and at first sight he seems no more ready than we are with a solution. The attentive reader who is on the alert for some unmistakable sign that now the story is going to pull itself together and make straight as an arrow its destination is still looking rather more blankly when the end comes.[48]

Introduced by the narrative fiction of the second half of the nineteenth century, these three processes that disintegrated the theatrical plot were to be found everywhere at the height of modernism after 1910.

New Characters

With the exception of Stendhal, no novelist of the early 1800s had dis-solved the *charakter;* after 1850, the imprint that once stabilized protago-nists now weakened or became problematic. Out of the vast expanse of possibilities, I will pick out four new solutions that were significant.

1. I begin with the one that Tolstoy adopted. Lukács describes it perfectly in one of his most beautiful essays:

His characters do not, any more than the personages of the naturalists, develop dramatically, as did Balzac's; but their movement through life, their conflicts with the external world nevertheless give them very well-defined outlines. These outlines, however, are by no means as strictly monolinear and clear-cut as those of the characters drawn by the old realists. Tolstoy's plots revolve around the "extreme possibilities" of the characters, possibilities which never become reality but which come to the surface again and again, thus affording each character many op-portunities of expressing their thoughts and emotions. Tolstoy describes the fleeting moods of his characters at least as sensitively and accurately as the most gifted of the newer realists, but nevertheless the figures never

---

48. Virginia Woolf, "Chekhov's Questions" (1918), in *The Essays of Virginia Woolf,* vol. 2, *1912–1918,* ed. Andrew McNeillie (London: Hogarth Press, 1987), 245. See also by Woolf: "Modern Fiction" (1919–1925) and "The Russian Point of View" (1925), in *The Es-says of Virginia Woolf,* 4:162–163, 183–185.

dissolve into mere clouds of moods, for they are placed within a precisely circumscribed space, a field of force within which all their moods must oscillate.[49]

Tolstoy's characters elude any rigid keynote: their behavior does not lend itself to establishing social and psychological types. They do not embody "the aristocratic," "the official," "the prostitute," "the hot-tempered man," "the hedonist," "the adulterous woman," or any sort of hybrid between human groups. For the same reasons, their behavior is never entirely predictable: you can never know how the hero will act in a given situation. Very often, the character's moods and desires change in the middle of a single episode in reaction to trivial, accidental events. But while individual action remains unpredictable from one moment to the next, the behavior of each character remains within the confines of a "magnetic field" (Lukács), a band of oscillation defined by the tendencies left inside the individual by the *milieu,* the *moment,* and the individual mental armor.

> One of the most beautiful and eloquent examples of this technique is in a minor episode in *Anna Karenina.* The leading roles are played by two secondary characters, Sergei Ivanovich Koznysev, Levin's brother, and Varenka, a young woman who is getting on in years, the daughter of a cook, who grew up in an aristocratic milieu as Mme. Stahl's protégée. The two meet in Levin's country house, where they are both guests. Sergei Ivanovich lives for his studies, considers himself old, and feels bound to the memory of a woman whom he loved and who passed away, named Marie; Varenka, who had a love affair a few years earlier, is poor, single, and has no life of her own. They are attracted to each other. Everybody who spends the summer at the Levins' realizes how Sergei Ivanovich and Varenka feel for each other and try to encourage them.
>
> One day, Sergei Ivanovich suggests to Levin and his guests that they go mushroom hunting. He knows that this is the right time to declare himself, as do Varenka and everybody else. The couple is left alone. The narrator focuses on Sergei and shows us the band of oscillation, the field of possibilities within which his thoughts move:

---

49. Lukács, *Tolstoi und die Probleme des Realismus* (1935); English translation "Tolstoy and the Evolution of Realism," in *Studies in European Realism,* 185.

He recalled any number of women and girls he knew, but could not re-call one who would combine to such a degree all, precisely all, the quali-ties that he, reasoning coldly, would wish to see in his wife. She had all the loveliness and freshness of youth, yet she was not a child, and if she loved him, she loved him consciously, as a woman should love: that was one thing. Another: she was not only far from worldliness, but obviously had a loathing for the world, yet at the same time she knew that world and had all the manners of a woman of good society, without which a life's companion was unthinkable for Sergei Ivanovich. Third: she was religious, and not unaccountably religious and good, like a child, like Kitty, for instance, but her life was based on religious convictions. Even to the smallest details, Sergei Ivanovich found in her everything he could wish for in a wife: she was poor and alone, so she would not bring a heap of relations and their influence into the house as he saw with Kitty, but would be obliged to her husband in all things, which he had also always wished for his future family life. And this girl, who combined all these qualities in herself, loved him. He was modest but he could not fail to see it. And he loved her. One negative consideration was his age. But his breed was long-lived, he did not have a single grey hair, no one would have taken him for forty, and he remembered Varenka saying that it was only in Russia that people considered themselves old at the age of fifty, that in France a fifty-year-old man considered himself *dans la force de l'âge*, and a forty-year-old *un jeune homme*.[50]

Rather than a rigid mold, the interior life is a field of forces: some dis-tance Sergei from Varenka (the memory of Marie, the fear of being too old), while others push him closer to declaring himself, and, ultimately, these prevail. Varenka talks less to herself, but from what the text says it is clear that she, too, is crossed by opposing forces: there is a sense of her undeniably low social position, which prompts her to not delude herself, but there is also the desire to change her life and the attraction of a man who is solid, respectable, and rich. Varenka is also divided, then, but the sum of what stirs inside her would certainly drive her to accept his pro-posal. The two are alone now. Sergei has mentally prepared a speech, but cannot find the right moment to deliver it. Meanwhile, to gain time, he talks about mushrooms:

50. Tolstoy, *Anna Karenina*, part 6, chap. 4, pp. 562–563.

They went on silently for a few steps. Varenka saw that he wanted to speak. She guessed what it was about and her heart was gripped by the excitement of joy and fear. They went far enough away so that no one could hear them, and still he did not begin to speak. It would have been better for Varenka to remain silent. After a silence it would have been easier to say what they wanted to say than after talking about mushrooms; but against her own will, as if inadvertently, Varenka said:

"So you didn't find any? But then there are always fewer inside the wood."

Sergei Ivanovich sighed and made no answer. He was vexed that she had begun talking about mushrooms. He wanted to bring her back to her first words about her childhood; but, as if against his will, after being silent for a while, he commented on her last words.

"I've heard only that the white boletus grows mostly on the edge, though I'm unable to identify it."

Several more minutes passed, they went still further away from the children and were completely alone. Varenka's heart was pounding so that she could hear it, and she felt herself blush, then turn pale, then blush again.

To be the wife of a man like Koznyshev, after her situation with Mme. Stahl, seemed to her the height of happiness. Besides, she was almost certain that she was in love with him. And now it was to be decided. She was frightened. Frightened that he would speak, and that he would not.

He had to declare himself now or never; Sergei Ivanovich felt it, too. Everything, in Varenka's gaze, colour, lowered eyes, showed painful expectation. Sergei Ivanovich saw it and pitied her. He even felt that to say nothing now would be to insult her. In his mind he quickly repeated all the arguments in favour of his decision. He also repeated to himself the words in which he wished to express his proposal; but instead of those words, by some unexpected consideration that occurred to him, he suddenly asked:

"And what is the difference between a white boletus and a birch bolutus?"

Varenka's lips trembled as she answered:

"There's hardly any difference in the caps, but in the feet." And as soon as these words were spoken, both he and she understood that the matter was ended, and that what was to have been said would not be said, and their excitement, which had reached its highest point just before then, began to subside.

"In the birch boletus, the foot resembles a two-day growth of beard on a dark-haired man," Sergei Ivanovich said, calmly now.

> "Yes, that's true," Varenka replied, smiling, and the direction of their
> walk changed inadvertently. They began going towards the children. Va-
> renka was both hurt and ashamed, but at the same time she had a sense
> of relief.
>
> On returning home and going through all the arguments, Sergei Iva-
> novich found that his reasoning had been wrong. He could not betray
> the memory of Marie.[51]

This scene could have concluded in two ways, both of which are plausible and both of which are compatible with Sergei and Varenka, with their
bands of oscillation. The decision came down to chance; the less desirable
outcome prevailed; individuals redefine their identities based on these accidental verdicts. The interior life is a magnetic field bounded by confines
but exposed to circumstances and, in the end, destiny is created by circumstances, not character.

2. The second device extends the analytical French tradition, that is, the
lineage of psychological narratives most successful in transiting through
the epochs—the only one that managed to pass from premodern structures of sense to modern ones while substantially preserving its continuity.
This apparatus of concepts and techniques, as I have said, owes much to
Montaigne and to the rediscovery of Augustine in the time of the Reformation and the Counter-Reformation. It took root during the second half
of the seventeenth century in the works of the *moralistes* and in *nouvelles,*
which created a vocabulary and syntax of inner analysis. At the beginning
of the nineteenth century, Constant and Stendhal explicitly laid claim to
this legacy, tracing themselves back to Madame de La Fayette. This tradition easily survived the development of the modern novel.

> One of the scenes that best expresses the unique analytical capacity of
> Proust is the episode with which he ends *The Guermantes Way,* the scene of
> the red shoes. The narrator meets Swann in Madame de Guermantes's house;
> Swann appears to be very ill. After the reception, Madame de Guermantes
> invites Swann to accompany her and her husband on a trip to Italy that
> will take place the following spring; Swann responds that this will not be
> possible, because he will already be dead in the spring. Madame de

51. Ibid., part 4, chap. 5, pp. 564–565.

Guermantes, who must attend a dinner and is late, finds herself caught between two obligations and stalls for time:

> "What on earth are you telling me?" the Duchesse burst out, stopping short for a second on her way to the carriage and raising her handsome, melancholy blue eyes, her gaze now fraught with uncertainty. Poised for the first time in her life between two duties as far removed from each other as getting into her carriage to go to a dinner party and showing compassion for a man who was about to die, she could find no appropriate precedent to follow in the code of conventions, and, not knowing which duty to honor, she felt she had no choice but to pretend to believe that the second alternative did not need to be raised, thus enabling her to comply with the first, which at that moment required less effort, and thought that the best way of settling the conflict would be to deny that there was one. "You must be joking," she said to Swann.
>
> "It would be a joke in charming taste, " replied Swann ironically. "I don't know why I'm telling you this. I've never mentioned my illness to you before. But since you asked me, and since now I may die at any moment. . . . But, please, the last thing I want to do is to hold you up, and you've got a dinner party to go to," he added, because he knew that for other people their own social obligations mattered more than the death of a friend, and as a man of considerate politeness he put himself in their place. But the Duchesse's own sense of manners afforded her, too, a confused glimpse of the fact that for Swann her dinner party must count for less than his own death. And so, while still moving toward her carriage, she said with a droop of her shoulders, "Don't worry about the dinner party. It's of no importance!" But her words put the Duc in a bad mood, and he burst out: "Come along, Oriane, don't just stand there with your chatter, whining away to Swann, when you know very well that Mme de Saint-Euverte makes a point of having her guests sit down at the table at eight o'clock sharp. We need you to make up your mind. Their horses have been waiting for a good five minutes now. Forgive me, Charles," he said, turning to Swann, "but it's ten minutes to eight. Oriane is always late, and it will take us more than five minutes to get to old Mother Saint-Euverte."[52]

52. Marcel Proust, *Le Côté de Guermantes* (1920–1921); English translation *The Guermantes Way,* translated with an introduction and notes by Mark Treharne, in *In Search of Lost Time,* general editor Christopher Prendergast (London: Penguin, 2003), 594–595.

Madame de Guermantes continues to say goodbye to Swann while repeating that she does not believe a word of what he has been saying. When she is about to enter the carriage, Monsieur de Guermantes realizes that his wife has put on black shoes with a red dress. Annoyed by the combination, he asks her to go home and put on the red shoes that match the dress. Madame de Guermantes is embarrassed by the presence of Swann, to whom she has just said goodbye:

"But, my dear," said the Duchesse softly, embarrassed to see that Swann, who was leaving the house with me but had stepped back to let the carriage pass out in front of us, had heard this, "given that we're late . . ."

"No, no, we have plenty of time. It's only ten to. It won't take us ten minutes to get to the Parc Monceau. And anyway, what does it matter? Even if we arrive at half past eight, they'll still wait for us, but you simply can't go there in a red dress and black shoes.

. . .

"They were by no means a disaster," said Swann. "I noticed the black shoes and I didn't find them remotely offensive."

"You may be right," replied the Duc, "but it looks more elegant to have them matching the dress. Anyway, you can set your mind at rest. No sooner had she got there than she would have noticed, and I would have been the one who had to come back and fetch the others, which means I wouldn't have eaten till nine o'clock. Goodbye, my dear boys," he said, thrusting us gently away, "off you go, now, before Oriane comes down. It's not that she doesn't like seeing you both. On the contrary, she's too fond of seeing you. If she finds you still here, she'll start talking again. She's already very tired, and she'll be dead by the time she gets to that dinner. And, quite frankly, I have to tell you that I'm dying of hunger. I had a miserable lunch this morning, when I came from the train. That *sauce béarnaise* was damn good, certainly, but in spite of that I won't be sorry, no two ways about it, to sit down to dinner. Five to eight! That's women for you! She'll give us both indigestion before the night's out. She's far less robust than people think."

The Duc had absolutely no qualms in speaking this way about his wife's petty discomforts and his own to a dying man, for, because they were what was uppermost in his mind, they seemed more important to him. And so, after he had gently steered us to the door, it was merely his jocund sense of good manners that led him to boom out after Swann, who was already in the courtyard, in a voice for all to hear:

"Now, mind you don't let all this damned doctors' nonsense get to you. They're fools. You're in strapping shape. You'll live to see us all in our graves!"[53]

The crowning work of the "century of psychological realism (1850–1950)"[54] is the culmination of a long heritage: the vocabulary and syntax that it uses for the mimesis of the mental world is inconceivable outside the literary genealogy embarked on by the "science of the heart" of the *âge classique*. Proust's psychoanalysis is held together by gestures typical of the *moralistes:* the magma of the interior life is put in order and split up into opposing elements; the hierarchy of the passions is turned upside down by a crudely analytical and realistic eye; the laws of the psychic life are set out in the form of maxims ("for other people their own social obligations matter more than the death of a friend"). In this passage, Madame de Guermantes's inner tension is related to the conflict between two asymmetric duties, which are arranged in a hierarchy by the commonly accepted morality (compassion for a friend should count infinitely more than one's social life). The psychological realism of the narrator overturns the scale of values and shows that, for Madame and Monsieur de Guermantes, not being late for dinner is more important and less burdensome than paying attention to a dying friend. Swann's reaction is forged around the same opposition (a member of fashionable society knows that, for others, their social life is more important than his death), as is Madame de Guermantes's reply to Swann ("But the Duchesse's own sense of manners afforded her, too, a confused glimpse of the fact that for Swann her dinner party must count for less than his own death.") And yet Madame de Guermantes continues to walk toward the carriage: her social obligations matter more than the death of a friend. In the next scene, the more obtuse Monsieur de Guermantes talks about his minor illnesses and those of his wife to someone who is terminally ill because the former are more interesting to him than the latter. Once again, the magma of the psychic life is ordered by oppositions.

53. Ibid., 596–597.
54. The expression comes from Dorrit Cohn, preface to *Transparent Minds.*

Proust thus adapts his own times to some of the structures of sense dating back to the culture of the *moralistes*. But in the two and a half centuries that separate *In Search of Lost Time* from Madame de Sévigné, Madame de La Fayette, and La Rochefoucauld, a great deal had happened. One of the most significant things to occur can be found as early as Stendhal's time: in *The Princesse de Clèves* the outside world never, or almost never, gets mixed up with self-analysis, but in the novels of Stendhal introspection is inseparable from the circumstances. The analysis of the hidden folds of the mind is placed within a richly textured context that influences life. In the episode of *The Red and the Black* commented on by Zola, for example, the narrator uses a psychological vocabulary akin to the tradition of the *moralistes,* which allows the dialectic between the interior planets and satellites to be examined ("His soul was flooded with happiness, not because he loved Madame de Rênal, but because a frightful torment had come to an end."); and to name the psychic forces ("frightful combat that duty fought against timidity").[55] But unlike what happens in the works of Madame de La Fayette, the attention is focused on contingent circumstances, and contingencies are involved in the action: the motion of the sun changes the atmosphere of the meeting; the clock that strikes ten spurs Julien to make his move; the movements of Madame Derville transform the balance of psychological forces. Proust perfects this rootedness of the passions in minutely detailed contexts.

However, simply binding the mechanics of the mental world to those of the outside world is not enough to transplant into the twentieth century the psychological vocabulary and syntax of the seventeenth. Compared to *The Princesse de Clèves,* it is not just the relation to circumstances that changes but also the form of the planets and satellites. Character molds are further shattered. If looked at from above, in a sort of existential blueprint, the human beings of *In Search of Lost Time* still have an internal logic, and the narrator's task is still to show every hidden detail of their mental maps. But subjective identity is by now so atomized that it has become a complex literary undertaking to provide plausible images of their interior landscapes. The difficulty in keeping the multiplicity of the psyche unified is revealed in a distinguishing feature of Proust's work: the expansion of the analytical sections. An immense introspective space is now required to reveal the

55. Stendhal, *The Red and the Black*, bk. 1, chap. 9, p. 62.

hidden or semi-hidden folds of the mind, and to connect them together in a logical way.

3. In 1923, a year after the death of Proust, while *In Search of Lost Time* was still partly unpublished, Gide collected his essays on Dostoevsky into a book.[56] Many of them were written for the centenary of Dostoevsky's birth in 1921. This was the beginning of the most important decade for modernist narrative fiction: five volumes of *In Search of Lost Time* were about to be published, as were *Ulysses* (1922), *Zeno's Conscience* (1923), *The Magic Mountain* (1924), *Mrs. Dalloway* (1925), *To the Lighthouse* (1927), *Berlin Alexanderplatz* (1929), *The Sound and the Fury* (1929), *As I Lay Dying* (1930), the first volume of *The Man without Qualities* (1930), and *The Sleepwalkers* (1931–1932). Gide considered Dostoevsky to be the most revolutionary novelist, a writer who had subverted the images of human beings and the world that had become fossilized in nineteenth-century narrative forms. One of his greatest innovations was his way of conceiving individuals:

> The principal charge brought against Dostoevsky in the name of our Western-European logic has been, I think, the irrational, irresolute, and often irresponsible nature of his characters, everything in their appearance that could seem grotesque and wild. It is not, so people aver, real life that he unfolds, but nightmares. In my belief this is utterly mistaken; but let us grant the truth of it for argument's sake, and refrain from answering after the manner of Freud that there is more sincerity in our dream-life than in the actions of our real existence.[57]

"It suddenly came into my mind," says the protagonist of *The Gambler* about an act of insolence that leads him to the brink of a duel, and he adds "I don't know why."[58] By keeping a part of themselves hidden or unconscious, Dostoevsky's characters are entitled to exhibit inconsistencies to which previous heroes of the European novel never had a right. When Fyodor Karamazov's first wife dies, some say that the widower began to

---

56. André Gide, *Dostoïevski* (1923); English translation *Dostoevsky* (New York: New Directions, 1961).

57. Ibid., 14.

58. Fyodor Dostoevsky, *Igrok* (1866); English translation *The Gambler*, trans. Constance Garnett (New York: Random House, 2003), 50.

run down the street in joy; others, that he wept like a little child. The narrator comments: "Both versions may very well be true—that is, that he rejoiced at his release and wept for her who released him, all at the same time."[59]

Dostoevsky's art of preserving shadows and inconsistencies distinguishes him from the entire European introspective tradition. Gide uses Balzac as his main term of comparison.

> The chief protagonists, he does not portray, leaving them to limn in their own portrait, never finished, ever changing, in the course of the narrative. His principal characters are always in the course of formation, never quite emerging from the shadows. In passing, note how profoundly different he is from Balzac, whose chief care seems ever to be the perfect consistency of his characters.[60]

But this difference can be perceived not only in comparison to a storyteller like Balzac, who uses bold strokes to describe his characters; according to Gide, when compared to Dostoevsky, all French narrative fiction exhibits an irremediable tendency toward simplification. The highly sophisticated technique used by the psychological culture descending from the moralists to dissect interior forces presupposed that the mystery of inner life could be captured by analytical discourses. In addition, the French psychological tradition was animated by a current of rationalism whose aim was to trace actions back to specific motivations. When La Rochefoucauld explains every behavior in relation to *amour propre*, writes Gide, "what is contradictory in the human soul escapes him."[61] However precise it may be, this anatomical art kills the unpredictable vitality of the psyche. French culture abhors formlessness; formlessness was Dostoevsky's favorite territory.

The fact that, at the beginning of one of the most important decades for European modernism, Gide juxtaposes Dostoevsky's psychology with the image of human beings found in nineteenth-century novels is telling. A significant part of modernist literature, from Gide to Faulkner (in Italy, from Tozzi to Pirandello), would learn a great deal from this paradigm, directly or indirectly. At mid-twentieth century, Nathalie Sarraute viewed Dostoevsky

59. Dostoevsky, *The Brothers Karamazov*, part 1, p. 9.
60. Gide, *Dostoevsky*, 17.
61. Ibid., 605.

as the precursor "for nearly all the European writers in our times," since he was the only nineteenth-century novelist who was able to represent the perpetual motion of our selves.[62] Between 1880 and 1923, between *The Brothers Karamazov* and the publication of Gide's essay, a new introspective theory had taken shape that, after struggling for a name, finally settled on "psychoanalysis." It is no coincidence that Gide would cite Freud to legitimize the irrational, irresolute, and irresponsible character of Dostoevsky's protagonists. The representational model of the interior life that we find in works such as *Notes from Underground, Crime and Punishment, The Idiot,* or *The Brothers Karamazov* is well suited to the idea of the subject implicit in depth psychology and in the epoch that made it possible.

4. The fourth possibility that opens with the crisis of the nineteenth-century character appeared a few years after Dostoevsky's model took form and responded to similar needs. In 1887, a writer associated with the poetics of the Symbolist movement, Édouard Dujardin, published a short novel called *Les lauriers sont coupés (We'll to the Woods No More)*. Forgotten for decades, the work reappeared in 1924, after Joyce publicly acknowledged its influence on his writing. Dujardin wrote an essay in the years that followed in which he claimed to have invented interior monologue.[63] It is true that precedents can be found in Dostoevsky (*Notes from Underground,* for example, or in his short story "A Gentle Creature") and in Tolstoy (the monologue of Anna Karenina before committing suicide); it is true that the expression *interior monologue* and the idea of pregrammatical speech that mimics thought precedes Dujardin;[64] it is also true that Bettina von Arnim had earlier loosened logical and syntactic connections in her *Dies Buch gehört dem König* (This Book Belongs to the King; 1843)[65]—but the fact

---

62. Nathalie Sarraute, "De Dostoïevski à Kafka" (1947); English translation "From Dostoevsky to Kafka," in *The Age of Suspicion: Essays on the Novel,* trans. Maria Jolas (New York: G. Braziller, 1963), 25.

63. Édouard Dujardin, *Le Monologue interieur: son apparition, ses origines, sa place dans l'oeuvre de James Joyce* (Paris: Messein, 1931).

64. They appear in *La Parole intérieure* (1881) by Victor Egger. See Laura Santone, *Voci dall'abisso. Nuovi elementi sulla genesi del monologo interiore* (Bari: Edipuglia, 1999), 7, 81ff.

65. See Peter Bürger, *Prosa der Moderne* (1988), in collaboration with von Christa Bürger (Frankfurt: Suhrkamp, 1992), 312ff.

remains that before Dujardin nobody had ever used this device to construct a novel.

Two types of interior monologue can be distinguished: the kind that mimics the confusion of an inner crisis, as in *Anna Karenina;* and the kind that mimics the multiplicity of daily life, as in *Ulysses.*[66] In both cases, what emerges is an image of people that differs from the assumption implicit in the very idea of *charakter:* the interest of the narrator is no longer focused on the supposedly rigid mold that distinguishes individuals, but on the chaotic plurality of consciousness, the preconscious, and the unconscious. Even when the trace of a mold remains visible (as in chapter 13 of *Ulysses,* where Gerty MacDowell's stream of consciousness intertwines with that of Bloom and vividly illustrates the difference between the two personalities), stream of consciousness is used to break up and complicate the life of the psyche. A stylistic sign that the genre of the Theophrastian character left on novels is the wide distribution of phrases like "he was one of those men, she was one of those women who . . ." by which individual difference is connected back to the universality of a type. Although very common in eighteenth-century novels founded on "moralistic" categories ("Mr. Allworthy was not one of those men whose hearts flutter at any unexpected and sudden tidings of worldly profit"[67]), they are also to be found in nineteenth-century novels based on historic and dynamic concepts[68] ("Madame de Rênal was one of those provincial women . . ."[69]). These expressions define, draw boundaries, and gather the dispersion of the self into a unity. Interior monologue represents the end of the Theophrastian character: it tends to shatter the I instead of uniting it within a rigid mold.

Tolstoy's model, developments in the French analytical tradition, Dostoevsky's model, and the mimesis of the psyche's chaotic jumble using interior monologue represent four possibilities that arose out of the crisis of the nineteenth-century paradigm. The order I have presented them in corresponds to their progressive distancing from the *charakter.* These degrees

66. Franco Moretti, *Opere mondo. Saggio sulla forma epica dal "Faust" a "Cent'anni di solitudine"* (1994); English translation *Modern Epic: The World System from Goethe to García Márquez* (London: Verso, 1996), 168ff.

67. Fielding, *The History of Tom Jones,* 281.

68. See Smeed, *The Theophrastan "Character,"* chap. 10.

69. Stendhal, *The Red and the Black,* 35.

of distance are also reflected in the techniques that the novelists adopted. As we have seen, in order to translate the interior life into language, our culture uses the genres of psychological analysis and the monologue: the former specializes in the description of enduring traits; the latter expresses inner conflicts. Now: while Tolstoy and the French analytical tradition present characters through the narrator's psychological analysis, and while Dostoevsky allows the protagonists of his novels to reveal themselves through action and first-person discourse, authors who employ stream of consciousness extend the tradition of the theatrical and epistolary soliloquy into a radical form, eliminating all links with the public dimension, even those implicit in the rules of grammar, punctuation, and syntax. If, as Ian Watt believed, *Ulysses* was the culmination of the formal trend beginning with Richardson, then the epistolary monologues of *Pamela* and *Clarissa* are the modern version of the epistolary monologues of the *Heroides* and, more generally, of the soliloquies of wounded, suffering, or conquered heroines and heroes. A frayed but recognizable genealogical line unites the soliloquy of Dido in book 4 of the *Aeneid* to the monologue of Anna Karenina. And when stream of consciousness later abandons crisis states to become the vehicle for expressing the normalcy of the everyday life of the psyche, this is when Anna Karenina's monologue can give rise to the last chapter of *Ulysses*.

Three Turning Points

In addition to developing new types of narrators, plots, and characters, the literary epoch that began around 1850 witnessed a changing balance between the elements of narrative texts. In the nineteenth-century paradigm, the essential is expressed through visible actions and audible speeches; in the mid-twentieth century, the barycenter started to migrate to other territories. For the first time, the noble forms of mimesis were able to locate the essential outside of public action. This transformation led to three turning points, freeing up new possibilities.

1. The most well known—the only one that has been defined as a turning point thus far—is the *inward turn*. The concept appears in a book by Leon Edel, *The Psychological Novel* (1955), where he speaks of an *inward-*

turning of the modernist novel.[70] Eighteen years later, *The Inward Turn of Narrative* (1973) by Erich Kahler was published. This was an expanded English version of the work that appeared in the *Neue Rundschau,* left unfinished due to the author's death.[71] Kahler describes the long-duration process that led Western narrative to abandon cosmogonies and theogonies to take up an interest in the sublunar world inhabited by human beings, and then to shift interest from public actions to psychological analysis.

The design, chronology, and vagueness of these books may be questionable, but there is no doubt that Edel's and Kahler's concepts illuminate a crucial aspect of modern literary history. An inward turn occurs when the essential part of a story no longer takes place in the segment of reality that everyone can see or hear, and is transferred instead to the unapparent sphere that lies nestled inside the protagonists like a hidden territory, their private realm. The Western way of viewing the ontological status of thoughts and passions oscillates between two ideas. On the one hand, the interior life is seen as the exclusive possession of the individual—according to a way of thinking implicitly signaled by the metaphor of "interiority." On the other hand, the interior life is seen as inhabited by suprapersonal and impersonal forces—according to a way of thinking that has come down through our culture, reappearing in radically different forms, from Homer to Gilbert Simondon and Gilles Deleuze.[72] But whatever paradigm we apply, thoughts and passions present us with a cognitive asymmetry: while our actions and words enter into the public sphere and are manifest to the senses, our thoughts and passions remain almost entirely concealed from other people until they are expressed. We cannot claim any hypothetical superiority for the actions we perform and the words we utter, because everyone can see them and hear them, while we can claim to know our

70. Edel, *The Psychological Novel, 1900–1950,* chap. 2.

71. Erich Kahler, *The Inward Turn of Narrative* (Princeton, NJ: Princeton University Press, 1973). See also Kahler *Die Verinnerung des Erzählens,* in *Die Neue Rundschau,* 68, 1957 and 70, 1959, and *Untergang und Übergang* (München: Deutscher Taschenbuch Verlag, 1970).

72. Gilbert Simondon, *L'Individu et sa genèse physico-biologique* (Paris: PUF, 1964); Gilles Deleuze, *Logique du sens* (1969); English translation *The Logic of Sense,* trans. Mark Lester with Charles Stivale (New York: Columbia University Press, 1990), 100ff.

thoughts and passions better than anyone else, at least until we transpose them into the public medium of words. Regardless of its nature, the *intus* to which interiority refers finds an ontological legitimacy in this cognitive imbalance.

Narrative turns toward the interior when interest shifts from what everyone can see or hear to what only individuals know, and what the narrative text takes upon itself to reveal. As a possibility that is always available, the inward turn traverses the history of the novel. The first example is in *The Princesse de Clèves,* a work that locates what is essential in the psyche of the characters and presents external behaviors as the secondary reflection of primary crises taking place *in interiore homine.* This is so much the case that social life seems like a show and "the return to the events of the heart is felt . . . like a return to reality."[73] Because the inward turn is associated with the Christian idea that the *intus* is the seat of divinity, it is a possibility of *longue durée.* Nevertheless, it became a crucial element in the Western narrative space only during the century of psychological realism, between the second half of the nineteenth century and modernism. This is when public plots became emptied of meaning, the narrative focus migrated to internal processes, and the characters attached enormous importance to events that, for others and for the public sphere, are trivial or nonexistent—as in the passage by Virginia Woolf that Auerbach writes about in the last chapter of *Mimesis:*

> The exterior events have actually lost their hegemony, they serve to release and interpret inner events, whereas before her time . . . inner movements preponderantly function to prepare and motivate significant exterior happenings.[74]

This transformation overturns relations between the public and private, between what is happening in the outside world and what matters for the private worlds of individuals. It thus becomes possible to construct novels around these ruptures or profane illuminations, fundamental for the protagonist and imperceptible for others, that Joyce called "epiphanies" and Proust "intermittences of the heart."

---

73. Rousset, *Forme et signification,* 21. See also Kahler, *The Inward Turn of Narrative,* 15ff.

74. Auerbach, *Mimesis,* 538.

2. During the same decades when *Verinnerung* became widespread, the novel underwent a complementary metamorphosis that made the inward turn possible. By analogy, I will call this the *essay turn*. The era when Western novels were being loaded with ideas spans the works Tolstoy and Dostoevsky published in the 1860s and those Musil and Broch published in the 1930s. As we have seen, the phenomenon did not originate during this period, but during these years it gained greater currency. With a few exceptions, early nineteenth-century narrative fiction used concepts to construct the invisible backstage surrounding the visible actions, keeping the latter at the center of the represented world. Instead, during the period we are considering, some crucial works shifted the text's barycenter toward a territory composed of collective regularities and suprapersonal laws. This space, which surrounds, crosses, traverses, and explains the acts of individuals, passes through the medium of the concept and takes the form of the novel-essay. This is what happens in the sections of *War and Peace* in which Tolstoy explains his philosophy of history or in the first part of *Notes from Underground*. This is what happens, even more obviously, in the continual reflective digressions in *In Search of Lost Time* and *The Man without Qualities,* or in the essay "The Disintegration of Values" that Broch inserts into the third part of *The Sleepwalkers*. Proust's aphorism comparing works of art that expound theories to an object with its price tag still attached is clearly a product of denial: if we broke *In Search of Lost Time* down into parts and calculated how much of the text is occupied by theorizing, chances are we would find that no other novel in the Western canon contains as many reflections, abstractions, and ideas. But in addition to revealing, through antiphrasis, an essential characteristic of the work in which it appears, Proust's maxim introduces an illuminating metaphorical field. A price tag defetishizes goods, depriving them of their magical aura and reducing them to their mere exchange value expressed by money, the universal equivalent that voids things of their difference and makes them comparable to each other. In the same way, theoretical remarks on the regularities that precede, surround, and traverse the lives of individuals defetishize stories, depriving them of all their specific differences and transforming them into particular cases of a law. Attention shifts from the individual object or single event to the general principle that makes all singularities equal and liquidates their pretensions. Like money, concepts presuppose the death of particularities: the

fact that ideas came to acquire more weight in the narrative economy means that the nineteenth-century gamble on interest being generated by the lives of people like us had been partly withdrawn. In the novel-essay, the stories of individuals need to stand on conceptual surfaces in order to generate a meaning and provide interest.

A method that achieves results similar to those of the novel-essay without using the vehicle of the concept is the allegorical use of narrative materials. When Joyce explains the internal characteristics of the chapters in *Ulysses* using the "Linati schema," he traces the form of his novel back to a preexisting idea that explains the text through an explicit pattern of correspondences. In a less pervasive but more general way, a similar effect is obtained using the principle of montage. The novel widely appropriated this technique between the second half of the nineteenth century and modernism—between the scene of the agricultural fair in *Madame Bovary* and Dos Passos's *U.S.A.,* passing by way of part 3 of *The Sleepwalkers* (*Huguenau, or The Realist*). Using this mechanism to bring the parts together is tantamount to subverting every *ordo naturalis*: it subordinates the plot to an idea that manifests in an oblique, silent form, in the authorial decision to put a certain sequence near another.

3. The third turning point is *estrangement.* Flaubert, as we have said, was the first to imagine narratives based on form, rather than on the appeal of the plot or the characters. The literature of the early nineteenth century had developed the ideal of transparent writing; instead, at a certain point novels began to circulate that were founded on the opacity of their style. Form no longer appears consubstantial with content, and thus natural and invisible; instead it draws attention to itself, revealing itself to be artificial mediation, creating a distancing effect on the habits of common sense and on the ordinary way of telling stories. It sets up a sort of screen between the story and the reader that is authorial and therefore subjective and lyrical—but its lyricism has no subject, crystallized into pure form, like a transcendental structure. In this case, too, interest is transferred from public action to the way of narrating the action, from what happens to the way it is being told. The importance writing assumes in some forms of the modernist novel (the work of Carlo Emilio Gadda, for example, in Italian literature) stems from this process.

Short Stories and Epiphanies

Another transformation that the serious mimesis of everyday life went through after 1850 involves the length of the texts. The nineteenth-century paradigm, as we have said, developed the utopia of universal narratability: any life can become the content of a story, any destiny can enthrall, and any situation is potentially loaded with interest. The great narrative cycles or polyhistorical novels of the 1800s furnished the architectonic equivalent of this project. Between the second half of the nineteenth century and the first half of the twentieth century, cyclical novels did not fade away. On the contrary, they met with remarkable success, from Zola's *Rougon-Macquart* (1871–1893), John Galsworthy's *Forsyte Saga* (1906–1921), and Martin du Gard's *Les Thibault* (1922–1940), to Louis Aragon's *Le Monde réel* (The Real World) (1934–1944). This phenomenon was contemporary with the new success of a genre that was in many respects diagonally opposed to it: the *short story.*

In the early nineteenth century, the importance and popularity of short narrative fiction were hardly comparable to the novel's. German and Russian literature were exceptions to this rule; but elsewhere, and especially in the two dominant European literatures, the short story was a secondary form mainly associated with fantastic tales. However, between the last decades of the nineteenth century and the first decades of the twentieth century, short narrative experienced a new development and joined in the mimesis of ordinary life. During this period, some of the greatest writers of the everyday expressed their narrative talent—or their finest narrative talent—in short forms (Maupassant, Chekhov, Katherine Mansfield, Sherwood Anderson, Luigi Pirandello). Others dedicated a significant part of their work to short narrative forms. What lies behind this phenomenon?

The first explanation is sociological: in many countries, newspapers and magazines began commissioning short stories, which later appeared side by side with the feuilleton, and in some cases replaced it. In Italy, for example, press commissions affected the literary choices and writing of Verga, Pirandello, and Tozzi.[75] But as always happens when we appeal to a mechanical

75. Gino Tellini, *La tela di fumo. Saggio su Tozzi novelliere* (Pisa: Nistri-Lischi, 1972), 15–43; Romano Luperini, "Il trauma e il caso. Sulla tipologia della novella moderna," in *L'autocoscienza del moderno* (Naples: Liguori, 2006), 171.

model of causality, the conceptual schema provides a good explanation for the dynamics of the event but does not shed light on the origin. All hegemonic phenomena inevitably arise out of a varying tangle of force and acquiescence:[76] no historical subject is strong enough to impose its will and desires on the social body if the social body does not already possess to some extent that will and those desires. If newspaper and magazine commissions had not amplified an interest in short forms that was already latent in a segment of readers, in the absence of an audience the practice of printing stories in newspapers would soon have faded out.

At a certain time, Western readers felt the desire to read short stories set in everyday environments. This happened because, in their eyes, narrative disruptions now had a more limited reach: the modern short story, like modern lyric poetry, originated from the idea that life is formed of long, monochromatic backgrounds of repetition interrupted by small, unprecedented events. While the melodramatic novel assumes that each day is a potential theater for major, externalized conflicts, while the *Bildungsroman* and the novel of personal destinies describe the progress or decline in people's existences through decisive scenes that make each person what he or she is, the short story imagines that under normal conditions daily life is static, disciplined, and unnarratable. Very often in lyric poetry and in modern short stories normalcy lies invisible inside the white spaces that separate the pages occupied by writing, while the words set down on paper record states of exception that interrupt the return of the identical. In some respects, this represents a return to the conception of life implicit in the premodern and early modern *novella*: daily existence juts out and becomes worthy of storytelling only on certain occasions. What changed was the context in which the protruding part of life is included, because all exemplary frame stories had disappeared, and because now we have the novel of personal destinies: every life, if observed well, can become narrative content.

According to the logic of the literary field, the position occupied by the short story stands opposite that of the great polyhistorical novel founded on the idea that situations worthy of attention abound. The collected stories of Maupassant, Chekhov, or Pirandello give the impression of human

---

76. See Antonio Gramsci, *Quaderni del carcere,* ed. Valentino Gerratana (Turin: Einaudi, 1975), Quaderno 19, §25, vol. 3, p. 2010. See also Quaderno 13, §37; vol. 3, p. 1638.

comedies constructed out of fragments: they embrace what the young Lukács would have called "the extensive totality of life," but they are composed of relatively short pieces. Ordinary lives become narratable only rarely and for short periods of time: surrounded by predictability and boredom, life offers only flickers—or episodes.

But this reduction in narratability is evident beyond the genre of the short story: it is also expressed inside literary works, in the role that epiphanies play in many modern novels.[77] Intermittences of the heart tend to last only an instant: even at the center of profuse works, what really counts, what enshrines the sense of a life, does not get played out over its entire duration but in the moment, and individual lives appear as long, monochromatic backgrounds of emptiness interrupted by brief revelatory intervals. Epiphanies also have two faces: they are crucial events for those who experience them and irrelevant to everyone else; they are peripheral satellites that become central only because they are overdetermined by a character, by the subjective meanings projected onto them.[78] The movement of a foot on the pavement in the courtyard of the Hôtel de Guermantes that provides Marcel with a vital illumination is a purely private experience: in the public sphere, on the objective stage of interhuman life, nothing has happened.

This approach has nineteenth-century precedents. Not by chance, the oldest of these arose out of lyric poetry: the illuminations of Baudelaire, in their auratic version ("Correspondances") and in their urbane, prosaic version ("The Swan," "To a Passerby"). But even as early as *War and Peace* some of the decisive twists in the story line take the form of an epiphany. We find some of the first great intermittences in well-known episodes of the same work. During the battle of Austerlitz, the French take the core of the Russian army by surprise and threaten to kill or capture Kutuzov. Andrei Bolkonsky watches his battalion being overpowered by the French; the Russians are fleeing. To reverse the outcome of the battle and cover

77. On the aesthetics of the epiphany in modernist literature, see Hugo Azérad, *L'Univers constellé de Proust, Joyce et Faulkner: le concept d'épiphanie dans l'esthétique du modernisme* (Bern: Lang, 2002), especially chap. 4.

78. See Franco Moretti, "'Un'inutile nostalgia di me stesso'. La crisi del romanzo di formazione europeo, 1898–1914 (1999)"; English translation "'A Useless Longing for Myself': The Crisis of the European *Bildungsroman*, 1898–1914," in *The Way of the World*, 233ff.; Romano Luperini, *L'incontro e il caso* (Rome-Bari: Laterza, 2007), chap. 7 and passim.

himself in glory, he picks up the standard and charges against the enemy so that his men will follow him and stop running away. Only minutes later he is wounded and falls to the ground with his face turned upward. The sky opens up above him, lofty and serene: watching it, Andrei understands the meaninglessness of the goals for which human beings fight.[79] Until that moment, Andrei had cultivated fantasies of military glory; the sky destroyed what was at stake in the battle and revealed the vanity of the whole undertaking. But, unlike medieval vanities, this illumination is not predicable to the masses: it remains a secret possession and is revealed in a scene that nobody except Andrei will ever be able to grasp. When Napoleon passes by to inspect the battlefield, he sees the lifeless body of Andrei and assumes that he is dead. Napoleon understands that Andrei was cut down in an act of bravery and says, "Voila une belle mort" (Now that is a beautiful death).[80] Up to that moment, in addition to being an enemy, he had also been Andrei's personal myth. But now, Napoleon's words no longer count for anything: in public, Andrei's gesture means a glorious death; for Andrei, it means the end of the layers of meaning that humans paper over the pure, indifferent sky. The same type of sudden, private revelation is repeated in book 2 of *War and Peace,* when the double meeting with an old oak is transformed by Andrei into a double epiphany.[81]

As a narrative adaptation of the tragic form, the melodramatic novel imagines the human world as a chain of showy actions, motivated by and tied to the need to compose a story line that develops over time. The exaggeration of the actions and passions is intended to signify—and before that, create—the absolute value of the events being described. The novel of personal destinies abandons this device and develops instead around objective, public plot twists that shape human paths: the reader can witness Natasha's triumph on the day of her first ball; the reader can see that Dorothea Brooke has finally found the right person. In the novel that develops around epiphanies, on the other hand, the key events are set outside the external world, transferring two prerogatives of modern lyric poetry into the narrative domain: the breaking of the chronological chain that binds instants of life to the course of life; and the breaking of the social

79. Leo Tolstoy, *War and Peace,* bk. 1, part 3, chap. 16, p. 281.
80. Ibid., 291.
81. Ibid., bk. 2, part 2, chaps. 1–3, pp. 419–420, 422–423.

chain that drives people to pursue the meaning of life in exchanges with others.

Worlds Apart

The serious mimesis of everyday life remained at the heart of the modern novel, but in the second half of the nineteenth century and in the first half of the twentieth century, new ways of conceiving action, the interior world, and ordinary life took hold in ways that segmented or emptied objective events, shifting the interest elsewhere. During the same decades, the narrative territories that were further removed from or peripheral to the core formed by everyday realism were expanded and reorganized.

In his preparatory notes for *Rougon-Macquart*, Zola develops a sort of theory of classes, distinguishing between the people, shopkeepers, the bourgeoisie, and the *grand monde* (high society). He then identifies "a world apart" whose members include "prostitute, murderer, priest, artist."[82] While Zola's map may not satisfy the criteria of sociology, it is accurate and illuminating for the criteria of narrative. The prostitute, the murderer, the priest, and the artist are in fact united by a similar position in society: they are not "people like us." For one reason or another, their lives evade the middle station of life—their experience is more adventurous or more reflective of what society normally reserves to *laboratores*. Telling the stories of the "world apart" means to seek out narrative interest in characters who do not fall within the bounds of average everyday experience, to venture instead into a territory that I will divide into three regions.

1. The first contains stories focused on *unconventional heroes,* on characters who have an adventurous existence that evades modern regulations and control: prostitutes and murderers, but also deviants, eccentrics, and the insane. Between the second half of the nineteenth century and the first half of the twentieth century, there were many novelists, from Dostoevsky to Faulkner, who resorted to unconventional characters in order to create nodes of narrative tension that ordinary life was no longer capable of generating, or in order to tell about ordinary life through states of exception.

---

82. Émile Zola, *La Fabrique des Rougon-Macquart: édition des dossiers préparatoires,* ed. Colette Becker, with Véronique Lavielle (Paris: Champion, 2003), 50.

2. The second region contains the stages of life that come before the regulated life of adulthood: *childhood, adolescence,* and *youth.* These periods of life, which entered into literature between the second half of the eighteenth century and the beginning of the nineteenth century thanks to autobiographical writing inspired by the model of Rousseau and the *Bildungsroman,*[83] gained significantly in importance between the 1850s and the early 1900s. In different ways, Tolstoy, George Eliot, and Dostoevsky (and Nievo in Italy) gave narrative depth to the unformed ages of life, the periods of discovery and experience. Between the end of the nineteenth century and the era of modernism, the European *Bildungsroman* was revitalized by the themes of childhood and adolescence.[84]

3. The third region contains one of the most important literary figures for writers: the *intellectual hero.* As we saw in Chapter 6, the *roman personnel,* the "artist novel," and the novel of the self-reflective protagonist are possibilities frequently employed in modern narrative fiction. Writers do so with the implicit or explicit knowledge that only special people whose depth of thought or experiences make them extraneous to the middle station of life can spark narrative interest. In the modernist period, and more generally in the twentieth century, the novel swelled with thinking heroes and heroines located on the margins of the *vita activa.* Some of these characters are professional intellectuals (Mattia Pascal, Malte Laurids Brigge, Stephen Dedalus, Édouard, Ulrich Anders, Peter Kien, Antoine Roquentin); others, like Marcel and Zeno Cosini, are intellectuals in disguise. It is not difficult to glimpse another metaphorical appearance of this figure in the outpouring of the "inept."

If it is true that intellectual heroes proliferate in all periods of modern fiction, simply because they represent the double of the author and allow him or her to write fictional autobiographies through a third person, it is equally true that some phenomena are peculiar to this epoch. The most interesting of these does not involve the character of the intellectual, but the intellectual makeup of the common protagonists. In the realistic novel

83. See Francesco Orlando, *Infanzia, memoria e storia da Rousseau ai romantici* (Padua: Liviana, 1966).
84. See Moretti, "'A Useless Longing for Myself,'" 229–245.

throughout the 1800s, people who are active in the practical world are still capable of deep thought: although they are not intellectuals, or disguised intellectuals, the Unnamed, Rastignac, Andrei Bolkonsky, and Dorothea Brooke all reflect with lucidity on the meaning of their lives, on the meaning of life in general, or on the state of the world. Their thinking is not restricted by preset limitations, nor is it filled with platitudes and clichés. Instead, starting at a certain time, the distance between practical beings and thinking beings began to grow. In the twentieth century it became increasingly difficult to encounter heroes and heroines who are able to reconcile praxis and theory. Instead, there is an abundance of intellectual heroes or the inept (which amounts to the same thing), who are detached from the life of action and devoted to thought.

A scene in *Buddenbrooks* symbolically marks this transition. The protagonists of the novel are members of the ruling class of the city of Lübeck: in the hierarchy of the social system that the book chronicles, they represent the elite. They therefore should have the capacity to express themselves with great depth on their personal lives and on the life of the city, as happens in many nineteenth-century novels—for example, as Wüllersdorf and Innstetten do in the closing scenes of *Effi Briest*. But Mann places a limit in front of the most intelligent and thoughtful member of the family, Thomas Buddenbrook. This barrier appears toward the end of the novel, in the fifth chapter of part 10. For a long time Thomas has contented himself with what he is able to accumulate through his family firm and manages his business affairs without enthusiasm. His wife is resentful toward him and spends her days playing music with a young man, in such a manner as to call attention to herself and raise suspicions. One day Thomas Buddenbrooks stays home from the office. Sitting on the terrace of his house, he begins to read a book that fell into his hands by chance. Although not named expressly, the book is *The World as Will and Representation*. Thomas is bowled over: so many of the things that he had confusedly felt now find their rightful place and a meaning in Schopenhauer's work:

> He was filled with an unfamiliar sense of immense and grateful contentment. He felt the incomparable satisfaction of watching an enormously superior intellect grab hold of life, of cruel, mocking, powerful life, in order to subdue and condemn it. What he felt was the satisfaction of a

sufferer who has always known only shame and the bite of conscience for hiding the suffering that cold, hard life brings, and who now, suddenly, from the hand of a great and wise man, receives elemental, formal justification for having felt such suffering in this world—in this best of all possible worlds, which by means of playful scorn was proved to be the worst of all possible worlds.[85]

Thomas spends the day in a state of gloomy desolation and goes to bed early, but he wakes up after three hours and begins to reflect on the absurdity of life, on the pain of individuation, on death as a deliverance from the prison of the self:

> He wept; he pressed his face into the pillow and wept. An intoxicating joy ran through him, lifted him up, and it was incomparably sweeter than the world's sweetest pain. This was it, this was the drunken darkness that had filled him since the afternoon, this was what had stirred in his heart in the middle of the night, awakening him, quickening like first love within him. And in being granted this understanding and realization—not in words and sequential thoughts, but in the sudden bliss of internal illumination—he was already free, was truly liberated from all natural and artificial bonds and barriers.[86]

Like the Unnamed on the night of the conversion, or like Andrei Bolkonsky as he watched the sky above Austerlitz, Thomas Buddenbrook seems to have come to an agonizing revelation. But the next day, this lucidity has vanished: Thomas wakes up "feeling slightly embarrassed by the intellectual extravagances of the night"[87] and returns to his regular habits. He would like to start reading again, but asks himself whether it is right, if that knowledge really suits him:

> Still fully intending to read further from that wonderful book, he nevertheless began to ask himself whether his experiences of the previous night were truly something for him and of lasting value and whether, if death were to arrive, they would stand up to the practical test. His middle-class instincts were roused now—and his vanity as well: the fear of being seen

85. Thomas Mann, *Buddenbrooks: Verfall einer Familie* (1901); English translation *Buddenbrooks: The Decline of a Family,* trans. John E. Woods (New York: Random House, 1994), 631.

86. Mann, *Buddenbrooks: The Decline of a Family,* 725.

87. Ibid., 726.

as eccentric and ridiculous. Would such ideas really look good on him? Were they proper ideas for him, Senator Thomas Buddenbrook, head of the firm of Johann Buddenbrook? . . .

And about two weeks after that remarkable afternoon, he had arrived at the point where he abandoned the whole idea and told the maid to fetch a book that for some reason was lying in the drawer of the garden table and put it back in the bookcase.

And so Thomas Buddenbrook, who had stretched his hands out imploringly for high and final truths, sank back now into the ideas, images, and customary beliefs in which he had been drilled as a child.[88]

Supreme truths are now the possession of specialists, attainable only through the mediation of a philosopher, "an enormously superior intellect." They are unacceptable if one is the head of the firm Johann Buddenbrook, if one has a practical role in life and is therefore forced to dwell in the commonplaces that one has assumed to be true since childhood—what Heidegger, in *Being and Time,* calls *das Man,* "the One" ("that is what one does or say," "that is what people have to do or say"). Over the course of the twentieth century, the gap separating the thinking hero from the practical hero often remained insurmountable. For this reason, novels that were able to credibly fill this breach exerted a peculiar fascination. One of the reasons behind the critical success of Philip Roth's latest books resides in his willingness to take seriously the kind of reflections on American history and life in general that an adman or the owner of a glove factory might have. The expedients used by Roth show that this is no easy task. His characters are never left alone: they are always accompanied by the interpreting voice of the narrator, or his double, Nathan Zuckerman, as if the truth of ordinary characters needed to be translated into a more complex language, as if this truth needed to be extracted.

What is the meaning of the metamorphosis represented by Thomas Buddenbrook's crisis? Perhaps what novelists transposed into writing was an objective feature of contemporary social structures. For a good part of the twentieth century, in major cities as well as in small provincial towns, the members of the ruling classes still had a robust intellectual function: the systemic complexity and the division of labor had not yet fully segmented human aggregates, separating the cultural worlds of the classes and social

88. Ibid., 727.

strata. However, there was an intermediate step between this change in the real world and the changes occurring in literature. The nineteenth-century paradigm adapted to the modern world archaic, premodern literary forms premised on the centrality and wholeness of people. In this sense, the ability to think deeply about the meaning of life and on the state of the world became the intellectual counterpart of the capacity that many nineteenth-century heroes preserved to perform showy actions or make eloquent speeches. This is not just a simple reflection, then, but one that filters through the internal logic of literature.

In any case, whatever its origin, this state of things could not last long for several reasons: first, over the course of the nineteenth century, European narrative developed mimetic forms foreign to the anthropocentrism inherited from the past by the early nineteenth century; second, because the complexity of the social systems, which was growing beyond all measure, created more distance between the mentalities of the social classes and strata. For the elite intellectuals of the twentieth century, for those who judged the *doxa* of the masses from the perspective of traditional humanistic culture, it became increasingly difficult to view the prevailing common sense of the practical man in a serious way. And while abstract thought and estrangement turned into specialized activities, this transformation was inscribed into the language of literature, separating the intellectual hero from the common hero.

The Modern Forms of the *Romance*

Narrative that uses special characters always, or almost always, respects the logic of the *novel*, but places the interest outside the middle station of life: it preserves the armature of the realistic paradigm but tells stories about protagonists who are completely divorced from *medietas,* as if ordinary life had lost its charm.

The development of this area, slightly peripheral to the center, is not the only line of flight from everyday life that the novel took in this period: in the second half of the nineteenth century there emerged *new forms of the romance*. In the language of literary criticism, for the past few decades a large portion of these forms of contemporary romance have been referred to as "genre fiction" to convey their rigid, codified nature. The primary templates of genre fiction are the fantastic (or, in the language of the culture industry, fantasy), crime fiction, and science fiction. By crossbreeding them, we get the intermediate forms. While contemporary fantasy is the more or less degraded continuation of the literature of the fantastic that arose or became established during the Romantic era, crime fiction and science fiction emerged as structured genres in the mid-nineteenth century.[89]

In addition to genre fiction, the second half of the nineteenth century witnessed the rise of a new form of romance, packed with hidden allegorical senses, but with a modern allegorism devoid of any fixed hermeneutic key. *Moby-Dick* (1851) is one of the first examples of this type. This narrative family has become remarkably important over the past fifty years. It could be defined using a formula Roland Barthes used to describe the work of Italo Calvino:

> [Calvino] has a very distinctive imagination: essentially, the kind that Edgar Allan Poe staged in his work. We might call it the imagination of a certain kind of mechanics, or viewing imagination in relation to mechanics. The idea may appear somewhat paradoxical, because from a Romantic point of view one would think that the imagination is, on the contrary, a force that is anything but mechanical, extremely "spontaneous." Quite the contrary. The imagination, or perhaps a great imagination, is always the development of a certain kind of mechanics. In this respect, although with huge differences in style, there's an Edgar Allan Poe side to Calvino, because [Calvino] sets up a situation . . . that's unrealistic in terms of its faithfulness to the world, but only as far as the initial conditions are concerned, and then this unrealistic situation is developed in an implacably realistic and implacably logical way.[90]

89. Ernest Mandel, *Delightful Murder: A Social History of the Crime Story* (Minneapolis: University of Minnesota Press, 1984), 18ff.; Elsa de Lavergne, *La Naissance du roman policier français: du Second Empire à la Première Guerre mondiale* (Paris: Classiques Garnier, 2009); Paul K. Alkon, *Science Fiction before 1900* (1994) (New York: Routledge, 2002), chap. 1; Martin Willis, *Mesmerists, Monsters, and Machines: Science Fiction and the Cultures of Science in the Nineteenth Century* (Kent, OH: Kent State University Press, 2006), chap. 1; Irène Langlet, *La Science-fiction: lecture et poétique d'un genre littéraire* (Paris: Colin, 2006), 134ff.

90. Roland Barthes, "La Mécanique du charme" (1978), in Italo Calvino, *Le Chevalier inexistant* (Paris: Seuil, 1984), 1–2. For a definition and map of this narrative territory, see Massimo Rizzante, *Non siamo gli ultimi. La letteratura fra fine dell'opera e rigenerazione umana* (Milan: Effigie, 2009), 74ff., which resumes and develops the theoretical insights presented in "La Mécanique du charme." Barthes's piece was originally a radio interview for France Culture that was transcribed and published in the French edition of *The Nonexistent*

Barthes insists on the link between romance and logic that we find in the works of Calvino and, before him, in the narrative current to which Calvino is related: in the more cerebral and less visceral part of Poe's work, for example; but also in Robert Louis Stevenson, Lewis Carroll, and Marcel Schwob; and in Nabokov, Borges, and the writers that Borges influenced.[91] This fiction of the imagination, but with a controlled irrationality, this interweaving of romance and *Aufklärung*, or of romance and metaliterature, constitutes one of the most important narrative fringes in recent centuries. When this textual space took on defined features, it became possible to read the preceding literary history in a new way and to interpret certain premodern and early modern authors and genres as precursors of the "mechanical imagination." With a retrospective movement, then, the works of Ariosto and Jonathan Swift or the eighteenth-century *conte philosophique* can thus be included in the genealogical lineage that Barthes describes. What Kafka creates in his short stories and novels is a different but related mode. The stories he introduces into the structures of ordinary life cannot be explained by the categories of daytime logic—they disturb the familiar framework of certainties that underpins common sense.

The Sense of a Transformation

I have tried to describe the narrative territory that took shape between the second half of the nineteenth century and the first half of the twentieth century. What is the overarching sense of this transformation?

The main change was the crisis of the nineteenth-century paradigm and, in particular, that of its symbolic core, the melodramatic model. Scott, Balzac, and Dickens transferred devices at work in genres like epic and tragedy, which enact public conflicts between cosmic-historical individuals, to private individuals. In doing so, the melodramatic novelists grafted a vision of the world and life belonging to the age of heroes onto the age of prose. While the primary *raison d'être* of a technique of this sort is intraliterary (the inert survival of schemas that came into being during other epochs), this memory of antiquity could not have lasted long if it

Knight. It was not included in the first and second editions of the complete works of Barthes, published by Seuil in 1993–1995 and in 2002.

91. See Rizzante, *Non siamo gli ultimi*, 75–76.

had not anchored itself to a fact of reality. The melodramatic novel arose in an era when secular forms of life had collapsed and were replaced by other forms, history had become a lived experience of the masses, and it was plausible to think that people, subjects, or witnesses of an unprecedented transformation were involved in absolute conflicts. At a certain point this paradigm proved to be unrealistic. This happened when the institutions and forms of life ceased to change at the same speed as before, and modern society seemed to harden, losing its fluidity and turning into the superpersonal mechanism that Weber described using the metaphor of the iron cage. Universal forces were no longer revealed in the experience of private persons, and particular individuals, now regulated and controlled, signified only themselves: they are little monads (but endowed with windows, permeable to the environment) enclosed in systems. Today, the great collective history has a purely mechanical relationship with small, subjective stories. Today the only universality to which people can aspire is not that of the cosmic-historical individuals, but that of private life as a universal condition of modern human beings as it unfolds in novels of personal destinies.

However, the crisis of the nineteenth-century paradigm did not stop at the crisis of melodrama. The change had a much larger reach that touched the very heart of the theatrical model. Beginning in the second half of the nineteenth century, the life of people like us began to appear under a different light. It became increasingly difficult to discern the sign of great universal forces in the actions of private individuals. The space for narrative disruptions gradually shrank; lives became more predictable; the form of life in which people were immersed tended to be perceived as an unchangeable background, or one that could be changed only on the basis of dynamics beyond people's control. This diminishment of individual action in the public space, and therefore of theatricality, corresponded to a different way of interpreting events. Because the world lacked a great central event, and because the way of the world was seen as indifferent to the trajectories of individuals, as erecting obstacles or creating confusion, a new decentralized, nonhierarchical mode of perceiving life was able to take shape: plots were populated with secondary actions, ruptures, and dead time. It also became possible to locate the essential outside the external world. The most pervasive shift, the first, great inward turn that led to a work like *The Princesse de Clèves,* happened at the same time as the courtization of warriors in the court society,[92] when the aristocracy gradually lost its ability to act and physical violence was transformed into symbolic violence, ceremony, and the cult of distinction. It was in the court society that the psychological approach to human action matured,[93] when identities and destinies were no longer defined through significant deeds, and desires and conflicts spilled over into private life. It was in this sphere that people compared and interpreted each other.

But the century of psychological realism originated from a second inward turn. When the objective space for performing actions narrowed, when the essential was transferred *in interiore homine,* the inner life became more complex. No longer constrained by the unilateralism of action, the psyche emerged from the molds that had previously defined it: "yes, a man of the nineteenth century ought, indeed is morally bound, to be essentially without character; a man of character, a man who acts, is essentially limited."[94] But the inward turn, as we have seen, was not an isolated incident: in fact, the century of psychological realism coincided with the period during which few novelists sought the essential in estrangement or in essayistic reflection. All these movements brought narrative interest outside the public existence of individuals like us. At the beginning of the nineteenth century it seemed plausible to tell stories about private people as if they still lived in the age of heroes; at the beginning of the twentieth century, the prose of modern life had now permeated the novelistic architecture.

92. Elias, *The Civilizing Process,* p. 387.
93. Ibid., 401.
94. Fyodor Dostoevsky, *Zapiski iz podpol'ya* (1864); *Notes from Underground,* trans. Jessie Coulson (London: Penguin Books, 2003), 7.

CHAPTER EIGHT

On Contemporary Fiction

After Modernism

We have so far identified three phases in the history of modern narrative (from 1800 to 1850, from 1850 to 1900, and from 1900 to 1940), all marked by striking internal evolutions. Between 1800 and 1940, ground-breaking devices widened the field of possibilities that lay before novelists when they started to write. Authors and readers of this epoch perceived literature as inclined toward novelty and transformation. The idea already present in the thought of Friedrich Schlegel that beauty, like fashion, should change along with the times was a controversial topic in Baudelaire's time, before becoming a topos of the historical avant-gardes and modernism. This was also the period when the evolutionary paradigm gained a foot-hold that has long dominated histories of modern literature: the notion that the artistic space lives under a regime of permanent revolution, a principle Ezra Pound set out in a maxim about another modern genre ("No good poetry is ever written in a manner twenty years old").[1] According to this view, authors like Flaubert and Joyce would thus belong to two completely different historical eras, and the task of criticism would be to describe the progressive movement that separates them, as if culture arose through a series of small, consecutive breaks with the past. Also tied to this principle is the conviction that in each period there exists only a limited number of artistic works and schools, while all the others (to borrow the

1. Ezra Pound, "Retrospect" (1913–1918), in *Literary Essays of Ezra Pound* (Westport, CT: Greenwood Press, 1979), 11.

expression Hegel used to explain the irrelevance of Africa and Siberia in Universal Becoming) lie "out of the pale of History."[2] Originally a product of Romantic historicism, this model gained currency with the nineteenth-century avant-gardes and with the radical tides of modernism. According to this way of thinking, the evolutionary stages of the novel are marked by Flaubert's *A Sentimental Education* (1869) and not by Hugo's *Les Miserables* (1862); by Joyce's *Ulysses* (1922) and not by Forster's *Passage to India* (1924); by Nathalie Sarraute's *Planetarium* (1959) and not by Pasternak's *Dr. Zhivago* (1957). Although these pairs of works appeared at the same times, they are viewed as belonging to different developmental stages, some of which are innovative, "at the height of their times," and authentically historical (Flaubert, Joyce, Sarraute); others of which are conservative, lagging behind the times, and antihistorical (Hugo, Forster, Pasternak). Literary history is expected to dwell on the extreme fringes and pass over the rest; or, to use the military metaphors typical of this paradigm, it must concern itself with the avant-garde and forget the rearguard.

The fourth phase of modern narrative history, however, the one beginning after the end of modernism, definitively resists any such notions. It is true that between the beginning of the twentieth century and the 1930s the novel underwent a transformation that, from a long-term perspective, could also be interpreted as a progressive, continuous motion, but the works written between the 1930s and the 1950s were often less technically advanced and less innovative than those written during the previous two decades. It was the first time this had happened in the modern era. The second wave of the twentieth-century avant-gardes, the one beginning to develop in the mid-1950s, was not able to reinstate the progressive schema of literary history that reigned before the 1930s. What had changed?

The Decline of the New

Between the beginning of the nineteenth century and the early decades of the twentieth century, a few literary inventions became predominant and

2. Georg Wilhelm Friedrich Hegel, *Vorlesungen über die Philosophie der Geschichte*; English translation *The Philosophy of History*, trans. John Sibree (Kitchener, ON: Batoche Books, 2001) 109ff.; this quote from p. 118. On the Hegelianism implicit in historiographical models of the nineteenth-century avant-gardes, see Arthur C. Danto, *After the End of Art* (Princeton, NJ: Princeton University Press, 1997).

grammaticalized. This transformation had two effects: it opened up new possibilities and sidelined others, pushing them "out of the pale of History." This approach would be codified by the artists and critics of the twentieth century, but the phenomenon existed before the 1900s, since the modernist and avant-garde perception of aesthetic becoming was the extreme version of an attitude whose essential traits date back to Romanticism—in other words, to the time when the idea of a linear, irreversible transformation of forms entered into the discourse of European aesthetics. When Balzac talks about the new possibilities that Sir Walter Scott introduced into European narrative, he adopts the same mental schemas that the culture of the early twentieth century would revive.

By 1850 the European novel had already grammaticalized some of its innovations: the theatrical plot, the transparent writing style, and the new conceptual ether sensitive to historical dynamics had become part of the narrative field, one of the possibilities always available for use. In the same process, a few of the devices dear to eighteenth-century taste had become obsolete and were marginalized. The insularity that a substantial part of British fiction suffered from in the first half of the nineteenth century was partly due to the survival of techniques in English narrative that the continental novel, prevalently French, considered outdated but that Dickens or Thackeray continued to use as a matter of course: the comic mimesis of everyday life, poetic justice, and a philosophical ether composed of static, moralistic categories.[3] Then, between the 1850s and the 1930s, the European novel absorbed into its grammar other groundbreaking devices: disjointed plots, new ways of imagining the psychic life, and new narrative mediations. These techniques were collectively accepted, altering the range of possibilities available to high-culture writers. At the same time, a few older possibilities (melodramatic plots, personages marked by a rigid *charakter*) passed into disuse: Balzac, writes Ortega y Gasset, sounds artificial and *à-peu-près* in 1925.[4]

In the 1930s this evolutionary schema began to crack: innovations continued to exist, of course, but they no longer became part of the narrative grammar in the way they used to. Even when the new avant-garde movements

3. See Franco Moretti, *The Way of the World*, 181ff.; and by the same author, *Atlas of the European Novel, 1800–1900*, 151ff.

4. José Ortega y Gasset, *Ideas sobre la novela*, in *Obras completas*, 165.

of the 1950s, 1960s, and 1970s reintroduced extremely experimental narrative, the new approaches no longer had the force to change the repertoire of shared manners and failed to become institutions. Proust, Kafka, Woolf, Joyce, and Musil transformed European narrative far more deeply than Sarraute, Beckett, Claude Simon, Uwe Johnson, or Perec. This is not because their innovations were more radical, but because these earlier techniques came to be part of the shared narrative vocabulary. At the same time, the ability to expel, exclude, push out of the pale of history forms that were considered outdated seems to have diminished. As we noted, Western narrative written between the late 1930s and the 1950s, if viewed from a distance like a faraway landscape, appears to be less revolutionary than the narrative written during the three previous decades. At the beginning of the twenty-first century, we can say that the innovations put forward by the second phase of the twentieth-century avant-gardes have remained confined to a big historical enclave. Furthermore, the imperative, binding character of novelty itself has dissolved: the idea spread that there exists a tradition of the new, a repertoire of experimentation that is equal and opposite to the repertoire of preservation, and that the art from the avant-garde belongs to a family, extends a genealogy, and is just as filled with epigones as art from the non-avant-garde. As a result, the new has lost prestige as a criterion of judgment, and works that might have been criticized for their technical backwardness at the time they were published, such as *Buddenbrooks, Dr. Zhivago,* and Grossman's *Life and Fate* (or, in Italy, Tomasi di Lampedusa's *The Leopard* and Elsa Morante's *History*), were less and less prone to these kinds of attacks. Contemporary arts form a disjointed region cohabited by diverse factions that evolves without following any telos.

Only during the past four decades has this perception become widespread, but the first signs of the discontinuity were perceptible as early as the late 1930s. They became fully visible at the same time that thought on the dialectic of enlightenment emerged—in other words when the crisis of the idea of progress became a theme of contemporary philosophical discussion. It became common currency during the years when tensions internal to mass societies, the development of totalitarianisms, and World War II transformed the way elite intellectuals in the West looked at history. The search for the new in the world of narrative already began to wane during the 1930s. But for the perception of this threshold to enter into common sense, the literary domain had to pass through another phase, one that was both artistic and political. This happened a few decades later, when the second wave of twentieth-century avant-gardes had become exhausted and mass trust in the future as progress or redemption had become tarnished. At this point, the understanding that arts in the West had entered a postmodernist period became pervasive. At the same time, discourses on the dwindling hope for a future radically different from the present extended from artistic domains into the form of life that incorporates these domains, and thought on artistic postmodernism became thought on the surpassing of the modern era, which is to say, on postmodernity.

A Multiple Archipelago

How should the medium-length phase that began during the 1930s be interpreted? While it is true that novelty was no longer integrated and institutionalized with the same enthusiasm, a steady, magmatic stream of individual innovations continued to appear. From a perspective of long duration, the structures of sense that originated during the Romantic period are still with us. One of these is the anarchic logic governing the arts: every creator or artist seeks to express himself or herself in an original way, so much so that at first glance the modern aesthetic space gives the impression of an endless, chaotic jumble of different works. Nevertheless, there were some waves of collective innovation in this apparently punctiform territory that generated large, unprecedented literary regions unknown to the novel of the nineteenth and early twentieth centuries and recognizable if viewed with farsighted eyes. Unlike what happened previously, these currents did not subvert the shared narrative grammar, nor did they extensively alter the way of telling stories, constructing characters, or managing the voice of the narrator. Instead, they produced rather large, relatively isolated territories that intersected with the preexisting forms, generating a ragged landscape.

An atlas of contemporary literary plurality has to begin with a preliminary observation: after World War II, the genre of the novel became truly planetary, since Europe and the United States began to steadily (and not just occasionally) absorb works coming from Eastern and colonial cultures, until the birth of a *global novel*. The first of the innovative narrative trends was magic realism, which developed outside Europe during the 1940s, and after the success of Gabriel García Márquez went on to become the dominant form of the postcolonial novel. The second were the clusters of experimentation that emerged between the late 1950s and the 1970s, especially in the literatures of continental Europe. These experiments reflected and extended the tradition of the first twentieth-century avant-gardes and modernism, but in extreme forms. The third was postmodernist narrative in a narrow sense, which developed in the United States between the 1960s and 1970s especially thanks to authors born between 1920 and 1940 (Gaddis, Vonnegut, Barth, Barthelme, Doctorow, DeLillo, Pynchon, and others). Through resemblance, their works then served to define the poetics of authors who were not American, such as Italo Calvino or Umberto Eco in Italy. Each of these currents introduced new techniques; each of them created a genealogy that is still alive at the beginning of the twenty-first century; and yet none of them was able to establish their devices as models with the same force or the same ability to create collective habits that the major innovations possessed between the beginning of the nineteenth century and the 1930s. A few decades ago it was thought that postmodernism would impose its own hegemony on high-culture literature just as the avant-gardes and modernism had done in the early 1900s; in the early 2000s, though, we know that magic realism, the second phase of the twentieth-century experimentations, and postmodernist narrative did no more than add provinces and islands to a variegated territory where diverse literary families make their collective home. At times remote from each other, at times hybridized, they are always, in any case, multiform. The archipelago of contemporary fiction is plural.

What has occurred over the past few decades allows us to observe it in a new way and discern a continuity of long duration. Some of the most interesting narrative works to appear between the end of the twentieth century and the beginning of the twenty-first century elude all the taxonomic categories and oppositional pairings invented by literary theory in order to group texts together. This includes both recent categories (postmodernism, avant-garde, and tradition) and those of medium duration (nineteenth-century realism, modernism). Which classification in literary history can be assigned to works like *Le Labyrinthe du monde* (*The World Is a Maze*) by Marguerite Yourcenar (1974–1988), the autobiographical trilogies by Elias Canetti (1977–1985) and Edmund White (1982–1997), *A Late Divorce* (1982) by A. B. Yehoshua, the short stories that Raymond Carver wrote between the 1970s and 1980s, those that Alice Munro wrote from the 1970s to date, *Flesh and Blood* (1995) by Michael Cunningham, the novels of Philip Roth, *The Elementary Particles* (1998) by Michel Houellebecq, *Boyhood* (1997) and *Youth* (2002) by J. M. Coetzee, *The Kindly Ones* (2006) by Jonathan Littell—in other words, some of the most important works of fiction to be written between the last decades of the twentieth century and the beginning of the twenty-first? Where do they get penciled in on our blueprints? One might try to pigeonhole them into known categories using the prefix *neo-*. From a technical point of view, *A Late Divorce* and *Flesh and Blood* owe a lot to Faulkner and Virginia Woolf: it would be legitimate to interpret them as neomodernist novels. And yet they lack an essential characteristic of modernism: their authors are not interested in experimenting with radically new narrative forms, nor do they want to discover or fully explore uncharted stylistic solutions. In *A Late Divorce* and *Flesh and Blood*, modernism seems to have become repertoire. Also, while a category of this sort can be adapted to certain books, it does not cover the entire area we are discussing. The authors we mentioned are not linked exclusively to modernist forms—their books are technically more backward, more conservative, than the models that inspire them. The common traits uniting these writers lie elsewhere: all of them offer serious treatments of episodes set in an everyday context against a backdrop with a sense of historical dynamics; none of them is attracted by novelty for the sake of novelty; all of them look to the past two centuries of Western narrative with the attitude of someone who feels free to reuse techniques appearing in the second half of the nineteenth century just as much as at the beginning of the twentieth century, in Tolstoy, in modernist literature, or in postmodernist literature. What are we to make of these characteristics and their peculiar mix?

First and foremost, they show that the three long-duration infrastructures that prevailed at the beginning of the nineteenth century still occupy the center of the modern literary space. Magic realism and postmodernist narrative had programmatically rejected them, the former by reintegrating forms of magic and adventure, the latter by overthrowing the hierarchy between playfulness and seriousness or by indulging in metaliterature. The fiction of the second avant-garde wave focused for its part on devices of estrangement in order to create new forms of narrative. Instead, the works we are talking about preserved a continuity with the novel that over the past few centuries has represented the conflicts of common life in a tragic and problematic mode. In other words, they move in the realm of the "serious realism of modern times [that] cannot represent man otherwise than as embedded in a total reality, political, social, and economic, which is concrete and constantly evolving."[5] Ways of problematically treating ordinary life have changed, but its background radiation has not faded out: the seriousness of everyday life has continued to form the core of literary history for the past two hundred years—the evolution we are experiencing is part of a systemic continuity. In the face of this subterranean persistence, other narrative modes are peripheral trends or short-term and medium-term fashions.

But the existence of works like the ones we have listed also attests to a changed relationship with the past. A few months after Jonathan Littell's *The Kindly Ones* came out, a reviewer attacked the novel in the following way:

> How can you write exactly as if you were in the nineteenth century? As if Joyce, Proust, Hammett, Faulkner, and Robbe-Grillet had never existed, not to mention Toni Morrison, Rushdie, and Houellebecq. Can you imagine for one second a contemporary artist who paints like Monet? The weirdness of literature—the creative domain that is the least aware of its own history. Littell may very well have brought off the *tour de force* of writing a novel on the Shoah in a deliriously anachronistic form, as if he were writing a century before the very event that changed the face of literature for all time.[6]

This string of *idées reçues* encapsulates a way of understanding the history of the arts that was typical of radical modernism and the avant-gardes. An entire literary landscape can be glimpsed against the backdrop of these few lines: the aesthetic myth of novelty, the conviction that there has to be a necessary correspondence between changing times and changing artistic forms, and a popularized and sketchy notion of nineteenth-century narrative. It even includes a reference to Adorno's comment on the relationship

---

5. Auerbach, *Mimesis*, 463.
6. Sylvain Bourmeau, "Bête à Goncourt," *Les Inrockuptibles* 569 (October 24, 2006): 69.

between the Holocaust and literature: nothing is left out. During the second experimental wave of the twentieth century, Robbe-Grillet argued that "to praise a young writer in 1965 because he 'writes like Stendhal' is doubly disingenuous. . . . Flaubert wrote the new novel of 1860, Proust the new novel of 1910. The writer must proudly consent to bear his own date."[7] In reality, Littell does not write exactly like in the nineteenth century, because *The Kindly Ones* is composed of a mix of elements. And yet it is true that the nineteenth-century narrative tradition (Stendhal, Flaubert, and especially Tolstoy) and its twentieth-century reinterpretations (Vasily Grossman) are technically essential to the architecture of *The Kindly Ones*. Between the end of the twentieth century and the beginning of the twenty-first, writers can pick up on devices that come from Tolstoy (Littell), from Woolf (Cunningham in *Flesh and Blood*, organized like *The Years*), or from Faulkner (Yehoshua in *A Late Divorce*). They may refuse to write the *nouveau roman* of 2000 and to instead reuse 150-year-old narrative materials. For this reason, the persistence of these sorts of works confirms that when thinking about literary history over the past few centuries, and, more generally, about the history of culture, we must imagine its evolution in a different way—leaving behind the paradigms that presuppose a perpetual renewal of forms.

If we look at literary history from the point of view of technical changes, the narrative possibilities used by novelists at the beginning of the twenty-first century for the most part originated between the second and fourth thresholds that we identified: between 1850 and 1940. From this perspective, the first generation of writers that are still contemporary is that of George Eliot, Flaubert, Dostoevsky, and Tolstoy. The storehouse of available techniques was expanded by other devices after them, but the ways of constructing characters, plots, and narrators that these novelists invented or perfected still furnish solutions that twenty-first century novels continue to use today. Their greatest works are still somehow contemporary to our epoch, while those of Scott, Balzac, or Manzoni show signs of an era that no longer speaks to us.

But beyond narrative techniques, what unites the tradition of the modern novel from the turning point that we nominally located in 1800 until today is the centrality of existential realism. As a constant of long duration, the

7. Robbe-Grillet, *For a New Novel*, 10.

serious mimesis of everyday life set against a historical and dynamic background gives form to the narrative of our times. Challenges, rejections, alternatives, and escapes have been and will be many, but in the end, from a perspective spanning centuries, in different versions that change continuously or return cyclically, this deep structure still occupies the center of the narrative space. To change this status would require a transformation comparable to what resulted in the phase of human history whose protracted twilight we are currently living through—the modern age.

Conclusion

A Theory of the Novel

The Genre of Particularity

In the Introduction to this book, speaking about the schemas that critical thought uses to imagine the causal relationship between forms of life and language games, I referred to Althusser and Jameson to distinguish between a mechanical paradigm, an expressive paradigm, and a structural paradigm. The first conceives of reality as a network of regional microevents linked by small relations of cause and effect (the influence of one author on another, of an environment on a group of writers, of an editorial choice on a work or genre). It has met with remarkable success in histories of culture with a philological and positivist slant, which for the past century and a half have proliferated in academic journals. Even today those who speak of "scientific rigor" in relation to literary criticism often refer to this model, which claims to export the truth protocols of the natural sciences into the domain of culture: the result is a tremendously impoverished scope of problems and phenomena. The expressive paradigm hierarchically distinguishes between planes of reality, separating original ones from derivative ones. This approach is typical of Marxist cultural history in its popularized version and it generates the distinction between structure and super-structure, between "the ultimately determining instance" of the economy and the consequences that this primary level is said to have on all the others. The third paradigm imagines that the totality is immanent in all its ways of being and that each plane of the real expresses an aspect of the whole. The three schemas are not mutually exclusive, and they all appear in this book, but the structural paradigm is unquestionably the cornerstone that holds up the construction.

Theory of the Novel presents a long-duration history of the ways in which European culture has articulated its stories. It also offers an interpretation of the relationship that mimesis, narrative, and the novel have entertained with other games of truth and, more generally, with the idea of truth itself. So far I have traced out the internal history of a genre; we now need to investigate the meaning of this process, what it allows us to understand about the form of life in which we are immersed. What contents lie crystallized in the novel? What history lies sedimented in these works?

The novel is the genre of particularity: it expresses a plane of being that for centuries was ignored or grasped only with difficulty by other discursive formations. Even when the invention of photography and cinema enabled the sensible appearance to be represented through the media of image and sound, the novel preserved its supremacy in the mimesis of the interior life and of the relations between human beings and the forces that traverse them. Telling stories about anything in any way whatsoever means affirming the centrality of singular individuals, reproducing their objective ways of being, imagining their subjective ways of being, and following the minute, anomic dispersion of all that exists. The genre we are talking about "carr[ies] the incommensurable to extremes in the representation of human life":[1] using words, it tells about all the appearances that particularities can assume. In the first place, it lingers on proper names, follows the paths of individuals, and multiplies the epicenters of sense that attribute a meaning and a *Stimmung* to what happens. Secondly, it places particular beings into regional and transitory forms of life. It is an "atmospheric" and "provincial" genre[2] that describes microcosms: "remembering the titles of a novel is like remembering a city where we once lived for some time."[3] It is a form that, in its own logic, introjects the objective fragmentation of the world into worlds. Contemporary with the age of exploration, the rise of modern states, the demographic growth of the West, the increase in social complexity and division of labor, it emerged

1. Benjamin, "The Storyteller: Reflections on the Works of Nicolai Leskov," 87.
2. Ortega y Gasset, *Ideas sobre la novela*, 185, 198.
3. Ibid., 195.

in the epoch when the spheres of life differentiated, rendering the effects of this fragmentation.

But there is a third aspect to particularity: in addition to telling stories about anything, novels tell stories in any way whatsoever. In classical and classicist literature, the style is set a priori by conventions: the epic voice already knows what to talk about and what form to adopt. Novelists, on the other hand, are not backed up by any collective norms that restrict the choice of stories or ways of telling them. In transmitting real or possible stories, the author chooses a few episodes from the infinite variety of beings that, for the community he or she belongs to, are equivalent to countless others, putting them into a form that can also be imagined differently. Multiple points of view and the theoretical possibility of telling things in a different way abound in every novel, because it is assumed that each person, in theory, has the right to represent the world according to his or her perceptual and ethical angle.

Since nothing legitimates a priori a certain story or a certain style, since these decisions are freely taken, the act of narrating embodies without filters or intermediate steps what happens in every form of mimesis. Writing a novel means choosing a few discontinuities out of an unlimited expanse of possible stories and condemning thousands of others to oblivion; it means assuming a responsibility toward the real and the possible. This responsibility is redoubled by the choice of how to tell the story, that is, how to judge the fragment that has been isolated out of the seriality. In both cases, what is latent in every mimetic act becomes manifest. The novel exhibits the subjective nature of our judgments on the world: it is the flagship that literature ranges against systematic thought, against science and philosophy. This is partly because in the language games of science and philosophy certain points of view are presented as better than others, but every point of novelistic view, even that of the most omniscient of narrators, always coexists with other epicenters of sense. This coexistence is asymmetric and symmetric at the same time. It is asymmetric because the narrator is always in a higher position with respect to the protagonists (he or she sees them from the outside, knows more than they do, and objectively transcends them); it is symmetric because what the characters think never entirely loses its value. This applies to narrative as a language game. As we saw in Chapter 1, even Hector and Priam can inspire our compassion; even an enemy's point of view can be embraced. In the novel, this

openness appears even clearer: not even the most authoritarian of narrators has a complete monopoly on sense. In the end, his or her version is
just one more point of view, one way of describing a microcosm that, in
theory, also provides for other possible outlooks.

Relativism and Perspectivism

The result of the threefold particularity that novels introject into their logic
is the relativistic and perspectivist nature of the *Weltanschauung* conveyed
by this game of truth. The modern success of the genre is mainly linked to
its ability to make us see the world through the eyes and conscience of
someone else, its ability to allow us to step into a possible life that is not
ours—and perhaps even to allow different and irreconcilable outlooks to
exist in the same text and on the same page, all of which are endowed with
a legitimacy and rightness of their own.

Novelistic relativism concerns not only the interweaving of worlds that
takes place in a single text, but also the accumulation of texts. When we
close a novel and then open up a new one, we change microcosms and
value spheres. Every reader may have his or her favorite novels, but the
worlds that the individual texts create are equivalent, because the intrinsic
meaning of the values is not essential to understand and appreciate the
stories:

> No horizon . . . is interesting because of its subject matter. Any horizon
> is interesting because of its *form,* because of its form of horizon, i.e., its
> cosmos or total world. Microcosm and macrocosm are both cosmos in
> the same way. . . . The relativity between horizon and interest—the fact
> that every horizon has its *own* interest—is the vital law that makes the
> novel possible in the aesthetic order.[4]

Modern novels do not offer models or *exempla.* There may exist an af-
finity between characters and readers, but more frequently this is not the
case: we would do very little reading if we identified only with the heroes
we resemble. In actuality, we very often feel compassion and fear for characters who have completely different opinions and needs from our own.
The ease with which the average reader identifies with a variety of entirely

---

4. Ibid., 198.

different characters, adapting his or her own horizon each time to constantly new horizons, is a sign that, in his or her eyes, the motivations that drive the protagonists of the modern novel have lost any substantial significance. The existence of a genre that allows the desires and the worlds of others to be shared without judging their intrinsic value is eloquent. This literary space within which it becomes possible to express points of view so different as to be irreconcilable is governed by the maxim that Thomas Buddenbrook applied to his own life: "All human endeavour is merely symbolic."[5] Since there no longer exists an absolute scale to which to appeal, "a man can be a Caesar in an old commercial city on the Baltic,"[6] the fate of a businessman from Lübeck deserves the same interest that other cultures might have reserved for the fate of a prince, and the story of the maid Pamela Andrews can move us with the force of a tragedy.

Few books express the deep logic of the novel as well as Tolstoy's major works. In *War and Peace* and *Anna Karenina,* the narrator goes into extraordinary detail in describing the bubbles of desires and meanings inside of which individuals move around. He locates them side by side on the same plane, without creating any hierarchies. The seriousness with which each person is treated and the way the details of his or her world are lingered on create an objectively relativistic structure that is at odds with the authoritative word of the narrator. What issues from this is a perpetually shifting balance between the perspectivism implicit in the structure of the whole and the judgments of the narrator. Above, around, and in the midst of this interweaving of human interests, world history takes up its place, following its own mechanisms, blind to the wishes of private individuals, and sweeping their fates along with it.

Consider one of the most beautiful scenes in *War and Peace,* in which Tolstoy tells the story of Natasha Rostova's first grand ball.[7] Although Natasha has been getting ready since eight in the morning, she is late. The Rostovs have decided to arrive at the ball at half past ten. Now it is ten: her mother and cousin Sonya are ready, but the skirt Natasha has chosen is too long. At the last moment, crouched on the ground, the housemaids

5. Mann, *Buddenbrooks*, bk. 6, chap. 7, p. 353.
6. Ibid., bk. 5, chap. 4, p. 270.
7. Tolstoy, *War and Peace*, bk. 2, part 3, chaps. 14–17.

try to shorten it, hoping the seam will hold. Natasha is so overwhelmed that she cannot even think. Once she is in the carriage and has calmed down for a moment, she reflects on what is happening. She is about to make her debut in society, before the sovereign and the most fashionable young men of Petersburg, dressed as an adult.

The carriage pulls up in front of the palace. Natasha gets out, enters the vestibule, goes up the stairs, and is blinded by the view; dazzled by the light and brilliance of the guests' images reflected in the mirrors, she loses her own. In the end, stunned and distraught, she crosses the threshold into the first room. The rite of presentations reassures her: she realizes she has made a good impression on the hostess and sees two people she knows among the guests, Pierre Bezukhov and Andrei Bolkonsky. Then, suddenly, the crowd divides down the middle; the orchestra begins to play, and the sovereign makes his entrance, followed by the host and hostess. The dancing can begin. More than half of the ladies already have a partner; Natasha is among those who remain waiting, pressed against the wall:

> She stood, her thin arms lowered, her barely defined bosom rising rhythmically, holding her breath, her shining, frightened eyes looking straight ahead with an expression of readiness either for the greatest happiness or for the greatest grief. She was interested neither in the sovereign nor in any of the important persons Mme Peronsky pointed out—she had one thought: "Can it be that no one will come up to me, can it be that I won't dance among the first, can it be that all these men won't notice me, who now don't even seem to see, and if they look at me, it's with such an expression as if they were saying: 'Ah! it's not her, there's no point in looking!' No, it can't be!"[8]

Nobody invites her for the first dance: Natasha remains alone with Sonya, "as if in a forest, in this crowd of strangers," while an adjutant of the sovereign asks them to step further aside so as not to disturb the dancers. Seeing herself relegated to a corner of the room with her mother and cousin, almost as if it were a family reunion, Natasha is about to cry when, right at that moment, by chance, Pierre Bezukhov notices her. He sees that the girl is desperate and asks Andrei Bolkonsky, who has the reputation of being a good dancer, to partner her. Everything changes: Natasha begins to

---

8. Ibid., chap. 16, p. 459.

dance magnificently; all kinds of people take note of her; after Bol-konsky, other young men step up to invite her. Natasha is unaware of anything, because she is illuminated by a childlike, totalizing serenity: "She was happier than she had ever been before in her life. She was in that highest degree of happiness when a person becomes perfectly kind and good, and does not believe in the possibility of evil, unhappiness, and grief."[9]

This scene provides a graphic summary of what we have discussed thus far. Over the course of an entire chapter, the reader participates in the story of a girl who is invited for the first time to a grand ball. We share in her anxiety about getting dressed and being late; her wonder at the palace as it opens its doors; the momentary calm that follows the presentations; and then the anguish of those who are not picked to dance, a pain which is intense for the person experiencing it but trivial when seen from the eyes of an outsider; the anguish of not making a good impression at this sort of social event; and finally, the subjectively limitless and objectively futile joy of someone who is admired and desired by others at a party. It is the night of New Year's Eve 1809: a few years previously and a few years later, Russia and Europe as a whole had been and would be shaken by the Napoleonic wars. In earlier chapters the narrator had described the battle of Austerlitz: he presented the scene, in the absolute terms of a sacred text, in which the wounded Andrei Bolkonsky, looking upward above the battling armies, sees the vanity of human endeavors and the beauty of a sky that offers neither salvation nor redemption. We will witness the advance of the French into Russia and the war. Some of the people who will die in battle are attending the New Year's Eve soirée: for example Anatoly Kuragin, who will try to seduce Natasha and who watches the women at the ball with haughtiness and self-assurance, because he knows that he is one of the most admired young men in Petersburg; and especially Andrei Bolkonsky, who will fall in love with the girl and ask her to marry him, but who will not survive the battle of Borodino. In parts of the novel, Tolstoy presents the thoughts and words of Napoleon, Emperor Alexander, and Kutuzov; in yet other parts he tells the story of Pierre and Andrei, the intellectual heroes who search for the meaning of life. A little after the ball scene, an essay written in conceptual language presents a philosophy of history, interrupting the narrative mimesis and the illusion that personal

9. Ibid., chap. 17, p. 462.

life is the only reality. But regardless of what we have witnessed and re-gardless of what is going to take place, page after page, we avidly follow the story of Natasha: the story of a girl who, blind to the affairs of the world, pursues her limited aims and desires, devoid of any substantial im-portance and irrelevant to the collective fate. Nevertheless, when this epi-sode is being told, we are ready to narrow our gaze. We understand that in the game of happiness and unhappiness, of balance and imbalance that agi-tates us, the contents we use to fill it up are valueless in themselves and have a meaning only for us, and we share the perspectivist conclusion that Pierre comes to during his captivity: "He had learned that . . . the man who suffers because one leaf is askew in his bed of roses, suffers as much as he now suffered falling asleep on the bare, damp ground, one side getting cold as the other warmed up."[10]

For us, the happiness of Natasha, the values of her world, the logic of her microcosm, take on the utmost importance in these pages, just as the desires of any other individual and the logic of any other microcosm do in novels that successfully engage our interest. This segmentation of the world into worlds is the first content crystallized in the genre of the novel. Swept away by the democratic leveling of personal aims and desires, hierarchies disappear.

An Analytics of Existence

Perspectivism is not the only content that lies sedimented in the novel, though. Another layer of meaning shines below the fragmentation into microworlds. In addition to talking about anything in any way whatso-ever, the novel *tells stories:* the dissemination of value spheres occurs ac-cording to the language game of narrative, and inscribed in the logic of this game is a discourse on finite beings—an analytics of existence. Choosing to tell a story (as opposed to engaging in abstract thought, or counting, or writing in a form that completely excludes plot and narrator) means to accept an ontology: it means to assume that reality is composed of particular beings who are subject to time, agitated by an imbalance, and located in a world. In narrative representation people are not abstract or self-centering or disembodied or static or alone, unlike what may occur in

10. Ibid., bk. 4, part 3, chap. 12, p. 1060.

language games like science, philosophy, or lyric poetry. Rather, they are proper names thrown into a here and now, placed in the midst of others, cut through by influences, exposed to circumstances and paths, and surrounded by a network of actions, words, and meanings that decide the meaning or meaninglessness, happiness or unhappiness, peace of mind or anxiety of every one of us. If the possibility of describing anything in any way contains a relativistic element, the existential analytic implicit in the narrative reflects an image of the world. There are two contents that get crystallized in the novel form: the idea that reality is inherently multifaceted due to the perspectivist multiplication of egos, and the idea that individuals, regardless of the content of their lives, are thrown into time and enclosed in a local sphere of forces, environments, and plots that decide the destiny of each person.

Of all the language games our culture has developed, the novel is the one that shows in the most detail what it means to exist in time and in a world. Think of the philosophical significance of the two images we use to unravel the logic of narratives: *point of view* and *plot*. The first descends from Renaissance thought on pictorial perspective and circulated in the philosophical vocabulary of the seventeenth century.[11] One might think that a metaphor of this sort could not be applied to an art like narrative, which is completely extraneous to the medium of the image; and yet, literary criticism appropriated "point of view" and transformed it into an indispensable concept. This happened because the metaphor incisively condenses the two contents crystallized in the narrative form: every finite being is an epicenter of sense (that is, a "point of view," an outlook on the real and the possible), and the beings are included in a world that embraces them as finite subjects, located in a specific place, and therefore endowed with a necessarily partial vision.[12] The presuppositions that made Nietzsche's *Perspektivismus* possible two centuries later took shape thanks to

11. James Elkins, *The Poetics of Perspective* (Ithaca, NY: Cornell University Press, 1994), chap. 1.

12. On the process of the "objectification of the subjective" that took place in perspective, see Erwin Panofsky, *Die Perspektive als "symbolische Form"* (1927); English translation *Perspective as Symbolic Form* (New York: Zone Books, 1991), 60. On the "perspective paradigm," see H. Damisch, *L'Origine de la perspective* (1987); English translation *The Origin of Perspective*, trans. John Goodman (Cambridge, MA: MIT Press, 2000), 19–20.

the vocabulary of pictorial perspective,[13] the same one that was appropriated by narrative theory. The image of plot (*intrigue* in French, *filo della storia* in Italian) points to the same dialectic. Personal trajectories interweave to compose a fabric that transcends the individual parts, that is moved by time, and that takes a definitive form only at the end.

Point of view and plot are connected to the systemic, environmental ontology that we examined in Chapters 4 and 6. They presuppose that human beings are structurally restless and out of balance. No moment, not even the most beautiful, can be stopped in stories because time and desire stir up every *nunc stans* and generate movement—hence the importance we give to the way the tension is relieved, to the ending. Literally or metaphorically, the endings of stories coincide with the two existential situations in which time, desires, and tension with the world disappear: happiness and death. These zones of stasis elude stories. If death is the archetype of narrative endings,[14] and if boredom projects death onto life ("deadly boring," *mourir d'ennui, tödliche Langeweile, aburrimiento mortal, noia mortale*), the experience of happiness is the most refractory to the story form, because every unhappy family is unhappy in its own way, but all happy families resemble each other. The relief communicated by a happy ending stems from the resolution of potential conflict between the self and reality. In commercial literature and in commercial movies, in the arts whose aim is entertainment and not knowledge, this type of conclusion is almost always obligatory.

Discursive Transformations

What changes might give rise to this sort of discursive formation? We could start with a historical reflection: precisely when the novel, literature, and mimesis emancipated themselves from the safeguards of Christian aesthetic Platonism, the cultural frameworks underwent several epochal changes. The rise of the novel genre must be understood within this wider horizon.

13. Antonio Somaini, *Rappresentazione prospettica e punto di vista. Da Leon Battista Alberti ad Abraham Bosse* (Milan: Cuem, 2004), 4ff.

14. Kermode, *The Sense of an Ending*; Ricœur, *Time and Narrative*, vol. 1; Peter Brooks, *Reading for the Plot: Design and Intention in Narrative* (Cambridge, MA: Harvard University Press, 1984), chap. 4.

1. In his *Aesthetics,* Hegel reflected on the past character of art. Human history has experienced periods during which works of art communicated an image of the world that contemporaries judged as primary and corresponding to the thing-in-itself, while for modern individuals true knowledge no longer appears in an aesthetic form, but rather through the medium of the concept. Art maintains an archaic relationship with truth. Following his philosophy of history, Hegel situates the beginning of this archaism at the height of Christianity.

In reality, the *Vergangenheitscharakter* of the aesthetic sphere is in the first place a consequence of Platonism and Western metaphysics: it is a sign that the narrative frontier discussed in the *Republic* continues to exert its influence on us. Still today, in order to receive a salary as legitimate bearers of knowledge about the world, we must present our knowledge through the medium of the concept, as do modern philosophers, scientists, specialists in the human sciences, and historians. Artists have a different public status: they are paid as experts in a *techne,* an *ars,* not as possessors of official knowledge. The relationship between mimesis and truth remains problematic for us: works of art still need to be explained; criticism and educational institutions continue to translate the language of art into the form of judgments and concepts; Western aesthetics can still be read as a continuous debate on the idea that poets are liars. The very existence of a philosophy of art is an organic offshoot of the discursive split sanctioned by the character of Socrates, who called for poets to be banned from the polis until their defenders were able to demonstrate, through reasoning, that the practice of mimesis is not only pleasurable but also useful to the life of the community.[15] By reflecting on the truth content of the arts, modern aesthetics and criticism respond to Plato in the form that Plato wanted.

But even if this split still remains, art has not taken on a past character. On the contrary: in very few historical periods has art had the importance it has commanded during the past two centuries. For modern culture, the aesthetic languages are not confined to embellishing the truths that philosophy, the natural sciences, the human sciences, and history express in pure form. Today, mimesis reveals aspects of the human condition that elude concepts, reasoning, and numbers; it holds an importance that it

15. Plato, *Republic* 10.607c–e.

never had after Plato; it has fully reclaimed its place as a book of life. That is why the main task of contemporary aesthetics and criticism is to transpose into the form of ideas the content of truth that lies deposited in mimesis, translating into the medium of the concept the image of the world that Virgil, Michelangelo, Proust, or Kubrick expressed in the medium of their specific language and that could not be fully articulated in any other way. This problem never presented itself for ancient aesthetics, or it did so in a different way: artists were masters of truth to the extent that they adorned and transmitted, in the form of allegories, *sententiae* and *exempla,* philosophical, religious, moral, historical, cosmological, and technical knowledge that already existed and that other discursive formations expressed directly. While the idea that a crucial part of the human condition eludes philosophy, theology, and science and that it reveals itself only in art is foreign to the culture of aesthetic Platonism and classicism, it is the *raison d'être* of the modern aesthetic. Where did this change arise from?

Each of the arts merits a specific answer to this question, but in this case the languages of the mimetic arts form a system. The reason mimesis has once again become so important and untranslatable is because we moderns can say that "nothing is important but life." What D. H. Lawrence meant by "life" was the existence of ordinary human beings: Adam, Eve, Sarah, Abraham, Isaac, Jacob, Samuel, David, Bathsheba, Ruth, Esther, Solomon, Job, Isaiah, Jesus, Mark, Judas, Paul, Peter, considered simply as "men alive."[16] The importance that we moderns give to the ontological region of particularities, to individual differences, to the nonidentical, makes mimesis resistant to the leveling that takes place whenever concepts, ideas, or numerals are used for conceiving the world of finite beings, turning the chaotic plurality of individual leaves into the general notion of "the leaf." The writers who transported Hegel's aesthetics into the twentieth century—starting with Theodor Adorno[17] and Peter Szondi—were also those who reflected on this transition.

16. Lawrence, "Why the Novel Matters," 191–198.
17. See Theodor W. Adorno, "Über epische Naivetät" (1943); English translation "On Epic Naiveté," in *Notes to Literature,* vol. 1, ed. Rolf Tiedemann; trans. Shierry Weber Nicholsen (New York: Columbia University Press, 1991), 3–23, and by the same author, *Aesthetic Theory,* 118ff.

Hegel does not seem to take into account the fact that particularity not only separates people in the present, but also unites them. Precisely because it is a law of the current condition—of the societies to which we are all subject—the representation of an individual in all the constraints of his or her world can be representative for all other individuals. . . . In actuality, modern art is the very expression of the world of particularity and antagonism that Hegel wanted to surpass, and not reflect, with his conception of dialectics and art. The Hegelian concept of art is a critique of our world: those who want to take it seriously cannot expect to apply it to this epoch.[18]

It is because particularity is the *proprium* of our era that depicting an individual in the full restriction of his or her world can become a representative gesture. The birth of narcissistic genres like modern autobiography, the diary, or modern poetry is the first effect of the cultural transmutation that justified the increasingly detailed imitation of contingency. The second effect, made possible by technology, is the multiplication of private images in the age of photography and, later, video. Ever since the realm of particularity became impossible to transcend, the entire system of mimesis was changed, because discursive formations that tell stories about contingency or depict it fully reverted to being the books of life. Starting from the second half of the eighteenth century, "the novel, the movie, and the TV program have, gradually but steadily, replaced the sermon and the treatise as the principal vehicles of moral change and progress."[19] This follows on a transformation that simultaneously affected the history of ideas and the history of publishing. Until the first half of the nineteenth century, the majority of published works were religious, devotional, and moralistic in nature; in the second half of the nineteenth century, the hegemony of fiction and autobiographical writings began.[20] The conditions that had allowed mimesis to emerge as a game of truth were recreated in a completely new context.

18. Peter Szondi, "Hegels Lehre von der Dichtung," in *Poetik und Geschictsphilosophie* (Frankfurt: Suhrkamp, 1974), 414–415.

19. Richard Rorty, *Contingency, Irony, and Solidarity* (Cambridge: Cambridge University Press, 1989), xvi.

20. See Jack Goody, "From Oral to Written: An Anthropological Breakthrough in Storytelling," in Moretti, *The Novel,* 1:29.

After being at the forefront of Greek culture in a premetaphysical age, in our postmetaphysical age the arts have resumed their battle for supremacy over legitimate knowledge. However, although linked by a similarity of position, these periods of cultural history are separated by profound changes. The first relates to the choice of content for mimesis. While the *epos* and cosmogonies allude to an aristocratic hierarchy of beings, ranking those who deserve to be represented and those who do not, the modern aesthetic space is egalitarian and, in theory, incorporates any singularity and any event. For the Homeric bards, the deeds of gods and heroes were sovereign actions because they founded, impersonated, or represented collective institutions and values; for modern narrators, every life in principle is sovereign because this ontological level has become sacred. The second change, which mirrors the first, concerns the choice of form: post-Romantic mimesis presupposes the principle of stylistic freedom, namely, the belief that every creator has the right to come up with his or her own manner, according to an aesthetic principle that, when taken literally, frees art from any connection with mimesis. This is what happens, for example, in the abstract visual arts or in "pure poetry." Today we can tell stories about, paint, film, and draw any fragment of pure contingency, because no life or form of life is judged unworthy of mimetic reproduction. But for the sake of our expressivist freedom we can also tell stories, paint, film, or draw using any style to the point of destroying any link with the common appearance of the external world. Both these currents are propelled by the same epochal drift.

2. Until the dawning of the modern age, as we have seen, art forms were conditioned by structures deriving from the logic of the concept. Allegorism, moralistic prefaces, poetic justice, and the self-correction of heroes served to introduce the unequivocal truths of normative ethics and philosophy into the potentially equivocal material of narrative. In order to do this, characters and plots were transformed into placeholders for concepts or *exempla:* mimesis moved in the shadow of ideas. Starting from a certain historical threshold, the reverse occurred: mental structures evoking the ontology characteristic of mimesis entered into the domain of conceptual knowledge.

Few revolutions have so deeply transformed philosophy as the emergence of the idea that truth and thought are dependent on the historical time and sociogeographical space that engender them. Modern historicism and localism are the result of a long process of transformation that began in the second half of the sixteenth century and came to completion in the second half of the nineteenth century, when historical thought jettisoned its Christian armature, dropped the notion of *telos,* and conceived becoming as a sequence of truths and contingent powers that emerge, do battle with other powers and truths, dominate, perish, and are replaced by others.

The most mature expression of this metamorphosis is to be found in the work of Nietzsche. Significantly, some of the most important twentieth-century interpreters of Nietzsche dedicated their thought to the implications of these changes: Leo Strauss, for example, and, with completely different aims, Deleuze and Foucault. Historicism and localism bring back into becoming, into changeability, everything that philosophy believed to be supratemporal. The search for permanent forms, for universal and eternal laws concealed inside and beneath the flow of phenomena, is displaced by the idea that everything, starting with concepts, is temporary and situated—because there are no constants, but rather only contingencies thrown into time and space, interwoven with other equivalent contingencies in a web of actions, conflicts, negotiations, victories, and defeats.[21] As forms of absolute immanentism, historicism and localism assail the assumption, essential for European metaphysics, that truth and thought can extract themselves from the influence of places and times and aspire to an eternal validity.[22] In doing so, they situate knowledge and expose human beings to a "radical dispersion that provides a foundation for all other histories," to a "finitude without infinity."[23] In discussing one of the extreme forms that the urge to situate thought assumes in modern philosophy, Deleuze observes that the internal rule Nietzsche's genealogical processes obey is tragic, in other words, theatrical: ideas are portrayed as conflicts between

21. Michel Foucault, "Nietzsche, la généalogie, l'histoire" (1971); English translation "Nietzsche, Genealogy, History" (1971), in *Language, Counter-Memory, Practice: Selected Essays and Interviews,* ed. Donald F. Bouchare, trans. Donald F. Bouchard and Sherry Simon (Ithaca, NY: Cornell University Press, 1977), 139–164.

22. Leo Strauss, *Natural Right and History* (Chicago: University of Chicago Press, 1953), 11ff.

23. Michel Foucault, *Les Mots et les Choses* (1966); English translation *The Order of Things* (New York: Vintage Books, 1994), 369, 372.

underlying forces, and these forces are treated as individuals that emerge in a certain place and at a certain time, and cross paths on an ideal stage. For this "method of dramatisation,"[24] the question "Who are you?" does not mean "What is your stable essence?" Rather, it means "How did your identity come to be?" "What is the accidental history of forces that made you what you are?" By relating thought to the subjects or dynamics that generated it, by interpreting ideas as actions that someone or something produced under certain circumstances, historicism and localism introduce a narrative type of ontology into the heart of philosophical theories—the same one that has always dwelt in every form of history. Our interest in ideas no longer resides in their claim to express an absolute truth, but in their nature as events; rather than converging toward the unity of universals, reality proliferates in potentially myriad plots. The Platonic image of philosophical speculation comes out of this obliterated: there are no essences, only vicissitudes (of thoughts, people, groups, and forces) immersed in worlds subject, in their turn, to vicissitudes. The gesture of historicizing and situating is steeped in relativistic skepticism, in a disbelief toward ideas and values, because "we view all concepts as having *become*."[25]

This attitude is clearly visible in the forms of genealogy belonging to the school of suspicion, but its most pervasive, mundane version is to be found in disciplines that relate human creations to the laws of mechanical causality, presupposing that these are the proper confines of thought. Few disciplines are based on such a thoroughly nihilistic foundation as philology. The image of the world etched into its premises views reality as a heap of particular events and minimal genealogies: the influence of one person on another, of one singular event on another, of a restricted environment on an individual. Indeed, while the schools of suspicion rest on a complex metaphysics accepted as true and removed from the game of historiciza-

---

24. Gilles Deleuze, *Nietzsche et la philosophie* (1962); English translation *Nietzsche and Philosophy*, trans. Michael Hardt (New York: Columbia University Press, 2006), 78–79.

25. "What divides us most radically from all Platonic or Leibnizian ways of thinking is this: we do not believe in eternal concepts, eternal values, eternal forms; and insofar as philosophy is science and not legislation, for us it represents simply the broadest extension of the concept of 'history.' Starting out from etymology and the history of language, we view all concepts as having *become*." Friedrich Nietzsche, *Nachgelassene Fragmente 1884–1885*, in *Friedrich Nietzsche: Sämtliche Werke*, ed. Giorgio Colli and Mazzino Montinari, vol. 11 (Munich: Deutsches Taschenbuch Verlag, 1988), 613.

tions and localizations (as it is in Marx and Freud, but also in Nietzsche), philology admits no other metaphysics than the obtuse, minimal one inscribed in the method of mechanical causality. It destroys every form of regularity that connect particular beings into larger assemblages. Philology is the most extreme example of how narrative has permeated the realm of concepts.

3. But the new importance mimesis has acquired as the book of life and the introduction of particularities into disciplines that should seek universal regularities entail more than the finitude without infinity of a thought that introjects narrative assumptions. These discursive changes are actually accompanied by opposite changes, by reflexive gestures that connect the chaos of particulars to a higher order. The same epoch in which time and space were introduced into the transcendental structures of thought, the same epoch that allowed disciplines of knowledge to proliferate along the line of flight of an infinite contingency, also witnessed the emergence of an analytic of finitude, in the form of a philosophical anthropology or an existential analytic.[26] These disciplines interpret multiplicity starting from a common structure rooted in the ontology of particular beings. These two types of knowledge are intertwined. It is the same dialectic that traverses stories: modern fiction acquires an unprecedented freedom to reproduce life, but its internal logic shows that the shifting surface of life is founded on a single grammar of existence.

This change is accompanied by another, even more important one. As we saw in Chapter 7, the development of the modern novel, poetry, and drama, the emancipation of mimesis from its safeguards, the rise of the arts to books of life were contemporary with the development of disciplines of knowledge that seek to solidify the inconstancy of accidental life into the medium of concepts, or even numbers. Between the mid-1600s and the early 1800s, the increased philosophical interest in particularities led to the emergence of disciplines dedicated to the conceptual study of contingencies. The novel attained its modern form precisely when the human sciences established themselves: in other words, when the sixteenth- and seventeenth-century "sciences of the soul" morphed during the eighteenth century into

---

26. Foucault, *The Order of Things*, 339ff., 369ff., 398ff.

the discipline of empirical psychology,[27] and when thought on the life of society, which began with Montesquieu and before him with Bodin, led to the emergence of sociology.[28] Auguste Comte, who invented this term, also extended the mechanical and biological concept of *milieu* to human life during exactly the same years when Balzac was completing an identical maneuver in *The Human Comedy*—almost as if sociology and the novel were bound by a symmetry and a secret competition.[29] But the historical parallelism is even more profound. The epoch during which the artistic representation of singularities was refined and writers became capable of describing the most minute details of consciences, destinies, and environments was the same period that applied the calculation of probabilities to life and saw the rise of statistics.[30] European literature became capable of describing the most subtle nuances of people just when, on the other end of the cognitive spectrum, sciences were dawning that were founded on the attempt to relate the diversity among individuals to mathematical laws. The opening to the chaos of differences occurred at the same time that the differences were being nullified in the chilling sameness of numbers. What do these specular transformations mean?

The Design of This Book

Theory of the Novel is the second part of a study that began with *Sulla poesia moderna* (On Modern Poetry).[31] Those who write philosophical works assume that it is possible to speak of the present by dialoguing with the works of other philosophers, in the conviction that philosophy is the present time crystallized in thought. *Sulla poesia moderna* and

27. See Vidal, *The Sciences of the Soul*, chap. 1.

28. See Raymond Aron, *Les Étapes de la pensée sociologique* (1967); English translation *Main Currents in Sociological Thought*, with a new introduction by Daniel J. Mahoney and Brian C. Anderson, foreword by Pierre Manent (New Brunswick, NJ: Transaction Publishers, 1998).

29. Spitzer, "Milieu and Ambiance"; Canguilhem, *Knowledge of Life*, chap. 5.

30. Ian Hacking, *The Emergence of Probability* (Cambridge: Cambridge University Press, 1975); Alain Desrosières, *La Politique des grands nombres: histoire de la raison statistique* (1993); English translation *The Politics of Large Numbers: A History of Statistical Reasoning*, trans. Camille Naish (Cambridge, MA: Harvard University Press, 2002).

31. Guido Mazzoni, *Sulla poesia moderna* (Bologna: Il Mulino, 2005); French version: *Sur la poésie moderne* (Paris: Classiques Garnier, 2014).

Theory of the Novel attempt to decipher a few aspects of the present, using two of the most important literary genres of our times as a point of departure and symptom. They do so in the belief that "art forms tell the history of human beings with more accuracy than historical documents."[32] This project is distantly related to the hermeneutic tradition that draws from the aesthetics of German idealism, particularly from the writings of Friedrich Schlegel and Hegel's lectures on aesthetics. Many of the twentieth-century works that offer a theory of an art form issued either directly or indirectly from this critical school: Lukács's *The Theory of the Novel*, Benjamin's *The Origin of German Tragic Drama* and his essay on "The Storyteller," Bakhtin's studies on the novel, Panofsky's *Perspective as Symbolic Form*, Adorno's *Philosophy of New Music*, Szondi's *Theory of Modern Drama*, and Arnold Gehlen's *Zeit-Bilder.* In spite of the differences separating these works, they share a resemblance because they consider aesthetic materials to be "symbolic forms" in which "spiritual meaning is attached to a concrete, material sign and intrinsically given to this sign." This is the formula Panofsky borrowed from Cassirer and used to define the essence of perspective.[33] If we wanted to express the same concept in Hegel's terms or to use more orthodox Hegelian vocabulary, we could say that, considering that "the sensuous aspect of art is *spiritualized,* since the spirit appears in art as made *sensuous,*"[34] forms of art transmit "sedimented contents"[35] in a medium other than that of thought.

But if the distant source is the critical tradition we have just described, *Sulla poesia moderna* and *Theory of the Novel* differ from the archetype in two ways: they adopt a different metaphysics—as readers who have reached this point in the book will be more than aware—and they have a different conception of the nature of their objects. The theories of artistic forms that we find in the works of Lukács, Benjamin, Adorno, or Gehlen owe part of their allure to the fact that their authors treat artistic genres and eras not as shadows, but as solid things. The "novel," the "Trauerspiel,"

---

32. See Theodor W. Adorno, *Philosophie der neuen Musik* (1949); English translation *Philosophy of New Music* (Minneapolis: University of Minnesota Press, 2006), 37.

33. Ernst Cassirer, *Philosophie der symbolischen Formen* (1923–1929); English translation *The Philosophy of Symbolic Forms,* trans. Ralph Manheim (New Haven, CT: Yale University Press, 1953); Panofsky, *Perspective as Symbolic Form,* 41.

34. Hegel, *Aesthetics,* vol. 1, p. 39.

35. Adorno, *Philosophy of New Music,* 37; also by Adorno, *Aesthetic Theory,* 144.

"storytelling," "tragedy," "new music," "modern drama," "modern painting," "Greece," "closed cultures," "the Baroque," "Romanticism," or "modernity" enter into discourse as if they were proper names, as unitary bodies so evident as to require no explanation, following an approach we find earlier in Schlegel or Hegel. Over the past forty years, a shift in historical time has distanced us from the intellectual gestures that founded these studies, propagating a pervasive, nebulized form of skepticism toward generalities and master narratives. Our culture has become increasingly incredulous of any consciously or unconsciously holistic, essentialist conceptions of cultural phenomena and epochs. Today, anyone wanting to reflect on language games and on historical periods must abandon certain gestures that are too immediately synthetic and delve into the analytical territory of philology. There are many reasons for this development, some of which are mechanical: social changes during the past few decades have multiplied the number of researchers and the amount of research being conducted; digital technology has multiplied the data to which we have access, and, with them, the chaos of details. But this is not the only explanation. Between their epoch and ours, there has been a change in the attitude of interpreters toward empirical data. The works of Lukács, Benjamin, Bakhtin, Adorno, Gehlen (Panofsky and Szondi are a case apart) are made possible by the assurance with which their authors can rely on a few master narratives to define epochs, to unify phenomena, to control the mass of details, and to ignore exceptions. This is the same gesture we find in Schlegel or in Hegel, which is encapsulated in a famous phrase attributed to the latter: "So much worse for the facts." The way Lukács, Benjamin, Bakhtin, Adorno, and Gehlen speak about their objects is intelligent but also vague; the synthetic power of some of their opinions is directly linked to the lack of details and to the assurance with which many facts are effectively ignored.

An approach of this sort presupposed a faith in the descriptive power of theories. Today the cultural atmosphere of our time no longer legitimizes these approaches. One of the harshest attacks directed against philosophies of cultural history that order facts according to a unitary principle is the one Ernst Gombrich launched in many of his books and summarized in his methodological lectures, published as *In Search of Cultural History* (1967):

> The cultural historian was much worse off than any other historian. His
> colleagues working on political or economic history had at least a crite-

rion of relevance in their restricted subject-matter. They could trace the history of the reform of Parliament, of Anglo-Irish relations, without explicit reference to an all-embracing philosophy of history. But the history of the culture as such ... could never be undertaken without some ordering principle, some centre from which the panorama can be surveyed, some hub on which the wheel of Hegel's diagram can be pivoted. Thus the subsequent history of historiography of culture can perhaps best be interpreted as a succession of attempts to salvage the Hegelian assumption without accepting Hegelian metaphysics.[36]

In Gombrich's view, although many histories of culture abandoned the Hegelian philosophy of history, they never gave up on a fundamental Hegelian assumption—the idea that an epoch is not dispersed in facts, microsystems, and heterogeneous elements, but is held together by a unitary principle. Usually, this unity is designated with a metaphor that serves as a model: body, spirit, logic, grammar, mentality, structure. In the century and a half or two that separate the invention of concepts like "spirit of the people" or "spirit of the time" from the invention of concepts like "metaphysical basis,"[37] "episteme,"[38] or "the cultural logic of an epoch,"[39] philosophical vocabularies did change, but the philosophical act, the gesture of aggregating the multiple, remained the same even when the intentions were entirely different. In the same way, many histories of culture assume that their objects are obvious, unitary entities. Today, statements like "The inner form of the novel has been understood as the process of the problematic individual's journeying towards himself"[40] or "The novel was the literary form specific to the bourgeois age. ... Realism was inherent in the novel"[41] sound vague. The intellectual impulses that move us force us to ask: "What type of novel are you talking about?" "What is meant by

---

36. Ernst H. Gombrich, *In Search of Cultural History* (Oxford: Clarendon Press, 1967), 25.

37. Martin Heidegger, "Die Zeit des Weltbildes" (1938); English translation "The Age of the World Picture," trans. William Lovitt, in *Concerning Technology and Other Essays* (New York: Garland, 1977), 115.

38. Foucault, *The Order of Things*.

39. Frederic Jameson, *Postmodernism, or, The Cultural Logic of Late Capitalism* (London: Verso, 1991).

40. See Lukács, *The Theory of the Novel*, 54.

41. Theodor W. Adorno, "Standort des Erzählers im zeitgenössischen Roman" (1954); English translation "The Position of the Narrator in the Contemporary Novel," in *Notes to*

'novel,' 'bourgeois age,' or 'realism'?" For us there is no way around philology, and not only because of the mechanical reasons we mentioned
earlier. There is no way around it because philology cuts across two deep
tendencies of our age, which are actually bound tightly together: suspicion toward master narratives, and the triumph of particularities qua particularities. *Sulla poesia moderna* and *Theory of the Novel* attempt to put
forward general interpretations while entering, as far as possible, into the
bad infinity of philology, and trying, as much as possible, to tackle the
dispersion of factual data. I have attempted to examine literary genres not
as obvious entities, but as universals *in re* that emerge, transform, and
evolve in different ways depending on the culture. Above all, I have
attempted to conceive of literary epochs and spaces as only partly continuous
and only partly ordered aggregates of various things: ideas, theories,
master narratives, disciplines, genres, standards, styles, gestures, manners,
habits, expectations, forms of attention, *habitus,* topoi, examples, canons,
watchwords, *auctoritates* that overlap, intertwine, and combine, creating
a temporary cohesiveness.

> I would like to briefly explain an expression that recurs frequently in this
> book: *structures of sense*. This is what I have called the elements that work
> together in various capacities to form a literary epoch or space. Christian
> aesthetic Platonism or the rule of the separation of styles, for example, are
> two large structures of sense that interweave and generate a series of pre-
> cise effects. What I mean by "structure of sense" is everything that makes
> a certain discourse or practice sensible—the adjective "sensible" being un-
> derstood in various ways depending on the context, and signifying "legiti-
> mate," "'instructive," "entertaining," "authoritative," "true," "nice," "in-
> teresting." Among all the available definitions, the most universal, it seems
> to me, is the one Wittgenstein uses to describe why we accept propositions
> or behaviors: "we just behave this way and then we feel satisfied."[42] *Be-*

Literature I, trans. Shierry Weber Nicholsen (New York: Columbia University Press,
1991), 30.

  42. Ludwig Wittgenstein, "Remarks on Frazer's Golden Bough," in *Philosophical
Occasions, 1912–1951* (Indianapolis: Hackett, 1993), 123. See also his *Philosophical Investigations,* §88: "No single ideal of exactness has been envisaged; we do not know what we
are to make of this idea—unless you yourself stipulate what is to be so called. But you'll find
it difficult to make such a stipulation—one that satisfies you."

friedigen here seems to be the equivalent of *to persuade* in ancient rhetoric. We are satisfied that a certain thing has been done, said, written in a certain way. We feel this way because we appeal, often unconsciously, to a living structure of sense: because the law says so or because we are imitating an authoritative model, because we have always done it this way or because our culture tells us that we need to change, because we are following the protocols of a certain discipline or because we are repeating a commonplace, because we are applying the *Stiltrennung* or because *il faut être absolument modernes.* The apparatus of the justifications is multifaceted, mobile, and only in part cohesive. Some structures of sense are very extensive (aesthetic Platonism, the *Stiltrennung*); others have a regional validity (the appeal to the normative value of ancient poetics between the mid-sixteenth and mid-eighteenth centuries; others are minimal. However, when some structures decline, a certain practice or a certain discourse stops satisfying us, and the field of the possibilities changes. Structures of sense are actually the expanded version of what topoi were in the system of classical rhetoric, namely, the places that everyone is expected to relocate in their minds and perceive as familiar or common. They are the crutches we rely on, often unconsciously, to justify our actions and our speech. Out of the shifting weave of these big and small elements there arises a paradigm, a field of possibilities, a literary space. Each of these sets is not the coherent expression of a unitary spirit of the time or an *episteme,* but a varying weave of patches: a patchwork. Moreover, contradictory structures of sense can exist in the same epoch, and every national culture can express the same epochal structures differently. Every field of possibility declines over time and space: a long-term constant (the literary heritage of the ancient culture) may include a medium-term constant (the European classicism of the early modern age between the humanistic rediscovery of the Greco-Roman culture and the second half of the eighteenth century) that takes on different forms depending on the nation (more rigid in France, less so in England). The fact remains that by reassembling the structures of sense through philology, and by comparing what it was considered sensible to write in a certain period with what it was considered sensible to write in another, historical boundaries and thresholds emerge.

On the Present State of Things

Let us return now to the question with which we ended the "Discursive Transformations" section. The art form we are talking about expresses a relativistic vision of the world, but it accepts a specific grammar of existence, as if it participated in diametrically opposed cultural transformations: some extol the chaos of private life, while others insist on the seriality of all beings. What do these specular transformations communicate? What story do they tell?

The modern era enshrines the right of individuals to constitute themselves as epicenters of sense, to pursue their own interests, to criticize what has been handed down to them, to participate, at least in theory, in the creation of a collective political will, and to construct an autonomous sphere of values. Between the sixteenth century and the eighteenth century a relatively solid social structure held together by relatively strong shared metaphysics, religion, ethics, politics, and aesthetics was torn apart by the gradual affirmation of a form of life that claimed the right of unbelonging: to exist only for oneself, to pursue exclusively personal or family aims. Today we are witnessing the outcome of this process in its entirety. From the perspective of the twenty-first century we have an excellent vantage point to reflect on the modern age, because the set of conditions that developed over the past three or four decades—what we call "postmodernism"—makes it possible to perceive and understand certain aspects of modernity that remained concealed in other historical periods. This is the case, for example, when Raymond Carver's common people allow us to see what was already implicit in the characters of Maupassant or Chekhov, and the nineteenth-century *petite bourgeoisie* reveals itself to be the origin, archetype, and figure of the neoliberal middle class.

The consecration of individuals, the right to subjective freedom, and the growth of material wealth accompanying the development of middle-class society produced one of the fundamental turning points in human history. Billions of individuals who lived in other times and other places viewed the Western, middle-class way of life as progressive, as the very definition of "progress." What made "progress" attractive to the masses of the Third World, to the inhabitants of totalitarian states, or to millions of European farmers living in substantially feudal conditions until the first half of the twentieth century was not democracy. Universal suffrage is an overly abstract value for most people and, under ordinary conditions, the liberal democracy of modern states is a fragile mechanism, stripped of its political effectiveness by the actions of economic powers external to states, by the actions of oligarchic groups, by unequal access to mass communication, and by resistance to political decisions created by bureaucratic mechanisms. More than the abstraction of democracy, what makes desirable the middle station of life—or its globalized twentieth-century extension, the *American way of life*—is the concrete capacity to construct small spheres of autonomy, security, and material prosperity around individuals and families. "Progress" has a Tocquevillian aspect to it: it allows private individuals to live for themselves and to pursue their own aims. No matter how insignificant, no matter how marginal and ephemeral they may be, subjective desires and aims are now treated with absolute importance: no culture has ever indiscriminately granted so much weight to individuals. What we call sacred is that which one cannot transcend or negotiate: in this sense, the particular life represents the only horizon of sacredness that modern culture still recognizes. According to a certain model of philosophy of history that emerged from the culture of German idealism, modern individualism arose out of the foundation of Christian theology: because each person is created in the image and likeness of God, he or she represents an infinite value. While there may be truth to this explanation, it is equally true that the cultural unconscious of the modern world pushed this genealogy aside and transformed life *ohne Eigenschaften* and without theological safeguards into an absolute value. The legal consequence of this process was the rise of human rights, the political consequence was democracy, the philosophical consequence was relativism, and the cultural consequence was the multiplication of traces that each and every life feels authorized to leave behind.

A system of this kind is traversed by two fractures. The first is the violence out of which the present state of things was born and by which it is maintained: the regime of class struggle; the competition between individuals that has become a norm and a value; power relations that condemned and continue to condemn billions of people to colonial or neocolonial subjugation, to exploitation, to selling one's time and work in exchange for subsistence wages. But this first crack—the enormous denial on the part of middle-class society, the barbarism on which our civilization rests—is almost always kept out of Western discourses, all the more since there has ceased to be a credible political alternative to the present state of things.

The second crack, which appears more often in discourses, is the constant, polymorphic discomfort emanating from the system's mechanisms. The consecration of private life produces contradictions that we see clearly today. One of these we see most distinctly is the disintegrative force implicit in modern individualism, the same one that fascinated and disturbed Hegel, Tocqueville, Marx, Herzen, Nietzsche, and Kojève. Western humanity lives in private little spheres that, for now, are quite protected; within each of these territories, individuals seek personal happiness or, more modestly, as in Jane Austen or Chekhov, tranquility—a form of balance between desires and world. The names of collective transcendences that the modern age inherited (God, Duty) or invented (Homeland, Revolution, Engagement, Community) are increasingly more difficult to pronounce without irony or without real or metaphorical quotation marks. This crisis of transcendences must not be thought of as a political and intellectual change with heroic features, but as a phenomenon with systemic, mediocre origins. The relativistic deflation of collective values is inscribed in the modern worship of personal and family life. Individualism is "the *most modest* stage of the will to power";[43] the simple private condition, the choice to give natural rights and an absolute value to all bare life, indiscriminately, contain a nihilistic core; the small objectives that "the soul clings to . . . end up obscuring the rest of reality from one's view."[44] By shutting itself up in a very restricted sphere of relations and by replacing public gods with personal demons, the modern, middle-class form of life brings with it a drive toward unbelonging. In part 3 of *Buddenbrooks,* the consul Buddenbrook writes to his daughter Tony:

> We are not born, my dear daughter, to pursue our own small personal happiness, for we are not separate, independent, self-subsisting individuals, but links in a chain; and it is inconceivable that we would be what we are without those who have preceded us and shown us the path that

---

43. Friedrich Nietzsche, *Nachgelassene Fragmente* (1885–1887), in *Friedrich Nietzsche: Sämtliche Werke,* ed. Giorgio Colli and Mazzino Montinari, vol. 12 (Berlin: de Gruyter, 1999), 502.

44. Alexis de Tocqueville, *De la démocratie en Amérique* (1835–1840); English translation *Democracy in America,* trans. Gerald Bevan (London: Penguin Books, 2003), 593.

they themselves have scrupulously trod, looking neither to the left nor to the right, but, rather, following a venerable and trustworthy tradition.[45]

In part 6, Thomas says to his brother Christian: "You do not belong just to yourself alone."[46] The heads of the Buddenbrook family defend the family, which is to say, the entity that binds each individual to a collective history. By behaving this way, they obey a bourgeois ethic modeled on the explicit example of the noble dynasties. In one of the most beautiful scenes in the novel, Hanno comes across the family book in which, in homage to an ancient tradition, all the major events of the lives of the Buddenbrooks are recorded, and he draws a line in it. This gesture is a harbinger of his premature death and, at the same time, a declaration of unbelonging. Hanno traces out a line because this boy with artistic talent, marked by disease, is alien to practical life, to its chain of responsibilities, to any link with a genealogy. A very similar image can be found in a famous passage by Tocqueville: "The thread of time is ever ruptured and the track of generations is blotted out. Those who have gone before are easily forgotten and those who follow are still completely unknown. Only those nearest to us are of any concern to us."[47] Tocqueville speaks of the disintegration of collective bonds that is inherent in modern, middle-class individualism. In the light of this similarity, Hanno's gesture takes on a wider metaphorical significance and the ethos of the Romantic and post-Romantic artist is revealed as the elitist forerunner of the expressivist individualism that would become a mass phenomenon over the course of the twentieth century.[48]

"Two things are certain: 1) people no longer care what happens to other people; 2) nothing makes any real difference any longer," says a character in a story by Raymond Carver.[49] In a specular fashion, the circle of personal interests ends up assuming an extraordinary weight. In the first two parts of *Daniel Deronda* (1876), George Eliot tells the story of Gwendolyn Harleth:

45. Mann, *Buddenbrooks*, part 3, chap. 10, p. 144.
46. Ibid., part 6, chap. 3, p. 314.
47. Tocqueville, *Democracy in America*, 563.
48. On the relationship between the ethos of the Romantic artist and the individualism of twentieth-century earth, see Taylor, *Sources of the Self*, parts 4 and 5.
49. Raymond Carver, "So Much Water So Close to Home," in *Furious Seasons and Other Stories* (Santa Barbara: Capra Press, 1977), 49.

Could there be a slenderer, more insignificant thread in human history than this consciousness of a girl, busy with her small inferences of the way in which she could make her life pleasant?—in a time, too, when ideas were with fresh vigour making armies of themselves, and the universal kinship was declaring itself fiercely: when women on the other side of the world would not mourn for the husbands and sons who died bravely in a common cause, and men stinted of bread on our side of the world heard of that willing loss and were patient: a time when the soul of man was waking to pulses which had for centuries been beating in him unfelt, until their full sum made a new life of terror or joy.

What in the midst of that mighty drama are girls and their blind visions? They are the Yea or Nay of that good for which men are enduring and fighting. In these delicate vessels is borne onward through the ages the treasure of human affections.[50]

In an age when "human affections" matter in themselves, and not in relation to their objective value, the small inferences of Gwendolyn can have the same weight as an immense tragedy. This is precisely the point: more than a true nihilism, the shortsightedness implicit in an attitude of this sort involves a shifting of weights. The struggle that each individual faces to find a balance has taken on an absolute value, equivalent to what other cultures attribute only to major public conflicts. We already came across this idea in the observations accompanying the rise of the novel between the seventeenth and eighteenth centuries: the happiness or unhappiness of a private man, wrote Lessing, moves us more than the destiny of a state.[51] Balzac picks up on this notion and amplifies it:

The unknown struggle which goes on in a valley of the Indre between Mme. de Mortsauf and her passion is perhaps as great as the most famous of battles (Le Lys dans la vallée). In one the glory of the victor is at stake; in the other it is heaven. The misfortunes of the two Birotteaus, the priest and the perfumer, to me are those of mankind.[52]

According to the melodramatic logic that governs Balzac's narrative, the battles that are fought within individuals embody battles between universal

50. George Eliot, *Daniel Deronda* (1876), ed. G. Handley (Oxford: Clarendon Press, 1984), bk. 2, chap. 11, p. 109.

51. Lessing, *Hamburgische Dramaturgie*, vol. 1, chap. 14, pp. 38–39.

52. Balzac, "Author's Introduction" to *The Human Comedy*, lxv.

powers. But the passage cited above also applies to texts that do not obey this logic: for us readers of novels, the destiny of the characters is tremendously important; even when we do not agree with the goals that the heroes are pursuing, we are able to recognize ourselves in the schema of their existence. We are like them: private beings, thrown into a world, occupied in seeking a balance between desires and reality. The personal aims and microcosms are different for everyone, but the attempt to quell our restlessness is the same and holds an absolute importance for us. This aspect of the present state of things is what makes possible identification with others, the preservation of a public ethic, and interest in lives other than our own. On the other hand, since what we share is not a set of contents but a form—a grammar of existence—the identification is never guaranteed. This second aspect of the present state of things makes possible indifference to lives other than our own, the destruction of all solidarity, and the impenetrable opacity of others.

Furthermore, the epoch during which the nominal importance of individual people increased and collective transcendences were pulverized is the same period during which human beings were bound into systems of mutual dependence, multiplying the chains of uncontrollable actions and reactions. Although individuals acquire independence and security inside the little spheres that surround them, the overall orography of their existential territories extends well beyond them. This has always been the case, but in the modern era displacement and dispossession have been multiplied. The crisis of collective transcendences corresponds to a strengthening of objective transcendences, namely, the dependence of individuals on suprapersonal powers, opinions, and mechanisms. The French Revolution and the Napoleonic wars, by transforming history into a lived experience of the masses, introduced a typical feature of modernity. Over the next two centuries, major conflicts with mandatory conscription, global economic cycles, and changes in manners and morals would reaffirm the contents of that experience, showing that the atmosphere in which the small worlds of individuals are immersed transcends individuals, eludes their control, and constitutes the only true Event. The culture of the nineteenth century—from Hegel to Tolstoy, and from Marx to Durkheim—would interpret in many ways the discovery that the suprapersonal life sedimented in history and in society is the true objective transcendence, the temporal and secularized form of the divine.

Therefore, the era in which the absolute value of each individual is affirmed has been the same as the period in which there emerged, with absolute clarity, the power of large impersonal forces—in planetary wars or global economic crises, in the mechanisms of capitalist markets, or in the changes of the *Zeitgeist*. This is also the age in which it has become clear that our life, the life that we have led ourselves to view as our own property, is always constitutively improper, *uneigentlich,* in the sense that Heidegger gives to this word. The ideas, habits, and behaviors that we have introjected precede us: they are products of the world that includes us; they do not really belong to us. If observed with an attitude of estrangement, they reveal that we are serial beings, like everyone else.

The antithesis between the nominal importance of individuals and their objective irrelevance divides the field of discursive formations. It shows up in the conflict between the forms of mimesis of singularity (autobiography, poetry, the novel, photography, film) and the language games that transfer personal experiences to the equalizing order of concepts or numbers (the human sciences, statistics). But the contradiction, in reality, is implicit in every discipline. Modern narrative fiction, for example, refined the artistic representation of singularity during the same period that it developed the form of the novel-essay: the greatness of *War and Peace* lies partly in its ability to bring these two currents together. During the age of modernism, then, the two lines became distinct and intertwined in various ways. In a chapter of *The Man without Qualities,* for example, Musil gives himself the challenge of describing a man who thinks. In the 1920s, when the book was written, the representation of the interior life was the typical theme of narrative that sought to express individual singularity in all its fragmentation and in all its idiosyncratic distinctiveness. Provocatively, Musil transforms psychological mimesis into essayistic reflection: he does not mimic Ulrich's interior monologue; rather, he meditates on the dynamics of thought in general.

> Unfortunately, nothing is so hard to achieve as a literary representation of a man thinking. . . . As long as the process of thinking is in motion it is a quite wretched state, as if all the brain's convolutions were suffering from colic; and when it is finished it no longer has the form of the thinking process as one experiences it but already that of what has been

thought, which is regrettably impersonal. . . . [A]nd this is manifestly why thinking is such an embarrassment for writers that they gladly avoid it.

But the man without qualities was now thinking. One may draw the conclusion from this that it was, at least in part, not a personal affair. But then what is it? World in, and world out; aspects of world falling into place inside a head.[53]

Musil's choice, by opposition, alludes to techniques to give form to the fluid, subjective aspect of the interior life that had been invented during the century of psychological realism in general, by the writers of Musil's generation in particular, and by Musil himself in an earlier phase of his work. *The Man without Qualities* was written immediately after *Ulysses* came out, during the years of debate on interior monologue and its revolutionary novelty.[54] In the third chapter of *Ulysses,* thinking about Aristotle, Stephen Dedalus reflects on gnoseological problems of perception while walking on a beach. His thoughts are captured as they rise up and then splinter off.

Ineluctable modality of the visible: at least that if no more, thought through my eyes. Signatures of all things I am here to read, seaspawn and seawrack, the nearing tide, that rusty boot. Snotgreen, bluesilver, rust: coloured signs. Limits of the diaphane. But he adds: in bodies. Then he was aware of them bodies before of them coloured. How? By knocking his sconce against them, sure. Go easy. Bald he was and a millionaire, *maestro di color che sanno.* Limit of the diaphane in. Why in? Diaphane, adiaphane. If you can put your five fingers through it, it is a gate, if not a door. Shut your eyes and see.[55]

The dialectic between essayism and minute introspective details well expresses the contrast between the gaze that through reflection grasps universal laws, and the gaze that seeks to focus on each person's particularities. The age of modernism saw the development of these two potentially

---

53. Musil, *The Man without Qualities*, bk. 1, chap. 23, pp. 115–116.

54. See Dujardin, *Le Monologue intérieur,* which also provides an account of contemporary discussion on interior monologue.

55. James Joyce, *Ulysses,* critical and synoptic edition prepared by Hans Walter Gabler with Wolfhard Steppe and Claus Melchior, vol. 1 (New York: Garland, 1986), 75.

opposing lines: a work like *In Search of Lost Time,* for example, contains both.

The conflict between universal and particular, between suprapersonal generalities and singular individualities, splits the cultural domain, cuts through the single games of truth, and expresses a dialectic without reconciliation. Inscribed in the ontological condition of finite beings, it ends up multiplied by the dynamics of the modern world. People have become an absolute *primum;* their fates can take center stage; every detail of their finitude counts. At the same time, the modern form of life takes it upon itself to show at every turn that this is not the whole story. Around and inside the individual there operates an objective transcendence made of regularities, universal trends, introjected attitudes, fields of forces; a transcendence that conceives individuals as simple, particular cases of general laws—the same laws that philosophy, the human sciences, and statistics seek to establish. This twofold truth, which is consubstantial with the present state of things, divides the cultural realm and traverses the individual discursive formations—but only the narrative form incorporates it into its structures. Only narrative fiction can show how particular beings are exposed to the world, and how their identity, happiness, and unhappiness depend on the way their paths cross with those of others, and the power of circumstances.

Our existences are private, contingent, and unstable. We pursue a balance between desire and reality in the local system where we are thrown; we live exposed to time, transcended by the influences that have made us what we are. Our life is improper: on the plane of being, it fluctuates between nothingness and seriality; on the plane of discourse, it fluctuates between silence (disinterest in what, at bottom, is the same as everything else) and concepts or numbers. And yet we take seriously the little, local bubble where we exist; for most of us, the struggle to find a form of happiness or tranquility inside this sphere is the whole world. Unlike the philosophies from Montaigne to Heidegger that insist on the constitutive unbelongingness of human beings to themselves, novelists do not usually adopt an estranged gaze: they accept the goals that their protagonists set for themselves. To not be interested in the forms of life in which one is immersed, just because these forms are contingent and improper, signifies preserving a trace of transcendence or nurturing nostalgia for it; it means taking the point of view of the absolute—an outlook that, for precarious beings like us, is academic and unreal. In ordinary life we are always caught up in our existence. We are always inside and rarely outside: the accidental and limited nature of what we are interests us to a certain point; the objective tragedy of our condition does not prevent us from playing an active part in the plot in which we are implicated. We live our impropriety properly,[56] as we inevitably must: a life that the anonymous powers and the game of systems have forged for us is ours nonetheless, and it is the only thing that we consider sacred. In narrative fiction, this passion for particularity exhibits itself according to its own logic. We follow the ups and downs of heroes, at the end of which, in one way or another, they will reach a form of tranquility. We follow them not so much because we are interested in the content of their desires, but because we share the form of their condition, the grammar of their existence.

Modern culture has no answer for the question "Why?" or "What for?" Those of us who are enclosed in the Western form of life can enjoy life with an unprecedented degree of autonomy and comfort as long as we remain immersed in the shortsightedness that normally envelopes us in the form of common sense; but when faced with thresholds and crises, we feel anguish. In the emphatic, capital-S understanding of the term, nothing makes Sense anymore. But outside the context of abstract thought and states of exception, if one observes how the problem appears in the logic of those who attempt to tell stories about particular beings, one arrives at a different conclusion. By telling stories about people immersed in local worlds who are occupied with reaching their goals and finding a balance between desire and reality in the midst of other individuals who are pursuing the same type of balance, novels present an idea of sense that runs closer to the one in ordinary experience. For the reader, the contents of the stories are all interchangeable and all potentially worthy of attention for as long as they continue to exist. Inside our small local worlds, everything at stake has an unquestionable value, as if there were no longer a sense, as if the word *sense* could no longer be in the singular, and instead, there were lots

---

56. See Giorgio Agamben, "La passione della fatticità" (1987); English translation "The Passion of Facticity: Heidegger and the Problem of Love" (1987), trans. Daniel Heller-Roazen, in *Potentialities* (Stanford, CA: Stanford University Press, 1999), 185–204.

of little, regional meanings—all absolute in their absolute relativity. This is the form our life has taken today, this product of impersonal forces, this improper concretion that we cannot go beyond, because it is our only property, the sole layer of existence that, for a certain span of time, distinguishes us from nothing. Nothing is important but life.

Theory of the Novel, 1995–2010

ACKNOWLEDGMENTS

INDEX

Acknowledgments

The University of Siena, the Italian Fulbright Commission, and the University of Chicago financially supported this work; Reading Room U at the Bibliothèque Nationale de France in Tolbiac made it possible. My thanks go to those who contributed to the writing of this book with their suggestions, comments, and help: Annalisa Agrati, Albert Ascoli, Vincenzo Bagnoli, Valentino Baldi, Alessio Baldini, Daniele Balicco, Piero Caracciolo, Alberto Casadei, Pietro Cataldi, Valeria Cavalloro, Raffaele Donnarumma, Céline Frigau, Maddalena Graziano, Clemens Härle, Laurent Jenny, Anne Lepoittevin, Romano Luperini, Marielle Macé, Maria Anna Mariani, Franco Moretti, Michel Murat, Francesco Orlando, Giulia Oskian, Thomas Pavel, Angela Piliouras, Martin Rueff, Elisa Russian, Guido Sacchi, Barbara Spackman, Justin Steinberg, Carlo Tirinanzi de Medici, Roberto Venuti, Elissa Weaver. A special thanks goes to those who read and discussed the final draft with me: Anna Baldini, Clotilde Bertoni, Daniela Brogi, Barbara Carnevali, Claudio Giunta, Pierluigi Pellini, Marina Polacco, Filippomaria Pontani, Matteo Residori, Gianluigi Simonetti, Paolo Tortonese, Enrica Zanin, Sergio Zatti. Finally, I am very grateful to Zakiya Hanafi for her meticulous translation.

Index

CPSIA information can be obtained
at www.ICGtesting.com
Printed in the USA
LVHW091636060322
712378LV00013B/66/J

9 780674 333727